Adobe

After Effects CS6
Visual Effects and Compositing

STUDIO TECHNIQUES

Mark Christiansen

Adobe

Adobe® After Effects® CS6 Visual Effects and Compositing Studio Techniques

Mark Christiansen

This Adobe Press book is published by Peachpit.
For information on Adobe Press books, contact:

Peachpit
1249 Eighth Street
Berkeley, CA 94710
(510) 524-2178
Fax: (510) 524-2221

To report errors, please send a note to errata@peachpit.com

Peachpit is a division of Pearson Education
Copyright © 2013 Mark Christiansen
For the latest on Adobe Press books, go to www.adobepress.com

Senior Editor: Karyn Johnson
Production Editor: Katerina Malone
Technical Editor: Todd Kopriva
Copy Editor: Harbour Hodder
Proofreader: Kelly Kordes Anton
Composition: Kim Scott, Bumpy Design
Indexer: Jack Lewis
Cover Design: Charlene Charles-Will
Cover Illustration: Alicia Buelow

ISBN-13: 978-0-321-83459-1
ISBN-10:   0-321-83459-3

9 8 7 6 5 4 3 2 1

Printed and bound in the United States of America

Contents

Scripting appendix by Jeff Almasol and After Effects JavaScript Guide by Dan Ebberts available on the accompanying DVD.

About the Author

Mark Christiansen is a San Francisco–based visual effects supervisor and creative director. Some of his Hollywood feature and independent film credits include *Avatar, All About Evil, The Day After Tomorrow* and *Pirates of the Caribbean 3: At World's End*. As a director, producer, designer, and compositor/animator, he has worked on a diverse slate of commercial, music video, live event, and television documentary projects for a diverse set of Hollywood and Silicon Valley clients. More recently he has been employed directly by Adobe to produce video marketing material. It was a brief stint advising on the set of *Beasts of the Southern Wild* that sparked the concept for Cinefex for iPad and foundation of the company that produced it—New Scribbler.

Mark has used After Effects since version 2.0 and has worked directly with the After Effects development and marketing teams over the years. He has written four previous editions of this book, and has contributed to other published efforts, including the *Adobe After Effects Classroom in a Book* and *After Effects 5.5 Magic* (with Nathan Moody).

Mark is a founder of Pro Video Coalition (providecoalition.com). He has created video training for Digieffects, lynda.com, and fxphd.com, and has taught courses based on this book at Academy of Art University. You can hear him on popular podcasts such as "The VFX Show" and you can find him at christiansen.com.

About the Contributors

 **Jeff Almasol** (Appendix: Scripting) is a senior quality engineer on the Adobe After Effects team by day and crafter of After Effects scripts at his redefinery.com site by night. His site provides numerous free scripts, reference material, and links to other scripting resources. Prior to Adobe, Jeff worked at Elastic Reality Inc. and Avid Technology on Elastic Reality, Marquee, AvidProNet, and other products; and at Profound Effects on Useful Things and Useful Assistants. You might find him talking in the third person on Twitter (redefinery) and other sites.

 **Dan Ebberts** (Chapter 10: Expressions and After Effects Javascript Guide) is a freelance After Effects script author and animation consultant. His scripting services have been commissioned for a wide range of projects, including workflow automation and complex animation rigging. He is a frequent contributor to the various After Effects forums and has a special interest in expressions and complex algorithms. Dan is an electrical engineer by training, with a BSEE degree from the University of California, but has spent most of his career writing software. He can be reached via http://motionscript.com.

 **Stu Maschwitz** (Foreword) is a writer and director, and the creator of the Magic Bullet Suite from Red Giant Software. Maschwitz spent four years as a visual effects artist at George Lucas's Industrial Light & Magic (ILM), working on such films as *Twister* and *Men in Black*. He cofounded and was CTO of The Orphanage, a San Francisco-based visual effects and film production company. Maschwitz has directed numerous commercials and supervised effects work on films including *Sin City* and *The Spirit*. Maschwitz is a guerilla filmmaker at heart and combined this spirit and his effects knowledge into a book: *The DV Rebel's Guide: An All-Digital Approach to Making Killer Action Movies on the Cheap* (Peachpit Press).

To the true spirit of collaboration.

Acknowledgments

This book wouldn't exist without the dedication of the After Effects team at Adobe to make the best software they can for more than two decades, which is nearly how long I've been working with it. I started with the CoSA After Effects 2.0 beta at LucasArts—back before I knew the term "compositor"—and was soon blowing minds with what I could do on a beige Mac.

In this edition, I also thank Adobe specifically in a couple of ways. There couldn't be a better technical editor than Todd Kopriva, who made time in his more-than-full schedule to review this book. And during the development of this book, I have had an office at Adobe, where I've had the opportunity take part in the tremendous step forward for video that is CS6. Thanks to Paramita Bhattacharya and Ellen Wixted for making me more of an insider than ever.

And, of course, I remain grateful to filmmaker Stu Maschwitz, who cofounded and was CTO of The (late, great) Orphanage, without whom the first edition of the book wouldn't have been what it was. Working with Stu directly on A-list feature films gave me the confidence that the techniques in this book were valid and worth sharing.

Maintaining that standard has been possible only with the collaboration of others. Thanks to Dan Ebberts for his work on Chapter 10, "Expressions," and his counterpart on the scripting side, Jeff Almasol. Jeff even contributed several useful scripts that he and I cooked up specifically for readers of this book. Thanks also to Sébastien Perier for revamping a few of the expressions examples for this edition.

I'm proud of the way this edition looks, and that's thanks in no small part to Jim Geduldick and Tyler Ginter, each of whom contributed high-speed action footage from the Phantom camera. If you haven't seen Tyler's project "Holi," find it on Vimeo—it's amazing. We also have footage, courtesy of Adobe, which was shot by Vincent LaForet. The LaForet footage is used for motion tracking and color look examples throughout the book; it's a treat to work with footage that is properly shot, well lit, and completely flat, ready to be manipulated. Bob Donlon of Wrecking Ball and Adam Shaening-Pokrasso of 12fps contributed the nightclub shots featuring the Afrolicious band. Thanks guys!

I learn from teaching and thank past students and collaborators at Academy of Art and fxphd.com for reminding me of the need for clear, patient, lucid descriptions of fundamentals.

Repeat thanks to Tyler McPherron, Chris Meyer, Eric Escobar, and Brendan Bolles for contributions retained from previous editions. In addition, I thank Mike Chance and Jesse Boots (of Project Arbiter), Pixel Corps, Artbeats, fxphd, Case Films, Creative COW, Kenwood Group, Inhance, Sony, ABC, Red Bull USA, and individuals such as Pete O'Connell, Benjamin Morgan, Matt Ward, Ross Webb, Luis Bustamente, Micah Parker, Fred Lewis, Jorge L. Peschiera, Shuets Udono, Eric E. Yang, Charlie Styr, Mike Sussman, Marco Abis, Håkan Dahlström, and Kevin Miller. Thanks to Flickr for the Creative Commons tag that allows incorporation of fantastic images from willing contributors around the world.

Alicia Buelow designed this book's cover with guidance from Charlene Charles-Will. Thanks to Peachpit for commissioning original artwork for the cover, and to the team for patiently working through a number of revisions. It was worth the trouble.

The people on the After Effects team at Adobe have made this application what it is. Dave Simons and Dan Wilk go all the way back, and Chris Prosser and Steve Forde now ably guide it forward (and offer smart, clear, concise responses to technical questions). One of the biggest thrills during this cycle was to travel to Seattle and have nearly the entire team come out for Thai food—we took over the restaurant.

This book relies on the commitment of Peachpit Press to manage the highest-quality publications possible in a world of increasing costs and continual shifts in the marketplace. My editor for three print editions now, Karyn Johnson, devoted long hours and extraordinary energy to everything from minuscule copyedits to coordination of the many pieces that need to come together to make a book. Karyn, the readers of this book get the benefit of your professionalism and genuine commitment to quality, while I have been the beneficiary of your sense of humor, fun—and patience! I hope some higher-ups at Pearson are listening—they are lucky to have you.

Finally, thank you to you, the people who read, teach, and bring the material in this book to life to collaborate on your own stories. Please let me know what you think at aestudiotechniques@gmail.com.

Foreword to This Edition

Face it, Bart, Sideshow Bob has changed.
No, he hasn't. He's more the same than ever!
—Lisa and Bart Simpson in "Brother from
Another Series," *The Simpsons*, Season 8

The first edition of this book was published in 2005, and I wrote the foreword for the third edition in 2008. I just read it, with an eye to updating it. I didn't change a word.

Everything I wrote then is even more true today. I'm seeing it every time I turn on my television—people are losing their preoccupation with realism and just telling stories. Certainly in many cases this is due to drastically reduced budgets. Nothing inspires creativity like limited resources. But if you can make your point as effectively with a stylized-but-beautiful animation, suddenly spending months of work to "do it photo-real" seems like more than just squandered resources; it seems to miss the point altogether.

Today, our phones come with 1080p video cameras, and our favorite visual effects application comes bundled with a 3D tracker. Every week on Kickstarter there's a new project designed to make some aspect of film production even more accessible. We're expected to make even more for even less.

The combination of Adobe After Effects CS6 and this book remains your best asset in that battle. What I wrote in 2008's foreword was controversial and challenging at the time, but today it just feels like common sense. When the season finale of a hit TV show is shot using a camera that you can buy at the corner camera store—when a professional cinematographer is willing to suffer through compression artifacts and other technical shortcomings of that camera because the images he makes with it create an emotional experience he can't achieve any other way— you're in the middle of a sea change. It's not the 100-artist facilities or the shops with investments in "big iron" that are going to come out on top. The victory will go to the artists who generate an emotional reaction by any means necessary. The filmmaker with an entire studio in her backpack. The visual effects artist who has an entire show's worth of shots slap-comped while the editor is still loading footage. The graphic designer who ignores the stale collection of stock footage and shoots his own cloud time-lapse using a $.99 iPhone app.

Four years ago it was fun to think about bringing the sex to your work. Today it's necessary for survival. Use what you learn in this book to make beautiful things that challenge and excite people. The tools have gotten better. It's up to you to translate that into a better audience experience.

—Stu Maschwitz

Foreword

I can't see the point in the theatre. All that sex and violence. I get enough of that at home Apart from the sex, of course.

—Tony Robinson as Baldrick, *Blackadder*

Who Brings the Sex?

"Make it look real." That would seem to be the mandate of the visual effects artist. Spielberg called and he wants the world to believe, if only for 90 minutes, that dinosaurs are alive and breathing on an island off the coast of South America. Your job: Make them look real. Right?

Wrong.

I am about to tell you, the visual effects artist, the most important thing you'll ever learn in this business: Making those velociraptors (or vampires or alien robots or bursting dams) "look real" is absolutely not what you should be concerned with when creating a visual effects shot.

Movies are not reality. The reason we love them is that they present us with a heightened, idealized version of reality. Familiar ideas—say, a couple having an argument—but turned up to 11: The argument takes place on the observation deck of the Empire State building, both he and she are perfectly backlit by the sun (even though they're facing each other), which is at the exact same just-about-to-set golden-hour position for the entire 10-minute conversation. The couple are really, really charming and impossibly good-looking—in fact, one of them is Meg Ryan. Before the surgery. Oh, and music is playing.

What's real about that? Nothing at all—and we love it.

Do you think director Alejandro Amenábar took Javier Aguirresarobe, cinematographer on *The Others*, aside and said, "Whatever you do, be sure to make Nicole Kidman look real?" Heck no. Directors say this kind of stuff to their DPs: "Make her look like a statue." "Make him look bullet-proof." "Make her look like she's sculpted out of ice."

Did It Feel Just Like It Should?

Let's roll back to *Jurassic Park*. Remember how terrific the T-rex looked when she stepped out of the paddock? Man, she looked good.

She looked good.

The realism of that moment certainly did come in part from the hard work of Industrial Light and Magic's fledgling computer graphics department, which developed groundbreaking technologies to bring that T-rex to life. But mostly, that T-rex felt real because she looked good. She was wet. It was dark. She had a big old Dean Cundey blue rim light on her coming from nowhere. In truth, you could barely see her.

But you sure could hear her. Do you think a T-rex approaching on muddy earth would really sound like the first notes of a new THX trailer? Do you think Spielberg ever sat with sound designer Gary Rydstrom and said, "Let's go out of our way to make sure the footstep sounds are authentic?" No, he said, "Make that mofo sound like the Titanic just rear-ended the Hollywood Bowl" (may or may not be a direct quote).

It's the sound designer's job to create a soundscape for a movie that's emotionally true. They make things feel right even if they skip over the facts in the process. Move a gun half an inch and it sounds like a shotgun being cocked. Get hung up on? Instant dial tone. Modern computer displaying something on the screen? Of course there should be the sound of an IBM dot-matrix printer from 1978.

Sound designers don't bring facts. They bring the sex. So do cinematographers, makeup artists, wardrobe stylists, composers, set designers, casting directors, and even the practical effects department.

And yet somehow, we in the visual effects industry are often forbidden from bringing the sex. Our clients pigeonhole us into the role of the prop maker: Build me a T-rex, and it better look real. But when it comes time to put that T-rex on screen, we are also the cinematographer (with our CG lights), the makeup artist (with our "wet look" shader), and the practical effects crew (with our rain). And although he may forget to speak with us in the same flowery terms that he used with Dean on set, Steven wants us to make sure that T-rex looks like a T-rex should in a movie. Not just good—impossibly good. Unrealistically blue-rim-light-outa-nowhere good. Sexy good.

Have you ever argued with a client over aspects of an effects shot that were immutable facts? For example, you may have a client who inexplicably requested a little less motion blur on a shot, or who told you "just a little slower" for an object after you calculated its exact rate of fall? Do you ever get frustrated with clients who try to art-direct reality in this way?

Well, stop it.

Your client is a director, and it's their job to art-direct reality. It's not their job to know (or suggest) the various ways that it may or may not be possible to selectively reduce motion blur, but it is their job to feel it in their gut that somehow this particular moment should feel "crisper" than normal film reality. And you know what else? It's your job to predict that they might want this and even propose it. In fact, you'd better have this conversation early, so you can shoot the plate with a 45-degree shutter, that both the actors and the T-rex might have a quarter the normal motion blur.

Was It Good for You?

The sad reality is that we, the visual effects industry, pigeonhole ourselves by being overly preoccupied with reality. We have no one to blame but ourselves. No one else on the film set does this. If you keep coming back to your client with defenses such as "That's how it would really look" or "That's how fast it would really fall," then not only are you going to get in some arguments that you will lose, but you're actually setting back our entire industry by perpetuating the image of visual effects artists as blind to the importance of the sex. On the set, after take one of the spent brass shell falling to the ground, the DP would turn to the director and say, "That felt a bit fast. Want me to do one at 48 frames?" And the director would say yes, and they'd shoot it, and then months later the editor would choose take three, which they shot at 72 frames per second "just in case." That's the filmmaking process, and when you take on the task of creating that same shot in CG, you need to represent, emulate, and embody that entire process. You're the DP, both lighting the shot and determining that it might look better overcranked. You're the editor, confirming that choice in the context of the cut. And until you show it to your client, you're the director, making sure this moment feels right in all of its glorious unreality.

The problem is that the damage is already done. The client has worked with enough effects people who have willingly resigned themselves to not bringing the sex that they now view all of us as geeks with computers rather than fellow filmmakers. So when you attempt to break our self-imposed mold and bring the sex to your client, you will face an uphill battle. But here's some advice to ease the process: Do it without asking. I once had a client who would pick apart every little detail of a matte painting, laying down accusations of "This doesn't look real!"—until we color corrected the shot cool, steely blue with warm highlights. Then all the talk of realism went away, and the shot got oohs and aahs.

Your client reacts to your work emotionally, but they critique technically. When they see your shot, they react with their gut. It's great, it's getting better, but there's still something not right. What they should do is stop there and let you figure out what's not right, but instead, they somehow feel the need to analyze their gut reaction and turn it into action items: "That highlight is too hot" or "The shadows under that left foot look too dark." In fact, it would be better if they focused on vocalizing their gut reactions: "The shot feels a bit lifeless," or "The animation feels too heavy somehow." Leave the technical details to the pros.

You may think that those are the worst kind of comments, but they are the best. I've seen crews whine on about "vague" client comments like "give the shot more oomf." But trust me, this is exactly the comment you want. Because clients are like customers at a restaurant, and you are the chef. The client probably wants to believe that "more oomf" translates into something really sophisticated, like volumetric renderings or level-set fluid dynamics, in the same way that a patron at a restaurant would hope that a critique like "this dish needs more flavor" would send the chef into a tailspin of exotic ingredients and techniques. Your client would never admit (or suggest on their own) that "oomf" is usually some combination of "cheap tricks" such as camera shake, a lens flare or two, and possibly some God rays—just like the diner would rather not know that their request for "more flavor" will probably be addressed with butter, salt, and possibly MSG.

The MSG analogy is the best: Deep down, you want to go to a Chinese restaurant that uses a little MSG but doesn't admit it. You want the cheap tricks because they work, but you'd rather not think about it. Your client wants you to use camera shake and lens flares, but without telling them. They'd never admit that those cheap tricks "make" a shot, so let them off the hook and do those things without being asked. They'll silently thank you for it. Bringing the sex is all about cheap tricks.

Lights On or Off?

There are some visual effects supervisors who pride themselves on being sticklers for detail. This is like being an architect whose specialty is nails. I have bad news for the "Pixel F*ckers," as this type are known: Every shot will always have something wrong with it. There will forever be something more you could add, some shortcoming that could be addressed. What makes a visual effects supervisor good at their job is knowing which of the infinitely possible tweaks are important. Anyone can nitpick. A good supe focuses the crew's efforts on the parts of the shot that impact the audience most. And this is always the sex. Audiences don't care about matte lines or mismatched black levels, soft elements or variations in grain. If they did, they wouldn't have been able to enjoy *Blade Runner* or *Back to the Future* or that one *Star Wars* movie—what was it called? Oh yeah: *Star Wars*. Audiences only care about the sex.

On a recent film I was struggling with a shot that was just kind of sitting there. It had been shot as a pickup, and it needed some help fitting into the sequence that had been shot months earlier. I added a layer of smoke to technically match the surrounding shots. Still, the shot died on the screen. Finally, I asked my compositor to softly darken down the right half of the shot by a full stop, placing half the plate along with our CG element in a subtle shadow. Boom, the shot sang.

What I did was, strictly speaking, the job of the cinematographer, or perhaps the colorist. The colorist, the person who designs the color grading for a film, is the ultimate bringer of the sex. And color correction is the ultimate cheap trick. There's nothing fancy about what a Da Vinci 2K or an Autodesk Lustre does with color. But what a good colorist does with those basic controls is bring heaping, dripping loads of sex to the party. The problem is—and I mean the single biggest problem facing our industry today—the colorist gets their hands on a visual effects shot only after it has already been approved. In other words, the film industry is currently shooting itself in the foot (we, the visual effects artists, being that foot) by insisting that our work be approved in a sexless environment. This is about the stupidest thing ever, and until the industry works this out, you need to fight back by taking on some of the role of the colorist as you finalize your shots, just like we did when we made those matte paintings darker and bluer with warm highlights.

Filmmaking is a battleground between those who bring the sex and those who don't. The non-sex-bringing engineers at Panavision struggle to keep their lenses from flaring, while ever-sexy cinematographers fight over a limited stock of 30-year-old anamorphic lenses because they love the flares. I've seen DPs extol the unflinching sharpness of a priceless Panavision lens right before adding a smear of nose grease (yes, the stuff on your nose) to the rear element to soften up the image to taste. Right now this battle is being waged on every film in production between the visual effects department and the colorists of the world. I've heard effects artists lament that after all their hard work making something look real, a colorist then comes along and "wonks out the color." In truth, all that colorist did was bring the sex that the visual effects should have been starting to provide on their own. If what the colorist did to your shot surprised you, then you weren't thinking enough about what makes a movie a movie.

In Your Hands

You're holding a book on visual effects compositing in Adobe After Effects. There are those who question the validity of such a thing. Some perpetuate a stigma that After Effects is for low-end TV work and graphics only. To do "real" effects work, you should use a program such as Nuke or Shake. Those techy, powerful applications are good for getting shots to look technically correct, but they do not do much to help you sex them up. After Effects may not be on par with Nuke and Shake in the tech department, but it beats them handily in providing a creative environment to experiment, create, and reinvent a shot. In that way it's much more akin to the highly respected Autodesk Flame and Inferno systems—it gives you a broad set of tools to design a shot, and has enough horsepower for you to finish it, too.

After Effects is the best tool to master if you want to focus on the creative aspects of visual effects compositing. That's why this book is unique. Mark's given you the good stuff here, both the nitty-gritty details as well as the aerial view of extracting professional results from an application that's as maligned as it is loved. No other book combines real production experience with a deep understanding of the fundamentals, aimed at the most popular compositing package on the planet.

Bring It

One of the great matte painters of our day once told me that he spent only the first few years of his career struggling to make his work look real, but that he'll spend the rest of his life learning new ways of making his work look good. It's taken me years of effects supervising, commercial directing, photography, wandering the halls of museums, and waking up with hangovers after too much really good wine to fully comprehend the importance of those words. I can tell you that it was only after this particular matte painter made this conscious choice to focus on making things look good, instead of simply real, that he skyrocketed from a new hire at ILM to one of their top talents. Personally, it's only after I learned to bring the sex that I graduated from visual effects supervising to become a professional director.

So who brings the sex? The answer is simple: The people who care about it. Those who understand the glorious unreality of film and their place in the process of creating it. Be the effects artist who breaks the mold and thinks about the story more than the bit depth. Help turn the tide of self-inflicted prejudice that keeps us relegated to creating boring reality instead of glorious cinema. Secretly slip your client a cocktail of dirty tricks and fry it in more butter than they'd ever use at home.

Bring the sex.

Stu Maschwitz
San Francisco, October 2008

Introduction

If you aren't fired with enthusiasm, you will be fired—with enthusiasm.

—Vince Lombardi

Why This Book?

This book is about creating visual effects. Specifically, it dives into the art and science of assembling disparate elements so that they appear as part of a single, believable scene. When people ask me what exactly the book is about, I tell them that it shows artists how to make a shot assembled on a computer look as if it was taken with a single camera. It also hints at how to make an ordinary shot extraordinary, without destroying the viewer's willing suspension of disbelief.

The subject matter in this book goes well beyond the obvious—and what is well documented elsewhere—and deep into core visual effects topics. We look closely at features such as color correction, keying, tracking, and roto that are only touched on by other books about After Effects, while leaving tools more dedicated to motion graphics (such as Text and Shape layers) largely alone. It's not that those tools aren't a powerful part of After Effects; it's just that they literally don't fit in this book.

As the author, I do not shy away from strong opinions, even when they deviate from the official line. These opinions and techniques—which have been refined through actual work in production at a few of the finest visual effects facilities in the world—are valid not only for such high-end productions but really anywhere you are compositing a visual effect. Where applicable, the reasoning behind using one technique over another is provided. I aim to make you not a better button-pusher but a more effective artist and technician.

Visual effects companies are typically protective of trade secrets, reflexively treating all production information as proprietary. Once you work on a major project, however, you will soon discover that even the most complex shot is made up largely of repeatable techniques and practices. The art is in how the results are applied, combined, and customized, and what is added (or taken away). Visual effects artists, meanwhile, can be downright open and friendly about sharing discoveries, knowing that it's the artistry and not a clever bag of tricks that ultimately make the greatest difference.

Each shot is unique, and yet each relies on techniques that are tried and true. This book offers you as many of the techniques as possible so that you can focus on the unique properties of each shot. There's not much here in the way of step-by-step instructions—it's more important for you to grasp how things work so that you can repurpose techniques for your individual shot.

This is *not* a book for beginners. Although the first section is designed to make sure that you are making optimal use of the software, it's not an effective primer on After Effects in particular or digital video in general. If you're new to After Effects, first spend some time with its excellent documentation or check out one of the many books available to help beginners learn the application.

On the other hand, if you're comfortable with Photoshop and familiar with the visual effects process—which is likely, if you've picked up this book—try diving into the redesigned Chapter 1 and let me know how it goes.

Organization of This Book and What's New

Each edition of the *After Effects Studio Techniques* series has been organized into three sections. Although each chapter has been refined and updated, the broad organization of the book remains as follows.

▶ Section I, "Working Foundations," is about After Effects itself, and how to make the most of its user interface. This is not a list of each menu and button but a shortcut to power use when compositing.

NOTES

This book's technical editor, Todd Kopriva, maintains an excellent blog called After Effects Region of Interest at Adobe, and he has assembled and maintained a page of resources for beginners entitled Getting Started with After Effects. Visit http://blogs.adobe.com/toddkopriva/2010/01/getting-started-with-after-eff.html.

If you're advanced, don't skip this section. It's virtually guaranteed to contain valuable information that you don't already know, and it has been freshened up with new data and figures pertaining to new features in CS6, including the revolutionary Global Performance Cache coverage in Chapter 4.

▶ Section II, "Effects Compositing Essentials," is about the fundamentals of effects compositing. Color matching, keying, rotoscoping, and motion tracking are the essentials, plus there's a chapter on the camera and 3D along with another on the expressions used to generate animated data with connections, logic, and math. The final chapter in that section introduces you to 32-bpc linear compositing and high dynamic range imaging pipelines.

This section is the true heart of the book. This edition contains dramatic rewrites of Chapters 7 through 9, due to the many new rotoscoping, tracking, and 3D features added to the application since version CS5.

▶ Section III, "Creative Explorations," is about the actual shots you are likely to re-create—the bread-and-butter techniques every effects artist needs to know. Some of these examples are timeless, but you will also find a substantial new section to get you up and running with Adobe SpeedGrade, a powerful new tool that most After Effects CS6 artists will have but few know how to use.

In all cases, instead of leading you step-by-step through a single example, the goal is to explain the fundamentals of how things work. You will then be able to put these techniques to use on your own shot, instead of taking a paint-by-numbers approach. While each shot is unique, they can all be grouped together as effectively the same in fundamental ways.

Artistry

While working on the first edition of this book, I would ride my bicycle home up the hill out of the Presidio, where The Orphanage studio was located. As I rode, I thought about what people really needed to know in order to move their work to the level of a visual-effects pro. Sometimes it was very late at night, when raccoons and skunks would cross my path. Here's what I came up with:

▶ **Get reference.** You can't re-create what you can't clearly see. Too many of us skip this step and end up making boring, generic choices. Nature is never boring, and if it appears that way, you're not looking at it closely enough.

▶ **Simplify.** To paraphrase Einstein, the optimum solution is as simple as possible, but no simpler.

▶ **Break it down.** Talented but inexperienced students learn how the software works but are not used to analyzing a shot or sequence and breaking it down into manageable, comprehensible steps. This is a book filled with those steps.

▶ **Learn to take criticism rather than expect perfection.** My former colleague Paul Topolos, now in the art department at Pixar, used to say, "Recognizing flaws in your work doesn't mean you're a bad artist. It only means you have taste." To err is human, to cut yourself a break and keep going, divine.

This is what I learned working at the best studios, and even if you're not currently working at one of them, this is how collaboration, criticism, and perseverance will be your teachers.

Compositing in After Effects

There's a good reason that Nuke, a node-based compositing application from The Foundry, has almost uniformly become the compositing application of choice at the feature film visual effects studios around the world. Nuke is designed for exactly what those artists need—and only what they need. In some areas, mostly the handling of 3D and stereo, Nuke is clearly ahead of After Effects. In other areas, such as animation and type handling, After Effects has the edge. For compositing fundamentals, the two applications are equally valid, but operations that are simple in Nuke can be complicated in After Effects, and vice versa.

Despite the impression that Nuke has taken over compositing, when you move beyond feature films, After Effects remains the ubiquitous application. They're both awesome tools, but the important takeaway is that Nuke is specialized while After Effects targets a broader set of users.

Some of the features that streamline After Effects for the generalist and animator (and which, paradoxically, can complicate workflows that are more straightforward for video-effects compositing in Nuke):

▶ Render order is established in the timeline and via nested compositions that consist of layers, not nodes. After Effects has Flowchart view, but you don't create your composition there the way you would with a tree/node interface.

▶ Transforms, effects, and masks are embedded in every layer. They render in a fixed order.

▶ After Effects has a persistent concept of an alpha channel in addition to the three color channels. The alpha channel is always treated as if it is straight (never premultiplied) once an image has been imported and "interpreted," as the application terms it.

▶ An After Effects project is not a script, although version CS4 introduced a text version of the After Effects Project (.aep) file, the XML-formatted .aepx file. Most of the text file's contents are inscrutable other than source file paths. Actions are not recordable and there is no direct equivalent to Shake macros.

▶ Temporal and spatial settings tend to be fixed and absolute in After Effects because it is composition- and timeline-based. This is a boon to projects that involve complex timing and animation, but it can snare users who aren't used to it and suddenly find pre-comps that end prematurely, are cropped, or don't scale gracefully. Best practices to avoid this are detailed in Chapter 4.

This book attempts to shed light on these and other areas of After Effects that are not explicitly dealt with in its user interface or documentation. After Effects itself spares you details that a casual user might never need to know about but that, as a professional user, you want to understand thoroughly. This book is here to help.

All compositing applications are, at root, nodal, as you can glimpse in the seldom-used Flowchart view .

The XML Gibson and pt_OpenSesame scripts by Sébastien Perier (http://aescripts.com/xml-gibson) make clever use of XML to make After Effects more like a script-based application.

What's on the DVD

The DVD included with this book provides a variety of helpful resources for the After Effects artist, many provided by friends and colleagues (thanks!).

Scripting Chapter: Jeff Almasol's scripting chapter is now an appendix, found on the disc as a PDF. This highly accessible resource on this complicated and much-feared topic walks you through three scripts, each of which builds upon the complexity of the previous. Scripting provides the ability to create incredibly useful extensions to After Effects to eliminate tedious tasks. Several of these are included in the scripts folder on the disc as exclusives to this book.

A few useful and free third-party scripts mentioned throughout the book are included as well. For more of these, see the script links PDF in the scripts folder on the disc.

JavaScript Guide: To focus on more advanced and applied topics in the print edition, Dan Ebberts kicked JavaScript fundamentals to a special JavaScript addendum, also included as a PDF. This is, in many ways, the missing manual for the After Effects implementation of JavaScript. It omits all the useless Web-only scripting commands found in the best available books and extends beyond the material in After Effects help.

Special-Purpose Topics: Certain sections that appeared in the print version of previous editions have been moved onto the disc as PDF files. The tools and techniques are still valid, but the material on topics such as morphing, warping, and color management is able to stand on its own to make way for new features that had to be integrated more directly into the rest of the book.

Footage: You'll also find HD footage you can use to experiment on and practice your techniques. There are dozens of example files to help you deconstruct the techniques described.

To install the additional chapters, lesson files, footage, and software demos included on the DVD, simply copy each chapter folder in its entirety to your hard drive (the desktop is fine). Note that all .aep files are located in the subfolder of each chapter folder on the disc.

NOTES

If you have comments or questions you'd like to share with the author, please email them to aestudiotechniques@gmail.com.

The Bottom Line

Remember, the tools are just the means for the skilled talented artist to apply the hard work required to inspire an audience with results. By thoroughly learning the tools, you can also learn to think with them, and in so doing, to sort of forget about them as they become second nature. This book will help you do that.

1

Composite in After Effects

All science touches on art; all art has its scientific side.
The worst scientist is he who is not an artist; the worst
artist is he who is no scientist.

— Armand Trousseau

Composite in After Effects

This book is about creating visual effects using Adobe After Effects, the world's most widely used compositing application. It helps you create believable, fantastic moving images using elements from disparate sources, and it allows you to do so with the least possible effort. This first section offers a jump-start (if you're relatively new) or a refresher (if you're already an After Effects artist) on the After Effects workflow.

Effective visual effects compositing uses your best skills as both artist and engineer. As an artist, you make creative and aesthetic decisions that are uniquely your own, but if you are not also able to understand how to implement those decisions effectively, your artistry will suffer. If I had to say what most often separates a great result from mediocrity, the answer is iteration—multiple passes—and solid technical skills enable these to happen most quickly and effectively, allowing your creative abilities to then take over.

This chapter and the rest of Section I focus on how to get things done in After Effects as effortlessly as possible. It is assumed that you already know your way around the basics of After Effects and are ready to learn to fly.

A Basic Composite

After Effects is full of so many panels, effects, and controls, not to mention custom tools and powerful modifiers such as scripts and expressions, that it's easy to feel overwhelmed. Let's take a look at a simple yet real-world composite to help reveal the true essentials of the application.

NOTES

If this book opens at too advanced a level for you, see the Introduction for more resources to help you get up to speed with the basic operations of After Effects.

You may have heard the expression, "If you can imagine it, you can create it in After Effects." I first heard it working alongside Trish Meyer in the era of After Effects 3.0, and I'm sure you can appreciate that it has only become more true with time. So, the following example is by no means comprehensive, nor is adding an element to a scene in this manner even necessarily what you'll be doing in After Effects. But the basic principle is that After Effects lets you go beyond what you can otherwise do editing footage by actually changing what appears in the scene itself.

Let's suppose your independent film just got a great opportunity from a commercial sponsor to add its product into a scene. The challenge is that the scene has already been shot, and so you must "fix it in post"—a process that has become so common it's now an on-set joke. It's also the reality of how all of the top-grossing movies of our time have been made, not to mention virtually every commercial and many television, Internet, industrial, and student projects.

Figure 1.1 shows the elements we have to work with: a background *plate* image sequence and the foreground element to be added.

Workspace Setup

To get to this starting point as shown in Figure 1.1, first do this: In Windows Explorer or Mac OS Finder, navigate to the source elements in this chapter's folder on the book's disc (which you moved to your local drive). Find the

The term "plate" stretches back to the earliest days of optical compositing (and even further to still photography) and refers to the glass plate that held the source footage. It now generally means the background onto which foreground elements are composited, although the foreground can also be the plate, and there are other kinds of plates such as effects plates.

Figure 1.1 This comp begins as simple as can be, with element A (the can image with an alpha channel, where source is displayed in the footage channel) laid over element B (the background clip).

01_a_over_b subfolder in the Chapter01 folder. Arrange your windows so that you can see both that Explorer/ Finder window and the After Effects Project panel, then drag both source items (jf_table and RBcan_jf_table.tif) into that panel. (You can actually drag them anywhere onto the After Effects user interface [UI], and they should end up there.)

Make a folder by clicking the New Folder icon along the bottom of the Project panel and label it by typing **Source** or **src** in the live text field. Drag those elements into that folder. If you've done it right, your Project panel should look something like the one you see in Figure 1.1.

How the After Effects UI looks at program startup depends on its most recent usage, if any. You probably see a menu labeled Workspace; if not, reveal the Tools panel (**Ctrl+1/ Cmd+1**) or just choose Window > Workspace (most everything in the application exists in more than one place, allowing you to pick your favorite approach and find the controls more easily). Choose the Standard workspace and then, further down the same menu, pick Reset Standard— you are now back to the factory defaults.

Does the user interface seem complicated? You can make it even more so—go to Window > Workspace (or the Workspace menu in the toolbar) and choose All Panels. You're likely to see a bunch of tabs crammed up and down the right side of the screen. Now breathe a sigh of relief, since I can tell you that there are a few in there I no longer even use—Wiggler and Smoother being two that have been effectively rendered obsolete by expressions (Chapter 10). In any case, I would never recommend leaving so many controls open at once. To swing radically in the opposite direction, try the Minimal workspace (and if necessary, Reset Minimal). This is closer to my own optimal workspace (but then, I don't generally object when labeled a minimalist).

The Standard workspace is also a fine place to start. In Standard, click on the Audio tab and close it—unless you're timing animations to sound or mastering an entire movie in After Effects, you won't need that panel.

Now try tearing off the Info panel. Hold down **Ctrl (Cmd)** as you drag it by its tab away from its current position. You can do this with any panel: It is now undocked. I often

NOTES

If these instructions present any difficulty, you can instead choose File > Import > Multiple Files (**Ctrl+Alt+I/Cmd+Opt+I**), choose the single TIFF image, and then go into the jf_table folder to select any of those TIFF images with TIFF Sequence checked at the bottom of the Import Multiple Files dialog—but see how much more complicated that is?

work with Info this way, letting it float above my Composition viewer panel so that the pixel and position values are directly adjacent. This may be too much hot-rodding for you right away, so now try dragging it over a few of the other panels without letting go. You'll see violet-colored hit areas—six of them—on each panel, and at the four edges of the screen, teal-colored gutters.

If you actually drop the Info panel into any of these areas you may notice a pretty major flaw in all of this freedom— poorly placed, the Info panel can generate a lot of extra wasted space. You can drag it elsewhere or **Ctrl** (**Cmd**) drag and drop it to tear it off again. You can combine it with the Preview panel to save space: Drag the Info panel over the Preview panel or vice versa using the tab at the upper left.

Now try choosing Window > Effects & Presets, or even better, use the shortcut **Ctrl+5** (**Cmd+5**). The Window menu contains all of the panels, and each can be opened and closed (toggled) here. The need for the Effects & Presets panel is only occasional, so why take up space with it (**Figure 1.2**)?

NOTES

The term "toggle" throughout this book means that properties or options can be revealed or concealed.

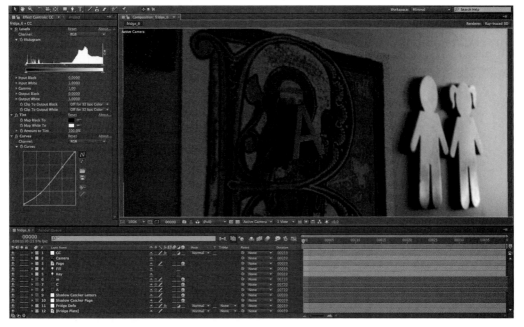

Figure 1.2 On a laptop, a modified Minimal layout groups Effect Controls and Project panels together next to the Composition viewer, with the Timeline taking maximum width. The Info panel floats above the image viewer and can even be opened and closed (Ctrl+2/Cmd+2).

TIP

Watch out for the default 30-fps setting for image sequences; it's highly unlikely to be the setting you want, but until you change it, 30 fps is the rate set by default under Preferences > Import > Sequence Footage.

Figure 1.3 Highlight an item in the Project panel and useful information appears adjacent to that item's thumbnail at the top.

NOTES

If details such as pixel aspect ratio seem arcane at this point, don't worry—they will be covered in greater detail later in the chapter, and you'll have more practice with them throughout the book.

Set Up the Composition

This is all a little abstract without working on the actual elements. I have done whole After Effects animations that have no source elements at all, type animations with solid, shape, and particle-based effects created right in the application. In other words, this is an approach more typical to motion graphics.

Let's have a look. Select jf_table in the Project panel and take a look at the information at the top of the panel (**Figure 1.3**). Listed are its pixel dimensions (1280 × 720), pixel aspect ratio (1 or square), duration (in frames or time, depending on your project settings—more on all of these later), frame rate, and color depth. If the frame rate isn't 24 fps (Figure 1.1 shows the After Effects default of 30 fps), click the Interpret Footage along the bottom of the panel and change it by typing 24 and clicking OK.

Now select the other layer, RBcan_jf_table.tif. It differs from the first in a couple of significant ways. As a still image, it has no duration or frame rate, although because it was rendered specifically for this scene it does have matching pixel dimensions and aspect ratio. Most significantly for our purposes, its pixel depth is Millions of Colors+ (that is After Effects-speak for 8-bit-per-channel RGBA, a 32-bit-per-pixel image with four 8-bit channels instead of three). This image includes an alpha channel to store transparency data, which is covered in depth in Chapter 3.

To get to work, place your elements in a composition, or comp. Start with whichever layer contains the plate—in this case, jf_table.tif—by dragging it to the New Composition icon. With no extra effort, you have automatically set a comp whose size, aspect, duration, and frame rate match those of the source.

Now add the Red Bull can. There are a few ways to do this. You can simply drag it into the Timeline panel to where you see a black line above the existing layer and drop it. You can also drag it to the Composition icon in the Project panel or, easiest of all, you can select the image and use **Ctrl+/ (Cmd+/)**.

Just as in Photoshop, simply positioning one layer above another in the stack—in this case, the Timeline panel instead of a Layer panel—creates a composite image. The operation is seamless only because the can was generated with an alpha channel, but this isn't the only way to combine layers in After Effects—not by a long shot. Chapter 3 introduces the full variety of options beyond this no-brainer, and even illustrates how this simplest of composites actually works.

Preview and Refine

Now is a good time to preview the composition and see how it looks. Here you can make use of the Preview panel, at least until you learn the one essential shortcut from it—0 (zero) on the numeric keypad (which is on the side or, on a laptop, embedded with the function key shortcuts) stands in for the RAM Preview icon . Beginners often mistakenly hit the spacebar to play compositions in After Effects. With faster and faster systems, this increasingly works, but only a RAM preview buffers the composition into memory and locks its playback to the correct frame rate. Only it takes advantage of multiprocessing to render multiple frames simultaneously, and includes audio playback.

Once the shot is looping, you can use the spacebar to stop it at any point, and then, with your cursor over the Composition panel, click the key at the upper left of your keyboard, just below Esc—it's usually called the tilde (~) key even though it's actually the backward accent (`) key. Let's call it the tilde—that's easier to say and remember, and other apps such as those from Autodesk use it as well. It brings the panel up full screen for easier examination.

The shot needs work. What do you see? If you said

- **color matching**—that is covered in Chapter 5
- **motion tracking**, so that it matches the slight camera move in the source shot—Chapter 8
- **adding a cast shadow**—this has a few components, which are addressed in Chapters 3, 7, and 12
- **foreground smoke**—fully addressed in Chapter 13
- **grain matching**—Chapter 9

> **TIP**
>
> You can tear off any panel and make it float by holding down **Ctrl (Cmd)** as you drag it away; I like to tear off the Render Queue panel and toggle it on and off via its shortcut (**Alt+Ctrl+0/Opt+Cmd+0**).

Just to complete the workflow, you can render this composition as a work-in-progress. With the composition selected, choose Composition > Add to Render Queue or press **Ctrl+Shift+/ (Cmd+ Shift +/)** to place it in the render queue, or you can even drag the Composition icon to the Render Queue panel from the Project panel. Once you've specified at least a name and location, as well as any other parameters (covered later in this chapter), click Render and an output file is created. We've made it from start to finish in just a few steps with an After Effects project (**Figure 1.4**). Now we spend the rest of the book refining that process.

Figure 1.4 A real-world "A over B" comp is rarely so simple and might mix multiple foregrounds, 2D and 3D, and actual and virtual source. In this case the virtual source is the refrigerator magnet that begins as a text layer.

Compositing Is A Over B… and a Bit More

Now let's proceed more deliberately through the workflow, considering more variables at each step and reducing the extra steps you may take many, many times in a normal After Effects workday.

Import and Organize Source

Getting a source file into After Effects so you can use it is no big deal. You can choose File > Import > File (or Multiple Files), or just drag footage directly from the Explorer or Finder into the Project panel. You can also double-click in an empty area of the Project panel.

Image sequences have a couple of specific extra rules but there are benefits that make them more reliable than QuickTime movies:

TIP

Prefer your workspace customizations to the defaults? Choose New Workspace in the Workspace menu and enter a new name to overwrite it; now After Effects will reset to your customized version.

Figure 1.5 The preferred After Effects monitor setup seems to be a pair of 2K or larger displays (top), although a single 30-inch display at a high resolution (bottom), used with the accent (tilde) key to zoom panels to full screen, is also quite luxuriant.

CLOSE-UP

Maximize the Screen

Which is best for After Effects, one big monitor or two smaller ones? Many After Effects artists like two HD-resolution displays side by side (**Figure 1.5**, top), although a single display can be optimal if it's large enough (**Figure 1.5**, bottom). However, you may notice that a floating panel (**Ctrl/Cmd-drag** the tab to make it float) lacks the Zoom button along the top to send the window to full screen. The shortcut **Ctrl+** (**Cmd+**) maximizes and centers any window. Press it again and even the top menu bar is hidden, filling the entire screen.

If you're stuck with a single small display, you can press the accent (tilde) key to maximize a single panel and do a RAM preview in full-screen mode by checking the Full Screen box in the Preview panel.

▶ An image sequence is less fragile than a QuickTime movie; if there is a bad frame in a sequence, it can be replaced, but a bad frame will corrupt an entire movie.

▶ You can interrupt and restart an image sequence render without then having to splice together multiple movies.

▶ QuickTime in particular has its own form of color management that isn't entirely compatible even with Apple's own applications, let alone the Adobe color management pipeline (explained in depth in Chapter 11).

Unfortunately, none of the Adobe applications (until SpeedGrade, at least) has ever become "smart" about recognizing sequences, let alone playing them back the way an application such as IRIDAS FrameCycler (now owned by Adobe, but not part of CS6) can.

Any single image sequence in a folder can simply be dragged in, if you're certain its frame rate is correct at the top of the Project panel (if not, see the sections on settings later in this chapter for the fix). If you instead intend to bring in that folder's contents as individual files, hold down the **Alt** (**Opt**) key as you drag it in.

Things get more complicated if you are dealing with multiple image sequences in a single folder. With the Import dialog, it doesn't matter which specific image in a sequence you select; they are all imported, provided you select only one. By holding the **Shift** or **Ctrl** (**Cmd**) key as you select more than one frame, however, you can

▶ specify a subset of frames to be imported instead of an entire sequence

▶ select frames from more than one sequence in the same folder; a Multiple Sequences check box appears as an option below to make certain this is really what you want to do

▶ specify sets of frames from multiple sequences (a combination of the above two modes).

This is, in many ways, a work-around for the fact that the After Effects importer doesn't group a frame sequence together the way other compositing applications do.

By default, if a sequence has missing frames (anywhere the count doesn't increment by 1), a color bar pattern is inserted with the name of the file presumed missing, which helps you track it down (see "Missing Footage" later in this chapter).

The Force Alphabetical Order check box in the Import dialog is for cases in which the frame does not increment by 1. Suppose you render "on twos," creating every other frame from a 3D application; check this box and you avoid color bars on every other frame.

Want to be rehired repeatedly as a freelancer or be the hero on your show? Make it easy for someone to open your project cold and understand how it's organized. On a more ambitious project, it's worth organizing a project template so that items are easy to find in predictable locations. Chapter 4 offers suggestions.

Context-Clicks (and Keyboard Shortcuts)

As you advance in your skills, by all means avoid the bar like a recovered alcoholic—the top menu bar, that is. I often refer to context-clicking on interface items. This is "right-clicking" unless you're on a Mac laptop or have an ancient one-button mouse, in which case you can hold down **Control**. Here's what happens when you context–click on

- a **layer in the Timeline**: Access to the full Layer menu, minus a few minor items; useful additional items include Reveal Layer Source in Project and Reveal Expression Errors
- a **layer in a Composition viewer**: Many of the same items appear, plus the Select option at the bottom of the menu displays a list of all of the items below your pointer.
- a **panel tab**: The Panel menu (also found at the upper right) houses a bunch of options that even advanced users hardly know exist, such as the View Options that allow you to show, for example, only motion path tangents
- an **item in the Project panel**: Besides the File menu, you can reveal a file in the Explorer or Finder, the system counterpart to the Project panel.

Keep these options right under your pointer and you may find yourself more focused as you work.

Missing Footage

After Effects links to any source footage file that can be located on your system or network. Any source can become unlinked (missing) if it moves or changes its name or location (**Figure 1.6**). To relink an item, find it in the Project panel and double-click it (or **Ctrl+H**/**Cmd+H**), or context-click and choose Replace Footage > File.

TIP

Waiting for a long 3D render from Maya or CINEMA 4D? Render the first and last 3D frames only, with their correct final sequence numbers, and import them using the Import dialog with Force Alphabetical Order unchecked. You now have a placeholder of the correct length that is fully set up as soon as the file is rendered.

TIP

If source needs replacing with an element that's not yet available, note a couple of extra options under the Replace Footage menu item, including Placeholder, which inserts color bars.

Figure 1.6 Missing Footage displays the telltale color bars.

If instead, you need only to reload or update a source, context-click and choose Reload Footage (**Ctrl+Alt+L/ Cmd+Opt+L**). You can even edit a file in its source application and update it automatically in After Effects with Edit > Edit Original (**Ctrl+E/Cmd+E**), as long as you don't try anything tricky like saving it as a new file.

Sometimes it's difficult to locate a missing file or frame in your project. You may have used the Find Missing Footage check box in older versions, and you may wonder where it has gone. You're not alone.

To search for particular types of footage in your project, including a missing source, use the search field (**Ctrl+F/ Cmd+F**) in the Project panel with the following commands (**Figure 1.7**):

- ▶ `missing` is the replacement for the Find Missing Footage check box

- ▶ `unused` gets you all of the source that isn't in any composition

- ▶ `used` is, self-evidently, just what it says

- ▶ text strings that appear in the Project panel (say, `tif` or `Aug 26`)

Figure 1.7 Missing footage is replaced with color bars, both in the Project thumbnail and anywhere the footage appears in the project. You can reveal all missing files in a Project by typing the word "missing" in the Project search field, highlighted in yellow.

The date column in the Project panel may be hidden by default; context-click to reveal it, then type in yesterday's date using a three-letter month abbreviation; the Project panel now displays only the items that were introduced or updated yesterday.

Because every project is likely to be moved or archived at some point (you are making backups, right?), it's best to keep all source material in one master folder. This helps After Effects automatically relink all of the related files it finds there at once, thus avoiding a lot of tedium for you.

Move, Combine, and Consolidate Projects

At some point you probably will need to

- ▶ move an entire After Effects project, including its source, or archive it
- ▶ merge or combine two projects
- ▶ clean up a project, getting rid of unused files or extra instances of a single file.

To move or archive a project with only its linked sources, choose File > Collect Files. This command allows you to create a new folder that contains a copy of the project and all of its source files. The source files are reorganized with a directory structure identical to that of the Project panel (**Figure 1.8**).

Figure 1.8 Collect Files resaves all source files from your project using the same organization and hierarchy as the project itself.

Let the computer do what it does best and automate a cleanup of your sources. Choose Collect Source Files > For Selected Comps; After Effects collects only the footage needed to create that composition. If you check Reduce Project as well, the unused source is also removed from the collected project.

If the projects being combined are organized using the same set of sub-folders, you can merge them with Redefinery's Merge Projects script, which is included on the book's disc (**Figure 1.9**).

Figure 1.9 Load the highly useful rd_MergeProjects.jsx script from the scripts folder on the book's disc into Adobe After Effects CS6> Scripts > ScriptUI Panels, and you can then reveal it at any time from the bottom of the Window menu. This script takes nested folders with the same name as those closer to the root and merges them, while consolidating duplicate footage. It's great for importing a project and maintaining a tidy structure.

TIP

Use Increment and Save when you reach a point where you're happy with a project and ready to move on to the next step; you can then choose File > Revert to get back there in one step instead of using a series of undos.

Select the master compositions in your project and choose File > Reduce Project; After Effects eliminates project items not used in the selected compositions. You even get a warning dialog telling you how many items were removed—not from the drive, only from your project.

You can also reduce only the source footage (keeping compositions and solids) with File > Remove Unused Footage, which deletes from the project any footage that hasn't made its way into a composition. If the same clips have been imported more than once, File > Consolidate All Footage looks for the extra instances and combines them, choosing the first instance, top to bottom, in the project. File > Remove Unused Footage rids a project of footage not included in any composition (but the files do remain on your drive).

Need to combine two or more projects? Import one into the other (just drag it in), or drag several into a new project. The imported project appears in its own folder labeled with the source name.

Advanced Save Options

After Effects projects are saved and overwritten completely separate from the elements they contain. They tend to be small, making it easier to save often so that you don't lose your work.

File > Increment and Save attaches a version number to your saved project or increments whatever number is already there, at the end of the filename. It helps the automation process if you make a habit of naming files with the version number at the end, right before the .aep extension.

Preferences > Auto-Save fills in the spaces between incremented versions; toggle it on and you'll never lose more than the number of minutes you specify (Save Every 20 Minutes is the default. Also indicate whatever number of most recent versions you prefer (**Figure 1.10**).

Name	Date Modified
▼ 📁 lws vfx	Today, 8:07 AM
▼ 📁 Adobe After Effects Auto-Save	Today, 8:07 AM
chloe_multiplicity_02 auto-save 2.aep	May 6, 2010 12:47 AM
chloe_multiplicity_02 auto-save 1.aep	May 6, 2010 12:27 AM
chloe_multiplicity_02.aep	Today, 7:58 AM
chloe_multiplicity_01.aep	May 4, 2010 10:29 AM

Figure 1.10 Auto-Save must be enabled (in Preferences > Auto-Save) in order for a folder to be created adjacent to the project that will contain the most recent saves of the project—you specify the number and gap between saves.

CLOSE-UP

Save Copy as CS5.5

Save a Copy creates a saved project while leaving the open project alone. You can also save a copy that opens in the previous version of After Effects. This function was added to After Effects CS5.5 (which can, in turn, Save Copy as CS5) so that you're not stuck as the early adopter when working with a collaborator who hasn't yet made the switch to the latest version. Unlike Photoshop or Illustrator files, After Effects projects are not otherwise backwards compatible.

SCRIPT

Paul Tuersley's OpenSesame brings backwards compatibility to After Effects, exporting projects that can be opened in any version from CS3 or later. Projects are exported as human readable text files that can also be edited in a text editor or spreadsheet, and any incompatible features are clearly logged.

Get Settings Right

After Effects includes a bunch of settings that you must understand in order to avoid getting in a fight with them. These have to do with essentials such as how time, color depth, transparency, pixel aspect ratio, and field data are handled. It's not necessarily fun—but it's the law.

Project Settings

The Project Settings dialog (**Ctrl+Alt+Shift+K/ Cmd+Opt+Shift+K**) contains three basic sections:

▶ Display Style determines how time is displayed— predominantly whether a composition's frame count is kept in integers (frames) or in timecode (hours, minutes, seconds, and frames). Broadly, film projects tend to work in frames, broadcast video projects in timecode. This won't affect the frame rates of your footage or compositions.

▶ The Color Settings section includes the project-wide color depth (8, 16, or 32 bits per channel), as well as color management and blending settings. Chapter 11 covers this in depth.

▶ Audio Settings affect only previews; lowering the rate can save RAM. I never touch this.

TIP

Instead of opening Project Settings, change Display Style by Ctrl- or Cmd-clicking on the timecode indicator in the timeline; change color depth by Alt- or Opt-clicking the bpc indicator in the Project panel.

Embedded Timecode

After Effects CS5.5 added timecode support; reference timing in hours, minutes, seconds, and frames can now be used to log source media when recorded and edited. Moving-image formats such as QuickTime and even DPX sequences can contain embedded timecode, although tapeless-format cameras such as Canon DSLRDSLRs (pre-5D Mark III) don't embed it when recording.

Clips that do include embedded timecode can be sorted in the Project panel according to reel and In or Out points, which restores them to shooting order. There is no way to change the timecode or reel name of a clip in After Effects, but whatever numbers appear with the In and Out points in a timeline also render as embedded into formats that support it.

The Timecode Effect automatically adds a timecode window that, by default, reads source Timecode directly. Window timecode, although definitely old school, is still useful in shared reviews; it allows you to refer to a specific frame and be certain that everyone is reviewing the same image.

If you're displaying timecode, you'll almost never want to change the default Auto setting unless you're working with footage containing more than one frame rate and need to conform everything to a particular standard.

If you're working with frames, it's often most helpful to start numbering them at 1, although the default is 0. This applies to imported image sequences, not compositions. Numbering in a composition is determined by the Start Frame number in Composition Settings (**Ctrl+K/Cmd+K**).

Interpret Footage

This book generally eschews the practice of walking through After Effects menus, but a well-designed UI helps you think, so focusing on the material in this section will give you access to the best analytical tools. Decisions about how footage is interpreted are both vital and somewhat tedious. This makes the Interpret Footage dialog box (**Figure 1.11**), where you can specify details for any source clip,

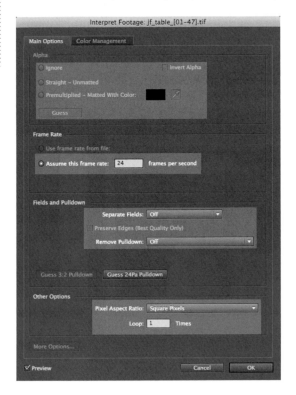

Figure 1.11 The Interpret Footage dialog box is a checklist for getting footage settings correct before you ever assemble a composition. Alpha determines transparency settings; Frame Rate is essential with an image sequence; Fields and Pulldown and Pixel Aspect Ratio (under Other Options) convert footage optimized for playback. The Color Management tab gets a complete treatment in Chapter 11.

even more vital as a preflight checklist for source footage. Here you'll determine

▶ Alpha Interpretation

▶ Frame Rate

▶ Fields and Pulldown

▶ Pixel Aspect Ratio (under Other Options)

▶ Color Management (under More Options with certain file types and the Color Management tab).

The Interpret Footage icon in the Project panel is the easiest way to open the Interpret Footage dialog. Select a clip in the Project panel and click it, or press **Ctrl+Shift+G** (**Cmd+Shift+G**). Or, you can context-click and select Interpret Footage > Main.

Alpha

Effective compositing requires a thorough understanding of alpha channels, but only when something goes wrong with them. **Figure 1.12** shows the most visible symptom of a misinterpreted alpha channel: fringing.

You can easily avoid these types of problems:

▶ If the alpha channel type is unclear, click Guess in the mini Interpretation dialog that appears when importing footage with alpha. This often (but not always) yields a correct setting.

▶ Preferences > Import contains a default alpha channel preference, which is fine to set on a project with consistent alpha handling. If you are in any doubt about that, set it to Ask User to avoid forgetting to set it properly.

More information on alpha channels and how they operate is found in Chapter 3.

TIP

After Effects does not interpret an alpha unless you specifically click Guess; if you merely clear the dialog (**Esc**) it uses the previous default.

TIP

You can change the default Frames Per Second setting for Sequence Footage under Preferences > Import. This should be among the first things you check when you are starting a new project so you don't have to continually change it.

Figure 1.12 It's not hard to distinguish a properly interpreted (left) from an incorrect (right) alpha channel. The giveaway is the contrasting fringe, caused in this case by the failure to remove the black background color premultiplied into edge pixels. The left image is unmultiplied; the right is not.

Figure 1.13 Useful information about any selected item appears atop the Project panel. The caret to the right of the filename reveals specific compositions in which it is used.

CLOSE-UP

Why an Image Sequence?

QuickTime (.mov) formats have the following flaws compared with image sequences:

▶ A bad frame in a rendered image sequence can typically be quickly isolated and replaced; a bad frame is a fatal flaw that can sink an entire QuickTime movie.

▶ It's easy to update a section of an image sequence precisely by overwriting a subset of frames instead of re-rendering the whole movie, cutting and pasting, or opening a nonlinear editor.

▶ Still image formats have more predictable color management settings than QuickTime. If Quick-Time is fast food—convenient but potentially bad for the health of your project, causing bloat and slowness—then image sequences are a home-cooked meal, involving more steps but offering more control over how they are made and consumed.

It's not always practical, particularly when making quick edits to video footage, to convert everything to image sequences, which don't play back as easily on your system or in your nonlinear editor. However, on larger or longer-form projects, they will preserve your work more effectively.

Frame Rate

I have known many experienced artists to be bitten by careless errors with frame rate, myself included. Misinterpreted frame rate is typically an issue with image sequences only, because unlike in QuickTime, the files themselves contain no embedded frame rate (not even formats such as .dpx, which have this capability). You can also override the QuickTime frame rate, which is exactly what After Effects does with footage containing any sort of pulldown (see next section).

The following two statements are both true:

▶ After Effects is flexible in allowing you to mix clips with varying frame rates and to change the frame rate of a clip that's already in a composition.

▶ After Effects is precise about how those timing settings are handled. If your true frame rate is 23.976 fps or 29.97 fps, don't round those to 24 and 30, or strange things are bound to happen: motion tracks that don't stick, steppy playback, and more.

The current frame rate and duration, as well as other interpretation information, is displayed at the top of the Project panel when you select a source clip (**Figure 1.13**).

Fields, Pulldown, and Pixel Aspect Ratio

One surprise for the novice is that video images are not typically made up of whole frames containing square pixels like stills. A video frame, and in particular one shot for broadcast, is often interlaced into two fields, and its pixels are stored nonsquare for the purpose of faster and more efficient capture and delivery.

A frame combines two fields by interlacing them together, vertically alternating one horizontal line of pixels from the first with one from the second. The result is half the image detail but twice the motion detail. **Figure 1.14** shows this principle in action.

If you're doing any compositing, transformation, paint/masking, or distortion—pretty much anything beyond basic color correction—match the Separate Fields setting

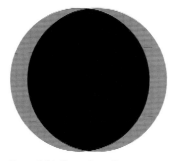

Figure 1.14 If a perfect ellipse were to travel horizontally at high speed, the interlaced result would look like this on a single frame. This contains two fields' worth of motion, alternating on vertical pixels of a single frame. If you see something like this in your composition, interlacing hasn't been removed on import.

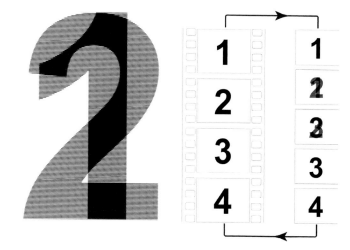

Figure 1.15 Pulldown allows 24-fps footage, the film frame rate, and enables it to play smoothly at 30 fps; without interleaving it into fields in this manner, the motion stutters, as it does if you try to go straight from 30 fps (no pulldown) to 24.

to that of the footage, causing After Effects to recognize the interlaced frame as two separate frames of video.

Pulldown allows 24-fps film footage to play smoothly at 29.97 fps by repeating one field every five frames (**Figure 1.15**). This creates a pattern that After Effects can accurately guess if there is sufficient motion in the first few frames of the footage. If not, the backup option (which still works) is trial-and-error. Do the following:

▶ Create a 23.976 composition with the source file in it.

▶ Try each initial pattern listed under Remove Pulldown until the field artifacts disappear.

There are two basic types of pulldown (3:2 and 24Pa), each with five potential initial patterns, so if none of these works to remove interlacing, there is some other problem with the footage.

Pixel aspect ratio (PAR) is another compromise intended to maximize image detail while minimizing frame size. The pixels in the image are displayed nonsquare on the broadcast monitor, with extra detail on one axis compensating for its lack on the other.

NOTES

To see interlaced footage in action with clips that contain interlacing, check out 01_interlaced_footage on the book's disc.

Your computer monitor, of course, displays square pixels, so any clip with a nonsquare PAR will look odd if displayed without compensating for the difference. Therefore, After Effects includes a toggle 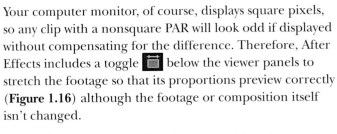 below the viewer panels to stretch the footage so that its proportions preview correctly (**Figure 1.16**) although the footage or composition itself isn't changed.

After Effects makes use of Mediacore, which is designed to predict the correct PAR and interlacing based on sampled data and source and target frame formats. Mediacore runs underneath all Adobe video applications. All settings can be overridden via Interpret Footage settings.

Source Formats

After Effects is capable of importing and exporting a wide array of footage formats, yet only a small subset of these occur regularly in production. **Table 1.1** contains a rundown of common raster image formats and some advantages and disadvantages of each. Which formats will you use most? Probably TIFF or DPX for source and JPEG (with a Quality setting of 7 or higher) for temporary storage when file space is at a premium.

TIFF offers lossless LZW compression, giving it an advantage over Adobe Photoshop format, especially when you

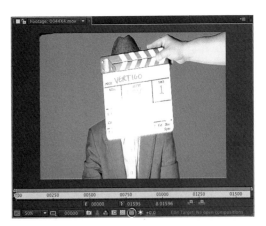

Figure 1.16 Think all of your problems with Pixel Aspect Ratio are gone with the demise of standard definition? Think again. Here is DVCPRO HD footage with Pixel Aspect Ratio Correction on (left) and off (right) via the toggle (circled in red). If subjects look anamorphic—long and skinny—toggle this, and if it looks OK, After Effects is handling it for you; no need to render a square pixel version.

TABLE 1.1 Raster Image Formats and Their Advantages

FORMAT	BIT DEPTH	LOSSLESS COMPRESSION	LOSSY COMPRESSION	ALPHA CHANNEL	OUTPUT FORMAT
TIFF	8/16/32	Y	N	Y (multiple via layers)	Y
PNG	8/16	Y	N	Y (straight only)	Y
CIN/DPX	10	N	N	N	Y (Cineon 4.5 or DPX; see Cineon settings)
CRW	12	N	N	N	N
EXR	16/32	Y	N	Y	Y
JPG	8	N	Y	N	Y

consider that TIFF can even store multiple layers, each with its own transparency. Other formats with lossless compression, such as TGA, don't support multiple bit depths and layers like TIFF does. PNG is more limited and slower, but the file sizes are smaller.

For film and computer graphics, it is normal to pass around CIN and DPX files (essentially the same format) and EXR. EXR was designed (and open-sourced) by ILM specifically to handle high-dynamic-range (HDR) renders with multiple channels of data. EXR channels can be customized to contain useful information such as Z depth and motion data). More on these formats is found in Chapters 11 and 12, which also include information on working with camera raw CRW images.

NOTES

After Effects includes EXR tools, which are highlighted in Chapter 12.

Photoshop Files

Although the PSD format does not offer any type of compression, it has a few unique advantages when used with After Effects. Specifically, PSD files can

▶ be imported directly as virtually identical After Effects compositions, with blending modes, layer styles, and editable text. In the Import File dialog, choose Composition or Composition-Retain Layer Sizes using the Import As menu (**Figure 1.17**)—you get a second chance in the Photoshop dialog that appears in After Effects itself after you click Import.

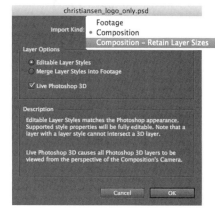

Figure 1.17 Composition-Retain Layer Sizes means "just like in Photoshop." The other option, Composition, reframes everything to the image area (all with the same center point)—and crops any pixels that fall outside frame. Choose Retain Layer Sizes to ensure that each layer has its own unique anchor point—and is not cropped.

Photoshop CS6 adds 3D features that are not supported in Adobe After Effects CS6. For this release, each team considered it more important to radically revamp 3D in the stand-alone app before making the two applications interoperable.

▶ be created from After Effects (File > New > Adobe Photoshop File or even Layer > New > Adobe Photoshop File).

Once your source footage is imported and organized (Chapter 4), the next step is to place it in a composition.

Composition Settings

My advice is to begin with your plate: the main footage, whether it's a background shot or a foreground yet to be keyed. To ensure that composition settings are exactly as they should be with the least effort, try one of the following:

▶ Use a prebuilt project template that includes compositions whose settings match the intended output; you can even create and save your own (see Chapter 4).

▶ Create a new composition by dragging the plate footage (often the background plate) to the Create a New Composition icon . This automatically matches pixel dimensions, Pixel Aspect Ratio, Frame Rate, and Duration, all of which are crucial.

Composition Settings contains an Advanced tab, which pertains to temporal and spatial settings (Chapter 4) and motion blur and 3D (Chapter 9).

Using the User Interface Like a Pro

How exactly does a professional work with footage in After Effects? I've noticed some good habits that experienced pros tend to share.

Resolution and Quality

A 2K plate is the minimum typical horizontal feature film resolution: approximately 2000 pixels, or more precisely 2048 pixels in width. HD video is 1920 pixels horizontal resolution.

First, keep in mind that you might never work at full resolution, but you should almost always leave layers set to Best quality. There are several effective ways to speed up previews and interactivity without ever setting a layer to Draft quality, which creates inaccurate previews by rounding off crucial values.

In rough order of preference, you can

▶ lower viewer Resolution to Half, or in extreme cases, Quarter (see Note)

▶ set Region of Interest (ROI) to isolate only the area that needs to be previewed

▶ use Shift+RAM Preview to skip frames (the default setting of 1 skips every second frame—see "Caching and Previewing" later in this chapter).

Half resolution allows four times as many frames to fill a RAM preview, and Shift+RAM Preview can reduce overhead further by skipping every nth frame (according to the Skip setting in the Preview panel). The default setting of 1 plays every other frame (**Figure 1.18**).

To quickly change the display resolution in the Composition panel, use the keyboard shortcuts shown in **Table 1.2**.

TABLE 1.2 Display Resolution/Size Shortcuts

RESOLUTION/SIZE	KEYBOARD SHORTCUT
Full	Ctrl+J or Cmd+J
Half	Ctrl+Shift+J or Cmd+Shift+J
Quarter	Ctrl+Shift+Alt+J or Cmd+Shift+Opt+J
Fit in viewer	Shift+/
Fit up to 100%	Alt+/ or Opt+/

Activate the Hand tool (H, spacebar, or middle mouse button) to move your view of a clip around. To zoom in and out, you can use

▶ **Ctrl+= (Cmd+=)** and **Ctrl+- (Cmd+-)**

▶ Zoom tool (**Z**) and **Alt+Z (Option+Z)**

▶ comma and period keys

▶ a mouse with a scroll wheel, or scrolling options on a track pad or tablet

Ever notice yourself focusing only on a particular section of a huge image? Use the Region of Interest (ROI) tool (**Figure 1.19**) to define a rectangular preview region. Only the layer data needed to render that area is calculated and buffered, allowing RAM to hold far more frames.

The Auto setting under the Resolution menu in the Composition panel downsamples the image so that resolution is never higher than the magnification.

Figure 1.18 Shift+RAM Preview is a secondary previewing option with unique settings. The default difference is a Skip setting of 1, which previews every other frame but can be changed to the pattern of your preference. To set a preview this way, either press Shift+0 (on the numerical keypad) or switch to Shift+RAM Preview in the Preview panel.

With the cursor over a specific area of the frame, hold the **Alt (Opt)** key as you zoom to keep that point centered.

Figure 1.19 Region of Interest crops the active view region. Want to keep this view? Crop Comp to Region of Interest (in the Composition menu).

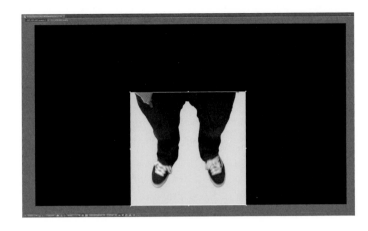

Figure 1.20 Disabling Live Update and enabling **Caps Lock** could be seen as desperation moves when interactivity becomes unacceptable, but the former is rarely necessary (you can do it temporarily with **Alt/Opt**) and the latter can actually be a handy way to do setup as quickly as possible without worrying about previews. The frame goes black as soon as you make an adjustment.

TIP

Working in a comp with Ray-traced 3D? Under the Fast Previews icon is a shortcut to Fast Previews Preferences. Click on the GPU Information button and you'll learn whether your machine renders on the CPU (slow for ray-tracing) and whether Fast Draft is available (the best option while working).

Responsiveness

Has your After Effects UI slowed to a crawl as you work on a big shot? Here's a quick triage you can try:

► **Deactivate Live Update (Figure 1.20).** On by default, this toggle enables real-time update in the viewers as you adjust controls. Deactivate it and updates occur only when you release the mouse.

► **Hold Alt (Opt) as you make adjustments.** With Live Update on, this toggle prevents views from updating. Deactivate Live Update and the behavior is inverted; the modifier keys instead enable real-time updates.

► **Activate Caps Lock.** If you don't mind working "blind" for periods of time, pressing the Caps Lock key on your keyboard prevents updates to any viewer.

In general, the more responsive you can make your user interface, the better the result, because you can make more decisions in a shorter period of time. Just leave time to double-check the result if you are in the habit of disabling screen viewers.

Multiprocessing

All modern desktop and laptop computers have multiple processors, each of which can in turn have multiple processor cores. In an ideal world, doubling the number of processor cores would double the speed of the system, but performance in the real world doesn't usually scale so neatly.

There are two basic methods that a system and its applications can employ to utilize multiple processors: via either *multiprocessing*, where whole instances of the application run in parallel on multiple processors as if several systems were working in tandem, and/or *multithreading*, where complex individual processes within a single application are run in parallel.

Because After Effects predates the multi-core era by well over a decade, multithreading is not part of its core processes to the same extent as within applications that were developed with multiple processors as an available resource. It is an oversimplification to say that After Effects is not multithreaded, since many effects and plug-ins are able to efficiently execute multiple threads, but it can be frustrating for an After Effects user to monitor processor activity on a render-intensive comp and not see those processors pegged.

After Effects CS5.5 was a big step forward in the use of multiprocessing. Granted, this is a bit of a brute-force approach compared to multithreading; whole instances of After Effects are run in parallel instead of individual threads, so each of them requires its own memory footprint. To try it, go into Preferences > Memory & Multiprocessing and enable Render Multiple Frames Simultaneously (disabled by default). You should be running a system with more than the barest of resources. Ideally, your system should have more than a couple of processors and at least 4 GB of physical memory (RAM).

With this option enabled, frames in a RAM preview will render out of sequence. The deal-killer for some people is that the CTI doesn't advance as each frame is drawn, so you have to wait until the work area is rendered (or you interrupt it) before seeing any result.

There are also a couple of adjustments you can make to tune this option. If you're running a system with eight or more cores, reserve a couple of them for other applications by setting CPUs Reserved for Other Applications in that same Preferences panel. Ideally, you can assign 2 GB per background CPU and still have a few GB of memory to reserve for other applications, as in **Figure 1.21**.

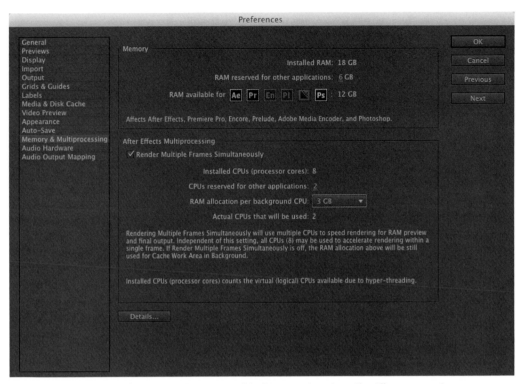

Figure 1.21 This dynamic Preferences panel contains useful information about how After Effects can use the resources on your specific system. Refreshingly, there's little here you need to adjust, other than enabling Render Multiple Frames Simultaneously, if you prefer that, and then optionally adjusting the amount of memory and number of processors reserved for other applications.

TIP

Initial results show that After Effects actually runs faster with fewer than the full number of cores on a system with eight or more cores. Reserve two for other applications and see if you get a speed boost.

Note that few other Adobe applications share the same protected memory pool as After Effects. Adobe Premiere Pro, Encore, Prelude, Photoshop, and Adobe Media Encoder don't count as "other applications," but have been tuned to cooperate using the same settings you give After Effects. You can work between these memory-hungry applications, editing and encoding simultaneously to compositing, without the need for further adjustments.

For more information on how the application is using your system resources, you can click the Details button at the bottom of Preferences > Memory & Multiprocessing. It won't monitor all of your applications, just the six that fall into its managed pool: the CS6 versions of After Effects, Photoshop, Prelude, Premiere Pro, Encore, and Media Encoder.

Caching and Previewing

After Effects automatically caches footage as you navigate from frame to frame (**Page Up**/**Page Down**) or load a RAM preview (**0** on the numeric keypad). The green line atop the Timeline panel shows which frames are stored for instant, real-time playback.

This green line used to be much more fragile than it is in After Effects CS6, thanks to the addition of the Global Performance Cache, which radically revamps caching. (This feature is on by default and detailed in Chapter 4.) You can recognize frames cached to disk by the blue line that appears above them (**Figure 1.22**).

Figure 1.22 The blue areas of the timeline are cached to disc in addition to the green areas cached into physical memory (RAM).

Preview Settings

Here are some cool customizations to a RAM preview:

▶ **Loop options** (Preview panel). Hidden among the playback icons atop Preview is a toggle controlling how previews loop. Use this to disable looping, or amaze your friends with the ping-pong option.

▶ **From Current Time** (Preview panel). Tired of resetting the work area? Toggle this on and previews begin at the current time and roll through to the end of the composition.

▶ **Full Screen** (Preview panel). Self-explanatory and rarely used, but a cool option, no?

▶ **Preferences** > **Video Preview** lets you specify the output device and how it is used. If you have an external video device attached with its own monitor, you can use it to preview. Third-party output devices, such as Kona and Blackmagic cards, are supported as well.

If refined motion is not critical, use Shift+RAM Preview—this skips frames according to whatever pattern is set in the Preview panel under the Shift+RAM Preview Options menu.

Backgrounds

You need to see what you're doing, and when you use a contrasting background it's like shining a light behind layer edges. You can customize the background color of the

TIP

To update an external preview device, press /.

TIP

The shortcut for Shift+RAM Preview is, naturally enough, **Shift+0** (on the numeric keypad). To set the Work Area to the length of any highlighted layers, use **Ctrl+Alt+B** (**Cmd+Opt+B**).

Figure 1.23 If the gradient behind a matted object is made a guide layer, you can clearly see the edge details of the foreground, but the gradient doesn't show up in any subsequent compositions or renders. If it's set as a Guide Layer  (Layer > Guide Layer or context-click the layer), it does not show up when rendered or nested in another composition.

TIP

To create a basic gradient background, apply the Ramp effect to a solid layer.

TIP

Use Preferences > Grids & Guides to customize the Safe Margins in the Title/Action Safe overlay or the appearance of grids and guides.

Composition viewer right in Composition > Compositing Settings or toggle the Transparency Grid icon ▨ beneath the Composition panel to evaluate edges in sharp relief.

You can even insert background or reference footage or a custom gradient background that you created (**Figure 1.23**).

Several other modes and toggles are available in the viewer panels. Some are familiar from other Adobe applications:

▶ **Title/Action Safe** overlays determine the boundaries of the frame as well as its center point. **Alt**- or **Opt**-click on the Grid & Guide Options icon ▦ to toggle it.

▶ **View > Show Grid** (**Ctrl+'**/**Cmd+'**) displays an overlay grid.

▶ **View > Show Rulers** (**Ctrl+R**/**Cmd+R**) displays not only pixel measurements of the viewer, but allows you to add guides as you can in Photoshop.

All of these are toggled via a single menu beneath the viewer panel (the one that looks like a crosshair). To pull out a guide, choose Show Rulers and then drag from either the horizontal or vertical ruler. To change the origin point (0 on each ruler), drag the crosshair from the corner between the two rulers.

Masks, keyframes, and motion paths can get in the way. You can

▶ hide them all using View > Hide Layer Controls (**Ctrl+Shift+H**/**Cmd+Shift+H**)

- ▶ use the Toggle Mask and Shape Path Visibility button at the bottom of the Composition panel

- ▶ customize what is shown and hidden with View > View Options (**Ctrl+Alt+U/Cmd+Opt+U**).

Beginning in Chapter 5 you'll be encouraged to study images one color channel at a time. The Show Channel icon exists for this purpose (keyboard shortcuts **Alt+1** [**Opt+1**] through **Alt+4** [**Opt+4**] map to R, G, B, and A, respectively). An outline in the color of the selected channel reminds you which channel is displayed (**Figure 1.24**).

Figure 1.24 The blue border indicates that only that color channel is displayed.

"Effects" in After Effects: Plug-ins and Animation Presets

After Effects contains about 200 default effects plug-ins, and third parties provide hundreds more. Personally, I use less than 20 percent of these effects around 80 percent of the time, and you probably will, too. So my opinion is that you don't need to understand them all in order to use the most powerful ones. And even cooler, once you thoroughly understand the core effects, you can use them together to do things with After Effects that you might have thought required third-party plug-ins.

Opened a project only to discover a warning that some effects are missing, and wondering which ones, and where to find them? The script pt_EffectSearch by Paul Tuersley (http://aescripts.com/pt_effectsearch/) helps you locate missing plug-ins and where they are used.

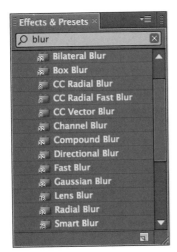

Figure 1.25 Type the word **blur** in the Effects & Presets search field and only effects with that text string in the name appear. You can also choose to display only effects with higher bit depths (when working at 16 or 32 bits per channel—see Chapter 11 for more on that).

TIP

Convert raw footage by dragging it directly to the Render Queue panel, no composition required (one is made for you). This is a quick and easy way to convert an image sequence to a QuickTime movie, or vice versa.

To apply an effect to a layer, my advice is to avoid the Effect menu and either context-click that layer, then use the Effect context menu, or double-click it in the Effects & Presets panel. The Effects & Presets panel helps beginners and pros alike by displaying effects alphabetically (without their categories) as well as offering a search field to help you look for a specific effect by name or for all the effects whose names include a specific word, such as "blur" or "channel" (**Figure 1.25**).

Animation presets allow you to save specific configurations of layer properties and animations, including keyframes, effects, and expressions, independent of the project that created them. Save your own by selecting effects and/or properties and choosing Animation > Save Animation Preset. Save to the Presets folder (the default location) and your preset will show up when After Effects is started.

Output: Render Queue and Alternatives

As you know, the way to get a finished shot out of After Effects is to render and export it. Here are a few things you might not already know about the process of outputting your work.

To place an item in the render queue, it's simplest either to use a shortcut (**Ctrl+Shift+/ or Cmd+Shift+/**) or drag items from the Project panel.

Each Render Queue item has both Render Settings (which controls how the composition itself is set when generating the source image data) and Output Module (which determines how that image data is then encoded and written to disk).

Render Settings: Match or Override the Composition

Render Settings breaks down to three basic sections (**Figure 1.26**):

▶ **Composition** corresponds directly to settings in the Timeline and Composition panels; here you choose whether to keep or override them. The more complex options, such as Proxy Use, are described in Chapter 4.

Figure 1.26 The Composition area of the Render Settings dialog gives details on how an individual frame is rendered while the Time Sampling section determines the timing of the whole sequence.

▶ **Time Sampling** gives you control over the timing of the render; not just frame rate and duration but the ability to add pulldown and fields—say, when rendering a 24-fps film composition for 29.97 video—as well as motion blur and frame blending (see Chapter 2).

▶ **Options** contains one super-important feature: Skip Existing Files, which checks for the existence of a file before rendering it. This is useful for splitting image sequences between sessions (see Chapter 4 for details on how to use this feature).

If you find that rendered output doesn't match your expectations, Render Settings is generally the place to look (unless the problem involves color management, compression, or audio). The output modules handle writing that output to a file.

Output Modules: Make a Movie

Output modules convert the rendered frame into an actual file. The main decisions here concern

▶ **format**—what file type is being created?

▶ **size**—should the pixel dimensions of the output differ from those of the composition being rendered?

▶ **audio**—on or off, and in what format?

TIP

Need to render several items to one location? Set up one item, then add the rest. The location of the first becomes the default.

TIP

Want the best looking half-resolution render? Use Stretch in Output Module, instead of half resolution in Render Settings (which typically renders faster).

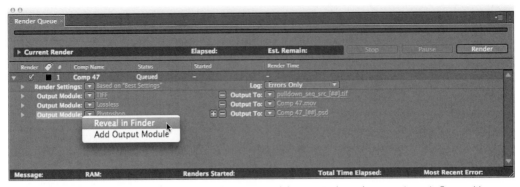

Figure 1.27 It's easy to miss that you can add multiple output modules to a single render queue item via Composition > Add Output Module or this context menu shown here. This is an immense time-saver, as each frame is rendered once and written as many times as you like.

Adobe Media Encoder

You can bypass the After Effects Render Queue entirely by dragging your render-ready .aep file into Media Encoder (AME), which uses Dynamic Link to peek inside the After Effects project, allowing you to select a comp to add to the Media Encoder's own queue.

Media Encoder has a bunch of advantages including:

▶ Runs in the background while you continue to work in After Effects

▶ Presets that correspond to popular formats

▶ A preview area to see before/after versions of compressed output

▶ Renders on 2-passes for formats such as H.264 that can thus possess higher image quality at lower data rates

The disadvantages are predominantly just a couple:

▶ Unlike Premiere, After Effects has no UI to send a timeline to AME, a minor inconvenience (that nonetheless causes 90 percent of After Effects users never to even think about AME).

▶ There is no relationship between AME and the Render Queue, so you can't move your settings from one to the other, and the AME settings are unfamiliar to AE users.

▶ **color management**—unavailable for some formats (QuickTime), essential for others (DPX and EXR).

Several elegant and easily missed problem-solving tools are embedded in output modules:

▶ Multiple output modules per render queue item avoid the need for multiple passes (**Figure 1.27**).

▶ Separate output modules can be changed at once by **Shift**-selecting the modules themselves (not the render queue items that contain them).

▶ A numbered image sequence can start with any number you like (**Figure 1.28**).

Figure 1.28 Custom-number a frame sequence here; no convoluted work-arounds needed.

▶ Scaling can be nonuniform to change the pixel aspect ratio.

▶ Postrender actions automate bringing the result back into After Effects. Chapter 4 tells all.

▶ A numbered image sequence must contain a string in the format [###] somewhere within its name. Each # sign corresponds to a digit, for padding.

▶ The Color Management tab takes effect with many still image formats. Chapter 11 tells all.

▶ Rendered files can include XMP metadata (if toggled on, as by default); this includes information that the file came from After Effects.

Save output modules early and often using the Make Template option at the bottom of the menu. If you intend to render with the same settings even once more, this will save time. Unfortunately, these cannot be easily sent to another user.

Optimized Output

Following are some suggested output settings (in Render Settings and Output Module) for specific situations:

▶ Final output generally should match the delivery format; it's usually an editor who decides this. Lossless, which is only 8-bit, is not sufficient if, for example, you've been working in 16 bpc to render a 10-bit final. For sending files internally, TIFF with lossless LZW compression is solid and can handle higher bit depths and color management.

▶ Low-loss output could be QuickTime with Photo-JPEG at around 75 percent. It works cross-platform, and at 100 percent quality it provides 4:4:4 chroma sampling, and at 75 percent 4:2:2 (see Chapters 6 and 11 for details on what that means).

▶ Online review typically should be compressed outside of After Effects; such aggressive compression formats as H.264 are most successful on multiple passes.

Assemble Any Shot Logically

Seasoned visual effects supervisors miss nothing. Fully trained eyes do not even require two takes, although in the highest-end facilities, a shot loops for several minutes while the team picks it apart.

This process, though occasionally hard on the ego, makes shots look good. A Chinese proverb in an earlier edition of this book read, "Men in the game are blind to what men

Naming Conventions

Part of growing a studio is devising a naming scheme that keeps projects and renders organized. It's generally considered good form to:

▶ Use standard Unix naming conventions (replacing spaces with underscores, intercaps, dashes, or dots).

▶ Put the version number at the end of the project name and the output file, and make them match. To add a version number to a numbered sequence, you can name the image sequence file something like foo_bar_[####]_v01.tif for version 1.

▶ Pad sequential numbers (adding zeros at the beginning) to keep things in order as the overall number moves into multiple digits.

And remember, After Effects itself doesn't always handle long filenames and paths particularly well, so a system that is concise makes key information easier to find in the Project panel.

Chapter 4 tells more about how to send your project to Adobe Media Encoder for multipass encoding.

After Effects offers a number of output formats and can be useful for simple file conversion; you need only import a source file and drag it directly to Render Queue, then add settings and press Render.

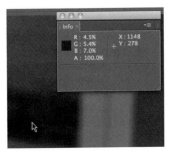

Figure 1.29 By moving the cursor over the area that appears black and examining the pixel values (here shown as Percentage), it becomes apparent that the black levels are not pure 0 percent black.

CLOSE-UP

Working with QuickTime

QuickTime is the most ubiquitous and universal playback format among video professionals, despite the fact that it is proprietary. There are design decisions behind QuickTime that don't change unless Apple decides to change them. Some of these amount to a gotcha:

▶ Color management of QuickTime can be a moving target, with MOV files appearing differently when they are moved from one platform, application, or even monitor, to another. "Application" includes those from Apple itself, which has not always been consistent on how to display the format.

▶ There's no reliable way to rescue a QuickTime movie with a corrupt frame.

On the other hand, QuickTime is a great review and delivery format that benefits from having been well designed at its inception and having stood the test of time. One great integration with After Effects: If you've rendered a QuickTime movie and wonder what project was used to create it, import the rendered QuickTime file and select Edit > Edit Original (**Ctrl+E/Cmd+E**). If the project can still be found on the available drives, it will open in the source After Effects project.

---

looking on see clearly." That may even go for women, too, who knows?

You can and should scrutinize your shot just as carefully in After Effects. Specifically, throughout this book I encourage you to get in the following habits:

▶ Keep an eye on the Info panel (**Figure 1.29**).

▶ Loop or rock-and-roll previews (or in Adobe lingo: ping-pong previews).

▶ Zoom in to the pixel level, especially around edges.

▶ Examine footage and compositions channel by channel (Chapter 5).

▶ Turn the Exposure control in the Composition viewer up and down to make sure everything still matches (Chapter 5).

▶ Assume there's a flaw in your shot; a trick to avoid getting too attached to your intentions.

▶ Approach your project like a computer programmer and minimize the possibility of bugs (careless errors).

▶ Aspire to design in modules that anticipate what might change or be tweaked.

This list may not mean a lot to you on the first read-through, so I suggest you check out the rest of the book and come back to it as your work continues to progress.

2

The Timeline

"The only reason for time is so that everything doesn't happen at once."

—Albert Einstein

The Timeline

The Timeline panel is something like After Effects' killer application within the overall program. More than any other feature, the Timeline panel extends the unique versatility of After Effects to a wide range of work, and differentiates it from less flexible node-based compositing applications. With the Timeline panel at the center of the compositing process, you can time elements and animations precisely while maintaining control of their appearance.

The Timeline panel is also a user-friendly part of the application that is full of hidden powers. By mastering its usage, you can streamline your workflow a great deal, setting the stage for more advanced work. One major subset of these hidden powers is the Timeline panel's set of keyboard shortcuts and context menus. These are not extras to be investigated once you're a veteran, but small productivity enhancers that you can learn gradually as you go.

If this chapter's information seems overwhelming on first read, I encourage you to revisit it often so that specific tips can sink in once you've encountered the right context in which to use them.

Dreaming of a Clutter-Free Workflow

The goal here is to get rid of everything you don't need and put what you do need right at your fingertips.

Column Views

You can context-click on any column heading to see and toggle available columns in the Timeline panel, or you can start with the minimal setup shown in **Figure 2.1** and then augment or change the setup with the following tools:

Figure 2.1 This most basic Timeline panel setup is close to optimal, especially if space is tight; it leaves everything you need within a single click, such as Toggle Switches/Modes. No matter how big a monitor you have, every artist tends to want more space for the keyframes and layers themselves.

▶ **Lower-left icons** : Most (but not quite all) of the extra data you need is available via the three toggles found at the lower left of the Timeline panel.

▶ **Layer switches** and **transfer controls** are the most used. If you have plenty of horizontal space, leave them both on, but the F4 key has toggled them since the days when 1280 × 960 was an artist-size display.

▶ **Time Stretch** toggles the space-hogging timing columns. The one thing I do with this huge set of controls is stretch time to either double speed or half speed (50% or 200% stretch, respectively), which I can do by context-clicking Time > Time Stretch.

▶ **Layer/Source (Alt or Opt key toggles)**: What's in a name? Nothing until you customize it; include clear labels and color (see Tip) and boost your workflow.

▶ **Parent**: This one is often on when you don't need it and hidden when you do (see "Animation: It's All About Relationships" later in this chapter); use **Ctrl+Shift+F4** (**Cmd+Shift+F4**) to show or hide it.

▶ I can't see why you would disable **AV Features/Keys**; it takes effectively no space.

The game is to preserve horizontal space for keyframe data by keeping only the relevant controls visible.

Color Commentary

When dissecting something tricky, it can help to use

▶ solo layers to see what's what

▶ locks for layers that should not be edited further

▶ shy layers to reduce the Timeline panel to only what's needed

▶ color-coded layers and project items

▶ tags in the comments field.

TIP

To rename an item in After Effects, highlight it and press Enter (Return) instead of clicking and hovering.

TIP

To change the visibility (rather than the solo state) of selected layers, choose Layer > Switches > Hide Other Video.

When multiple layers are solo, Alt/Opt-click on a solo layer to make it the only solo layer.

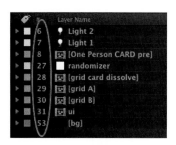

Figure 2.2 Shy layers can greatly reduce clutter in the Timeline panel, but if they ever trick you, study the Index numbers; if any fall out of sequence, there's a hidden shy layer.

Comments are generally the least-used column in the Timeline panel, but that could change if more people start using a script called Zorro—The Layer Tagger by Lloyd Alvarez (http://aescripts.com/zorro-the-layer-tagger/). This script manages the process of adding tags to layers and using them to create selection sets, which are more flexible than oft-requested layer folders (as are found in Photoshop).

Solo layers make other layers that are not solo invisible. They allow you to temporarily isolate and examine a layer or set of layers, but you can also keep layers solo when rendering (whether you intend to or not).

It can make a heck of a lot of sense to lock (**Ctrl+L/Cmd+L**) layers that you don't want "nudged" out of position, such as adjustment layers, track mattes, and background solids (but once they're locked, you can't adjust anything until you unlock them). If you're a super-organized person, you can use layer locks effectively to check layers in and out, with the locked ones completed—for now.

Shy layers are a fantastic shortcut in an often-cluttered Timeline panel. Layers set to Shy are hidden from the layer stack (once the Timeline panel's own Shy toggle is enabled) but remain visible in the Composition viewer itself (**Figure 2.2**). Even if you keep the number of layers in a composition modest (as you must for effective visual effects compositing work—see Chapter 4 for more on how), a composition containing an imported 3D track from such software as SynthEyes or Boujou may arrive with hundreds of null layers. I tend to make these Shy immediately, leaving only the camera and background plate ready for compositing.

Colors are automagically assigned to specific types of layers (such as cameras, lights, and adjustment layers) according to Preferences > Label. I often apply unique colors to track matte layers so I remember not to move them. On someone else's system, the colors may be different according to local user preferences, although they will correspond overall.

Layer and composition markers can hold visible comments. You can add a layer marker for a given point in time with the **asterisk (*)** key on your numeric keypad, meaning you can add them while looping up a RAM preview in real time. Composition markers are added using **Shift** and the numbers atop your keyboard or using the asterisk key with nothing selected. I sometimes double-click them to add short notes.

Navigation and Shortcuts

Keyboard shortcuts are essential for working speedily and effortlessly in the Timeline panel.

Time Navigation

Many users—particularly editors, who know how essential they are—learn time navigation shortcuts right away. Others primarily drag the current time indicator, which quickly becomes tedious. See if there are any shortcuts here you don't already know:

- **Home**, **End**, **PgUp**, and **PgDn** correspond to moving to the first or last frame of the composition, one frame backward or one frame forward, respectively.

- **Shift+PgUp** and **Shift+PgDn** skip ten frames backward or forward, respectively.

- **Shift+Home** and **Shift+End** navigate to the work area In and Out points respectively, and the **B** and **N** keys set these points at the current time.

- **I** and **O** keys navigate to the beginning and end frames of the layer.

- Press **Alt+Shift+J** (**Opt+Shift+J**) or click on the current time status at the upper left of the Timeline panel to navigate to a specific frame or timecode number. In this dialog box, enter values such as +47 to increment 47 frames or +−47 to decrement the same number; if you entered −47, that would navigate to a negative time position instead of offsetting by that number.

Layers Under Control

We were reviewing film-outs of shots in progress from *The Day After Tomorrow* at The Orphanage when my shot began to loop; it looked out a window at stragglers making their way across a snow-covered plaza and featured a beautiful matte painting by Mike Pangrazio. About two-thirds of the way through the shot came a subtle but sudden shift. At some point, the shot had been lengthened, and a layer of noise and dirt I had included at approximately 3% transparency (for the window itself) had remained shorter in a subcomposition. Gotcha!

TIP

Laptop users in particular may prefer **Ctrl+Left Arrow** or **Right Arrow** (**Cmd+Left Arrow** or **Right Arrow**) as an alternative to **PgUp** and **PgDn**.

NOTES

Don't bother with punctuation when entering time values into a number field in After Effects. When in Timecode mode, 1000 is ten seconds (10:00).

TIP

The increment/decrement method, in which you can enter +47 to increase a value by 47 or +−47 to reduce it by 47, operates in most number fields throughout After Effects (including Composition Settings).

TIP

The keyboard shortcut **Ctrl+/** (**Cmd+/**) adds selected items as the top layer(s) of the active composition.

TIP

To trim a composition's duration to the current work area, choose Composition > Trim Comp to Work Area. Combine this with Ctrl+Alt+B (Cmd+Opt+B) to quickly trim a comp to a given layer.

After Effects allows you to time the entrance and exit of layers in a way that would be excruciating in other compositing applications that lack the notion of a layer start or end. To avoid the accompanying gotcha when a layer or composition comes up short, it's wise to make elements way longer than you ever expect you'll need—overengineer in subcompositions and trim in the master composition.

To add a layer beginning at a specific time, drag the element from the Project panel to the layer area of the Timeline panel; a second time indicator appears that moves with your cursor horizontally. This determines the layer's start frame. If other layers are present and visible, you can also place the layer in order by dragging it between them.

Here are some other useful tips and shortcuts:

▶ **Ctrl+/** (**Cmd+/**) adds a layer to the active composition.

▶ **Ctrl+Alt+/** (**Cmd+Opt+/**) replaces the selected layer in a composition (as does **Alt**-dragging or **Opt**-dragging one element over another—note that this even works right in the Project panel and can be hugely useful).

▶ **J** and **K** navigate, respectively, to the previous or next visible keyframe, layer marker, or work area start or end.

▶ **Ctrl+Alt+B** (**Cmd+Opt+B**) sets the work area to the length of any selected layers. To reset the work area to the length of the composition, double-click it.

▶ **Numeric keypad numbers** select layers with that number.

▶ **Ctrl+Up Arrow** (**Cmd+Up Arrow**) selects the next layer up; the **Down Arrow** works the same way.

▶ **Ctrl+]** (**Cmd+]**) and **Ctrl+[** (**Cmd+[**) move a layer up or down one level in the stack. **Ctrl+Shift+]** and **Ctrl+Shift+[** move a layer to the top or bottom of the stack.

▶ **Context-click > Invert Selection** to invert the layers currently selected. (Locked layers are not selected, but shy layers are selected even if invisible.)

▶ **Ctrl+D** (**Cmd+D**) to duplicate any layer (or pretty much any selected item).

▶ **Ctrl+Shift+D** (**Cmd+Shift+D**) splits a layer; the source ends and the duplicate continues from the current time.

▶ The bracket keys [and] move the In or Out points of selected layers to the current time. Add **Alt** (**Opt**) to the bracket keys to set the current frame as the In or Out point, trimming the layer.

▶ **The double-ended arrow icon** over the end of a trimmed layer lets you slide it, preserving the In and Out points while translating the timing and layer markers (but not keyframes).

▶ **Alt+PgUp** or **Alt+PgDn** (**Opt+PgUp** or **Opt+PgDn**) nudges a layer and its keyframes forward or backward in time. **Alt+Home** or **Alt+End** (**Opt+Home** or **Opt+End**) moves the layer's In point to the beginning of the composition, or the Out point to the end.

Timeline Panel Views

After Effects has a great keyframe workflow. These shortcuts will help you work with timing more quickly, accurately, and confidently:

▶ The semicolon (;) key toggles all the way in and out on the Timeline panel, from single frame to all frames. The slider at the bottom of the Timeline panel zooms in and out more selectively.

▶ The scroll wheel moves you up and down the layer stack.

▶ **Shift-scroll** moves left and right in a zoomed Timeline panel view.

▶ **Alt-scroll** (**Opt**-scroll) zooms dynamically in and out of the Timeline panel, remaining focused around the cursor location.

▶ The backslash (\) key toggles between a Timeline panel and its Composition viewer, even if previously closed.

▶ The Comp Marker Bin contains markers you can drag into the Timeline panel ruler. You can replace their sequential numbers with names.

▶ **X** scrolls the topmost selected layer to the top of the Timeline panel.

NOTES

For those who care, a preference controls whether split layers are created above or below the source layer (Preferences > General > Create Split Layers Above Original Layer).

TIP

It can be annoying that the work area controls both preview and render frame ranges, because the two are often used independently of one another. Dropping your work composition into a separate "Render Final" composition with the final work area set and locked avoids conflicts between working and final frame ranges and settings.

TIP

Hold down the **Shift** key as you drag the current time indicator to snap the current time to composition or layer markers or visible keyframes.

Timing: Keyframes and the Graph Editor

Transform controls live under every layer's twirly arrow (or caret). There are keyboard shortcuts to each Transform property. For a standard 2D layer, these are

- ▶ **A** for Anchor Point, the center pivot of the layer
- ▶ **P** for Position, by default the center of the composition
- ▶ **S** for Scale (in percent of source)
- ▶ **R** for Rotation (in revolutions and degrees)
- ▶ **T** for Opacity, or if it helps, "opaci-T" (which is not technically spatial transform data but is grouped here because it's essential)

Once you've revealed one of these, hold down the **Shift** key to display another (or to hide another one already displayed). This keeps only what you need in front of you. A 3D layer reveals four individual properties under Rotation to allow full animation on all axes.

Add the **Alt** (**Opt**) to each of these one-letter shortcuts to add the first keyframe; once there's one keyframe, any adjustments to that property at any other frame generate another keyframe automatically.

There are corresponding selection tools to perform Transform adjustments directly in the viewer:

- ▶ **V** activates the Selection tool, which also moves and scales in a view panel.
- ▶ **Y** switches to the Pan-Behind tool, which moves the anchor point.
- ▶ **W** is for "wotate"—it adjusts Rotation. Wascally wotation!

Once you adjust with any of these tools, an Add Keyframe option for the corresponding property appears under the Animation menu, so you can set the first keyframe without touching the Timeline panel at all.

Graph Editor

The examples folder on this book's accompanying disc contains a simple animation, bouncing ball 2d (project 02_bouncing_ball.aep) that can be created from scratch;

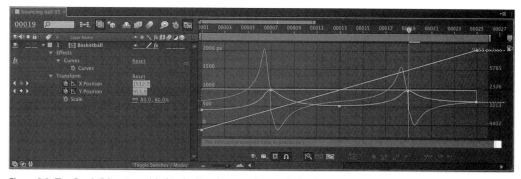

Figure 2.3 The Graph Editor is enabled in the Timeline panel instead of default Layer view. There is no option for viewing them together.

you can also see the steps below as individual numbered compositions.

To enable the Graph Editor, click its icon in the Timeline panel or use the shortcut **Shift+F3**. Below the grid that appears in place of the layer stack are the Graph Editor controls (**Figure 2.3**).

Show Properties

By default, if nothing is selected, nothing displays in the graph; what you see depends on the settings in the Show Properties menu . Three toggles in this menu control how animation curves are displayed in the graph:

▶ **Show Selected Properties** displays whatever animation property names are highlighted.

▶ **Show Animated Properties** shows everything with keyframes or expressions.

▶ **Show Graph Editor Set** displays properties with the Graph Editor Set toggle enabled.

Show Selected Properties is the easiest to use, but Show Graph Editor Set gives you the greatest control. You decide which curves need to appear, activate their Graph Editor Set toggle, and after that it no longer matters whether you keep them selected.

To begin the bouncing ball animation, include Position in the Graph Editor Set by toggling its icon. **Alt+P** (**Opt+P**) sets the first Position keyframe at frame 0; after that, any changes to Position are automatically keyframed.

TIP

To work in the Graph Editor without worrying about what is selected, disable Show Selected Properties and enable the other two.

TIP

The other recommended change prior to working through this section is to enable Default Spatial Interpolation to Linear in Preferences > General (**Ctrl+Alt+;** or **Cmd+Opt+;**). Try this if your initial animation doesn't seem to match that shown later in Figure 2.4.

Basic Animation and the Graph View

Figure 2.4 shows the first step: a very basic animation blocked in using Linear keyframes, evenly spaced. It won't look like a bouncing ball yet, but it's a typical way to start when animating, for new and experienced animators alike.

To get to this point, do the following:

▶ Having set the first keyframe at frame 0, move the ball off the left of the frame.

▶ At frame 24, move the ball off the right of the frame, creating a second keyframe.

▶ Create a keyframe at frame 12 (just check the box, don't change any settings).

▶ Now add the bounces: At frames 6 and 18 move the ball straight downward so it touches the bottom of the frame.

This leaves five Position keyframes and an extremely unconvincing-looking bouncing ball animation. Great—it always helps to get something blocked in so you can clearly see what's wrong. Also, the default Graph Editor view at this point is not very helpful, because it displays the speed graph, and the speed of the layer is completely steady at this point—deliberately so, in fact.

To get the view shown in Figure 2.4, make sure Show Reference Graph is enabled in the Graph Options menu . This is a toggle even advanced users miss, although

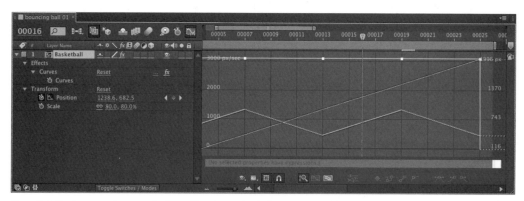

Figure 2.4 The layer travels across the frame like a bouncing ball, going up and down.

it is now on by default. In addition to the not-very-helpful speed graph, you now see the value graph in its X (red) and Y (green) values. However, the green values appear upside-down! This is the flipped After Effects Y axis in action; 0 is at the top of frame so that 0,0 is in the top-left corner, as it has been since After Effects 1.0, long before 3D animation was even contemplated.

Ease Curves

The simplest way to "fix" an animation that looks too stiff like this is often to add eases. For this purpose, After Effects offers the automated Easy Ease functions, although you can also create or adjust eases by hand in the Graph Editor.

Select all of the "up" keyframes—the first, third, and fifth—and click Easy Ease (**F9**). When a ball bounces, it slows at the top of each arc, and Easy Ease adds that arc to the pace; what was a flat-line speed graph now is a series of arcing curves (**Figure 2.5**).

NOTES

The Auto Select Graph Type option in the Graph Options menu selects speed graphs for spatial properties and value graphs for all others.

WARNING

Mac users beware: The F9 key is used by the system for the Exposé feature, revealing all open panels in all applications. You can change or disable this feature in System Preferences > Exposé & Spaces.

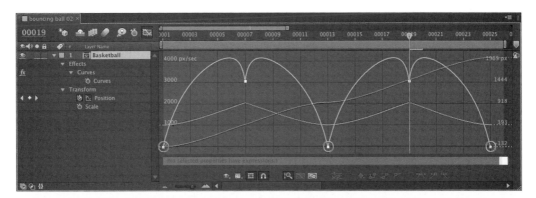

Figure 2.5 Easy Ease is applied (top) to the mid-air keyframes; Layer view (bottom) also shows the change from linear to Bezier with a changed keyframe icon.

Technically, you could have applied Easy Ease Out (**Ctrl+Shift+F9/Cmd+Shift+F9**) to the first keyframe and Easy Ease In (**Shift+F9**) to the final one, because the ease in each case only goes in one direction. The "in" and "out" versions of Easy Ease are specifically for cases in which there are other adjacent keyframes and the ease should only go in one direction (you'll see one in a moment). In this case, it's not really necessary.

Meanwhile, there's a clear problem here: The timing of the motion arcs, but not the motion itself, is still completely linear. Fix this in the Composition viewer by pulling Bezier handles out of each of the keyframes you just eased:

1. Deselect all keyframes, but leave the layer selected.

2. Make sure the animation path is displayed (**Ctrl+Shift+H/Cmd+Shift+H** toggles).

3. Click on the first keyframe in the Composition viewer to select it; it should change from hollow to solid in appearance.

4. Switch to the Pen tool by pressing the **G** key; in the Composition viewer, drag from the highlighted keyframe to the right, creating a horizontal Bezier handle. Stop before crossing the second keyframe.

5. Do the same for the third and fifth keyframes (dragging left for the fifth).

The animation path now looks more like you'd expect a ball to bounce (**Figure 2.6**). Preview the animation, however, and you'll notice that the ball crudely pogos across the frame instead of bouncing naturally. Why is that?

Separate XYZ

The Graph Editor reveals the problem. The red X graph shows an unsteady horizontal motion due to the eases. The problem is that the eases should be applied only to the vertical Y dimension, whereas the X animation travels at a constant rate.

It's not immediately apparent that you can animate X and Y (or, in 3D, X, Y, and Z) animation curves separately. This

Figure 2.6 You can tell from the graph that this is closer to how a bouncing ball would look over time. You can use **Ctrl+Shift+H** (**Cmd+Shift+H**) to show and hide the animation path, or you can look in the Composition panel menu > View Options > Layer Controls.

allows you to add keyframes for one dimension only at a given point in time, or to add keyframes in one dimension at a time.

Select Position and click Separate Dimensions ![icon]. Where there was a single Position property, there are now two, marked X Position and Y Position. Now try the following:

1. Disable the Graph Editor Set toggle for the Y Position so that only the red X Position graph is displayed.

2. Select the middle three X Position keyframes—you can draw a selection box around them—and delete them.

3. Select the two remaining X keyframes and click the Convert Selected Keyframes to Linear button ![icon].

Now take a look in the Composition viewer—the motion is back to linear, although the temporal eases remain on the Y axis. Not only that, but you cannot redraw them as you did before; enabling Separate Dimensions removes this ability.

Instead, you can create them in the Graph Editor itself.

1. Enable the Graph Editor Set toggle for Y Position, so both dimensions are once again displayed.

2. Select the middle Y Position keyframe, and you'll notice two small handles protruding to its left and right. Drag each of these out, holding the Shift key if necessary to keep them flat, and notice the corresponding change in the Composition viewer (**Figure 2.7**).

TIP

Show Graph Tool Tips displays values of whatever curve is under the mouse at that exact point in time.

TIP

Separate Dimensions does not play nicely with eases and cannot easily be round-tripped back, so unfortunately you're best to reserve it for occasions when you really need it.

Figure 2.7 If Separate Dimensions is activated, pull out the handles to create the motion arcs right in the Graph Editor; the handles are no longer adjustable in the Composition viewer.

3. Select the first and last Y Position keyframes and click Easy Ease; the handles move outward from each keyframe without affecting the X Position keyframes.

4. Drag the handles of the first and last Y Position keyframes as far as they will go (right up to the succeeding and preceding keyframes, respectively).

Preview the result and you'll see that you now have the beginnings of an actual bouncing ball animation; it's just a little bit too regular and even, so from here you give it your own organic touch.

Transform Box

The transform box lets you edit keyframe values in all kinds of tricky or even wacky ways. Toggle on Show Transform Box and select more than one keyframe, and a white box with vertices surrounds the selected frames. Drag the handle at the right side to the left or right to change overall timing; the keyframes remain proportionally arranged.

So, does the transform box help in this case? Well, it could, if you needed to

▶ scale the animation timing around a particular keyframe: Drag the anchor to that frame, then **Ctrl**-drag (**Cmd**-drag)

▶ reverse the animation: **Ctrl**-drag/**Cmd**-drag from one edge of the box to the other (or for a straight reversal, simply context-click and choose Keyframe Assistant > Time-Reverse Keyframes)

▶ diminish the bounce animation so that the ball bounces lower each time: **Alt**-drag (**Opt**-drag) on the lower-right corner handle (**Figure 2.8**)

NOTES

There is a whole menu of options to show items that you might think are only in Layer view: layer In/Out points, audio waveforms, layer markers, and expressions.

NOTES

The Snap button snaps to virtually every visible marker, but not—snap!—to whole frame values if Allow Keyframes Between Frames is on.

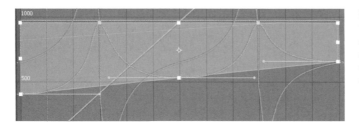

Figure 2.8 How do you do that? Add the **Alt** (**Opt**) key when dragging a corner of the transform box; this adjustment diminishes the height of the ball bounces proportionally over time.

If you **Ctrl+Alt**-drag (**Cmd+Opt**-drag) on a corner, it will taper values at one end. If you **Ctrl+Alt+ Shift**-drag (**Cmd+Opt+Shift**-drag) on a corner, it will skew that end of the box up or down. I don't do that kind of stuff much, but with a lot of keyframes to scale proportionally, it's a good one to keep in your back pocket.

Holds

At this point you may have a fairly realistic-looking bouncing ball; maybe you added a little Rotation animation so the ball spins forward as it bounces, or maybe you've hand-adjusted the timing or position keys to give them that extra little organic unevenness. Hold keyframes won't help improve this animation, but you could use them to go all *Matrix*-like with it, stopping the ball mid-arc before continuing the action. A Hold keyframe 🔲 (**Ctrl+Alt+H/ Cmd+Shift+H**) prevents any change to a value until the next keyframe.

Drag all keyframes from the one at the top of the middle arc forward in time a second or two. Copy and paste that mid-arc keyframe (adding one for any other animated properties or dimensions at that point in time) back to the original keyframe location, and toggle it to a Hold keyframe (**Figure 2.9**).

Figure 2.9 Where the graph line is flat-lined, the bounce stops mid-air—the result of Hold keyframes, which have the benefit of ensuring no animation whatsoever occurs until the next keyframe.

Beyond Bouncing Balls

In the reasonably likely case that the need for a bouncing ball animation never comes up, what does this example show you? Let's recap:

▶ You can control a Bezier motion path in the Composition viewer using the Pen tool (usage detailed in the next chapter).

▶ Realistic motion often requires that you shape the motion path Beziers and add temporal eases; the two actions are performed independently on any given keyframe, and in two different places (in the viewer and Timeline panel).

Animation can get a little trickier in 3D, but the same basic rules apply (see Chapter 9 for more).

Three preset keyframe transition types are available, each with a shortcut at the bottom of the Graph Editor: Hold, Linear, and Auto Bezier. Adjust the handles or apply Easy Ease and the preset becomes a custom Bezier shape.

Copy and Paste Animations

Yes, copy and paste; everyone knows how to do it. Here are some things that aren't necessarily obvious about copying and pasting keyframe data:

▶ Copy a set of keyframes from After Effects and paste them into an Excel spreadsheet or even an ordinary text editor, and behold the After Effects keyframe format, ready for hacking.

▶ You can paste from one property to another, as long as the format matches (the units and number of parameters). Copy the source, highlight the target, and paste.

▶ Keyframes respect the position of the current time indicator; the first frame is always pasted at the current time (useful for relocating timing, but occasionally an unpleasant surprise).

▶ There's a lock on the Effect Controls tab to keep a panel forward even when you select another layer to paste to it.

TIP

You can use an Excel spreadsheet to reformat underlying keyframe data from other applications; just paste in After Effects data to see how it's formatted, and then massage the other data to match that format (if you have Excel skills, so much the better). Once done, copy and paste the data back into After Effects.

Roving Keyframes

Sometimes an animation must follow an exact path, hitting precise points, but progress steadily, with no variation in the rate of travel. This is the situation for which Roving keyframes were devised. **Figure 2.10** shows a before-and-after view of a Roving keyframe; the path of the animation is identical, but the keyframes proceed at a steady rate.

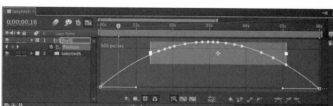

Figure 2.10 Compare this graph with the top one in Figure 2.5; the speed graph is back to a flat-line because the animation runs at a uniform pace. You may not want to bounce a ball, but the technique works with any complex animation, and it maintains eases on the start and end frame.

▶ Copy and paste keyframes from an effect that isn't applied to the target, and that effect is added along with its keyframes.

Pay close attention to the current time and what is selected when copying, in particular, and when pasting animation data.

Layer vs. Graph

To summarize the distinction between layer bar mode and the Graph Editor, with layers you can

▶ block in keyframes with respect to the overall composition

▶ establish broad timing (where Linear, Easy Ease, and Auto-Bezier keyframes are sufficient)

The Graph Editor is essential to

▶ refine an individual animation curve

▶ compare spatial and temporal data

▶ scale animation data, especially around a specific pivot point

▶ perform extremely specific timing (adding a keyframe in between frames, hitting a specific tween point with an ease curve)

In either view you can

▶ edit expressions

▶ change keyframe type (Linear, Hold, Ease In, and so on)

▶ make editorial and compositing decisions regarding layers, such as start/stop/duration, split layers, order (possible in both views, easier in Layer view)

By no means, then, does the Graph Editor make Layer view obsolete; Layer view is still where the majority of compositing and simple animation is accomplished.

Shortcuts Are a Professional Necessity

The following keyboard shortcuts have broad usage when applied with layers selected in the Timeline panel:

▶ **U** toggles all properties with keyframes or expressions applied.

▶ **UU** (U twice in quick succession) toggles all properties set to any value besides the default;, or every property in the Timeline panel that has been edited.

▶ **E** toggles all applied effects.

▶ **EE** toggles all applied expressions.

The term "toggle" in the above list means that not only do these shortcuts reveal the listed properties, they can also conceal them. With the **Shift** key, they can also be used in combination with one another and with many of the shortcuts detailed earlier (such as the Transform shortcuts **A**, **P**, **R**, **S**, and **T** or the Mask shortcuts **M**, **MM**, and **F**). You

NOTES

You must enable Allow Keyframes Between Frames in the Graph Editor or they all snap to exact frame increments. However, when you scale a set of keyframes using the transform box, keyframes will often fall in between frames whether or not this option is enabled.

want all the changes applied to masks and transforms, not effects? **UU**, then **Shift+E**. Lose the masks? **Shift+M**.

The **U** shortcut is a quick way to find keyframes to edit or to locate a keyframe that you suspect is hiding somewhere. But **UU**—now that is a full-on problem-solving tool all by itself. It allows you to quickly investigate what has been edited on a given layer, is helpful when troubleshooting your own layer settings, and is nearly priceless when investigating an unfamiliar project.

Highlight all the layers of a composition and press **UU** to reveal all edits. Enable Switches, Modes, Parent, and Stretch columns, and you see everything in a composition, with the exception of

The term "überkey" apparently plays on Friedrich Nietzsche's concept of the "übermensch"—like such an individual, it is a shortcut more powerful and important than others.

▶ contents of nested compositions, which must be opened (**Alt/Opt**-double-click) and analyzed individually

▶ locked layers

▶ shy layers (disable them at the top of the Timeline panel to show all)

▶ composition settings themselves, such as motion blur and frame rate.

In other words, this is an effective method for understanding or troubleshooting a shot.

Dissect a Project

If you've been handed an unfamiliar project and need to make sense of it quickly, a couple of other tools may help.

Composition Mini-Flowchart, aka Miniflow (with the Timeline panel, Composition panel, or Layer panel active, press the Shift key; see **Figure 2.11**, bottom) quickly maps any upstream or downstream compositions and allows you to open any of them simply by clicking on one.

If you're looking for a whole visual map of the project instead, try Flowchart view (**Ctrl+F11**/**Cmd+F11** or the tree/node icon in the Composition viewer). You have to see it to believe it: a nodal interface in After Effects (**Figure 2.11**, top), perhaps the least nodal of any of the major compositing applications.

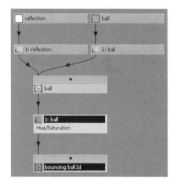

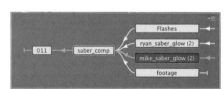

Figure 2.11 The tree/node interface in Flowchart (top) is a diagnostic rather than a creative tool. The gray nodes are compositions, the red source clips, and the yellow is an effect, but there is no way to apply or adjust an effect in this view. Its usage has largely been superseded by the new Miniflow (bottom), which focuses interactively on the current composition.

Nerd-Based Compositing

Flowchart, the After Effects nodal view, reveals the truth that all compositing applications are, at their core, nodal in their logic and organization. However, this particular tree/node view is diagnostic and high-level only; you can delete but not create a layer.

If keyframes are "hiding" outside the Timeline panel—you know they're there if the keyframe navigation arrows stay highlighted at the beginning or end—select all of them by clicking the Property Name, **Shift-drag** a rectangular selection around those you can see, and delete the rest.

This view shows how objects (layers, compositions, and effects) are used, and in what relationship to one another. The + button above a composition reveals its components; for the cleanest view, toggle layers and effects off at the lower left. Click the ⬚ icon to switch the view to flow left to right, which fits well on a monitor, or **Alt**-click (**Opt**-click) it to clean up the view. You can't make any edits here, but you can double-click any item to reveal it where you can edit it—back in the Timeline panel, of course.

Keyframe Navigation and Selection

Although no shortcut can hold a candle to the all-encompassing überkey, there are several other useful essentials:

- ▶ **J** and **K** keys navigate backward and forward, respectively, through all visible keyframes, layer markers, and work area boundaries; hide the properties you don't want to navigate.

- ▶ Click Property Name to select all keyframes for a property.

- ▶ Context-click keyframe > Select Previous Keyframes or Select Following Keyframes to avoid difficult drag selections.

- ▶ Context-click keyframe > Select Equal Keyframes to hit all keyframes with the same setting.

- ▶ **Alt+Shift**+Transform shortcut, or **Opt+Shift**+Transform shortcut (**P**, **A**, **S**, **R**, or **T**), sets a keyframe; no need to click anywhere.

- ▶ Click a property stopwatch to set the first keyframe at the current frame (if no keyframe exists), or delete all existing keyframes.

- ▶ **Ctrl-click** (**Cmd-click**) an effect stopwatch to set a keyframe.

- ▶ **Ctrl+Alt+A** (**Cmd+Opt+A**) selects all visible keyframes while leaving the source layers, making it easy to delete them when, say, duplicating a layer but changing its animation.

- ▶ **Shift+F2** deselects keyframes only.

Read on; you are not a keyframe Jedi—yet.

Keyframe Offsets

To offset the values of multiple keyframes by the same amount in Layer view, select them all, *place the current time indicator over a selected keyframe* (that's important), and drag the setting; all change by the same increment. If, instead, you type in a new value, or enter an offset, such as +20 or +-47, with a numerical value, all keyframes take on the (identical) new value.

With multiple keyframes selected you can also

- **Alt+Right Arrow** or **Alt+Left Arrow** (**Opt+Right Arrow** or **Opt+Left Arrow**) to nudge keyframes forward or backward in time

- Context-click > Keyframe Assistant > Time-Reverse Keyframes to run the animation in reverse without changing the duration and start or end point of the selected keyframe sequence

- **Alt**-drag (**Opt**-drag) the first or last selected keyframe to scale timing proportionally in Layer view (or use the transform box in the Graph Editor).

Animation: It's All About Relationships

3D animators are familiar with the idea that every object (or layer) has a pivot point. In After Effects, there are two fundamental ways to make a layer pivot around a different location: Change the layer's own anchor point, or parent it to another layer.

After Effects is generally designed to preserve the appearance of the composition when you are merely setting up animation, toggling 3D on, and so forth. Therefore, editing an anchor point position with the Pan Behind tool triggers the inverse offset to the Position property. Parent a layer to another layer and the child layer maintains its relative position until you further animate either of them. If you set up your offsets and hierarchy before animating, you may find fewer difficulties as you work—although this section shows how to go about changing your mind once keyframes are in place.

Keyframe multiselection in standard Layer view (but not Graph Editor) is inconsistent with the rest of the application: you Shift-click to add or subtract a single frame from a group. **Ctrl**-clicking (**Cmd**-clicking) on a keyframe converts it to Auto-Bezier mode.

The 02_parent_offset_setup project on this book's disc is for you to use to follow along with the examples.

To simply frame your layers, Layer > Transform (or context-click a layer > Transform) includes three methods to fill a frame with the selected layer:

▶ **Ctrl+Alt+F** (**Cmd+Opt+F**) centers a layer and fits both horizontal and vertical dimensions of the layer, whether or not this is nonuniform scaling.

▶ **Ctrl+Alt+Shift+H** (**Cmd+Opt+Shift+H**) centers but fits only the width.

▶ **Ctrl+Alt+Shift+G** (**Cmd+Opt+Shift+G**) centers but fits only the height.

Those shortcuts are a handful; context-clicking the layer for the Transform menu is nearly as easy.

Anchor Point

The Pan Behind tool (**Y**) repositions an anchor point in the Composition or Layer viewer (and offsets the Position value to compensate). This prevents the layer from appearing in a different location on the frame in which you're working.

The Position offset is for that frame only, however, so if there are Position keyframes, the layer may appear offset on other frames if you drag the anchor point this way. To reposition the anchor point without changing Position:

▶ Change the anchor point value in the Timeline panel.

▶ Use the Pan Behind tool in the Layer panel instead.

▶ Hold the **Alt** (**Opt**) key as you drag with the Pan Behind tool.

Any of these options lets you reposition the anchor point without messing up an animation by changing one of the Position keyframes.

You can also animate the anchor point, of course; this allows you to rotate as you pan around an image while keeping the view centered. If you're having trouble seeing the anchor point path as you work, open the source in the Layer panel and choose Anchor Point Path in the View menu (**Figure 2.12**).

Figure 2.12 Switch the default Masks to Anchor Point Path for easy viewing and manipulation of the layer anchor point. For the bouncing ball, you could move the anchor point to the base of the layer to add a little cartoonish squash and stretch, scaling Y down at the impact points.

Parent Hierarchy

Layer parenting, in which all of the Transform settings (except Opacity, which isn't really a Transform setting) are passed from parent to child, can be set up by revealing the Parent column in the Timeline panel. There, you can choose a layer's parent either by selecting it from the list or by dragging the pick whip to the parent layer and using the setup as follows:

▶ Parenting remains valid even if the parent layer moves, is duplicated, or changes its name.

▶ A parent and all of its children can be selected by context-clicking the parent layer and choosing Select Children.

▶ Parenting can be removed by choosing None from the Parent menu.

▶ Null Objects (**Ctrl+Alt+Shift+Y/Cmd+Opt+Shift+Y**) exist primarily to serve as parent layers; they are actually 100×100 pixel layers that do not render.

You probably knew all of that. But what happens when you add the **Shift** or **Alt** (**Opt**) key to Parent settings?

▶ Hold **Shift** as you pickwhippick whip or choose a Parent menu item and the child layer snaps to the position, rotation, and scale of the parent (and zeros out its own transform values).

▶ Hold **Alt (Opt)** as you pickwhippick whip or choose a Parent menu item and the transform values offset those of the child, effectively adding the two sets of values together.

▶ Hold **Shift** as you select the None option and the child layer's transform values zero out.

▶ Hold **Alt (Opt)** as you select the None option and the transform values of the parent are removed, effectively resetting it to its pre-parent position.

Figure 2.13 Until you know the trick, setting up a series of layers as an array seems like a big pain. The trick is to create the first layer, duplicate, and offset; now you have two. Duplicate the offset layer and—this is the key—**Alt**+Parent (**Opt**+Parent) the duplicate to the offset. Repeat this last step with as many layers as you need; each one repeats the offset.

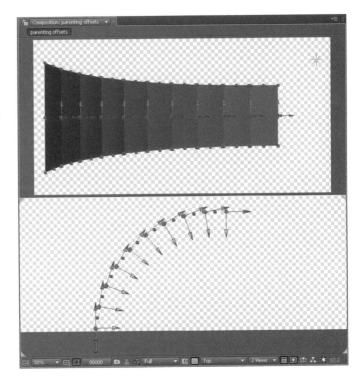

The option to alt/opt + parent is a very cool and easily missed method for arraying layers automatically. You duplicate, offset, and parent to create the first layer in a pattern, then duplicate that layer and **Alt+**Parent (**Opt+**Parent) it to the previous duplicate—provided you start at zero. It behaves like the Duplicate and Offset option in Illustrator (**Figure 2.13**).

Accurate Motion Blur

Motion blur is clearly essential to a realistic shot with a good amount of motion. It is the natural result of movement that occurs while a camera shutter is open, causing objects in the image to be recorded at every point from the shutter opening to closing. The movement can be from individual objects or the camera itself. Although motion blur essentially smears clean imagery in a composition, it is generally desirable; it adds to persistence of vision and relaxes the eye. Aesthetically, it can be quite beautiful.

CLOSE-UP

Blurred Vision

Motion blur occurs in your natural vision, although you might not realize it—stare at a ceiling fan in motion, and then try following an individual blade around instead and you will notice a dramatic difference. There is a trend in recent years to use extremely high-speed electronic shutters, which drastically reduce motion blur. It gives the psychological effect of excitement or adrenaline by making your eye feel as if it's tracking motion with heightened awareness.

The idea with motion blur in a realistic visual effects shot is usually to match the amount of blur in the source shot, assuming you have a reference; if you lack visual reference, a camera report can also help you set this correctly. Any moving picture camera has a shutter speed setting that determines the amount of motion blur. This is not the camera's frame rate, although the shutter does obviously have to be fast enough to accommodate the frame rate. A typical film camera shooting 24 fps (frames per second) has a shutter that is open half the time, or $\frac{1}{48}$ of a second.

Decoding After Effects Motion Blur

The Advanced tab of Composition Settings (**Ctrl+K/Cmd+K**) contains Motion Blur settings (**Figure 2.14**):

Figure 2.14 These are the default settings; 16 is really too low for good-looking motion blur at high speed, but a 180-degree Shutter Angle and –90 degree Shutter Phase match the look of a film camera. Any changes you make here stick and are passed along to the next composition, and even the next project, until you change them.

▶ **Shutter Angle** controls shutter speed, and thus the amount of blur.

▶ **Shutter Phase** determines at what point the shutter opens.

▶ **Samples Per Frame** applies to 3D motion blur and Shape layers; it sets the number of slices in time (samples), and thus smoothness.

▶ **Adaptive Sample Limit** applies only to 2D motion blur, which automatically uses as many samples as are needed up to this limit (**Figure 2.15**).

Here's a bit of a gotcha: The default settings that you see in this panel are simply whatever was set the last time it was adjusted (unless it was never adjusted, in which case there are defaults). It's theoretically great to reuse settings that work across several projects, but I've seen artists faked out by vestigial extreme settings such as 2 Samples Per Frame or a 720-degree blur that may have worked perfectly in some unique, previous case.

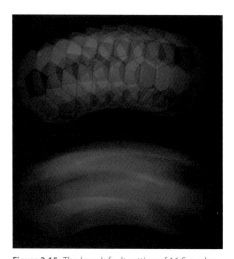

Figure 2.15 The low default setting of 16 Samples Per Frame creates steppy-looking blur on a 3D layer only; the same animation and default settings in 2D use the higher Adaptive Sample Limit default of 128. The reason for the difference is simply performance; 3D blur is costlier, but like many settings it is conservative. Unless your machine is ancient, boost the number; the boosted setting will stay as a preference.

Figure 2.16 The 180-degree mechanical shutter of a film camera prevents light from exposing film half the time, for an effective exposure of $^1/_{48}$ of a second. In this abstraction, the dark gray hemi-circular shutter spins to alternately expose and occlude the aperture, the circular opening in the light gray plate behind it.

NOTES

The 02_motion_blur folder and project on the disc contains relevant example comps. The 02_shutter_angle_diagram project contains an animated version of the graphics used to create Figure 2.16.

Shutter Angle refers to an angled mechanical shutter used in older film cameras; it is a hemisphere of a given angle that rotates on each frame. The angle corresponds to the radius of the open section—the wedge of the whole pie that exposes the frame (**Figure 2.16**). A typical film shutter is 180 degrees—open half the time, or $^1/_{48}$ of a second at 24 frames per second.

Electronic shutters are variable but refer to shutter angle as a benchmark; they can operate down in the single digits or close to a full (mechanically impossible) 360 degrees. After Effects motion blur goes to 720 degrees simply because sometimes mathematical accuracy is not the name of the game, and you want more than 360 degrees.

If you don't know how the shutter angle was set when the plate was shot, you can typically nail it by zooming in and matching background and foreground elements by eye (**Figure 2.17**). If your camera report includes shutter speed, you can calculate the Shutter Angle setting using the following formula:

shutter speed = 1 / frame rate * (360 / shutter angle)

This isn't as gnarly as it looks, but if you dislike formulas, think of it like this: If your camera takes 24 fps, but Shutter Angle is set at 180 degrees, then the frame is exposed half the time (180/360 = ½) or $^1/_{48}$ of a second. However, if the shutter speed is $^1/_{96}$ per second with this frame rate, Shutter Angle should be set to 90 degrees. A $^1/_{1000}$ per second shutter would have a 9-degree shutter angle in order to obey this rule of thumb.

Shutter Phase determines how the shutter opens relative to the frame, which covers a given fraction of a second beginning at a given point in time. If the shutter is set to 0, it opens at that point in time, and the blur appears to extend forward through the frame, which makes it appear offset.

The default –90 Shutter Phase setting (with a 180-degree Shutter Angle) causes half the blur to occur before the frame so that blur extends in both directions from the current position. This is how blur appears when taken with a camera, so a setting that is –50% of Shutter Angle

Figure 2.17 The white solid tracked to the side of the streetcar has been eye-matched to have an equivalent blur by adjusting Shutter Angle; care is also taken to set Shutter Phase to −50% of Shutter Angle so that the layer stays centered on the track.

is essential when you're adding motion blur to a motion-tracked shot. Otherwise, the track itself appears offset when motion blur is enabled.

Enhancement: Easier Than Elimination

Although software may one day be developed to resolve a blurred image back to sharp detail, in 2012 it remains much, much harder to sharpen a blurred image elegantly than it is to add blur to a sharp image. Motion blur comes for free when you keyframe motion in After Effects; what about when there is motion but no blur and no keyframes, as can be the case in pre-existing footage?

If you have imported a 3D element with insufficient blur, or footage shot with too high a shutter speed, you have the options to add the effect of motion blur using

- ▶ Directional Blur, which can mimic the blur of layers moving in some uniform X and Y direction
- ▶ Radial Blur, which can mimic motion in Z depth (or spin)

▶ Timewarp, which can add motion blur without any retiming whatsoever

Yes, you read that last one correctly. There's a full section on Timewarp later in this chapter, but to use it to add procedural motion blur

▶ set Speed to 100

▶ toggle Enable Motion Blur

▶ set Shutter Control to Manual

Now raise the Shutter Angle and Shutter Samples (being aware that the higher you raise them, the longer the render time). The methodology is similar to that of the plug-in, Reel Smart Motion Blur by RE:Vision Effects; try the demo version on the book's disc (in the REVision Effects folder) and compare quality and render time.

Timing and Retiming

After Effects is more flexible when working with time than most video applications. You can retime footage or mix and match speeds and timing using a variety of methods.

Absolute (Not Relative) Time

After Effects measures time in absolute seconds, rather than frames, whose timing and number are relative to the number per second. If frames instead of seconds were the measure of time, changing the frame rate on the fly would pose a much greater problem than it does.

Change the frame rate of a composition and the keyframes maintain their position in actual time, so the timing of an animation doesn't change (**Figure 2.18**), only the position of the keyframes relative to frames. Here's a haiku:

keyframes realign
falling between retimed frames
timing is unchanged

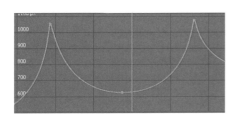

Figure 2.18 The bounce animation remains the same as the composition frame rate changes; keyframes now fall in between whole frames, the vertical lines on the grid.

Likewise, footage (or a nested composition) with a mismatched frame rate syncs up at least once a second, but the intervening source frames may fall in between composition frames. Think of a musician playing 3 against 4; one second in After Effects is something like the downbeat.

Time Stretch

Time Stretch lets you alter the duration (and thus the speed) of a source clip—but it doesn't let you animate the retiming itself (for that, you need Time Remap or Time-warp). The third of the three icons at the lower left of the Timeline panel reveals the In/Out/Duration/Stretch columns.

I mostly change the Stretch value and find the interrelated settings of all four columns redundant. I also never use a Time Stretch setting that is anything but an integer multiple or division by halves: 300%, 200%, 50%, or 25%. You can do without the columns altogether using the Time Stretch dialog (context-click > Time > Time Stretch). **Ctrl+Alt+R** (**Cmd+Opt+R**) or Layer > Time > Time-Reverse Layer sets the Stretch value to –100%. The layer's appearance alters to remind you that it is reversed (**Figure 2.19**).

Layer > Time > Freeze Frame applies the Time Remap effect with a single Hold keyframe at the current time.

Frame Blend

Suppose you retime a source clip with a Stretch value that doesn't factor evenly into 100%; the result is likely to lurch in a distracting, inelegant fashion. Enable Frame Blend for the layer and the composition, and After Effects averages the adjacent frames together to create a new image on frames that fall in between the source frames. This also works when you're adding footage to a composition with a mismatched frame rate. There are two modes:

▶ Frame Mix mode overlays adjoining frames, essentially blurring them together.

▶ Pixel Motion is based on optical flow technology, which uses motion vectors to track the motion of actual pixels from frame to frame, creating new frames that are something like a morph of the adjoining frames.

Confusingly, the icons for these modes are the same as Draft and Best layer quality, respectively (**Figure 2.20**), yet there are cases where Frame Mix may be preferable instead of merely quicker. Pixel Motion can often appear too blurry, too distorted, or contain too many noticeable frame

Figure 2.19 The candy striping along the bottom of the layer indicates that the Stretch value is negative and the footage will run in reverse.

The 02_frame_blend folder and project on the disc contain example comps to help you try frame blending on your own.

Figure 2.20 The Frame Blend switches for the composition and layer (the overlapping filmstrips to the right of frame). Just because Pixel Motion mode uses the same icon as Best in the Quality switch, to the left, doesn't mean it's guaranteed to be the best choice.

The optical flow in Pixel Motion and Timewarp is licensed from the Foundry. The same underlying technology known as Kronos is also used in Furnace plug-ins for Shake, Flame, and Nuke.

NOTES

Effect > Time > Posterize Time can also force any layer to take on the specified frame rate, but effects in the Time category should be applied before all other effects in a given layer. Posterize Time often breaks preceding effects.

artifacts. If this happens you can move back to Frame Mix, or move up to the Timewarp effect, for greater control of the same technology (detailed later in this chapter).

Nested Compositions

Time Stretch (or Time Remap) applies the main composition's frame rate to a nested composition; animations are not frame-blended; instead the keyframe interpolation is resliced to this new frame rate. If you put a composition with a lower frame rate into a master composition, the intention may be to keep the frame rate of the embedded composition. In such a case, go to the *nested* composition's Composition Settings > Advanced panel and toggle Preserve Frame Rate When Nested or in Render Queue (**Figure 2.21**). This forces After Effects to use only whole frame increments in the underlying composition, just as if the composition were pre-rendered with that frame rate.

Figure 2.21 The highlighted setting causes the subcomposition to use its own frame rate instead of resampling to the rate of the master composition, if they are different from one another.

Time Remap

For tricky timing, Time Remap trumps Time Stretch. The philosophy is simple: A given point in time has a value, just like any other property, so it can be keyframed, including eases and even loops. Basically, it operates like any other animation data.

Ctrl+Alt+T (**Cmd+Opt+T**) or Layer > Time > Enable Time Remapping sets two Time Remap keyframes: at the beginning and one frame beyond the end of the layer. Time remapped layers have a theoretically infinite duration, so the final Time Remap frame effectively becomes a Hold

TIP

The final Time Remap keyframe is one greater than the total timing of the layer (in most cases a non-existent frame) to guarantee that the final source frame is reached, even when frame rates don't match. To get the last visible frame, you must often add a keyframe on the penultimate frame.

keyframe; you can then freely scale the layer length beyond that last frame.

Beware when applying Time Remap to a layer whose first or last frame extends beyond the composition duration; there may be keyframes you cannot see. In such a case, I tend to add keyframes at the composition start and end points, click Time Remap to select all keyframes, Shift-deselect the ones I can see in the Timeline panel, and delete to get rid of the ones I can't see.

Timewarp

The Foundry's sophisticated retiming tool known as Kronos provides the technology used in Pixel Motion and Timewarp. Pixel Motion is an automated setting described earlier, and Timewarp builds this up by adding a set of effect controls that allow you to tweak the result. Timewarp uses optical flow technology to track any motion in the footage. Individual, automated motion vectors describe how each pixel moves from frame to frame. With this accurate analysis, it is then possible to generate an image made up of those same pixels, interpolated along those vectors, with different timing. The result is new frames that appear as if in between the original frames. When it works, it has to be seen to be believed.

What's the difference between Time Remap, which requires little computational power, and the much more complex and demanding Timewarp? Try working with the keyed_timewarp_source sequence on the disc (02_timewarp folder) or open the associated example project where it's already done. **Figure 2.22** shows the basic difference between Frame Mix and Pixel Motion.

So flipping the Frame Blend toggle in the Timeline panel (Figure 2.20) to Pixel Motion with Time Stretch or Time Remapping gets you the same optical flow solution as Timewarp with the same Pixel Motion method. What's the difference?

▶ All methods can be used to speed up or slow down footage, but only Time Remapping and Timewarp dynamically animate the timing with keyframes.

TIP

There is also a Freeze Frame option in After Effects; context-click a layer, or from the Layer menu choose Time > Freeze Frame, which sets Time Remap (if not already set) with a single Hold keyframe.

NOTES

The Foundry's Kronos tool is now available as a standalone plug-in that uses the GPU to outperform Timewarp and provides other features. A demo version can be found on the book's disc in the The Foundry folder.

NOTES

To transfer Time Remap keyframes to Source Frame mode in Timewarp, enable an expression (see Chapter 10) for Source Frame and enter the following:

```
d = thisComp.
➥frameDuration
timeRemap * 1/d
```

Figure 2.22 Frame Mix (left) simply cross-dissolves between adjacent whole frames, whereas Pixel Motion (right) analyzes the actual pixels to create an entirely new in-between frame.

▶ All methods can access all three Frame Blending modes (Whole Frames, Frame Mix, and Pixel Motion).

▶ Time Remapping keyframes can even be transferred directly to Timewarp, but it requires an expression (see note) because Timewarp uses frames and Time Remapping uses seconds.

Timewarp is worth any extra trouble in several ways:

▶ It can be applied to a composition, not just footage.

▶ It includes the option to add motion blur with the Enable Motion Blur toggle.

▶ The Tuning section lets you refine the automated results of Pixel Motion.

To apply Timewarp to the footage, enable Time Remapping and extend the length of the layer when slowing footage down—otherwise you will run out of frames. Leave Time Remapping with keyframes at the default positions and Timewarp will override it.

The example footage has been pre-keyed, which provides the best result when anyone (or anything) in the foreground is moving separate from the background. Swap in the gs_timewarp_source footage and you'll see some errors. Add the keyed_timewarp_source layer below as a reference, set it as the Matte Layer in Timewarp, and the

NOTES

Roto Brush (see Chapter 7) is a highly effective tool to create a foreground Matte Layer for Timewarp. This helps eliminate or reduce motion errors where the foreground and background move differently.

errors should once again disappear, with the added benefit of working with the full unkeyed footage.

You can even further adjust the reference layer and pre-comp it (for example, enhancing contrast or luminance to give Timewarp a cleaner source), and then apply this precomposed layer as a Warp Layer. It then analyzes with the adjustments, but applies the result to the untouched source.

The Tuning section is where you trade render time and accuracy, but don't assume that greater accuracy always yields a better result—it's just not so. These tools make use of Local Motion Estimation (LME) technology, which is thoroughly documented in the *Furnace User Guide*, if you ever want to fully nerd out on the details.

Now try a shot that needs more tuning that shows more of the flaws of Pixel Motion and how Timewarp can help solve them. The footage in the 02_rotoSetup_sk8rboi folder on the disc features several planes of motion—the wheels of the minivan, the van itself, the skater. At the climatic moment where the skater pulls the 360 flip, the board utterly lacks continuity from one frame to the next, a classic case that will break any type of optical flow currently available (**Figure 2.23**).

Here are a few tweaks you can try on this footage, or your own:

▶ While raising Vector Detail would seem to increase accuracy, it's hard to find anywhere in this clip where it helps. Not only does a higher number (100) drastically increase render time, it simply increases or at best shifts artifacts with fast motion. This is because it is analyzing too much detail with not enough areas to average in.

▶ Smoothing relates directly to Vector Detail. The Foundry claims that the defaults, which are balanced, work best for most sequences. You can raise Global Smoothness (all vectors), Local Smoothness (individual vectors), and Smoothing Iterations in order to combat detail noise, but again, in this case it changes artifacting rather than solving it.

Figure 2.23 With complex motion such as an object that re-orients itself rapidly over time (left), Timewarp cannot fabricate the changes in perspective that can be captured at high speed, as with a Phantom camera (right).

▶ During the skateboard ollie itself, the 360 flip of the board is a tough one because it changes so much from frame to frame. Build From One Image helps quite a bit in a case like this—instead of trying to blend two nonmatching sets of pixels, Timewarp favors one of them. The downside is that sudden shifts occur at the transition points—the pixels don't flow.

▶ There's no need in this clip to enable Correct Luminance Changes—it's for sudden (image flicker) or gradual (moving highlights) shifts in brightness.

▶ Error Threshold evaluates each vector before letting it contribute; raise this value and more vectors are eliminated for having too much perceived error.

▶ Block Size determines the width and height of the area each vector tracks; as with Smoothing, lower values generate more noise, higher values result in less detail. The Foundry documentation indicates that this value should "rarely need editing."

- ▶ Weighting lets you control how much a given color channel is factored. As you'll learn in Chapter 5, the defaults correspond to how the eye perceives color to produce a monochrome image. If one channel is particularly noisy—usually blue—you can lower its setting.

- ▶ Filtering applies to the render, not the analysis; it increases the sharpness of the result. It will cost you render time, so if you do enable it, wait until you're done with your other changes and are ready to render.

The biggest thing you could do overall to improve results with a clip such as sk8rboi is to use Roto Brush (see Chapter 7) to separate out each moving element—the van, skater, and background.

NOTES

Twixtor (RE:Vision Effects) is a third-party alternative to Timewarp; it's not necessarily better but some artists—not all—do prefer it. A demo can be found on the disc in the REVision Effects folder.

What a Bouncing Ball Can Teach You About Yourself

I remember getting mad when I asked Graham Annable, an animator at LucasArts, how to learn character animation and he told me to start with a bouncing ball. It didn't seem to contain any room for personal expression. Years later I read in *The Illusion of Life*, the seminal book by Frank Thomas and Ollie Johnston, that the standard animation test for all beginning artists at Disney Animation in the golden age of the 1930s and 1940s was to draw a bouncing ball.

TIP

Did you notice back in the Motion Blur section that Timewarp can be used to generate procedural motion blur without retiming footage (**Figure 2.24**)?

Figure 2.24 Footage that is shot overcranked (at high speed, left) typically lacks sufficient motion blur when retimed. Timewarp can add motion blur to speed up footage; it can even add motion blur to footage with no speed-up at all, in either case using the same optical flow technology that tracks individual pixels. It looks fabulous.

"The assignment was merely to represent the ball by a simple circle, and then, on successive drawings, to have it drop, hit the ground, and bounce back into the air, ready to repeat the whole process... all manner of variations were tried, each revealing something about the man who had done the animation and what he considered important in the scene. Some men added distinction by starting with a big bounce, followed by shorter and shorter ones as the ball gradually lost its spring. Some put the action in perspective to show how well they could figure a complicated assignment, or they added a stripe around the ball to show how much it turned during the whole action. These men were grabbed quickly by the Effects Department..."

From this, I realized not only that each animation was unique, but also how much of what you do as an animator comes up when you just re-create the seemingly simplest motions. Any viewer, whether or not that person is herself an animator, can tell if you've gotten it right, so finely tuned is the human sense of motion.

If you're learning computer graphics, it's worth knowing that not everyone is an animator. In fact, most compositors that I've met are not big on animation, other than the ones who end up focused on motion graphics (which also incorporates visual design).

After Effects is more animation-friendly than the typical compositing application. The exercises in this chapter can tell you whether you're the type of artist who can spend long stretches of time watching a short repeated motion until it looks right to you, and meanwhile, cover just about every main tool in the Timeline. Now that you've worked through them, you probably know if you're the type of artist who can spend long stretches of time perfecting natural motion. Either way, you should now have a good deal of control over timing and placement of elements, whether or not you ever end up expressing your own unique artistry through animation.

3

Selections:
The Key to Compositing

There is no abstract art. You must always start with something. Afterward you can remove all traces of reality.

— Pablo Picasso

Selections: The Key to Compositing

A particle physicist works with atoms, bakers and bankers each work with their own form of dough, and compositors work with selections—many different types of selections, even thousands, each derived one at a time.

If compositing were simply a question of taking pristine, perfect foreground source A and overlaying it onto perfectly matching background plate B, there would be no compositor in the effects process; an editor could accomplish the job before lunchtime. Instead, compositors break sequences of images apart and reassemble them, sometimes painstakingly, first as a still frame and then in motion. Often, it is one element, one frame, or one area of a shot that needs special attention. By the clever use of selections, a compositor can save the shot by taking control of it.

This chapter focuses on how a layer merges with those behind it. Then Section II of this book, "Effects Compositing Essentials" (in particular Chapters 6 and 7), examines specific ways to refine selections, create high-contrast mattes, and pull color keys (aka greenscreen mattes).

Beyond A Over B: How to Combine Layers

You may already be familiar with all of the ways to create layer transparency or the effect of one layer blended with another. However, it's worth a look just to be certain you're clear on all of the options in After Effects to begin with.

Mattes

In the book *CG 101: A Computer Graphics Industry Reference*, a matte is defined as "a grayscale single-channel image used to hold out a portion of a composite element when it is placed over a background plate… The pixel values of a matte channel therefore represent the opacity of the corresponding image data." Typically, pure white areas of the matte correspond to pure opacity, black pixels to pure transparency, and gray areas are partially transparent (or partially opaque, if you prefer).

As you know, After Effects uses a layer-based metaphor similar to that of Photoshop (and of the two, After Effects had them first). Many users of both applications are first introduced to mattes by beginning with elements that have mattes already included. Mattes can also be created by keying out the green or blue background from a visual effects shoot (**Figure 3.1**), but there are other ways to procedurally generate a matte, such as a high-contrast (or hi-con) matte using carefully manipulated luminance data. Chapter 6 covers these processes in depth.

Figure 3.1 This split-screen image shows a blue-screen shoot (left) and the resulting matte.

Alpha Channel

An alpha (or transparency) channel is contained within an image; in computer-generated images, the alpha channel is generated in the rendering process. After Effects itself can,

Figure 3.2 A computer-generated baseball's color and alpha channels.

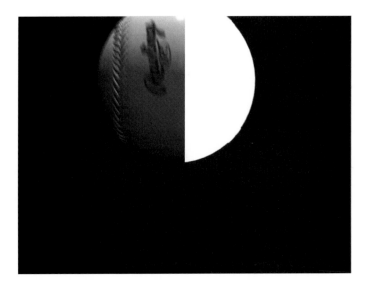

of course, also create alpha and transparency channels in rendered images (**Figure 3.2**).

Here's the important part: Like Photoshop but unlike many other compositing applications, After Effects has a persistent concept of a fourth alpha or transparency channel alongside three channels of color data. After Effects assumes (also unique among other compositing applications) that edge premultiplication is automatically removed before image combination or manipulation is begun. Internally then, all alphas in After Effects are processed as straight (see Chapter 1 for a review of how interpretation is determined on import). This may never be an actual problem for you, until you work in an application such as Nuke that has you manage this process more directly.

NOTES

The built-in assumption of unmultiplied edge pixels can, in some cases, make life more difficult should things not go as planned. The "Transparency and How to Work With It" section later in this chapter offers the lowdown on changing edge multiplication midstream.

Mask

A mask in After Effects is a shape made up of points and vectors (**Figure 3.3**). As a vector shape, it can be infinitely scaled without losing any definition, but as it is generally drawn by hand, hand-animating the selection (a process known as *rotoscoping*, detailed in Chapter 7) is much more involved than generating a matte procedurally.

Figure 3.3 This split-screen view shows the garbage matte mask that was added to remove areas of the stage not covered by the blue screen.

There are also procedural methods to create animated selections by tracking raster data (pixel values):

▶ **Roto Brush**—this much talked-about feature that was added to After Effects CS5 can automatically generate and track an animated mask (**Figure 3.4**). The advantages are that it works well and can be automatically tracked; however, it is far from perfect and the result is its own effect-based selection instead of a standard After Effects mask. More about this in Chapter 7.

Figure 3.4 Before the introduction of Roto Brush (left), which analyzes pixels from user-generated brushstrokes, the closest thing to automatic mask generation in After Effects was Auto-trace, which uses simple luminance criteria to generate masks—lots of them, as is apparent from all the colored outlines (right).

▶ **mocha shape**—a shape tracked in mocha AE (mocha for After Effects) can be brought in and applied using the mocha shape plug-in. It is capable of automatically generating a mask that can include per-vertex feathering in many (but by no means all) situations. You can also use mocha shape as an effect-based selection tool that is unfortunately incompatible with the standard After Effects mask. More on this in Chapters 7 and 8.

▶ **mocha AE Copy/Paste**—it's also possible to copy a shape tracked in mocha AE and paste it directly into After Effects as a mask shape. This offers most of the advantages of mocha shape (other than per-vertex feathering), and because it is applied as mask data, it integrates with all of the many effects and plug-ins that rely on selections in that format. More on this in Chapters 7 and 8.

▶ **Laye**r > **Auto-trace**—While technically impressive, Auto-trace is problematic as a selection tool because it typically creates dozens of masks on anything but the simplest live-action shot. It also offers less control than the other methods, so there are only benefits if you want to do something stylized (motion graphics) with those masks. If this has a use for effects compositing, I haven't found it.

Blending Modes

Blending modes (Add, Screen, Multiply, Difference, and so on) do not, by and large, generate alpha channel transparency; most apply a specific mathematical formula to the compositing operation of a given layer. They are essential to re-create the phenomena of real-world optics.

For example, when compositing an element that is made up more of light or shadows than reflective surfaces, such as fire shot in a blackout environment, it is vital to use blending modes instead of a luminance matte—don't try keying out the black (see Chapter 14 for more details). You can, of course, use selections combined with blending modes to get the best of both worlds. Blending modes—which ones you can ignore, which ones are essential, and how to use them—are discussed in depth later in this chapter.

Effects

Effects and plug-ins can also generate transparency: some (such as Levels and Curves) by offering direct adjustment of the alpha channel, others (in the Channel category) by creating or replacing the alpha channel. Some even generate images from scratch that may include an alpha channel (**Figure 3.5**).

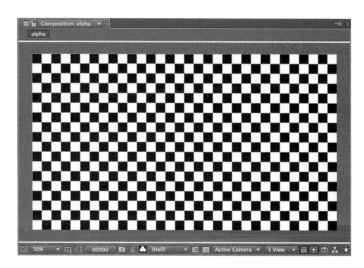

Figure 3.5 The Checkerboard effect is one of a few that is generated in the alpha channel (displayed here) by default.

Combined Selection Techniques

An ordinary effects shot may use more than one, or even all, of the above techniques. Suppose you have greenscreen footage of a vintage race car (say a stylish Ford GT40) and want to replace the number on the side. You might key out the greenscreen to create a matte channel for the car, paint out the existing number (you can even paint into an alpha channel), import the number decal via a Photoshop or Illustrator file with an alpha channel or other transparency data already included, create masks for the areas you couldn't key (such as where the wheels make contact with the floor), blend in some smoke coming out of the exhaust with layers using Add and Multiply modes, and create some heat ripple using a Displacement Map effect (Chapter 14).

Knowing which approach to apply in a given situation makes you a skilled and sought-after talent, and for this there is no substitute for knowledge and experience.

Close-Up: The Compositing Formula

The act of laying one object on top of another is so natural—A over B—it's hard to remember that re-creating this phenomenon on a computer means that something mathematically sophisticated occurs wherever there is transparency. The foreground pixel values are first multiplied by the percentage of transparency, which, if not fully opaque, reduces their value. The background pixels are multiplied by the percentage of opacity (the inverse of the foreground layer's transparency), and the two values are added together to produce the composite. Expressed as a formula, it looks like

$(Fg * A) + ((1-A)*Bg) = Comp$

With real RGB pixel data of R: 185, G: 144, B: 207 in the foreground and R: 80, G: 94, B: 47 in the background, calculating only one edge pixel would look like

$[(185, 144, 207) 3 .6] + [.4 3 (80, 94, 47)] = (143, 124, 143)$

The result is a weighted blend between the brightness of the foreground and the darker background.

Other effects compositing programs, such as Nuke or Shake, do not take this operation for granted the way that After Effects and Photoshop do. You can't simply drag one image over another in a layer stack—you must apply an Over function to create this interaction.

This is not a disadvantage of After Effects—it actually makes basic compositing simpler and faster—but it can obscure important related details such as edge pixel premultiplication (detailed later in this chapter).

Edges on Camera (and in the Real World)

What exactly occurs in a simple A over B composite? In After Effects, it is as natural as laying one object on top of another. In most other compositing applications even A over B is an individualized compositing *operation*, and that is closer to the truth—a truth that After Effects obscures in order to make the process easier. Not only that, but there is more to what is going on than might be obvious, because of the phenomena of optics. The four stages of image gathering and viewing—the physical world itself, camera optics, human vision, and the display device and its environment—exhibit phenomena that are interdependent.

As a compositor, you are not supposed to re-create actual reality, but instead the way the camera (and the eye) gathers visual data from the world. This affects something as fundamental as how the edges of objects should look in order for the eye to accept them as believable.

Bitmap Alpha

A *bitmap* can be defined as an image made up of pure white or black pixels (ones and zeros, if you will). A bitmap selection is made up of pixels that are either fully opaque or fully transparent. This is the type of selection generated by the old Magic Wand tool in Photoshop. You can feather or blur the resulting edge, but the initial selection contains no semitransparent pixels.

This type of selection may have an occasional use, but it truly belongs to the world of primitive computers, not complex nature (or optics). An edge made up of pixels that are either fully opaque or invisible cannot describe a curve or angle smoothly, and even a straight line looks unnatural in a natural image if it completely lacks edge thresholding (**Figure 3.6**).

Feathered Alpha

Although it's easy enough to see that a bitmap edge does not occur in nature, it's hard to imagine that hard objects should have transparent, feathered edges. Look around you at the edges of hard-surface items; they appear sharp.

But study an image of the same scene more closely, and you'll find some degree of edge softness. Adding softness, threshold, or "feather" to an edge approximates this softness in the hard digital world of single pixels, which are square and either on or off. Properly feathered edges can

▶ approximate organic curves (**Figure 3.7**); we're used to this in *raster images*—digital images made up of pixels

▶ mimic the natural behavior of optics; edges are rarely 100% sharp

Optics can be observed in any photo with no compositing whatsoever (**Figure 3.8**). Viewed close up, areas at the edge of objects become a fine wash of color combining the foreground and background. This is not due to inaccuracy in the camera; it is what happens to light as it travels around objects in the physical world and then through the lens of the camera (or your eye).

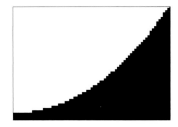

Figure 3.6 This bitmap image contains no threshold pixels. Compare this result with that of Figure 3.7 to see how your monitor displays a curved shape.

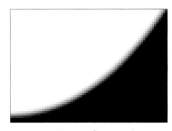

Figure 3.7 Zoom in far enough on a diagonal or curve and you see square pixels, yet further away your eye accepts the illusion.

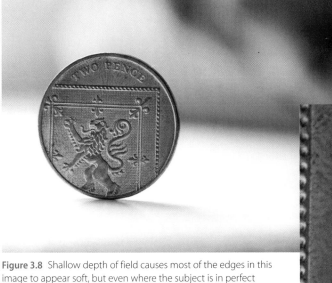

Figure 3.8 Shallow depth of field causes most of the edges in this image to appear soft, but even where the subject is in perfect focus (inset) the edge displays surprising characteristics where it meets the defocused background. Lesson? A soft edge is not necessarily a mistake, since nature never makes any of those.

TIP

Ctrl+Alt (Cmd+Opt) and the + or – key (on the numeric keypad) raises or lowers layer opacity by 1%. As everywhere in After Effects, add the **Shift** key and the increment is 10x or 10%.

Opacity

Transparent foreground objects transmit light, and After Effects is designed to mimic the way these objects behave when layered. Take two identical layers, with no alpha or transparency information for either layer. Set each layer to 50% opacity, and the result does not add up to 100%. Here's why.

Figure 3.9 shows light filtering through two overlapping sheets of paper. (No expense is spared bringing you these real-world simulations.) Let's suppose that each sheet is 75% opaque; 25% of the background light passes through. Add a second sheet and 25% of 25%—roughly 6%—passes through both layers. It's not a lot of light, but it's not zero; it would take a few more layers of paper to completely block out the light.

Figure 3.9 Although a single sheet of paper is more than 50% opaque, two sheets of paper layered one on top of another are not 100% opaque. This is how overlapping opacity is calculated in After Effects.

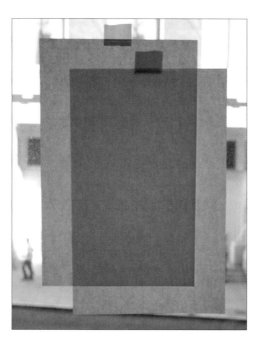

NOTES

The After Effects model of combining opacity values fractionally, instead of simply adding the values together, is not how it's handled in most other compositing applications, and it takes even some veterans by surprise.

After Effects re-creates this behavior, adding fractional rather than whole opacity values of two or more layers. It's Zeno's paradox—you are only getting a fraction of the way closer to the destination of 100% opacity when stacking layers whose opacity is less than 100%.

Transparency and How to Work With It

One major source of confusion with After Effects has to do with its handling of alpha channels and edge multiplication against a solid background color, a process known as *premultiplication*. After Effects has a persistent concept of the alpha channel as part of every image, and this channel is always expected to be unmultiplied within After Effects, whether it originated that way or not.

Any color multiplied into edge pixels is to be removed upon import (in the Alpha section of the Interpret Footage dialog), and reintroduced only on output. Provided those Alpha settings are correct, this works surprisingly well. At some point, however, you may need to better understand how to take control of edge multiplication within After Effects.

Premultiplication Illustrated

Premultiplication exists for one reason only: so that rendered images have realistic, anti-aliased edges *before they are composited*. **Figure 3.10** (left) shows an image rendered against black without edge multiplication; it just doesn't look very nice. **Figure 3.10** (right) looks more natural, but the edge pixels are now mixed with the background color and must effectively be uncomposited from it before they are composited against some other image.

How Edge Multiplication Works

Imagine the background value to be 0,0,0 or solid black. An edge pixel is multiplied by 0 (making it pure black) and then added back to the source, in proportion to the amount of transparency in the alpha channel pixel. Removing edge multiplication with the Premultiplied setting subtracts this extra black from those edge pixels.

The 03_edge_multiplication folder and project on the disc contain example comps to illustrate this concept.

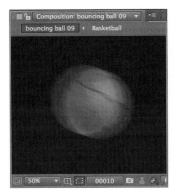 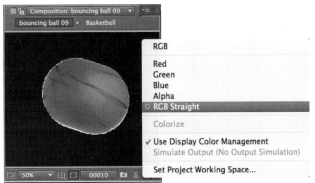

Figure 3.10 The purpose of premultiplication is principally so that images rendered against black, such as this motion-blurred basketball from Chapter 2 (left), appear natural by blending the semitransparent edge pixels. You have the option to choose RGB Straight under the Channel menu and view the image the way After Effects works with it (right).

NOTES

Most computer-generated images are premultiplied, unless specific steps are taken to counteract the process. The Video Output section of the Output Module settings for items in the Render Queue includes a menu to specify whether you render with Straight or Premultiplied alpha; by default, it is set to Premultiplied.

NOTES

After Effects attempts to guess not only the setting but the background color of a premultiplied image; generally this is black or white, but watch out for situations where a 3D artist has become creative and rendered against canary yellow or powder blue. This is bad form, but it's also the reason there is an eyedropper adjacent to the Matted With Color setting (Figure 3.11).

Figure 3.11 Be careful here: Many experienced artists assume that After Effects has already made a guess (here, Straight) when it is merely using whatever was set the last time. It's better to find out what the correct setting is from the application (or artist) that created the image and set this yourself.

When you ask After Effects to "guess" how to interpret the footage (on import, by choosing Guess in the Interpret Footage dialog box, or pressing **Ctrl+Alt+G/Cmd+Opt+G**), it looks for sections of uniform color that are mixed into edge pixels, indicating that the correct setting is Premultiplied.

Back in Chapter 1, Figure 1.13 presented two versions of the same foreground image with two alpha interpretations, one interpreted correctly, the other not. A misinterpreted alpha either fails to remove the background color from the edge pixels or does the opposite, removing shading that should actually be present.

You may find that fringing appears in your comps despite your careful managing of the alpha channel interpretation on import. This does not indicate some bug in After Effects, but rather a mystery for you to solve. There are two basic ways it can occur:

▶ An alpha channel is misinterpreted in Interpret Footage.

▶ Edge multiplication can materialize within After Effects, probably unintentionally, when a matte is applied to a layer that has already been comped against black.

Unfortunately, artists who misunderstand the underlying problem will resort to all sorts of strange machinations to fix the black edge, ruining what may be a perfectly accurate edge matte.

Get It Right on Import

Preferences > Import > Interpret Unlabeled Alpha As determines what happens when footage with an unlabeled alpha channel is imported; the default is Ask User.

The Ask User dialog has three choices, one of which is selected, along with a Guess button (**Figure 3.11**). This is confusing, as it seems as if After Effects has already guessed, when it has not: *It is merely using whatever was set the previous time.*

The Guess option is not accurate 100% of the time; if the foreground and background are similar, it can be fooled.

Ideally you will work on a project whose images are consistent (in terms of edge multiplication and background color); in that case, you can set an Import preference. Typically, however, it's best to be able to find out from whoever created the source whether it contains edge multiplication and what settings to use.

When that's not possible, examine the image and look for the symptoms of a misinterpreted alpha: dark (or bright) fringing in the semi-opaque edges of the foreground.

Solve the Problem Internally

The really gnarly fact is that premultiplication errors can be introduced within a composition, typically by applying a matte to footage that is already somehow blended—multiplied—with a background.

If you see edge fringing, you can try the Remove Color Matting effect (**Figure 3.12**). This effect has one setting only, for background color, because all it does is apply the unpremultiply calculation (the antidote to premultiplication) in the same manner that it would be applied in Interpret Footage.

TIP

RGB Straight displays the image in straight alpha mode, as After Effects views it internally (**Alt+Shift+4/ Opt+Shift+4** on the main keyboard or use the Show Channel menu at the bottom of a viewer panel).

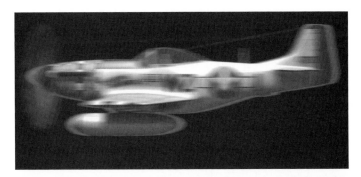

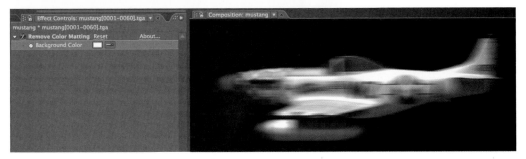

Figure 3.12 The plane was matted against a white background, but transparency has been applied via a track matte (the equivalent of a straight alpha), so white fringing appears against black (top). Remove Color Matting, with Color set to pure white, corrects the problem (bottom), but only when applied to a precomp of the image and matte.

The Remove Color Matting effect will not work properly on a layer with a track matte; be sure to precompose the layer and its track matte prior to applying Channel > Remove Color Matting.

NOTES

Shape layers are directly related to masks; they are drawn with the same tools. If a layer that can receive a mask is selected, then After Effects draws a mask; otherwise, it creates a new Shape layer.

An even better option in cases where you have an element against black and no alpha channel is to use the Channel Combiner effect, with Max RGB as the From value and Alpha Only as the To value. Follow this with the Remove Color Matting effect. This one-two punch uses black areas of the image to create transparency and removes the multiplied black from the resulting transparent pixels. You can save it by choosing Animation > Save Animation Preset.

Mask Options and Variable Mask Feather

Masks in After Effects are available to any layer (provided it's not a camera, light, or null object); just twirl down the layer in the Timeline and there they are. These are vector shapes that you draw by hand, and they are the fundamental method used to hand-animate a selection. There are five basic shapes (the **Q** key cycles through them) and the Pen tool (**G**) for drawing free-form.

You can draw a mask in either the Composition viewer or Layer viewer. In Layer viewer, the source image persists in its default view; there is a Render toggle next to the Masks selection in the View menu to disable all mask selections. Artists may want to see a masked layer in the context of the comp but find it difficult to adjust the mask in that view—in such a case, the Layer and Composition views can be arranged side by side (**Figure 3.13**).

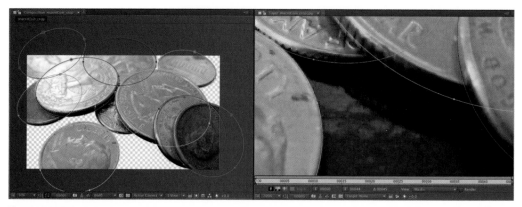

Figure 3.13 With the Composition and Layer panels side by side, you can leave the mask enabled in the Composition panel but uncheck Render in the Layer panel.

When you draw a mask directly in the Composition viewer, a selection is created as soon as the shape is closed. This allows you to examine the composited selection, but it conceals anything you might have missed. If the layer is rotated in 3D space, the mask shape is also rotated.

When using any predefined mask shape tool, it's possible to

▶ double-click the tool (in the Tools panel) to set the boundaries of the mask shape to match those of the layer

▶ press **Shift** to constrain proportions when drawing or scaling

▶ use **Ctrl** (**Cmd**) to draw from the center (with the Rectangle, Rounded Rectangle, and Ellipse tools)

▶ click Shape under Mask Path (**M**) in the Layer Switches column to open the Mask Shape dialog; here, you can enter exact mask dimensions (although I have to say I rarely ever work this way)

▶ double-click the shape with the Selection tool to activate Free Transform mode, then

   ▶ **Shift**-drag a corner to scale the mask proportionally

   ▶ **Shift**-drag an outside corner to snap rotation to 45-degree increments

   ▶ **Shift**-drag anywhere else to transform on one axis only

▶ press the **M** key twice, rapidly, to reveal all Mask options for the selected layer

▶ press the **F** key to solo the Mask Feather property so feather is applied everywhere equally on the mask, equidistant inward and outward from the mask shape

▶ use the Mask Expansion property to expand or contract (given a negative value) the mask area; two masks can be used together, one contracted, one expanded, to create an edge selection

Chapter 7 offers more specifics about drawing precise masks; big, soft masks are referenced throughout the book for all kinds of lighting, smoke, and glow effects.

Mask shapes can be edited to create more precise custom shapes; for example, you can make a half-circle by deleting one vertex and adjusting two vertices of an ellipse.

Easter egg alert! *Simpsons* fans, try this: **Hold Ctrl+Alt+Shift** (**Cmd+Opt+Shift**) and click on Mask Expansion. The property disappears. Now enter **MM** for a humorous reference to Season 3, Episode 13.

Chapter 7 contains details about making use of variable-width mask feather to specify where on a mask feather is applied, and in which direction.

Bezier Masks

Bezier masking in After Effects CS6 is finally streamlined for maximum speed and minimum tool switching. The keyboard shortcuts make sense and are way, way simpler to use, making drawing and refining shapes much quicker and simpler.

I often like to start by placing points at key transitions and corners using the Pen tool (**G**), 🖋, without worrying about fine-tuning the Beziers. When you draw a point, before moving on to the next point, you can

▶ drag to move the vertex

▶ hold and drag out a Bezier tangent

and a keyboard shortcut is no longer needed for either. Once you close a basic shape, keep the Pen tool active. It's now so intuitive I barely need to explain it to you, but you can simply click a point to move it (no need to switch tools)

🖋₊ click a segment between points to add a point

⌐ (**Alt**-click or **Opt**-click) on a point to enable the Convert Vertex tool; on a point with no Bezier, even, tangential handles are created, and on a point with handles, they are removed to make a sharp corner

⌐ (**Alt**-click or **Opt**-click) on a Bezier handle to break tangency and adjust the two handles independently

(**Alt**-click or **Opt**-click) on a mask vector to move the entire mask

▶ the **Shift** key is used to select multiple points and snap them as you drag

🖋₋ **Ctrl**-click (**Cmd**-click) on a point to delete it with a single click

Ctrl-click (**Cmd**-click) on a vertex to move it

Do these shortcuts seem straightforward? This is an absolute first in After Effects: full control over a mask with no need to switch tools or deselect a mask entirely to continue working.

Context-click on a mask path and you reveal the Layer context menu for a mask, including the Mask submenu. Everything from the Timeline is here along with a couple of special extras. There are Motion Blur settings just for the mask (optionally separate from the Layer; bet you didn't know that). The Mask and Shape Path submenu contains special options to close an open shape, set First Vertex (more on this later in this chapter), and toggle RotoBeziers (Chapter 7).

Shape Tool and Shape Layers

The Shape tools are a little bit of a secret weapon. They add functionality that you might normally obtain from importing files from Adobe Illustrator directly into After Effects, but with a few distinct advantages.

▶ A mask shape can be a precise star, polygon, or rounded rectangle, and its vertices can be edited as normal Beziers.

▶ As you draw, hold down the mouse and use the arrow keys to adjust the number of points and inner and outer roundness (where applicable—a star shape is a good one to try).

Shape layers can be a little annoying in a VFX context, because you sometimes draw them by mistake simply because you didn't have a target layer selected when you thought you were drawing a mask. But there's no pure line between VFX and motion graphics, so you will find a use for some of the advantages.

▶ Shapes have adjustable Fill and Stroke, and you don't have to go into a different application to adjust them. With a shape active, **Alt**-click (**Opt**-click) on Fill and Stroke in the toolbar to cycle through the options (also available in the Timeline).

▶ Shapes include effects such as Pucker & Bloat, Twist, and Zig Zag that procedurally deform the entire shape. You can also animate them—although that's pretty much a motion graphics thing.

▶ Shapes can be instanced and repeated in 2D space; **Alt**-drag (**Opt**-drag) to duplicate (as in Illustrator) or use a Repeater operation to instance and array a shape. This is a way to draw complex patterns such as custom checkerboards and radial targets—that's the secret weapon part.

Figure 3.14 The sprocket holes in this film are a simple example of a patter made with a Rounded Corner shape and a Repeater. You could easily make the sprockets extend across hundreds of frames, just by changing the Repeat values.

Preferences > User Interface Color > Cycle Mask Colors assigns a unique color to each new mask. This feature is disabled by default, so enable it to make masking better.

The 03_blend_mode_stills folder and project on the disc contain relevant example comps.

Chapter 7 demonstrates how effective rotoscoping involves multiple simple masks used in combination instead of one big complex mask.

Remember that you have shapes when you need a repeatable pattern of some type, as in **Figure 3.14**. Using the Repeater, you only have to adjust a single shape to edit all instances of it and how it is arrayed.

Using shapes is the gateway to creating certain types of basic 3D shapes, by extruding them. Check out Chapter 9 for more on that.

Mask Modes and Combinations

You will, of course, draw multiple masks. You will even want to do more than simply add a bunch of masks together. By default, all masks are drawn in Add mode (**Figure 3.15**), so the contents of the mask are added to the existing selection and the area outside all of the masks is excluded.

Ninety-nine percent of the time, you will use one of three modes: Add or Add with Invert for the first mask, and Add or Subtract (**Figure 3.16**) for the masks that follow. The After Effects developers are skilled mathematical logicians and have you covered for every possible combination. It's not impossible that you'll come up with a use for Intersect for overlaps (**Figure 3.17**) or Difference for overlap holdouts (**Figure 3.18**), it's just unlikely.

And as a bonus, None mode disables a mask, in case you've been looking for the on/off switch (**Figure 3.19**).

The Mask Opacity property (**TT**) attenuates the strength of a mask; setting any mask other than the first one to 0% disables it. A single Add mask set to 0% Mask Opacity causes the entire layer to disappear, inside or outside the mask.

My Masks Look Wrong When They Overlap

"Density" is a film term describing how dark (opaque or "dense") the actual film grain is at a given area of the image: the higher the density, the less light is transmitted. Masks and alpha channels are also referred to in terms of "density," and when two masks or mattes overlap, density can build up when it should not (with masks) or fail to build up.

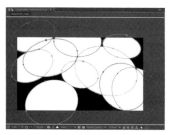

Figure 3.15 Add mode combines the luminance values of overlapping masks.

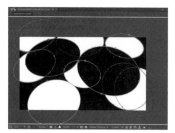

Figure 3.16 Subtract mode is the inverse of Add mode.

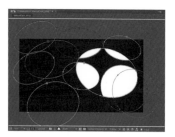

Figure 3.17 Intersect mode adds only the overlapping areas of opacity.

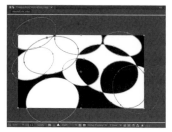

Figure 3.18 The inverse of Intersect, Difference mode subtracts overlapping areas.

Figure 3.19 With None mode, the mask is effectively deactivated.

CLOSE-UP

To Keep Multiple Masks Organized

▶ enable Preferences > User Interface Color > Cycle Mask Colors to assign a unique color to each new mask

▶ press the **Enter** (**Return**) key with a mask selected in the timeline and type in a unique name

▶ edit Mask Color swatch (click to the left of the name) to make it more visible or unique

▶ context-click > Mask > Locked, Mask > Lock Other Masks, or Mask > Hide Locked Masks to keep masks you no longer want to edit out of your way.

Figures 3.20 and **3.21** show a common problem and its simple solution; the Darken and Lighten mask modes prevent any pixel from becoming more dense than it is in the semitransparent areas of either matte. These modes should be applied to the masks that are below overlapping masks in the stack in order to work.

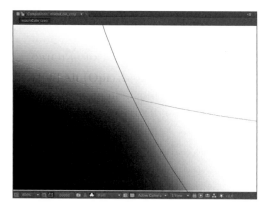

Figure 3.20 Two soft Add masks don't look bad when they overlap, but all detail in the overlap area is gone.

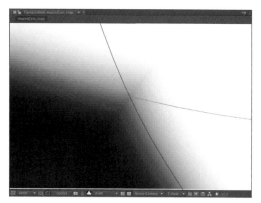

Figure 3.21 A Lighten mask (left) uses only the lighter (higher) value where threshold (semi-opaque) pixels overlap; it's more appropriate.

Overlap Inverted Layers Seamlessly

Suppose it's necessary to break out a selection into segments, adjust each segment as a separate layer, then combine them in the final result. A gap will appear along the threshold areas of the matte for the reasons explained in the "Opacity" section earlier; two overlapping 50% opaque pixels do not make a 100% opaque combined pixel.

Just as the name implies, the Alpha Add blending mode directly adds transparent pixels, instead of scaling them proportionally (**Figure 3.22**). You can cut out a piece of a layer, feather the matte, and apply the inverted feathered matte to the rest of the layer. Recombine them with Alpha Add applied to the top layer, and the seam disappears.

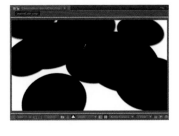

Figure 3.22 Comp a layer with matte A (upper left) over one with matte B (upper right) and you get a halo along the overlapping, inverted threshold edge pixels—around the wheels (bottom left in the image). Alpha Add does just what the title implies, adding the alpha values together directly (bottom right).

NOTES

If a pasted mask targets a layer with dimensions unique from the source, the mask stretches proportionally.

SCRIPT

ReverseMaskPath by Charles Bordenave (http://aescripts.com/reversemaskpath/) reverses the direction of selected masks without altering the shape, which is useful in any situation where point direction matters, including with effects that use open mask shapes such as Stroke and Trapcode 3D Stroke.

Animated Masks

Following are some basics to put a mask in motion. **Alt+M (Opt+M)** sets a mask keyframe to all unlocked layer masks. Mask movement can be eased temporally, but there are no spatial curves; each mask point travels in a completely linear fashion from one keyframe to the next. An arced motion requires many more keyframes.

You can only adjust a mask point on one keyframe at a time, even if you select multiple Mask Path keyframes before adjusting. If you must arc or offset the motion of an entire mask animation, one work-around is to duplicate the masked layer and use it as an alpha track matte for the source layer, then keyframe the track matte like any animated layer.

Move, Copy, and Paste Masks

Copy a mask path from virtually anywhere in Adobe-land:

- ▶ a Mask Path property from a separate mask or layer
- ▶ a Mask Path keyframe from the same or a separate mask
- ▶ a mask path from a separate Adobe application such as Illustrator or Photoshop

and paste it into an existing Mask Path channel, or paste it to the layer to create a new mask. Any keyframes are pasted in as well, beginning at the current time.

To draw an entirely new shape for an existing, keyframed mask path, use the Target menu along the bottom of the Layer panel to choose the existing mask as a target, and start drawing. This replaces the existing shape (**Figure 3.23**).

First Vertex

When pasting in shapes or radically changing the existing mask by adding and deleting points, you may run into difficulty lining up the points. Hidden away in the Layer > Mask (or Mask context) menu, and available only with a single vertex of the mask selected, is the Set First Vertex command.

If your mask points twist around to the wrong point during an interpolation, setting the First Vertex to two points that definitely correspond should help straighten things out. This also can be imperative for effects that rely on mask shapes, such as Reshape (described in Chapter 7).

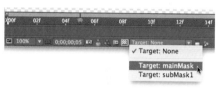

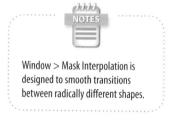

Figure 3.23 The Target menu along the bottom of the Layer panel makes it easy to create a new mask path that replaces the shape in the target mask. If the target mask has keyframes, After Effects creates a new keyframe wherever the new shape is drawn.

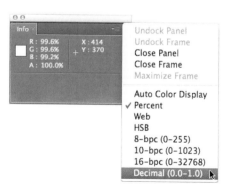

Figure 3.24 You're not stuck with your current color mode in the Info panel. Whichever mode you select also carries over to the Adobe Color Picker and all other color controls within After Effects.

Normalized Pixel Values

Most digital artists become used to color values in the 8 bpc range of 0 to 255, but the internal math of compositing is all done with pixel values normalized to 1, not 255, and this is a more helpful way to understand Blending Mode equations (**Figure 3.24**). A pure monitor white value of 255 is expressed as 1, and black is 0. Chapter 11 shows how values above 1 and below 0 are also possible.

Composite With or Without Selections: Blending Modes

After Effects includes 38 blending modes, each created with a specific purpose. As with anything, for visual effects work, the 80/20 rule is in full effect—a few of them, featured in this section, do most of the work, while special modes such as Pin Light may only be good for stylized motion graphics (I challenge you to find a use for Dancing Dissolve).

Figure 3.25 These examples show the color chart and real-world views of a few blending modes to inspire experimentation on your part. Add and Screen are not the same, particularly blending colors with a 1.0 gamma, which makes Add work properly (Chapter 11 has more on that).

To help you understand what the various blending modes are doing, **Figure 3.25** features text and a gradient over an image of a Macbeth color chart, while **Figure 3.27** (on page 96) has text on a monochrome banner, over a spectrum of hues. Contextual examples using these blending modes follow in the next section. (The 03_blend_mode_stills folder and project on the disc contain the examples shown.)

The difference between Add and Screen is more fully illuminated in the discussion of a linearized working space in Chapter 11.

Linear Dodge is Photoshop's name for Add. The two blending modes are identical.

Add and Screen

Add and Screen modes both effectively brighten the lighter areas of the layer where they overlap with light areas of the image behind them. They also subdue darker pixels and eliminate the blacks altogether. Screen mode yields a subtler blend than Add mode in normal video color space, but it's something like a cheat; only Add with linear blending mimics real illumination (details in Chapter 11).

The Add blending mode is every bit as simple as it sounds; the formula is

$$newPixel = A + B$$

where A is a pixel from the foreground layer and B is a background pixel. The result is clipped at 1 for 8-bit and 16-bit pixels.

Add is incredibly useful with what After Effects calls a linearized working space, where it perfectly re-creates the optical effect of combining light values from two images, as with a film double-exposure (if that analog reference has any resonance in this digital era). It is useful for laying fire and explosion elements shot in negative space (against black) into a scene, adding noise or grain to an element, or any other element that is made up of light and texture, as in Figure 3.25.

Screen mode yields a result similar to Add, but via a slightly different formula. The pixel values are inverted and multiplied together, and the result is inverted in order to prevent clipping (pushing values above 1, which is the upper limit in 8 or 16 bpc):

$$newPixel = 1-((1-A) * (1-B))$$

Once you discover the truth about working linearized with a 1.0 gamma, you understand that Screen is a work-around, a compromise for how colors blend in normal video space. Screen is most useful in situations where Add would blow out the highlights too much—glints, flares, glow passes, and so on; check out the subtle but evident difference in Figure 3.25.

Multiply

Multiply is another mode whose math is as elementary as it sounds; it uses the formula

```
newPixel = A * B
```

This formula normalizes color values between 0 and 1 (see the earlier sidebar "Normalized Pixel Values"). Multiplying two images together, therefore, typically has the effect of reducing midrange pixels and darkening an image overall, although pixels that are fully white in both images remain fully white, because, after all, $1 \times 1 = 1$.

Multiply or Add has the inverse effect of Screen mode, darkening the midrange values of one image with another. It emphasizes dark tones in the foreground without replacing the lighter tones in the background, which is useful for creating texture, shadow, or dark fog, as in Figure 3.26 (which features that type of foreground element generated with simple Fractal Noise—Chapter 13—instead of fire).

Overlay and the Light Modes

Overlay uses the Screen or Multiply formula, depending on the background pixel value. Above a threshold of 50% gray (or .5 in normalized terms), a Screen operation is used, and below the threshold, it's Multiply. Hard Light does the exact same thing but bases the operation on the top layer, so the two have an inverse effect if combined.

These modes, along with Linear and Vivid Light, can be most useful for combining a layer that is predominantly color with another layer that is predominantly luminance, or contrast detail, as in Figure 3.25. In *Spy Kids 3-D*, we needed lava that looked like it came from a video game, so we used Hard Light to combine a hand-painted color heat map with moving fractal noise patterns. More refined uses are also possible.

Difference

Difference inverts a background pixel in proportion to the foreground pixel. I don't use it as much in my actual comps as I do to line up two identical layers (**Figure 3.26**).

NOTES

Overlay and the various Light modes do not work properly with values above 1.0, as can occur in 32 bpc linearized working spaces (see Chapter 11).

NOTES

Reversing layer order and swapping Overlay for Hard Light yields an identical result.

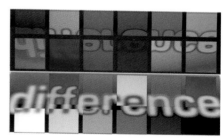

Figure 3.26 This layer is Difference matted over itself—in this image it is offset just slightly, creating contrasting outlines where the edges don't match up. When two layers with identical image content become completely black in Difference mode, you know they are perfectly aligned. This is also a great way to evaluate compressed output vs. the source.

HSB and Color Modes

The Hue, Saturation, and Brightness modes each combine one of these values (H, S, or B) from the foreground layer with the other two from the background layer. Color takes both the hue and saturation from the top layer, using only the luminance (or brightness) from the underlying background (Figure 3.27).

These modes are often useful at an Opacity setting below 100% to combine source HSB values with ones that you choose.

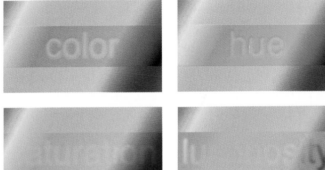

Figure 3.27 Color modes are not intuitive at first, but once you see what they do, you are likely to find uses for them.

Stencil, Silhouette, and Preserve Transparency

Commonly overlooked, Stencil and Silhouette blending modes operate only on the alpha channel of the composition. The layer's alpha or luminance values become a matte for all the layers below it in the stack. Stencil makes the brightest pixels opaque, and Silhouette affects the darkest.

TIP

Stencil Alpha and Silhouette Alpha are useful to create custom edge mattes (a technique detailed in Chapter 6) as well as a light wrap effect, demonstrated in Chapter 12.

Suppose you have a foreground layer that is meant to be opaque only where the underlying layers are opaque, as in **Figure 3.28**. The small highlighted toggle labeled Preserve Underlying Transparency makes this happen, much to the amazement of many who've wished for this feature and not realized it was already there.

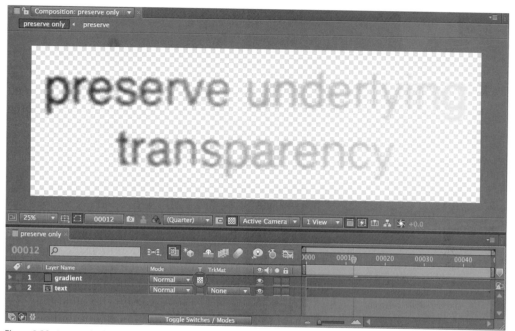

Figure 3.28 Among the hardest-to-find and most-easily-forgotten features in the Timeline is the Preserve Underlying Transparency toggle, circled above. This re-creates behavior familiar to Photoshop users, in which a layer's own transparency applies only where it intersects with that of the underlying layer. Here, the same gradient is simply placed over a text layer; without this mode, the gradient would fill the frame as a solid.

Luminescent Premultiply

Luminescent Premultiply is one method you can use to remove premultiplication on the fly from source footage, retaining bright values in edge pixels that are otherwise clipped. Premultiplication over black causes all semi-transparent pixels to become darker; removing it can cause them to appear dimmer than they should.

Luminescent Premultiply is used to remove premultiplication (for cases in which edges have somehow become multiplied within After Effects). In **Figure 3.29**, the source text over black has been matted using the same layer—white text over black—as a luma matte, which means that black remains multiplied into the background unless this mode is set.

CLOSE-UP

Adjustment Layers and Blending Modes

Here's something I didn't used to know, and you may not either—when you apply a blending mode to an Adjustment layer, that layer's effects are first applied and then the result is comped over the underlying layers with that mode applied. In other words, if you create an Adjustment layer with a Levels effect in Add mode, the Levels effect is applied to underlying layers and that result is then added to them. Leave Levels at the default in this scenario and the area defined by the Adjustment layer—usually the entire underlying image—is added to itself.

 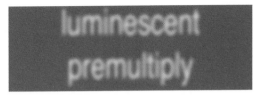

Figure 3.29 Did you create edge multiplication by luma matting a layer against black with itself (left)? Luminescent Premultiply fixes this (right).

Share a Selection with Track Mattes

Track mattes allow you to use the alpha or luminance information of one layer as the transparency of another layer (**Figure 3.30**). It's a simple enough concept, yet one that is absolutely fundamental as a problem-solving tool for complex composites.

Figure 3.30 The alpha of layer 1 is set as the alpha of layer 2 via the circled menu. The small icons to the left indicate which is the image and which is the matte.

The perceptual difference between an alpha channel and a track matte isn't, for the most part, too difficult to grasp. In both cases, you have pixels with an 8-bit value between 0 and 255, whether derived from a grayscale alpha matte or the grayscale average of three channels of color, a luma matte. With color, the three channels are simply averaged together to make up a single grayscale alpha. With 16 and even 32 bpc, it's finer increments in the same range.

To set a track matte, place the layer that contains the transparency data directly above its target layer in the Timeline and choose one of the four options from the Track Matte menu:

- ▶ **Alpha Matte**: The alpha channel of the track matte layer is the alpha
- ▶ **Alpha Inverted Matte**: The same, but the black areas are opaque
- ▶ **Luma Matte**: Uses the average brightness of red, green, and blue as the alpha
- ▶ **Luma Inverted Matte**: The same, but the black areas are opaque

By default, the visibility of the track matte layer is disabled when you activate it from the layer below by choosing one of these four modes. This is generally desirable. Some clever uses of track mattes require them to be on. For example, by matting out the bright areas of the image, turning on the matte, and setting it to Add mode, you can naturally brighten those areas even more.

Track mattes solve a lot of compositing problems. They also help overcome limitations of After Effects. Chapter 7 describes more uses for them.

Gotchas

Even an advanced user has to pay attention when working in a composition with track mattes. Unlike parented layers, track mattes do not stay connected with their target if moved around; they must occupy the layer directly above in order to work.

After Effects does help manage changes in certain ways. Duplicate a layer (**Ctrl+D/Cmd+D**) with a track matte activated and it moves up two layers, above the track matte layer. Include the track matte when you duplicate and it also moves up two layers, so layer order is preserved (**Figure 3.31**).

Share a Matte

Node-based compositing programs make it easy for a single node to act as a selection for as many others as needed without being duplicated. The way to do this in After Effects is using the Set Matte effect, detailed below, which has the disadvantage of having no visible reference in the Timeline or Flowchart views. In After Effects, the standard way to provide a one-to-many operation is to precomp the matte being shared and then duplicate the nested comp layer as needed, but this complicates dynamic adjustments such as animating the matte layer in the master composition.

Figure 3.31 Select and duplicate two layers that are paired to make use of a track matte (as in Figure 3.31), and the two duplicate layers leapfrog above to maintain the proper image and matte relationship.

There is a work-around that allows a matte layer to be anywhere in the Timeline, but it offers its own perils. Effect > Channel > Set Matte not only lets you choose any layer in the comp as a matte, it keeps track if that layer moves to a different position. It also offers a few custom matte-handling options regarding how the matte is scaled and combined. However, nothing you add to the other layer, including Transform keyframes, is passed through; these would need to be added in a precomp.

Combine a track matte and an image with an alpha channel, and the selection uses an intersection of the two.

If you're not certain whether your edits to the matte are being passed through, save the project and try cranking them up so it's obvious. Then undo or revert. If it's not working, precomp the matte layer.

Chapter 9 focuses on 3D compositing; for now, keep in mind that while you might want to use a 2D layer as a track matte for a 3D layer, or even a 3D layer to matte a 2D layer, rarely will you want to matte a 3D layer with another 3D layer. The reason is that the matte is applied to the underlying layer, and then any animation is added to both layers—so it becomes a double 3D animation (or possibly a glimpse into the ninth dimension, we can't be sure—either way it doesn't usually look right).

Right Tool for the Job

So there you have it. Even when reviewing the fundamentals, there are less-obvious options to combine one layer with another. Combining moving images is more or less the definition of compositing, so we all have reason to hope you were paying attention.

Often there's not just one "right" way to do this. Besides, the one that looks best, there's also the question of which offers the most direct and flexible workflow as you continue to tweak the shot, and which one is most comprehensible as you attempt to dissect a complex shot. In fact, tweaking and dissecting come close to being the "definition" of compositing.

Now we move on to solving specific workflow issues in depth, including those that pertain to render order. The timeline is not only a great animation interface, it is an environment in which to solve visual problems. The next chapter and Chapter 11 at the end of Section II are the most technical in the book, so get ready to nerd out.

4

Optimize Projects

Build a system that even a fool can use and only a fool will want to use it.

—George Bernard Shaw

Optimize Projects

This chapter examines in close detail how image data flows through an After Effects project. It's full of the information you need to help you make the most of After Effects.

Sometimes you take the attitude of a master chef—you know what can be prepped and considered "done" before the guests are in the restaurant and it's time to cook the meal. At other times, you're more like a programmer, isolating and debugging elements of a project, even creating controlled tests to figure out how things are working. This chapter helps you both artistically and technically (as if it's possible to separate the two).

After Effects CS6 received the most substantial performance increase of any single upgrade thanks to Global Performance Cache, a scheme to preserve more individual render data indefinitely, not just when it's buffered into the RAM cache. This addition doesn't obviate the need for a solid understanding of how to work with multiple compositions and when to precomp, nor for specific strategies to optimize render time. It does, however, cut down on a good deal of redundancy on the After Effects side of the equation, leaving it up to you to avoid the possibility of PEBKAC (Problem Exists Between Keyboard and Chair).

Work With Multiple Comps and Projects

It's easy to lose track of stuff when projects get complicated. This section demonstrates

- ▶ how and why to work with some kind of project template
- ▶ how to keep a complex, multiple-composition pipeline organized

> ▶ shortcuts to help maintain orientation within the project as a whole.

These tips are especially useful if you're someone who understands compositing but sometimes finds After Effects disorienting.

Precomping and Composition Nesting

Precomping is often regarded as the major downside of working in After Effects, because vital information is hidden from the current comp's timeline in a nested comp. Artists may sometimes let a composition become unwieldy, with dozens of layers, rather than bite the bullet and send a set of those layers into a precomp. Yet precomping is both an effective way to organize the timeline and a key to problem solving and optimization in After Effects. Motion graphics comps can involve the animation and coordination of hundreds of animated elements. In a visual effects context, however, if your main composition has more than 20 or so layers, you're not precomping effectively, making work way less efficient overall.

Typically, precomping is done by selecting the layers of a composition that can sensibly be grouped together, and choosing Precompose from the Layer menu (**Ctrl+Shift+C/Cmd+Shift+C**). Two options appear (the second option is grayed out if multiple layers have been selected): to leave attributes (effects, transforms, masks, paint, blending modes) in place, or transfer them into the new composition.

Why Precomp?

Precomping prevents a composition from containing too many layers to manage in one timeline, but it also lets you do the following:

▶ Reuse a set of elements.

▶ Fix render order problems. For example, masks are always applied before effects in a given layer, but a precomp can contain an effect so that the mask in the master comp follows that effect in the render order.

▶ Organize a project by grouping interrelated elements.

NOTES

Precomping is the action of selecting a set of layers in a master composition and assigning it to a new subcomp, which becomes a layer in the master comp. Closely related to this is *composition nesting*, the act of placing one already created composition inside of another.

Cache Work Area in Background

One reward for making effective use of precomping is the ability to then save the entire precomp to the disk cache for immediate playback. This happens automatically when you preview the master sequence containing the precomp in question, but you can also select the precomp in the Project panel or open its timeline and choose Composition > Cache Work Area in Background to make After Effects immediately pre-render it in the background. As explained later in the chapter, the resulting cache remains available even if the project is reopened at a later time on the same system.

rd: Pre-compose by Jeff Almasol (http://aescripts.com/rd-pre-compose/) displays a dialog to precomp one or more layers, just like the regular After Effects dialog, but adds the ability to trim the precomp to the selected layer's duration, including trim handles.

The 04_comp_templates folder and project on the disc contain relevant example comps.

▶ Specify an element or set of layers as completed (and even pre-render them, as discussed later in this chapter).

Many After Effects artists are already comfortable with the idea of precomping but miss that last point. As you read through this, think about the advantages of considering an element finished, even if only for the time being.

The Project Panel: Think of It as a File System

How do you like to keep your system organized—tidy folders for everything or files strewn across the desktop? Personally, I'm always happiest with a project that is well organized, even if I'm the only one likely to ever work on it. When sharing with others, however, good organization becomes essential. The Project panel mirrors your file system (whether it's Explorer or Finder), and keeping it well organized and tidy can clarify your thought process regarding the project itself.

I know, I know, eat your vegetables, clean your room. Imagine that the person next opening your project is you, but with a case of amnesia. Actually, that basically is you after a sufficient period of time.

Figure 4.1 shows a couple of typical project templates containing multiple compositions to create one final shot, although these could certainly be adapted for a group of similar shots or a sequence. When you need to return to a project over the course of days or weeks, this level of organization can be a lifesaver.

Here are some ideas to help you create your own comp template:

▶ **Create folders,** such as Source, Precomps, and Reference, **to group specific types of elements.**

▶ **Use numbering to reflect comp and sequence order** so that it's easy to see the order in the Project panel.

▶ **Create a unique Final Output comp** that has the format and length of the final shot, particularly if the format is at all different from what you're using for work (because it's scaled, cropped, or uses a different frame rate or color profile).

Figure 4.1 A complex project such as a shot for a feature film might be generically organized (left) to include numbering that reflects pipeline order and multiple output comps with no actual edits, just the necessary settings. At minimum (right), you should have Source and Precomps folders, as well as a Reference folder, to keep things tidy.

- ▶ **Use guide layers and comments** as needed to help artists set up the comp (**Figure 4.2**).

- ▶ **Organize Source folders** for all footage, broken down as is most logical for your project.

- ▶ Place each source footage clip into a precomp. Why? Unexpected changes to source footage—where it is replaced for some reason—are easier to handle without causing some sort of train wreck.

Figure 4.2 Here is a series of non-rendering guide layers to define action areas and color.

The basic organization of master comp, source comp, and render comp seems useful on a shot of just about any complexity, but the template can include a lot more than that: custom expressions, camera rigs, color management settings, and recurring effects setups.

Manage Multiple Comps from the Timeline

Ever had that "where am I?" feeling when working with a series of nested comps? That's where Mini-Flowchart, or Miniflow, comes in. Access it via ▶◀ in the Timeline panel, or simply tap the **Shift** key with the Timeline panel displayed to enable it.

TIP

If nothing else, a locked, untouchable Final Output comp prevents losing a render to an incorrectly set work area (because you were editing it for RAM previews).

SCRIPT

Arrange Project Items into Folders (http://aescripts.com/arrange-project-items-into-folders/) looks for project items with a matching prefix and groups them together in a folder. Load Project or Template at Startup (http://aescripts.com/load-project-at-startup/) loads a project or template each time you start After Effects—this can really help if you need several people in a studio to follow a certain organizational style. Both scripts are by Lloyd Alvarez.

NOTES

The Always Preview This View toggle lets you work entirely in a precomp but switch automatically to the master comp (if this is on in that comp) when previewing.

Miniflow (**Figure 4.3**) shows only the nearest neighbor comps, but click on the flow arrows at either end and you navigate up or down one level in the hierarchy. Click on any arrows or items in between the ends and that level is brought forward. You're even free to close all compositions (**Ctrl+Alt+W**/**Cmd+Opt+W**) and reopen only the ones you need using this feature.

Figure 4.3 By default, the comp order is shown flowing right to left. The reason for this is probably that if you open subcomps from a master comp, the tabs open to the right; however, you may want to choose Flow Left to Right in Miniflow's panel menu instead.

What about cases where you'd like to work in the Timeline panel of a subcomp while seeing the result in the master comp? The Lock icon at the upper left of the Composition viewer lets you keep that Composition viewer forward while you open another composition's Timeline panel and close its view panel. Lock the master comp and double-click a nested comp to open its Timeline panel; as you make adjustments, they show up in the master comp.

Ctrl+Alt+Shift+N (**Cmd+Opt+Shift+N**) creates two Composition viewers side by side, and locks one of them, for any artist with ample screen real estate who wants the best of both worlds.

To locate a comp in the Project panel, you can

▸ select an item in the Project panel; click the caret to see where the item is used, along with the number of times, if any, the item is used in a comp (**Figure 4.4**)

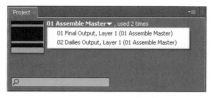

Figure 4.4 Click the caret next to the total number of times an item is used to see a list of where it is used.

▸ context-click an item in the Project panel and choose Reveal in Composition; choose a composition and that comp is opened with the item selected

▸ context-click a layer in the timeline and choose Reveal Layer Source in Project to highlight the item in the Project panel

▸ context-click in the empty area of a timeline—and choose Reveal Composition in Project to highlight the comp in the Project panel (**Figure 4.5**)

▸ type the name of the comp in the Project panel search field.

Figure 4.5 Find the empty area below the layers in the timeline and context-click; you can reveal the current comp in the Project panel.

Ways to Break the Pipeline

Precomping solves problems, but it can also create more problems—or at least inconveniences. Here are a few ways that render order can go wrong:

▸ Some but not all properties are to be precomped, but others must stay in the master comp? With precomping it's all-or-nothing, leaving you to rearrange properties manually.

▸ Changed your mind? Restoring precomped layers to the master composition is a manual (and thus error-prone) process, due to the difficulty of maintaining proper dependencies between the two (for example, if the nested comp has also been scaled, rotated, and retimed).

▸ Do the layers being precomped include blending modes or 3D layers, cameras, or lights? Their behavior changes depending on the Collapse Transformations setting (detailed in the next section).

▸ Is there motion blur, frame blending, or vector artwork in the subcomp? Switches in the master composition affect their behavior, as do settings on each individual nested layer, and this relationship changes depending on whether Collapse Transformations is toggled on.

▸ Layer timing (duration, In and Out points, frame rate) and dimensions can differ from the master comp. When this is unintentional, mishaps happen: Layers end too soon or are cropped inside the overall frame, or keyframes in the precomp fall between those of the master, wreaking havoc on tracking data, for example.

TIP

You may already know that a double-click opens a nested comp, and **Alt**–double-click (**Opt**–double-click) reveals it in the Layer viewer.

SCRIPT

The script preCompToLayerDur.jsx from Dan Ebberts (found on the book's disc) starts a precomped layer at frame 1 even if the layer to be precomped is trimmed to a later time.

True Comp Duplicator (http://aescripts.com/true-comp-duplicator/) was created by Brennan Chapman to address the biggest bugbear of working with nested comps in After Effects—in a node-based app, you can duplicate an entire nested tree and all of the components are unique, but duplicate a comp in After Effects and its subcomps are the same as in the source. This script can reside in a panel ready to create an entire new hierarchy. Highly recommended.

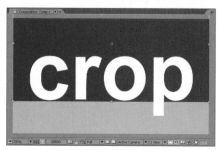

Figure 4.6 The nested comp has a blue background and the leg of the letter "p" extends outside its boundaries (top); a simple quick fix is to enable Collapse Transformations, and the boundaries of the nested comp are ignored (bottom).

▶ Are you duplicating a comp that contains subcomps? The comp itself is new and completely independent, but the nested comps are not (see Script on this page).

No wonder people avoid precomping. But there is hope if you recognize any difficulty and know what to do, so that inconveniences don't turn into deal-killers.

Boundaries of Time and Space

Each composition in After Effects contains its own fixed timing and pixel dimensions. This adds flexibility for animation but if anything reduces it for compositing. Most other compositing applications such as Nuke and Shake have no built-in concept of frame dimensions or timing and assume that the elements match the plate, as is often the case in visual effects work.

Therefore it is helpful to take precautions:

▶ Make source compositions longer than the shot is ever anticipated to be, so that if it changes, timing is not inadvertently truncated.

▶ Enable Collapse Transformations for the nested composition to ignore its boundaries (**Figure 4.6**).

▶ Add the Grow Bounds effect if Collapse Transformations isn't an option (see sidebar on next page).

Collapse Transformations is the most difficult of these to get your head around, so it's worth a closer look.

Collapse Transformations

In After Effects, when a comp is nested in another comp, effectively becoming a layer, the ordinary behavior is for the nested comp to render completely before the layer is animated, blended, or otherwise adjusted (with effects or masks) in the master comp.

However, there are immediate exceptions. Keyframe interpolations, frame blending, and motion blur are all affected by the settings (including frame rate and timing) of the master comp—they are calculated according to its settings (which can become tricky; see the next section). 3D position data and blending modes, on the other hand, are not passed through unless Collapse Transformations is enabled. Enable the toggle and it is almost as if the pre-composed layers reside in the master comp—but now any 3D camera or lighting in the subcomp is overridden by the camera and lights in the master comp.

Not only that, but layers with Collapse Transformations lose access to blending modes—presumably to avoid conflicts with those in the subcomp. Now here comes the trickiest part: Apply any effect to the layer (even Levels with the neutral defaults, which doesn't affect the look of the layer) and you force After Effects to render the collapsed layer, making blending modes operable. It is now what the Adobe developers call a *parenthesized* comp. Such a nested comp is both collapsed and not: You can apply a blending mode, but 3D data is passed through (**Figure 4.7**).

To collapse transformations but not 3D data, apply any effect—even one of the Expression Controls effects that don't by themselves do anything—to parenthesize the comp.

NOTES

The 04_collapse_transformations folder and project on the disc contain relevant example comps.

TIP

Annoyed to find sequences importing at the wrong frame rate? Change the default Sequence Footage Frames per Second under Preferences > Import.

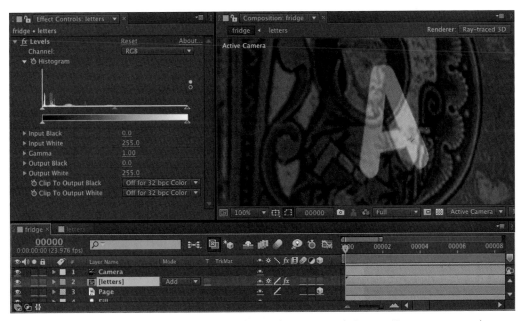

Figure 4.7 You're not supposed to be able to apply blending modes to ray-traced 3D scenes. You can precomp such a scene and enable Collapse Transformations so that all of its ray-traced 3D qualities are passed through, but you still can't apply a blending mode such as Add (shown here). However, if you add a simple effect such as Levels, unadjusted, transformations and shading are still passed through, but they no longer interact in 3D with the master comp.

Grow Bounds

Sometimes, enabling Collapse Transformations is not desirable—for example, if you set up 3D layers with a camera in a subcomp and don't want their position to be changed by a camera in the master comp. The Grow Bounds effect overcomes one specific (and fairly rare) problem (in which the embedded layer is too small for an applied effect), but it is also useful in cases where other effects create a comp boundary that leads visual data to appear cropped.

The Posterize Time effect will force any layer to the specified frame rate.

Alpha channel effects change the alphas of the layers below, not of the adjustment layer itself.

Nested Time

After Effects is not rigid about time, but digital video itself is. You can freely mix and change frame rates among compositions without changing the timing, as has been shown. However, because your source clips always have a very specific rate, pay close attention when you

- ▶ import an image sequence
- ▶ create a new composition
- ▶ mix comps with different frame rates.

In the first two cases, you're just watching out for careless errors. But you might want to maintain specific frame rates in subcomps, in which case you must set them deliberately on the Advanced tab of the Composition Settings dialog.

Advanced Composition Settings

In addition to the Motion Blur settings covered in detail in Chapter 8, Composition Settings > Advanced contains two toggles that influence how time and space are handled when one composition is nested into another.

Preserve Frame Rate maintains the frame rate of the composition wherever it goes—into another composition with a different frame rate, or into the render queue with different frame rate settings. So if a simple animation cycle looks right at 4 frames per second (fps), it won't be expanded across the higher frame rate, but will preserve the look of 4 fps.

Preserve Resolution When Nested controls what is called *concatenation*. Typically, if an element is scaled down in a precomp and the entire composition is nested into another comp and scaled up, the two operations are treated as one, so that no data loss occurs via quantization. This is concatenation, and it's usually a good thing. If the data in the subcomp is to appear pixilated, as if it were scaled up from a lower-resolution element, this toggle preserves the chunky pixel look.

Special Case: Adjustment and Guide Layers

Two special types of layers, adjustment and guide layers, offer extra benefits that might not be immediately apparent, and are often underused.

Adjustment Layers

From a nodal point of view, adjustment layers are a way of saying "at this point in the compositing process, I want these effects applied to everything that has already rendered." Because render order is not readily apparent in After Effects until you learn how it works, adjustment layers can seem trickier than they are.

The *adjustment layer* is itself invisible, but its effects are applied to all layers below it. It is a fundamentally simple feature with many uses. To create one, context-click in an empty area of the Timeline panel, and choose New > Adjustment Layer (**Ctrl+Alt+Y/Cmd+Opt+Y**) (**Figure 4.8**).

Adjustment layers allow you to apply effects to an entire composition without precomping it. That by itself is pretty cool, but there's more:

▶ Move the adjustment layer down the stack and any layers above it are unaffected, because the render order in After Effects goes from the lowest layer upward.

▶ Shorten the layer and the effects appear only on frames within the adjustment layer's In/Out points.

▶ Use Opacity to attenuate any effect; most of them work naturally this way. Many effects do not themselves include such a direct control, even when it makes perfect sense to "dial it back 50%," which you can do by setting Opacity to 50%.

▶ Apply a matte to an adjustment layer to hold out the effects to a specific area of the underlying image.

▶ Add a blending mode and the adjustment layer is first applied and then blended back into the result (**Figure 4.9**).

It's a good idea 99% of the time to make sure that an adjustment layer remains 2D, and you will most often also want it to be the size and length of the comp, as when applied. It's rare that you would ever want to move, rotate, or scale an adjustment layer in 2D or 3D, but it is possible to do so accidentally. If you enlarge the composition, resize the adjustment layers as well.

Figure 4.8 The highlighted column includes toggle switches, indicating an adjustment layer. Any layer can be toggled, but the typical way to set it is to create a unique layer. An adjustment layer created under Layer > New > Adjustment Layer (or via the shortcuts) is a white, comp-sized solid.

(a)

(b)

(c)

Figure 4.9 Here, the source plate image **(a)** is shown along with two alternates in which Camera Lens Blur has been applied via an adjustment layer, held out by a mask. With the adjustment layer blending mode set to Normal **(b)**, there is a subtle bloom of the background highlights, but changing it to Add **(c)** causes the effect to be applied as in **(b)** and then added over source image **(a)**.

Guide Layers

Like adjustment layers, *guide layers* are standard layers with special status. A guide layer appears in the current composition but not in any subsequent compositions or the final render (unless it is specifically overridden in Render Settings). You can use this for

- ▶ foreground reference clips (picture-in-picture timing reference, aspect ratio crop reference)
- ▶ temporary backgrounds to check edges when creating a matte
- ▶ text notes to yourself
- ▶ adjustment layers that are used only to check images (described further in the next chapter); a layer can be both an adjustment and a guide layer.

Any image layer can be converted to a guide layer either by context-clicking it or by choosing Guide Layer from the Layer menu (**Figure 4.10**).

Figure 4.10 Check out all the guide layers that won't render, but do help you work: One pushes up gamma to check blacks, and two provide crops for different aspects (1.85:1 and 2.35:1, the common cinematic formats). A picture-in-picture layer shows timing reference from the plate, along with a text reminder that does not render. None of this is visible in another composition or in the render.

Image Pipeline, Global Performance Cache, and Render Speed

The *render pipeline* is the order in which operations happen; by controlling it, you can solve problems and overcome bottlenecks. For the most part, render order is plainly displayed in the timeline and follows consistent rules:

▶ 2D layers are calculated from the bottom to the top of the layer stack—the numbered layers in the timeline.

▶ Layer properties (masks, effects, transforms, paint, and type) are calculated in strict top-to-bottom order (twirl down the layer to see it).

▶ 3D layers are instead calculated based on distance from the camera; coplanar 3D layers respect stacking order and should behave like 2D layers relative to one another.

So to review: In a 2D composition, After Effects starts at the bottom layer and calculates any adjustments to it in the order that properties are shown, top to bottom. Then, it calculates adjustments to the layer above it, composites the two of them together, and moves up the stack in this manner (**Figure 4.11**). Although effects within a given layer are generally calculated prior to transforms, an adjustment layer guarantees that its effects are rendered after the transforms of all layers below it.

Track mattes and blending modes are applied last, after all other layer properties (masks, effects, and transforms) have been calculated, *and* after their own mask, effect, and transform data are applied. Therefore, you don't generally need to pre-render a track matte simply because you've added masks and effects to it.

Global Performance Cache: Way Faster!

We're over 100 pages into the book and just now getting into the most revolutionary addition to the latest version of After Effects. You don't technically need a book to experience what can be extraordinary benefits from how After Effects CS6 preserves your work in progress for instant playback; you probably already know and love this feature, but as a reader of a book like this you probably also want

Figure 4.11 2D layers render starting with the bottom layer, rendering and compositing each layer above in order. Layer properties render in the order shown when twirled down; there is no direct way to change the order of these categories.

to know as much as you can about how it works so you can maximize what it does for you.

The feature name "Global Performance Cache" is a generic term for what is, in fact, a set of interrelated technologies:

▶ a Global RAM cache that is smarter about dividing your work to save as many individual processes as possible

▶ a persistent disk cache that saves those precalculated processes for continual reuse

▶ an updated graphics pipeline that makes greater use of OpenGL to present and stream images onscreen, including the UI overlays that are a constant when working in After Effects

You have to hand it to the After Effects development team here. Engineers too easily assume they need to tear technology apart and rebuild it from scratch in order to modernize it. Global Performance Cache is the result of looking at what modern hardware can deliver that simply was not possible a few years ago, and figuring out how to make use of that hardware:

▶ **cheap and plentiful RAM**, and the ability of a 64-bit operating system to access far more of it (up to 192 GB on Windows 7, and well in excess of the 2 GB per processor core recommended for After Effects)

▶ **fast attached storage**, including SSD drives that routinely double the access speed of even the fastest HDD drive or array

▶ **high-end graphics cards** with GPUs that accelerate performance year after year at rates that way, way outstrip Moore's Law

In the past, After Effects has rather notoriously failed to take advantage of these advantages. Lots of RAM is no good if your RAM preview disappears each time you make an edit; fast storage doesn't mean spacebar play of a timeline in real-time; and until CS6, the high-end graphics card that you purchased to work in Maya or CINEMA 4D hardly made a dent in After Effects interactivity.

Each of these areas of performance is directly addressed in After Effects CS6. The result is completely subjective, but can be quantified as a routine 10–20x acceleration of RAM previews. Depending on how often you review playback during your workday, this means either you can keep working that much faster, or the whole way that you work with the application is changed.

Memory Acceleration: Global RAM Cache

After Effects has always loved plenty of RAM, but until CS6 it used it in a much more brute-force way. You have always needed lots of RAM to store and play back a given large-format clip using physical memory and perform operations on that large frame. The brute-force part is that as soon as you made even a teeny change to all of that cached data, it all tended to be blown away, only to be recreated more or less from scratch the next time you previewed a frame or sequence.

By slicing a clip with its many selections and effects into discrete chunks and storing each of those render steps individually, After Effects CS6 greatly reduces the amount of re-rendering of cached footage. You can change a given effect setting or range of keyframes without disrupting other parts of the image and clip that are unrelated to that change.

Reusable frames are recognized anywhere on the timeline: when you use loop expressions (Chapters 8 and 10), remap time, or copy and paste keyframes. Duplicated layers or whole duplicated comps are also recognized.

The net result is that you can try something, preview the result without rendering from scratch, and undo the change without penalty. Since this, in essence, is how you spend your working day as an After Effects artist, the resulting 5–15x speed increase ripples throughout the process, allowing you not only to get to a result more quickly but to try more options without worrying about the time cost.

This tends to work a lot better with 2D layers than with a ray-traced 3D comp. It is easy to consider an effect or setting in a 2D layer to be an island unto itself, but in 3D, light, reflection, shadows, refraction, and translucency are all considered to be influenced by the adjustment of a single element such as a light or the position of a layer.

After Effects CS6 Persistent Disk Cache has been called "the closest thing After Effects will ever get to a cure for cancer."

Continuous Access: Persistent Disk Cache

Data in the RAM cache is now much less fragile because it is constantly backed up in a *persistent disk cache*. If you run out of RAM, increment and save to a new version of the project, or even quit the application and reopen the project. Its cache is available for instant playback and immediate rendering (**Figure 4.12b**).

Persistent disk cache is also the most tweakable of the Global Performance Cache options, and the one for which your choice of hardware may make the greatest difference. Here's a list of the most effective tweaks, followed by a breakdown:

▸ dedicate **fast attached storage** to the After Effects cache

▸ use the **Cache Work Area in Background** command as you work

▸ incorporate **Dynamic Link** with Premiere Pro

▸ render locally

Want to see how caching behaves on individual layers? Under the Timeline panel menu, hold down Ctrl/Cmd and click Show Cache Indicators, even if it's already checked. Now each layer has its own blue or green bar if it's cached (**Figure 4.12a**). Turn it off when you have a good sense of how it works, because it will slow down your renders.

A

B

Figure 4.12 With Layer Cache Indicators on, you begin to see how After Effects breaks down the RAM cache into individual layers and even effects (**a**). With fast attached storage, you will see those green lines turn blue as they move from RAM to the disk (**b**).

Before drawing out the first three points in more detail, note that the persistent disk cache cannot be considered sharable or portable. Place the cache on a shared drive and point two systems to it and all you do is introduce the likelihood of instability; the two systems will not recognize those cached files in the same way and will simply continue to generate their own cache data. This data is designed to be accessed instantly and is cleverly designed to track a given comp and layers even as project versions change on a given system (**Figure 4.13**).

This is not to say that I haven't tried and succeeded at replacing the disk cache on a given system with one that's already preloaded with a bunch of rendered frames and effects, but I wouldn't make that standard practice. The disk cache is designed to be local to a given system. The benefit is that a cached comp may render faster locally than it will even on a large render network. The downside, if you want to think of it that way, is that the render network has essentially no opportunity to take advantage of a disk cache, at least not on the first pass.

Disk Cache Boost 1: Get Fast Attached Storage

The permanent disk cache can be a little like a huge RAM extension providing much longer memory and far greater capacity. As such, it's in your interest to maximize its performance and, if possible, capacity. Why? Not only because faster is better; After Effects actively evaluates whether it's in the application's best interests to commit a given process to disk. The greater the difference between processor and cache speed, the more likely a frame gets the blue cache indicator, ready to turn green at any time (and the faster it turns green, ready for real-time).

Let's start at the low end, with you laptop people. I know, I know, you are the cutting edge. But your single, slow hard disk drive will make you long for something better—something like a dedicated solid state drive, which at this writing is sparking a laptop evolution in which nearly useless DVD drives are replaced with a sled holding a high-capacity SSD. Yes, there is a cost involved. It will also set you free.

Figure 4.13 If you were thinking the disk cache is a bunch of easily recognized files you can share and edit, think again!

How do I get more stuff to cache?

You've followed the tip above to show layer cache indicators, and are dismayed to find a number of layers that don't cache, presumably because they don't pass the After Effects evaluation that it's not a faster option than re-rendering. You then have three options: load up, cheat, or get faster storage.

Add render-heavy effects to a given 2D layer, and at some point it will cache. Similarly, you can hack the preferences file (using instructions later in this chapter) and change the "proclivity" preference, the basic metric for caching.

The real, practical solution is to get more and faster attached storage. The faster the physical disk you have available for the hard-disk cache, the more likely that it will pass the test for providing better speed than simple re-rendering of elements.

Also, while a ray-traced 3D scene does cache nicely, ready to be replayed when you restart After Effects, changes to such a scene tend to wipe out the cache, because ray-tracing creates dependencies between all 3D elements in a scene.

Figure 4.14 The revolutionary power of fast attached storage.

At the other end—the high one—the release of After Effects CS6 coincided neatly with the debut of Fusion ioFX (**Figure 4.14**). It's not easy to quantify, but it's being regarded in After Effects circles as something like a half-terabyte extension to SDRAM, with the disk cache ready to fill it with your inspirations and missteps alike. It's all part of the process, and way less hard on your body than amphetamines, which never let you get out of the studio in time for a dinner date.

And in the middle, that striped RAID array you have attached to your system is still going to help you a bunch. Any drive other than the internal boot drive will work better, and if you edit footage professionally, you already have just such a dedicated drive available.

Bottom line? Everyone wins. Even on a laptop you can see 10–15x speed increases that will make you hungry to feed the disk cache more and faster storage space.

Disk Cache Boost 2: Commit a Comp

Disk caching in After Effects need not be a passive response, like Aslan, only appearing when not expected and most needed. It's true, you get all of the subcomps associated with the comp that you cache committed to disk as well (assuming After Effects judges them faster to render if committed to storage), so caching a master comp gets you a lot of free material to work with. But sometimes, for whatever reason, that master comp doesn't commit to disk when previewed, or more often, it needs way longer to render than you want to wait watching it draw frames.

I just realized as I typed the last sentence that the days of waiting and watching a RAM preview progress frame by frame could, in fact, be completely over if you want them to be. Composition > Cache Work Area in Background (**Ctrl/Cmd+Return**) renders a comp into the disk cache while you continue to work.

If you really hate waiting for a comp to preview, and have a half-decent system and something better to do with your time, you can select a whole set of comps in the Project panel and cache them. Yes, if you're on a non-CUDA-enabled Macbook Pro and those comps are all full of HD ray-traced 3D animations, your system is going to sound like a jet preparing for takeoff and your laptop will scorch your lap. On the other hand, if you're on one of those systems that has more processor cores than you can count when you open up their little capacity meters in the system, well, you are finally going to get your money's worth.

Caveats? Downsides? You gotta pay to play. This is where gobs of low-latency storage is going to be your new best friend, other than the actual best friend that you get to spend time with when you are done for the day and not already burning the midnight oil. But there's always that CBB.

Disk Cache Boost 3: Rethink Dynamic Link

Odds are better than even that, alongside After Effects, sit a number of other apps (or *programs* as you Windows people and characters in Tron apparently call them) that also begin with the word "Adobe." Go ahead, take a look, I'll wait.

Oh, you're back! And you have just discovered that fully half the contents of the applications (programs) begin with A? Welcome to the world of video, in which company names start with A. While you wonder why you installed Flash Builder with no plans to build anything in Flash, go back, scroll down, and note the little nonlinear editor that could. I'm talking about Premiere Pro.

No longer solely the favorite among wedding videographers (and I say that with no disrespect, but let's face it, After Effects is not big with that group), Premiere Pro CS6 has become many people's favorite NLE, mine included. Like many others, I treated Premiere Pro as a utility, not a place I wanted to spend time working, and for me the CS6 version changes that. I find that I actually like working in it.

Premiere Pro has a unique ability to link directly to an After Effects comp. Dynamic Link is a feature that allows Adobe Premiere Pro to actually look inside an After Effects project for an existing comp that it can import (**Figure 4.15**), or designate a clip in a sequence as the basis for a new After Effects comp.

NOTES

CBB stands either for Can't Be Bothered or Could Be Better. Both apply in visual effects circles, but unfortunately it's the latter that got the moniker.

Figure 4.15 If you've never witnessed the power of Dynamic Link to peer inside an After Effects Project from Adobe Premiere Pro or Adobe Media Encoder, it may seem like magic.

Preferences > General > Dynamic Link with After Effects Uses Project File Name with Highest Number is unchecked by default, but it could instead simply be called Make Dynamic Link Usable in the Real World.

With either approach, there is an actual, live After Effects comp sitting in a Premiere Pro sequence. After Effects invisibly provides the ability to render it, headlessly, in the background. As any change is made to the comp on the After Effects side, it remains up to date in the Premiere edit.

In the past, the difficulty with this approach has been that Premiere Pro has no real concept of render management, and the steps that you take for granted to make a preview render faster in After Effects, working at half or quarter resolution, aren't available. Imagine that every time you wanted to play something back, you had to render it at full resolution.

If you're thinking that Global Performance Cache helps in such a case, you are correct. Suppose you have a heavy comp that requires 10 seconds to render each frame at full resolution. If you cache the comp at full, Premiere Pro has access to those cached frames *even if After Effects isn't open*. Render the sequence and that clip is ready for real-time playback in seconds, not minutes or hours.

Note that you do, however, still have to render to get rid of the red line above that clip, even if it's completely cached at full resolution. And, when you do so, it doesn't add to the After Effects cache. The way to make this work is to generate a preview in After Effects. This still requires you to perform an edit, but once you do so, it helps speed up the Premiere Pro timeline just as it does in After Effects.

Proxies, Previews, and Network Renders

Previous editions of this book advocated the use of proxies and previews as ways to accelerate the previewing and rendering process. This is exactly where Global Performance Cache changes the game, but only as long as you work on the "one artist, one project, one system" model, given that the cache is neither portable nor sharable.

For this reason, the old ways are still valid in any case where a project needs to be moved or shared, even if only for rendering purposes. The good news is that the cached data helps even this process to happen much more efficiently, because it is also used to render on the system that generated it.

Post-Render Options

Tucked away in the Render Queue panel, but easily visible if you twirl down the arrow next to Output Module, is a menu of three post-render actions to incorporate a render into a project. After the render is complete, you can use

▶ **Import** simply to bring the result back into the project

▶ **Import & Replace Usage** to replace the usage of the source comp in the project without blowing it away

▶ **Set Proxy** to add a proxy to the source (the most elegant solution, but the most high-maintenance)

The latter two options even let you use the pick whip icon adjacent to the menu to connect whatever item in the Project panel needs replacement. If you've already created a pre-render or proxy, you can target that (**Figure 4.16**).

Proxies and Pre-Renders

Let's face it, dutifully rendering proxies is boring and will seem completely unnecessary with all of the new cache features—right up until the moment when you're in a rush and no longer have access to that cache, either when rendering remotely or handing off the project. Are you willing to buy some insurance on that cache? If so, this section is for you.

Preferences > Display > Show Rendering Progress in Info Panel and Flowchart shows what is happening on your system. It is disabled by default because it requires some extra processing power, but you may find you get that time back from the ability to spot and solve an obvious bottleneck.

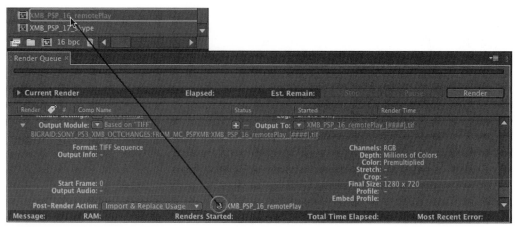

Figure 4.16 Virtually any project item can be the target for replacement or a proxy; click and drag the pick whip icon to choose the item to be replaced by the render.

Figure 4.17 The black square icon to the left of an item in the Project panel indicates that a proxy is enabled; a hollow square indicates that a proxy is assigned but not currently active. Both items are listed atop the Project panel, the active one in bold.

Any image or clip in your Project panel can be set with a proxy, which is an imported image or sequence that stands in for that item. Its pixel dimensions, color space, compression, even its length and frame rate, can differ from the item it replaces. You can have a quick-and-dirty still or low-res, compressed, low-frame-rate clip stand in for a render-heavy comp.

To create a proxy, context-click an item in the Project panel and choose Create Proxy > Movie (or Still). A render queue item is created and, by default, renders at Draft quality and half-resolution; the Output Module settings create a video file with alpha, so that transparency is preserved and Post-Render Action uses the Set Proxy setting.

Figure 4.17 shows how a proxy appears in the Project panel. Although the scale of the proxy differs from that of the source item, it is scaled automatically so that transform settings remain consistent. This is what proxies were designed to do: allow a low-resolution file to stand in, temporarily and nondestructively, for the high-resolution final.

There's another use for proxies. Instead of creating low-res temp versions, you can instead generate final quality pre-rendered elements. With a composition selected, choose Composition > Pre-render and change the settings to Best for Quality and Full for Resolution, making certain that Import and Replace Usage is set for Output Module.

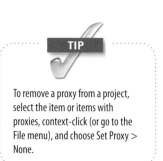

TIP

To remove a proxy from a project, select the item or items with proxies, context-click (or go to the File menu), and choose Set Proxy > None.

Here's the key. By default, the source file or composition is used to render unless specifically set otherwise in Render Settings > Proxy Use. Choose Use Comp Proxies Only, Use All Proxies, or Current Settings (**Figure 4.18**) and proxies can be used in the final render.

Background Renders

Rendering from the render queue ties up the application and much of the machine's processing power, which used to mean that renders were left until lunchtime or off-hours. On a modern system with multiple processors, you can do much better than that (but take breaks anyway, they're good for you).

Adobe Media Encoder

It is easily overlooked that Adobe provides a background rendering application. Adobe Media Encoder (AME) has, for a couple of versions, been the best option to render certain video formats optimally—including Flash video (FLV and F4V), H.264, and MPEG-2—that don't work well with the frame-by-frame rendering model of After Effects. H.264, for example, is a "long GOP" format that relies on keyframes with lots of image data surrounded by in-between frames containing only shorthand for the changes for those keyframes, and it requires all of the frames to be rendered before it can work its magic. Only Adobe Media Encoder collects frames to compress them, and offers the option to render an After Effects comp on two passes.

Drag and drop an After Effects project into Adobe Media Encoder and you are able to look inside the project for renderable comps (**Figure 4.19**). You then choose render settings by either selecting them from the Preset Browser

Figure 4.19 Dynamic Link allows other Adobe applications to see your Project panel; Adobe Media Encoder uses this to let you render comps for heavily compressed video formats directly from the project.

BG Renderer by Lloyd Alvarez (http://aescripts.com/bg-renderer/) may be the most universally used After Effects script. Not only does it automatically set up a background render by creating the command line for you, but it offers you a user interface for extra variables you might miss that determine the priority and number of processors used to render (**Figure 4.20**).

Figure 4.20 BG Renderer uses ScriptUI, which means that it looks like it's part of the interface and can remain in an open panel as you work. When you're ready to render, you can specify priority and number of processors; click the button and a terminal window opens that shows the render progress, line by line. You may miss the progress bar of the render queue, but if you can live without that, the benefit is that you can keep working while your machine renders.

or customizing the settings by clicking on the Preset for the render item and specifying your own (which you can then save as a preset).

The best thing about Adobe Media Encoder, in addition to multipass rendering, is that it provides the option to render in the background while you continue to work in After Effects, which a regular render doesn't permit. The challenge to AME is that it has a lot of presets without a lot of clues to which is the best for your situation. Worst of all, the layout for these settings is unfamiliar if you are accustomed to After Effects, and that alone stops a lot of people.

aerender

Background rendering allows a render to occur without the user interface, allowing you to continue working with it. The aerender application is found alongside the After Effects CS6 application on your system but runs via a command line (in Terminal Unix shell on Mac OS, or the command shell in Windows). You can drag it into the shell window to run it, or press **Enter** (**Return**) to reveal its Unix manual pages. This lists the arguments that can be added in quotes to the command aerender, and the location string of the project file.

But that's all such geeky gobbledygook when you have the BG Render script, which gives you access to all of these options via a panel in the After Effects UI, with no need to type any code.

Network Rendering

The aerender command is also used by third-party rendering solutions that work a lot like BG Renderer but are distributed across multiple machines on a network. These programs can manage renders on multiple machines and do tricky stuff like pause a render until an updated element from 3D is done, or automatically re-queue failed renders. Because these third-party rendering options— Rush Render Queue, Pipeline's Qube!, Überware's Smedge, or Muster by Virtual Vertex, to name a few—also support other terminal-friendly applications such as Maya and Nuke, it's an investment facilities that are large enough to have a render farm don't have to think twice about making.

These are not one-click installs and they're generally justified only by dedicated machines and a dedicated nerd to manage it all. If that's beyond your facility at this point, you can still take advantage of all of this technology via the Cloud, or via a service such as Render Rocket. You upload your source files and get back rendered output. The downside for compositors is that we generally require a lot of source data to produce final shots, compared with 3D artists who can sometimes create a final cinematic image with virtually no source.

Watch Folder

The myopic and slightly dotty granddaddy of network rendering on After Effects is Watch Folder (File > Watch Folder). Watch Folder looks in a given folder for projects ready to be rendered; these are set up using the Collect Files option. The Adobe Help topic "Network rendering with watch folders and render engines" includes everything you need to know.

Watch Folder is kind of okay on small, intimate networks, but it requires much more hands-on effort than dedicated

Multiple After Effects Versions

When desperate, you can open more than one After Effects on Mac OS or Windows. This is memory intensive and not ideal for rendering (for which BG Renderer is much preferred), but it lets you work with two projects at once.

On Mac OS, locate Adobe After Effects CS6.app and duplicate it (**Cmd+D**); both will run after you clear the warning that the application has moved. On Windows, go to the Start menu, choose Run, type cmd, and click OK. In the DOS shell that opens, drag in AfterFX.exe from your Programs folder and then add –m (that's a space, a dash, and m as in "multiple"). Voilà, a second version initializes.

Suppose you just have one machine and a big render. You want it to keep running but shut down the system when it's done, and even notify you remotely that the render was a success. Render, Email, Save, and Shutdown by Lloyd Alvarez (http://aescripts.com/render-email-incremental-save-and-shutdown/) exists for this purpose; just queue up your render and fire one of them off.

Setting Preferences and Project Settings

Here are a few default preferences I always change.:

▶ **Preferences > General > Levels of Undo:** Got RAM? Set this to 99.

▶ **Preferences > General:** Check the options Allow Scripts to Write Files and Access Network.

▶ **Preferences > General:** Toggle Default Spatial Interpolation to Linear.

▶ **Preferences > General:** Dynamic Link with After Effects Uses Project File Name with Highest Number.

▶ **Preferences > Display:** Check all four boxes (unless you love those little thumbnails; they can slow you down on a network).

▶ **Preferences > Import:** 29.97 for broadcast, 24 fps for film, 23.976 for both (film for broadcast), and 25 fps for PAL-derived systems.

▶ **Preferences > Media & Disk Cache:** Choose a folder on a fast, attached disk.

▶ **Preferences > Appearance:** Cycle Mask Colors; on.

▶ **Preferences > Auto-Save:** On.

TIP

Press **Alt+Ctrl+Shift** (**Opt+Cmd+Shift**) immediately after launching After Effects to reset Preferences. Hold **Alt** (**Opt**) while clicking OK to delete the shortcuts file as well.

render management software, and it breaks easily, at which point it requires human intervention. Since individual systems have become so powerful, it's easy to become lazy about taking the trouble required to set up a Watch Folder render, but if you're up against a deadline, don't have the dedicated software, and want to maximize multiple machines, it will do the trick.

Optimize a Project

Here are a few more workflow tweaks to get the best performance out of After Effects.

Hack Shortcuts, Text Preferences, or Projects

Some people are comfortable sorting through lines of code gibberish to find editable tidbits. If you're one of those people, After Effects Shortcuts and Preferences are saved as text files that are fully editable and relatively easy to understand. Unless you're comfortable with basic hacking (learning how code works by looking at other bits of code), however, I don't recommend it. The files are located as follows:

▶ Windows: [drive]:\Users\[user name]\AppData\ Roaming\Adobe\After Effects\11.0

▶ Mac: [drive]:/Users/[user profile]/Library/ Preferences/Adobe/After Effects/11.0/

Mac OS X started hiding the User/Library folder with the release of 10.7 (Lion). The easiest way to reveal it from the Finder is to select Go > Go to Folder and then type Library. The names of the files are

▶ Adobe After Effects 11.0-x64 Prefs.txt

▶ Adobe After Effects 11.0 Shortcuts

These can be opened with any text editor that doesn't add its own formatting and works with Unicode. Make a backup copy before editing by simply duplicating the file (any variation in the filename causes it not to be recognized by After Effects). Revert to the backup by giving it the original filename should anything start to go haywire after the edit.

The Shortcuts file includes a bunch of comments at the top (each line begins with a # sign). The shortcuts themselves are arranged in a specific order that must be preserved, and if you add anything, it must be substituted in the exact right place.

Be extra careful when editing Preferences—a stray character in this file can make After Effects unstable. Most of the contents should not be touched, but here's one example of a simple and useful edit (for studios where a dot is preferred before the number prefix instead of the underscore): Change

```
"Sequence number prefix" = "_"
```

to

```
"Sequence number prefix" = "."
```

This is the format often preferred by Maya, for example.

In other cases, a simple and easily comprehensible numerical value can be changed:

```
"Eye Dropper Sample Size No Modifier" = "1"
"Eye Dropper Sample Size With Modifier" = "5"
```

In many cases, the value after the = is a binary yes/no value, expressed as 0 for no and 1 for yes, so if you're nostalgic for how the After Effects render chime sounded in its first several versions, find

```
"Play classic render chime" = "0"
```

and change the 0 to a 1. Save the file, restart After Effects, and invoke those 20th-century glory days of the beige Mac. Ask an After Effects veteran sometime what that chime evokes, and get ready to buy that warrior a beer.

XML

After Effects projects can be saved as .aepx files. These work the same way but are written in plain Unicode text; you can edit them with an ordinary text editor. Most of what is in these files is untouchable; the main use is to locate and change file paths to swap footage sources without having to do so manually in the UI. If that means nothing to you, you're probably not the shell scripting nerd for whom a feature like that was created.

A fantastic script for specifying your own modifier keys called KeyEd Up was developed specifically for After Effects by Jeff Almasol, author of other scripts included with this book. Find it on Adobe After Effects Exchange at http://tinyurl.com/6cu6nq.

Batch Search-n-Replace Paths by Lloyd Alvarez (http://aescripts.com/batch-search-n-replace-paths/) may save you the need to dig around in an .aepx file to change footage source locations; it also makes use of regular expressions to make the matching process more sophisticated than what is possible with an ordinary text editor.

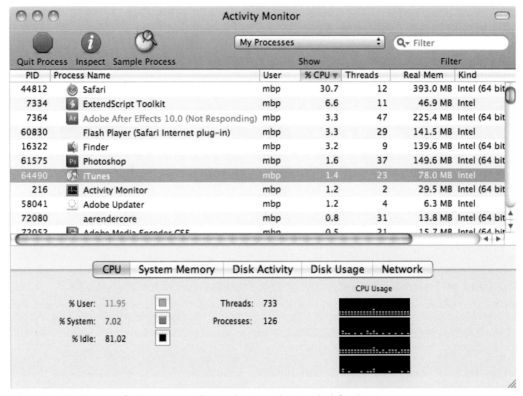

Figure 4.21 The Process ID for the nonresponding application is shown in the left column.

On the Mac: Force a Crash

When After Effects does crash, it attempts to do so gracefully, offering the option to save before it exits. The auto-save options, if used properly, further diminish the likelihood of losing project data. On Mac OS X, an extra feature may come in handy when the application becomes unresponsive without crashing.

Open Activity Monitor and look for After Effects to get its PID number (**Figure 4.21**). Now open Terminal, and enter kill –SEGV ### where "###" is replaced by the After Effects PID value. This should cause the application to crash and auto-save.

Memory Management

Chapter 1 included advice about running After Effects with multiprocessing enabled on a system with multiple cores and a good deal of physical memory. If you see your system's wait icon come up—the hourglass in Windows, the spinning ball on a Mac—that means there is a fight going on somewhere for system resources. In addition to following the advice in Chapter 1 to leave memory available for outside applications, you may have to quit any application that is both resource-intensive and outside the memory pool managed by After Effects (in other words, any app besides Adobe Premiere Pro, Encore, Prelude, Adobe Media Encoder, or Photoshop).

The best idea is to provide the system with more physical memory. As a rule of thumb, 2 GB of RAM per processor core is not a bad guide. You can go below this to, say, 1.5 GB per core, but much lower and your system will be less efficient unless you also limit the number of cores After Effects uses (in Preferences > Memory & Multiprocessing).

These Are the Fundamentals

You've reached the end of Section I (if you're reading this book linearly, that is), and we've done everything we could think of to raise your game with the After Effects workflow. Now it's time to focus more specifically on the art of visual effects. Section II, "Effects Compositing Essentials," will teach you the techniques, and Section III, "Creative Explorations," will show you how they work in specific effects situations.

So here comes the fun part.

Although the RAM cache is less likely to become full or fragmented with 64-bit processing, Throttle-n-Purge by Lloyd Alvarez (http://aescripts. com/throttle-n-purge/) provides a UI panel with a one-button solution to clear all caches and get maximum efficiency out of a preview render (**Figure 4.22**). It also lets you switch bit depths, more easily than the Project panel, and it lets you turn multiprocessing on and off without opening Preferences.

Figure 4.22 Throttle-n-Purge exposes controls to help you manage memory usage as well as offering a one-button option to purge all caches (undos and image buffers) and start over.

5

Color Correction

There are two main strategies we can adopt to improve the quality of life. The first is to try making external conditions match our goals. The second is to change how we experience external conditions to make them fit our goals better.

— Mihaly Csikszentmihalyi

Color Correction

When you picture a compositor, you may think of an artist behind a workstation, busily extracting greenscreen footage, but if I had to name the number one compositing skill, it would be color matching. The ability to authoritatively and conclusively take control of color, so that foreground and background elements seem to inhabit the same world and shots from a sequence are consistent with one another, and so that their overall look matches the artistic direction of the project, is more than anything what would cause you to say that a compositer has a "good eye."

The compositor, after all, is often the last one to touch a shot before it goes into the edit. Inspired, artistic color work injects life, clarity, and drama into standard (or even substandard) 3D output, adequately (or even poorly) shot footage, and flat, monochromatic stills. It draws the audience's attention where it belongs—into the action—and away from the artifice of the shot.

So whether or not you think you already possess a "good eye," color matching is a skill that you can practice and refine even with no feel for adjusting images—even if you're color-blind. And despite the new color tools that appear each year to refine your ability to dial in color, for color matching in After Effects three color correction tools are consistently used for most of the heavy lifting: Levels, Curves, and Hue/Saturation (in many ways, Levels and Curves overlap in functionality). These features have endured from the earliest days of Photoshop because they are stable and fast, and they will get the job done every time.

A skeptic might ask:

▶ Why these old tools when there are so many cool newer ones?

▶ Why not use Brightness & Contrast to adjust, you know, brightness and contrast, or Shadow and Highlight if that's what needs adjustment?

▶ What do you mean I can adjust Levels even if I'm color-blind?

This chapter holds the answers to these questions and many more. First, we'll look at optimizing a given image using these tools, and then we'll move into matching a foreground layer to the optimized background, balancing the colors. The goal is to eliminate the need to hack at color work and build skills that eliminate a lot of the guesswork.

This chapter also introduces topics that resound throughout the rest of the book. Chapter 11 deals specifically with HDR color, and then Chapter 12 focuses on specific light and color scenarios, while the last two chapters in the book describe how to create specific types of effects shots using these principles.

Color Correction and Image Optimization

What constitutes an "optimized" clip? What makes a color-corrected image correct? Let's look at what is typically "wrong" with source footage levels and the usual correction methods, in order to lay the groundwork for color matching. As an example, let's look at the brightness and contrast of a single *plate* image, with no foreground layers to match.

Levels

Levels is one of the most-used tools in After Effects. It consists of five basic controls—Input Black, Input White, Output Black, Output White, and Gamma—each of which can be adjusted in five separate contexts (the four individual image channels R, G, B, and A, as well as all three color channels, RGB, at once). There are two different ways to adjust these controls: via their numerical sliders or by dragging their respective caret sliders on the histogram (the more typical method).

NOTES

The term *plate* stretches back to the earliest days of optical compositing (and indeed, of photography itself) and refers to the source footage, typically the background onto which foreground elements will be composited. A related term, *clean plate*, refers to the background with any moving foreground elements removed.

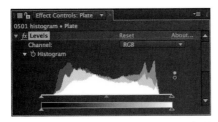

Figure 5.1 The Levels effect can be used to display its histogram (since unlike Photoshop there is no Histogram panel in After Effects) in color or black and white. The toggle is to the right of the graphic.

Contrast: Input and Output Levels

Four of the five controls—Input Black, Input White, Output Black, and Output White (**Figure 5.1**)—determine brightness and contrast, and combined with the fifth, Gamma, they offer more precision than is possible with the Brightness & Contrast effect.

To begin, try adjusting contrast only in the blacks with the Levels effect. Move the black caret at the lower left of the histogram—the Input Black level—to the right, and values below its threshold (the numerical Input Black setting, which changes as you move the caret) are pushed to black. The further you move the caret, the more values are "crushed" to pure black.

Move the Input White caret at the right end of the histogram to the left, toward the Input Black caret. The effect is similar to Input Black's but inverted: More and more white values are "blown out" to pure white (**Figure 5.2**).

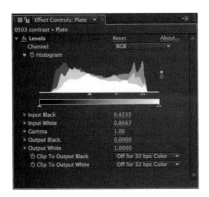

Figure 5.2 Raising Input Black and lowering Input White has the effect of increasing contrast at either end of the scale; at an extreme adjustment like this, many pixels in an 8-bpc or 16-bpc project are pushed to full white or black or "crushed."

Either adjustment effectively increases contrast, but note that the midpoint of the gradient also changes as each endpoint is moved in. In Figure 5.2, Input Black has been adjusted more heavily than Input White, causing the horizon of the gradient to move closer to white and the shadows to darken. You can re-create this adjustment with Brightness & Contrast, but without direct control of the midpoint (gamma) of the image it can be impossible to balance an entire image (**Figure 5.3**).

Reset Levels (click Reset at the top of the Levels effect controls) and try adjusting Output Black and Output White, whose controls sit below the gradient. Output Black specifies the darkest black that can appear in the image; adjust it upward and the minimum value is raised.

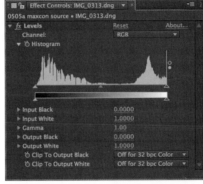

Figure 5.3 The image can resolve both sky and foreground, but on an image with so little midrange, Brightness & Contrast cannot; with no adjustment to the midpoint (gamma), you have to choose between the sky (Brightnesss –86, Contrast 64) and the foreground (Brightness 41, Contrast 32).

TIP

You can reset any individual effect control (any property that has its own stopwatch icon 🕑) by context-clicking it and choosing Reset. You know it's an individual property if it has its own stopwatch.

Lowering Input White is something like dimming the image, cutting off the maximum white value at the given threshold. Adjust both and you effectively reduce contrast in the image. Bring them alongside one another, and the gradient becomes a solid gray (**Figure 5.4**).

So Input and Output controls have inverse effects. But you will find situations where you might use them together, first balancing the image, then reducing contrast in the whites, blacks, or both.

As is the case throughout After Effects, the controls operate in the order listed in the interface. In other words, raising the Input Black level first raises black density, and a higher Output Black level raises all of the resulting black levels together (**Figure 5.5**). If you've crushed the blacks

Figure 5.4 Raising Output Black and lowering Output White reduces contrast in the dark and light areas of the image, respectively; this is useful for a hazy image, fog, and smoke.

Figure 5.5 Here, Output first clips the image, and then Input stretches out the reduced dynamic range; the adjustments do not round-trip when applied on the single instance of Levels as they would with multiple effects in 32-bpc mode (featured in Chapter 11).

with Input Black, they remain crushed, and they all just appear lighter (unless you work in 32 bpc—Chapter 11 has the details on that).

If you're thinking, "So what?" at this point, just stay with this until we make our way from the theoretical to the real world.

Brightness: Gamma

As you adjust the Input Black and White values, you may have noticed the third caret that maintains its place between them. This is the Gamma control, affecting midtones (the middle gray point in the gradient) without touching the white and black points. Adjust gamma of the gradient image and notice that you can push the grays in the image brighter (by moving it to the left) or darker (by moving it to the right) without changing the black and white levels.

Many images have healthy contrast, but a gamma boost gives them extra punch. Similarly, an image that looks a bit too "hot" may be instantly adjusted simply by lowering gamma. As you progress through the book, you will see that gamma plays a crucial role not only in color adjustment but also in how an image is displayed and how your eye sees it (more on that in Chapter 11).

In most cases, the image itself rather than the histogram offers the best clue as to whether the gamma needs adjustment (see the upcoming section "Problem Solving Using the Histogram," as well as **Figure 5.6**). So what is the guideline for how much to adjust gamma, if at all? I first learned that I'm free to deliberately go too far before dialing back, which is especially helpful when learning. An even more powerful gamma adjustment tool that scares novices away is Curves (coming up).

By mixing these five controls together, have we covered Levels? No—because there are not, in fact, five basic controls in Levels (Input and Output White and Black plus Gamma), but instead, five times five (RGB, Red, Green, Blue, and Alpha).

CLOSE-UP

What Is Gamma, Anyway?

It would be nice but inaccurate simply to say, "Gamma is the midpoint of your color range" and leave it at that. The more accurate the discussion of gamma becomes, the more purely mathematical it becomes. Plenty of artists out there understand gamma intuitively and are able to work with it without knowing the math behind it—but here it is anyway. Gamma adjustment shifts the midpoint of a color range without affecting the black or white points. This is done by taking a pixel value and raising it to the inverse power of the gamma value:

```
newPixel = pixel (1/gamma)
```

You're probably used to thinking of pixel values as fitting into the range 0 to 255, but this formula works with values *normalized* to 1. Here, 0 is 0, 255 is 1, and 128 is 0.5—which is how the math "normally" operates behind the scenes in computer graphics.

Gamma operates according to the magic of logarithms: Any number to the power of 0 is 1, any number to the power of 1 is itself, and any fractional value (less than 1) raised to a higher power approaches 0 without ever reaching it. Lower the power closer to 0 and the value approaches 1, again without ever reaching it. Not only that, but the values distribute proportionally, along a curve, so the closer an initial value is to pure black (0) or pure white (1) the less it is affected by a gamma adjustment.

Figure 5.6 Proper shooting with a low-dynamic-range digital video camera such as a DSLR requires that you shoot a flat-looking image with low contrast and then bracket the histogram's white and black points, as it's always possible to add contrast to optimize an image but not possible to remove it without losing detail. The only difference between the left and right sides of the image is a Levels adjustment transforming the flat source, left, into the richer image on the right.

Same Difference: Levels (Individual Controls)

The Levels effect and the Levels (Individual Controls) effect contain identical controls. The sole difference is that Levels lumps all adjustments into a single keyframe property, which expressions cannot use. Levels (Individual Controls) is particularly useful to

▸ animate and time Levels settings individually

▸ link an expression to a Levels setting

▸ reset a single Levels property (instead of the entire effect)

Levels is more commonly used, but Levels (Individual Controls) is sometimes essential.

Individual Channels for Color Matching

Some After Effects artists completely ignore the menu at the top of the Levels control, which slows adjustment of the five basic Levels controls on an individual channel, but this is where its powers for color matching lie. Let's take a look at these controls on the gradient image to reveal what exactly is going on.

Reset any Levels effect applied to the Ramp gradient. Pick Red, Green, or Blue in the Channel menu under Levels and adjust the Input and Output carets. The grayscale image takes on color. With the Red channel selected, move Red Output Black inward to tint the darker areas of the image red. Adjust Input White inward to make the midtones and highlights pink (light red). If, instead, you adjust Input Black or Output White inward, the tinting moves in the opposite direction—toward cyan—in the corresponding shadows and highlights.

As you probably know, each primary on the digital wheel of color (red, green, or blue) has an opposite (cyan, magenta, or yellow, respectively). As your color skills progress you will notice when your method of, say, reducing green spill

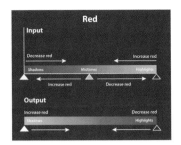 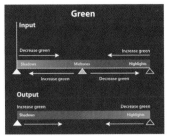 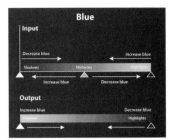

Figure 5.7 These charts were devised by John Dickinson at Motionworks (www.motionworks.com.au) after he read an earlier edition of this book; it shows the relationship of each color to its opposite when adjusting the Levels Effect.

has made flesh tones too magenta, but when you're starting out it's enough simply to be aware that adjustments to each color channel proportionally affect its opposite (**Figure 5.7**). See the file Motionworks_ levels_and_curves.pdf, in the Chapter05 folder on the book's disc for a reference on color adjustments to channels.

Gradients are one thing, but only a real image will help develop the habit of studying footage on individual color channels as you work. This is the key to effective color matching.

Along the bottom of the Composition panel, all of the icons are monochrome by default save one: the Show Channel menu. It contains five selections: the three color channels as well as two alpha modes. Each one has a shortcut that, unfortunately, is not shown in the menu: **Alt+1** through **Alt+4** (**Opt+1** through **Opt+4**) toggle each color channel. A colored outline around the edge of the Composition panel reminds you which channel is displayed (**Figure 5.8**); toggling the active channel returns the image to RGB.

Try adjusting a single channel of the gradient in Levels while displaying only that channel. The effect of brightness and contrast adjustment on a grayscale image is readily apparent. This is the way to work with individual channel adjustments, especially when you're just beginning or if you have difficulty distinguishing colors. As you work with actual images instead of gradients, the histogram can offer valuable information about the image.

TIP

Hold down **Shift** with the **Alt+1–3** (**Opt+1–3**) shortcut for color channels, and each will display in its color. Shift with **Alt+1–4** (**Opt+1–4**) displays the image with a straight alpha channel, as After Effects uses it internally.

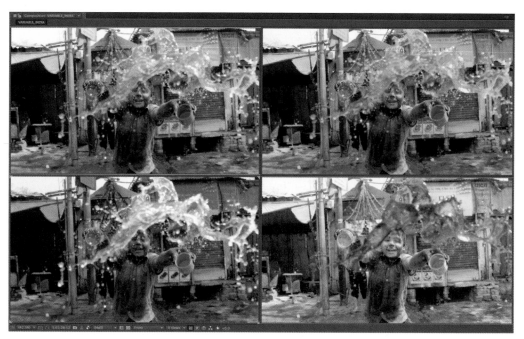

Figure 5.8 Four Views mode was designed for 3D, but why not use it for RGB, particularly when getting started with color matching? Note differences in the three channels and the colored outline to identify each.

Levels: Histograms and Channels

You might have noticed the odd appearance of the histogram with an unadjusted gradient. If you were to try this setup on your own, depending on the size of the layer to which you applied Ramp, you might see a histogram that is flat along the top with spikes protruding at regular intervals.

The histogram is exactly 256 pixels wide:, it is a bar chart made up of 256 little one-pixel-wide bars, each corresponding to one of the 256 possible levels of luminance in an 8-bpc image. These levels are displayed below the histogram, above the Output controls. In the case of a pure gradient, the histogram is flat because of the even distribution of luminance from black to white. If the image height in pixels is not an exact multiple of 256, certain pixels double up and spike.

In any case, it's more useful to look at real-world examples, because the histogram is useful for mapping image data that isn't plainly evident on its own. The point is to help you assess whether any color changes are liable to improve or harm the image. There is in fact no single typical or ideal histogram—they can vary as much as the images themselves, as seen back in Figure 5.6.

Despite that fact, you can try a simple rule of thumb for a basic contrast adjustment. Find the top and bottom end of the RGB histogram—the highest and lowest points where there is any data whatsoever—and bracket them with the Input Black and Input White carets. To "bracket" them means to adjust these controls inward so each sits just outside its corresponding end of the histogram. The result stretches values closer to the top or bottom of the dynamic range, as you can easily see by applying a second Levels effect and studying its histogram (**Figure 5.9**).

Try applying Levels to any image or footage from the disc and see for yourself how this works in practice. First densify the blacks (by moving Input Black well above the lowest black level in the histogram), and then pop the whites (moving Input White below the highest white value). Don't

TIP

Auto Levels serves up a result similar to bracketing Input White and Input Black to the edges of the histogram. If that by itself isn't enough to convince you to avoid using Auto Levels, or really any "Auto" correction, consider also that they are processor-intensive (slow) and resample on every frame. The result is not consistent from frame to frame, as with auto-exposure on a video camera—reality television amateurism.

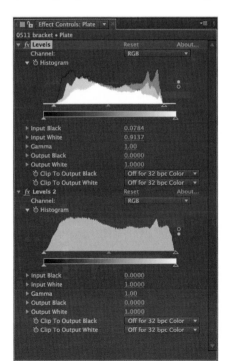

Figure 5.9 The bracketed histogram often yields what could be considered the ideal neutral image.

TIP

Footage is by its very nature dynamic, so it is essential to leave headroom for the whites and foot room for the blacks until you start working in 32 bits per channel. You can add contrast, but once the image blows out, that detail is gone.

NOTES

LCD displays, as a whole, lack the black detail that can be captured on film. The next time you see a movie in a cinema, notice how much detail you can see in the shadows and compare.

Figure 5.10 Push an adjustment far enough and you may see quantization, which appears as banding in the image. Those big gaps in the histogram are expressed as visible bands on a gradient. Switching to 16 bpc from 8 bpc is an instant fix for this problem in most cases.

go too far, or subsequent adjustments will not bring back that detail—unless you work in 32-bpc HDR mode (see Chapter 11). Occasionally a stylized look calls for crushed contrast, but generally speaking, this is bad form.

Black and white are not at all equivalent in terms of how your eye sees them. Blown-out whites can be ugly and a dead giveaway of an overexposed digital scene, but your eye is much more sensitive to subtle gradations of low black levels. These low, rich blacks account for much of what traditionally made film look like film, and they can contain a surprising amount of detail, none of which, unfortunately, shows up on the printed page. Look for it in the images themselves.

The occasions on which you would optimize an image by raising Output Black or lowering Output White controls are rare, as this lowers dynamic range and the overall contrast. However, there are many uses in compositing for lowered contrast, such as softening overlay effects (say, fog and clouds) or high-contrast mattes, and so on. Examples follow in this chapter and throughout the rest of the book.

Problem Solving Using the Histogram

You may have noticed that the Levels histogram does not update as you make adjustments. After Effects lacks a panel equivalent to Photoshop's Histogram panel, but you can, of course, apply a Levels effect just to view the histogram.

Spikes at either end of a histogram (which is there just to evaluate the adjustment of the first) indicate clipping at the ends of the spectrum. Clipping is both something to avoid and part of life (and the reflection of life in the final image), like rainy days in Paris and parking tickets in San Francisco.

The histogram can itself be a problem-solving tool, showing loss of detail where there are gaps or spikes. Such gaps are not a worry when surrounded by a good amount of healthy data, but in more extreme cases, in which there is no data in between the spikes whatsoever, you may see a prime symptom of overadjustment, known as *banding* (**Figure 5.10**).

Banding is typically the result of limitations inherent in 8-bpc color. To address this problem, 16-bpc color mode was added a long time ago, to After Effects 5.0. You can switch to 16 bpc by **Alt**-clicking (**Opt**-clicking) on the bit-depth identifier along the bottom of the Project panel (**Figure 5.11**) or by changing it in File > Project Settings. Chapter 11 explores this in more detail.

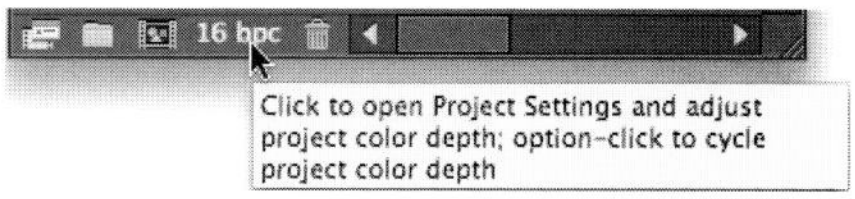

Figure 5.11 An entire project can be toggled from the default 8-bpc color mode to 16-bpc mode by **Alt**-clicking (**Opt**-clicking) the project color depth toggle in the Project panel; this prevents the banding seen in Figure 5.13.

Curves: Gamma and Contrast

Curves rocks. I still heart curves, even though it is shunned—and completely missing—in Adobe's new color application, SpeedGrade. The Curves control is particularly useful for gamma correction:

▶ Curves lets you fully (and visually) control how adjustments are weighted and roll off.

▶ You can introduce multiple gamma adjustments to a single image or restrict the gamma adjustment to just one part of the image's dynamic range.

▶ Some adjustments can be nailed with a single well-placed point in Curves, in cases where the equivalent adjustment with Levels might require coordination of three separate controls.

It's also worth understanding Curves controls because they are a common shorthand for how digital color adjustments are depicted.

Curves does, however, have drawbacks, compared with Levels:

▶ It's not immediately intuitive and can easily make a complete hash of things if you don't know what you're doing. There are plenty of artists who aren't comfortable with it.

▶ Unlike Photoshop, After Effects doesn't offer numerical values corresponding to curve points, making it a purely visual control that can be hard to standardize.

▶ In the absence of a histogram, you may miss obvious clues about the image (making Levels more suitable for learners).

The most daunting thing about Curves may be its interface, a simple grid with a diagonal line extending from lower left to upper right. There is a Channel selector at the top, set by default to RGB as in Levels, and there are some optional controls on the right allowing you to draw, save, and retrieve custom curves. To the novice, the arbitrary map is an unintuitive abstraction that you can easily use to make a complete mess of the image. Once you understand it, however, you can see it as an elegantly simple description of how image adjustment works. You'll find a project containing the equivalent Curves graph to the previous Levels corrections on the book's disc.

Figure 5.12 shows the more fully featured Photoshop Curves, which better illustrates how the controls work.

Figure 5.12 Photoshop's more deluxe Curves includes a histogram, built-in presets, displays of all channels together, and fields for input and output values for a given point on the curve.

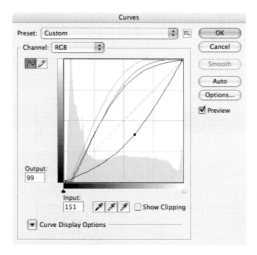

Figures 5.13 shows some basic Curves adjustments and their effect on an image. **Figure 5.14** uses linear gradients to illustrate what some common Curves settings do. I encourage you to try these on your own.

There are certain types of adjustments that only Curves allows you to do—easily, at least. I came to realize that most of the adjustments I make with Curves fall into a few distinct types that I use over and over.

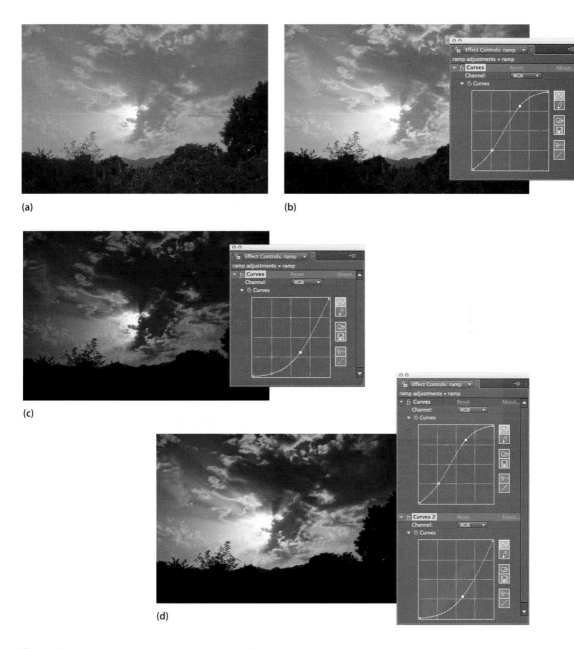

Figure 5.13 What you see in an image can be heavily influenced by gamma and contrast. **(a)** The source image. **(b)** An increase in gamma above the shadows. **(c)** A decrease in gamma. **(d)** Both corrections combined.

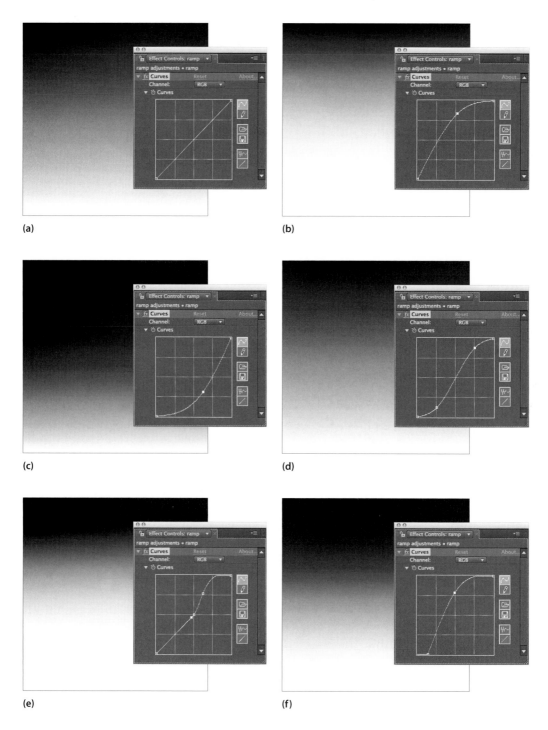

(a)

(b)

(c)

(d)

(e)

(f)

Figure 5.14 This array of Curves adjustments applied to a gradient shows the results of some typical settings. **(a)** The default gradient and Curves setting. **(b)** An increase in gamma. **(c)** A decrease in gamma. **(d)** An increase in brightness and contrast. **(e)** Raised gamma in the highlights only. **(f)** Raised gamma with clamped black values.

The most common adjustment is simply to raise or lower the gamma with Curves, by adding a point at or near the middle of the RGB curve and then moving it upward or downward. **Figure 5.15** shows the result of each. This produces a subtly different result from raising or lowering the Gamma control in Levels because of how you control the roll-off (**Figure 5.16**).

The classic S-curve adjustment, which enhances brightness and contrast and introduces roll-offs into the highlights and shadows (**Figure 5.17**), is an alternative method to get the result of the double curves in the image labeled D in Figure 5.14.

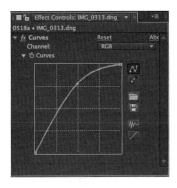

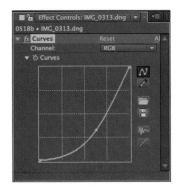

Figure 5.15 Two valid (and common) single-point gamma adjustments in Curves, in this case heavily favoring either foreground or background.

Figure 5.16 Both the gradient itself and the histogram demonstrate that you can push the gamma harder, still preserving the full range of contrast, with Curves rather than with Levels, where you face a choice between losing highlights and shadows some-what or crushing them.

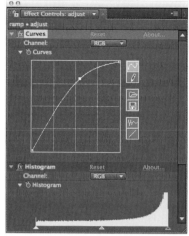

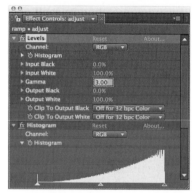

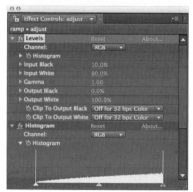

Some images need a gamma adjustment only to one end of the range—for example, a boost to the darker pixels, below the midpoint, that doesn't alter the black point and doesn't brighten the white values. Such an adjustment requires three points (**Figure 5.18**):

▶ one to hold the midpoint

▶ one to boost the low values

▶ one to flatten the curve above the midpoint

A typical Curves methodology is to begin with a single-point adjustment to adjust gamma or contrast, then to modulate it with one or two added points. More points quickly become unmanageable, as each adjustment changes the weighting of the surrounding points. Typically, I will add a single point, then a second one to restrict its range, and a third as needed to bring the shape of one section back where I want it.

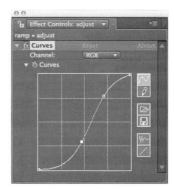

Figure 5.17 The classic S-curve adjustment: The midpoint gamma in this case remains the same, directly crossing the midpoint, but contrast is boosted.

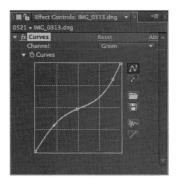

Figure 5.18 Study this curve and you'll see that it's almost two separate curves, raising gamma in the shadows and lowering it in the highlights around a center pivot. It's a quick way to get the most out of an image like this.

Hue/Saturation: Color and Intensity

The third essential color correction tool in After Effects is Hue/Saturation. Use this one to

▶ desaturate an image (or increase its vibrancy)

▶ colorize a monochrome image

▶ shift the overall hue of an image

▶ de-emphasize or remove an individual color channel (for example, to reduce green spill; see Chapter 6).

NOTES

Chapter 12 details why Tint or Black and White, not Hue/Saturation, is appropriate to convert an entire image to grayscale.

The Hue/Saturation control allows you to do something you can't do with Levels or Curves—directly control the hue, saturation, and brightness of an image. The HSB color model is merely an alternate numerical array of the same RGB color data. All "real" color pickers include RGB and HSB as two separate but interrelated modes that use three values to describe any given color.

You could arrive at the same color adjustments using Levels and Curves, but Hue/Saturation is more directly effective. Desaturating an image brings the red, green, and blue values closer together, reducing the relative intensity of the strongest of them; the saturation control lets you do this in one step.

Often colors are balanced but too juicy (not a strictly technical term), and lowering the Saturation value somewhere between 5 and 20 can be a direct and effective way to pull an image adjustment together (**Figure 5.19**).

TIP

When in doubt about the amount of color in a given channel, try boosting its Saturation to 100%, blowing it out—this makes the presence of tones in that range very easy to spot.

The other quick fix with Hue/Saturation is a shift to the hue of the whole image or of one of its component channels. The Channel Control menu for Hue/Saturation has red, green, and blue as well as their chromatic opposites of cyan, magenta, and yellow. In RGB color, these secondary colors work in direct opposition, so that lowering blue gamma effectively raises yellow gamma, and vice versa.

The HSB model includes all six individual channels, which means that if a given channel is too bright or oversaturated, you can dial back its Brightness & Saturation levels, or you can shift Hue toward a different part of the spectrum without unduly affecting the other primary and secondary colors. This can be an effective secondary color correction method, even for reducing green or blue spill (Chapter 6).

Compositors Match Colors

Now, having laid the groundwork with the toolset, it's time for the bread-and-butter work of compositing: to match separate foreground and background elements so that the scene appears to have been shot all together at once.

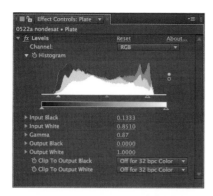

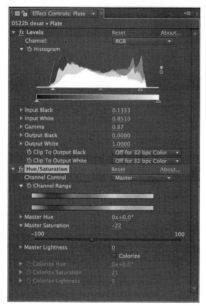

Figure 5.19 Boosting a saturated image's contrast can leave it a bit juiced up with saturated color (top). If you recognize this, a simple and modest pullback in overall Saturation (with the Hue Saturate and Brightness effect) is a quick solution.

You can learn this skill and produce measurable, objective results. The process obeys such strict rules that you can do it without an experienced eye for color. You can satisfactorily complete a shot on a monitor that is nowhere near correctly calibrated, and the result will not even suffer from color-blindness on your part.

How is that possible?

It's simply a question of breaking down the problem. In this case, the job of matching one image to another obeys rules that can be observed channel by channel, independent of the final, full-color result.

Of course, compositing goes beyond simply matching color values; in many cases that is only the first step. Observation of nature plays a part. And even with correctly matched colors, any flaws in edge interpretation (Chapter 3), a procedural matte (Chapter 6), lighting (Chapter 12), camera view (Chapter 9), or motion (Chapter 8) can sink an otherwise successful shot.

These same basic techniques can also be used to match clips from a source precisely—for example, color correcting a sequence to match a *hero* shot (based on such essentials as facial skin tones), a process also sometimes known as *color timing*.

The Fundamental Technique

Integration of a foreground element into a background scene often follows the same basic steps:

1. **Match overall contrast** without regard to color, using Levels (and likely examining only the Green channel). Align the black and white points, with any necessary adjustments for variations in atmospheric conditions.

2. Next, study each color channel individually as a grayscale image and use Levels to **match the contrast of each channel.**

3. **Align midtones (gamma)**, also channel by channel, using Levels or Curves. This is sometimes known as *gray matching* and is easiest when foreground and background contain areas that are something like a colorless mid-gray.

4. **Evaluate the overall result** for other factors influencing the integration of image elements—lighting direction, atmospheric conditions, perspective, and grain or other ambient movement (all of which follow as specific topics later in this book). Here you get to work a bit more subjectively, even artistically.

This uncomplicated approach will motivate you to make adjustments your brain doesn't necessarily understand because of its habit of stereotyping based on assumptions. An image that "looks green" may have a good deal of blue in the shadows with yellowish highlights, but a less experienced eye might not see these (and even a veteran can miss them). The choices are bolder than those derived from noodling around, and the results can be stunning—as we'll see on a subtle example here, followed by a couple of radical ones thereafter.

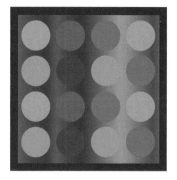

Truthfully, even an experienced artist can be completely fooled by the apparent subjectivity of color because of how human vision works. **Figure 5.20** shows an example in which seeing is most definitely *not* believing. Far from some sort of crutch or nerdy detail, channel-by-channel analysis of an image provides fundamental information as to whether a color match is within objective range of what the eye can accept.

Ordinary Lighting

We begin with a simple example: comp a neutrally lit 3D element into an ordinary exterior day-lit scene. **Figure 5.21** shows a simple A over B result in which the two layers are close enough in color range that a lazy or hurried compositor might be tempted to leave it as is, other than adding a bit of motion blur to match the car entering the frame. For the inexperienced, this shot is a bit of a challenge, as it may be difficult with the naked eye to say exactly how or why the color doesn't match.

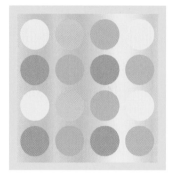

To begin, make certain that you are working in 16-bpc mode (**Alt**- or **Opt**-click on the indicator at the bottom of the Project panel to select a mode). This prevents banding and enhances accuracy when adjusting the color of low-dynamic-range images. Now reveal the Info panel, and choose Decimal (0.0—1.0) under the panel menu at the upper right ▼≡ to align with the settings used in this section. If you like, tear off the Info panel by **Ctrl**-dragging (**Cmd**-dragging) it over the Composition viewer.

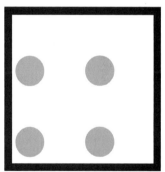

Figure 5.20 There are no yellow dots in the top image, and no blue dots in the middle image; the four dots shown in the bottom image are identical to their counterparts in the other two images.

This particular background plate helps us a lot, as it's filled with monochromatic elements: a concrete landscape and a silver car, black shadows and car tires, little white details such as a sign, license plate, reverse lights, and the stripe of a loading zone. The foreground aircraft is also

Figure 5.21 An unadjusted foreground layer (the plane) over a day-lit background.

predominantly monochromatic, with many black details and white highlights. This comped image is a single 8-bpc image, although the full animation with multiple passes will be used later in the book for more precise adjusting.

The first step is to match overall contrast with the Levels effect, so apply that to the foreground layer. This adjustment can be performed while viewing regular RGB but it may be easier with only the green channel displayed (**Alt+2/Opt+2**, or select from the menu). Move the cursor over the highlight areas along the top of the plane (or just look at the Levels histogram) and you'll notice that some of the highlights are clipped to 1.00 on all three color channels, as are highlights. Clipping is part of life and not necessarily a bad thing, unless those highlights need to be recovered for some reason. In this case, let's suppose we don't need to worry about Levels and just want to match the clipped foreground to the clipped background.

Here, the white foreground contrast doesn't appear hot enough for the outdoor lighting of the background. Even the road surface blacktop is close to pure white in the direct sunlight, so clearly the highlights on the plane

NOTES

This example can be found on the disc in the 05_color_match_01_basic folder.

NOTES

For simplicity's sake, the example on the disc uses still images only, but a multipass render of the plane and a full background plate are included to allow you to complete the shot. For more information on working with a multipass source, see Chapter 12.

Figure 5.22 Just because the Info panel and histogram clearly indicate clipping in the foreground doesn't mean you can't clip highlights further if it helps properly match it to the background. Shadows appear to match reasonably well on the green channel.

should, if anything, be pushed further. Lower Input White to at least the top of the visible histogram, around 0.82 (**Figure 5.22**).

Black contrast areas, the shadows, are at least as subjective. Again the histogram indicates that some blacks are already clipped; the question is whether the shadows, for example, under the back wing, need to be deeper (or lighter). Move the cursor to the shadows underneath the cars and they are clearly deeper—as low as 0.04. But higher up on the building, reflected light from the surface lightens the shadows under the overhangs to something like we see under the wings, in the range between 0.2 and 0.3 on all channels. Subjectively, you can try raising Output Black slightly to get more of the effect of shadows lightened by reflected light, or you can crush the shadows more with Input Black to match those under the cars. Try each before leaving them close to neutral.

Having aligned contrast, it's time to balance color by aligning contrast on each channel. Move your cursor back over shadow areas and notice that although the foreground plane's shadows are neutral, the background shadows are

TIP

The human eye is most sensitive to green, so begin by matching overall RGB contrast while viewing the green channel, then adjusting the other two channels to accommodate that adjustment.

155

approximately 20% more intense in the blues than greens, and around 20% less intense in red versus green. The goal is not so much to match the blacks to the exact levels of the background as to match these proportions on the red and blue channels.

Place the cursor under the big plane wing and you'll notice that the green value of that shadow is around 0.2. Switch Levels to Red under the Channel menu and raise Red Input Black just a hint, to something like 0.025, until the red value under the wing is approximately 0.18, or 20% lower than green. Now switch Levels to Blue; this time you'll raise Blue Output Black to lift the darkest blue shades slightly, maybe even just 0.015 (**Figure 5.23**). Double-check with your cursor under the wing; the red, green, and blue proportions are now similar to those of the background blacks.

Now for the whites. Take a look at the RGB image again, and notice the silver car left of frame and the difference between it and the plane. It's not clear that they should be the exact same shade, but here let's assume that they are both neutral gray and should be made much more similar, which can be accomplished by adjusting just white contrast on all three channels.

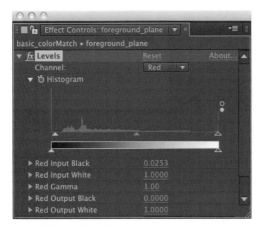 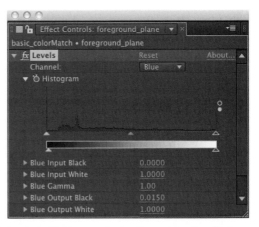

Figure 5.23 Black levels for Red and Blue in the foreground are taken just a hint in opposite directions, raising the effective black level in blue and lowering it in red (left). These adjustments are a little too subtle in this case to perform with the naked eye, so they were arrived upon using values shown in the Info panel.

Starting with the Blue channel, notice that the plane looks a little dull overall compared with the car. Bring Blue Input White down to at least 0.95 while viewing the Blue channel (**Alt+3/Opt+3**) and see if it doesn't appear to be a better match. Switch the view and Levels control to Red, and, conversely, the side of the plane looks bright compared to the car. Bring Red Output White down about the same amount, to 0.95. A final look at the Green channel shows that the same adjustment there, of Green Output White to 0.95, helps the match. Notice that these edits influence not just the highlights but also midtones, so there's no need to adjust gamma directly.

Et voilá, back to RGB—you'll see the result, which you can compare with the source image from Figure 5.24 simply by toggling Levels, in **Figure 5.24**. Motion blur can be roughed in by adding Fast Blur, setting Blur Dimensions to Horizontal, and raising Blurriness to approximately 100.0 to match the car entering frame right. The plane is now more effectively integrated into the scene, and these subtle changes make a huge difference (toggle the before and after to see for yourself).

This example can be found on the disc in the 05_color_match_02_bridge folder.

Figure 5.24 Compare this integration to that of Figure 5.21.

Dramatic Lighting

If you're working with a cinematographer shooting in available light, or heed the advice in the Foreword, you'll be happy to know that this matching technique is even more impressive with strong lighting.

Figure 5.25 Not only is it clear that the can does not belong in the color environment of the background, the mismatch is equally apparent on each color channel. (Plate courtesy of Shuets Udono via Creative Commons license.)

The composite in **Figure 5.25** clearly does not work; the foreground element lacks the scene's dominant color and is white-lit. That's fine; it better demonstrates the effectiveness of the following technique.

It helps that both the foreground and the background elements have some areas that you can logically assume to be flat gray. The bridge has concrete footings for the steel girders along the edges of the road, while the can has areas of bare exposed aluminum.

The steps to color-match a scene like this are as follows:

1. Apply Levels to the foreground layer.

2. Switch the view in the Composition panel to Green (**Alt+2/Opt+2**). Not only is this the dominant color in this particular scene, but it is dominant in human vision, so green-matching is the first step in most scenes.

NOTES

This section discusses colors expressed as percentages; to see the same values in your Levels effect, use the Wing menu of the Info panel to choose Percent for the Color Display.

3. Begin as if you are working with a black-and-white photograph, and match the element to this dark contrasty scene using Levels in the RGB channel. If the element needs more contrast in the shadows and highlights, as this one does, raise Input Black and lower Input White; if it needs less, adjust the Output controls instead. Finally, adjust the gamma; in this scene, should it come down to match the darkness of the scene, or up so the element stands out more? The result should look like a monochrome photo whose elements match believably (**Figure 5.26a**).

4. Switch the view (**Alt+1/Opt+1**) and the Levels control to the Red channel and repeat the grayscale matching process. Clearly, the foreground element is far too bright for the scene. Specifically, the darkest silver areas of the can are much brighter than the brightest areas of the concrete in the background. Adjust the gamma down (to the right) until it feels more like they inhabit the same world. Now have a look at the highlights and shadows; the highlights look a little hot, so lower Red Output White (**Figure 5.26b**).

5. Now move over to Blue in the view (**Alt+3/Opt+3**) and in Levels. In this case, there is almost no match whatsoever. The can is much brighter and more washed out than the background. Raise Input Blue and bring gamma way down. Now the can looks like it belongs there (**Figure 5.26c**).

It's strange to make all of these changes without ever looking at the result in full color. So now, go ahead and do so. Astoundingly, that can is now within range of looking like it belongs in that scene; the remaining adjustments are subjective. If you want the can to pick up a little less green from the surroundings as I did, lower Green Input White. Back in the RGB channel, adjust Gamma according to how much you want this element to pop. And of course, finish the composite: Defocus slightly with a little fast blur, add a shadow, and you may start to buy it (**Figure 5.27**).

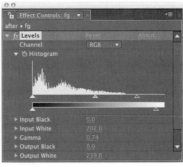

(a)

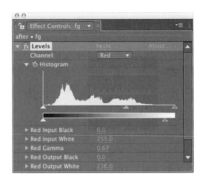

(b)

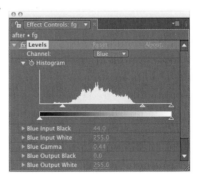

(c)

Figure 5.26 It's fun and satisfying to pull off an extreme match like this, channel by channel. The Levels settings come from looking for equivalent black/white/midpoints in the image and just analyzing whether the result looks like a convincing black-and-white image on each channel.

Figure 5.27 The result of all your previous efforts includes a subtle shadow that has been color-matched as well as a final adjustment to the white contrast.

No Clear Reference

Life doesn't always cooperate and provide nice white, black, and mid-gray references in the foreground and background source; the world is much more interesting than that.

Figure 5.28 contains a scene so strongly lit with one color, it's hard to tell what anything besides the glass would look like under white light, and even that is suspect.

The basic technique still works in this case, but it requires a bit more artistry. Instead of carefully matching specific

This example can be found on the disc in the 05_color_match_03_ red_interior folder.

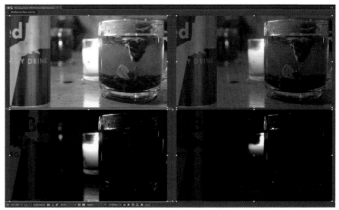

Figure 5.28 Sometimes a source scene will have completely crazy lighting. Once you are confident about how to match it, you may say to an image that is blown out and overbalanced in one direction, "Bring it on." This one requires as much intuition as logic, but the channel-by-channel approach works.

values, this time you must go channel by channel and simply make each image look plausible in grayscale black and white.

This time, begin with the red, not the green, channel, because it is clearly dominant. The foreground needs little adjustment to RGB to work in Red; just a slight reduction in Output White, to 0.85, and it looks pretty good. (We'll address matching the strong grain in Chapter 9.)

Move over to the green channel and it's a whole different story. Were it not for the light of the candle, this channel might be black, and matching the foreground clearly means bringing Green Output White way, way down (as low as 0.15). Now it's hard to tell what's even happening, so raise the exposure control in the viewer until the scene is somewhat illuminated (up as high as 10.0); the foreground now looks washed out compared with the extreme contrast of the background. Crush black and white contrast by raising Green Input Black up toward 0.3 and lowering Green Input White down to about 0.55. Great, but now the black level needs to be lifted just a touch, to 0.005 (you'd never notice it except that it's so overexposed). Click the exposure control icon to reset that, and it's looking pretty good.

Blue is the same story only more so, and yowza, is there a lot of grain here. Similar Blue Output White and Blue Input Black levels as for green will work, but there's no clear reason to increase white contrast in this channel, so leave Blue Input White where it is, and likewise Blue Output Black. Flashing with the exposure control reveals all.

Now for the moment of truth: Switch back to RGB to reveal a darned good color match happening here. With grain and maybe a little specular kick on the side, this element could look as though it had been there all along.

So even in cases where it's not really possible to be scientific about matching color, there are clear procedures to follow that allow you to make confident, bold, even radical color adjustments in composites.

NOTES

It can be a good idea to take a break when attempting fine color adjustment. Upon return, a clear first impression supersedes a lot more noodling.

Direction and Position

An element generated in 3D will ideally contain multiple passes for more control. Even with that, if the lighting direction and perspective of an element are wrong, there's no practical way to make it match (**Figure 5.29**).

Figure 5.29 All of the 2D compositing trickery in the world can't change the fact that this element is angled wrong. It is also lit from the wrong side. (Source clip from *Jake Forgotten*, courtesy of John Flowers.)

On the other hand, compositing frees artists from hanging around trying to solve everything in 3D software. **Figure 5.30** shows the simplest solution to the previous problem: Match the camera angle and basic lighting by observing what's in the scene. From looking at the pool balls and shadows, it seems apparent that there are a couple of overhead lights nearby and that the one off camera right is particularly strong.

NOTES

This example can be found on the disc in the 05_color_match_04_pool_interior folder.

Figure 5.30 The angle and lighting have been roughly matched in 3D; rather than tweaking it further there, work on getting a quicker and more accurate result in 2D.

The angle can be matched by placing the background shot into the background of the 3D software's camera view, making sure that there are a couple of lights roughly matched to that of the scene to produce the correct shading and specular highlights. This element does not match perfectly, but I am done with what I need to do in 3D.

More complex and dynamic perspective, interactive lighting, animation, and other variables certainly can be done in 3D, yet at the end of the day, the clever computer graphics artist moves a scene over to 2D as soon as the elements are within shooting distance (**Figure 5.31**).

Figure 5.31 The color-matched final includes a shadow.

Gamma Exposure Slamming

True story: When *Return of the Jedi* had its debut on national television in the 1980s, the emperor appeared with black rectangular garbage mattes dancing around his head, inside the cloak. All of this happened prior to the digital age, and these optical composites clearly worked fine on film—they were done at ILM by the best optical compositors in the business—but on video, those blacks were flashed and the illusion broke.

Don't lose your illusion, Axl, use it. Now that you know how to match levels, put them to the test. *Slam the exposure* of the image: Just adjust the Exposure control at the lower right of the viewer upward. *Slamming* (**Figure 5.32**) exposes areas of the image that might have been too dark to distinguish on your monitor; if the blacks still match with the gamma exposure slammed up, you're in good shape.

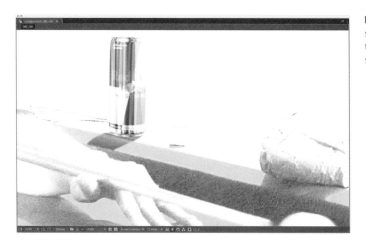

Figure 5.32 Slamming gamma is like shining a bright light on your scene. In this case it reveals a mismatch in the shadow color and the need for grain.

Everything must match, whether the image is blown out or dimmed way down.

Get into this habit anywhere that you find subtle discrepancies of contrast; you can use it to examine a color key, as you'll learn in the next chapter, or a more extreme change of scene lighting. Any reputable effects studio typically examines footage this way before it's sent for final editing.

Beyond the Ordinary, Even Beyond After Effects

Those, then, are the goods on color matching like a pro. Master these skills in a variety of compositions and you're already way above average with the most essential skill set you can learn as a compositor. With these tools under your belt, you're on your way to developing that key characteristic of a talented visual effects artist, a "good eye."

There is, of course, more to winning artistic fame and fortune than getting A and B to match, no matter how far B forces you to take A. There are special conditions like atmospheric haze and other environmental conditions that you can read more about in Chapter 13. There are special things to do to match how images behave on a camera that Chapter 9 will help illuminate. Chapter 11 is all about how higher dynamic range and greater color precision helps your result become even more awesome. And Chapter 12 gets into the specifics of how a mastery of light and shadows, depth cueing, and multipass rendering allow you to make jaws drop.

Looks and Colorista II

Red Giant Software was the first to deliver three-way color correction to After Effects in the form of its Magic Bullet Colorista plug-in, which it followed with the more fully featured and unique Magic Bullet Looks, which has now been followed by the deluxe Colorista II. These are worth mentioning not only because they're ubiquitous, but because Looks in particular works according to a unique UI metaphor. It offers tools that correspond to all five points from source to image: the subject, any matte box filters, the lens, the recording medium, and postproduction effects. It can be fun to concoct your own recipe from these modular ingredients, or to rely on one of the presets that comes with the application or can be purchased as add-on packages from Red Giant.

Chapter 12 includes an overview of the SpeedGrade toolset and how to make use of it. There are also excellent overview videos available at tv.adobe.com; just search "SpeedGrade" (or "Patrick Palmer," SpeedGrade's passionate product manager).

Chapter 12 is also where we get to look at tools you can use in conjunction with After Effects to enhance color, and thus enhance the result of your comp. As Stu Maschwitz, the author of the Foreword, has made abundantly clear, making it look "right" is nowhere near as good as getting a gut emotional reaction, and more than anything else, color finishing skills will get an otherwise perfectly executed shot to that point.

Color Finishing Outside After Effects

The tools that we just spent this chapter getting to know intimately are great for accuracy. For artistic expression with color, artists have tended to use tools beyond what is supplied in the shipping version of After Effects.

That kind of emotional magic is best created with tools outside of After Effects. As the publisher and I have always agreed, this book has focused almost exclusively on tools that are included in the shipping version of the application, even if that's not everyone's real-world experience, so in the past this part of the discussion has tended to be a bit thin. Sure, Red Giant Software tools such as Colorista and Looks have been so popular as an After Effects color solution you could almost call them ubiquitous, but we were faced with the dilemma of giving them substantial space in the book at the expense of features that are in the hands of everyone who uses the application.

This dilemma has been shared by After Effects artists as well, who also see their work graded in DaVinci Resolve, to name one tool with no connection whatsoever to the After Effects workflow. But now Adobe has responded by adding a toolset to CS6 Production Premium that is in the same class: SpeedGrade. This tool has been added to the discussion throughout the rest of this book, in particular into Chapter 11, about LUTs, and Chapter 12, on color looks.

SpeedGrade, of course, no doubt deserves its own book. Color finishing is an art, and SpeedGrade is a tool that works like no other software offered by Adobe. That will cause some initial resistance to working with it, and although overcoming that resistance is beyond what can be done in these pages, the difference that can be made with SpeedGrade is too great to ignore.

CHAPTER

6

Color Keying

Slow down, I'm in a hurry.

— Franz Mairinger (Austrian equestrian)

Color Keying

Color keying was devised in the 1950s as a clever means to combine live-action foreground footage with backgrounds from virtually anywhere. What was once a fragile and expensive proposition is now fully mainstream. Whole films have come to rely on this technique, while *The Colbert Report* invites anyone with a computer—and more than likely, a copy of After Effects—to try the "Greenscreen Challenge," which runs entries from none less than John Knoll.

The process goes by many names: color keying, bluescreening, greenscreening, pulling a matte, color differencing, and even chroma keying—a term from analog color television, a medium defined by chroma and heavily populated with weather forecasters.

The purpose of this chapter is to help you not only with color keying of bluescreen and greenscreen footage, but with all cases in which pixel values (hue, saturation, and brightness) stand in for transparency, allowing compositors to effectively separate the foreground from the background based on color data.

All of these methods extract luminance information that is then applied to the alpha channel of a layer or layers. The black areas become transparent, the white areas opaque, and the gray areas gradations of semi-opacity. Here's an overall tip: It's the gray areas that matter.

Procedural Mattes for the Lazy (and Diligent)

A *procedural matte* is generated by making adjustments to controls, instead of *rotoscoping* it by hand. You could say that the selection is generated mathematically rather than manually. Each artist has a threshold of tolerance to

NOTES

Example footage and comps for this chapter are all gathered together in the 06_keying folder on the disc.

NOTES

For those reading nonlinearly, this chapter extends logically from fundamental concepts about mattes and selections in Chapter 3.

continue to solve a matte procedurally or rotoscope it. My own threshold is high—I tend to avoid roto at all costs—so I have learned many methods for making the procedural approach work, and I share as many as possible here.

Following is some top-level advice to remember when creating any kind of matte.

▶ **Create contrast for clarity.** Use a bright, saturated, contrasting background (**Ctrl+Shift+B**/**Cmd+Shift+B**) such as yellow, red, orange, or purple (**Figure 6.1**). If the foreground is to be added to a dark scene, a dark shade is okay, but in most cases bright colors better reveal matte problems. Solo the foreground over the background you choose.

Figure 6.1 This plate is, on first glance, well lit and staged, yet all kinds of challenges become evident after selecting the background color with Keylight: vignetting, rig removal, tracking marker removal, reflection in the costume (knee and crotch area), and motion blur of fine detail. It is subtle corrections in these areas that make this matte believable.

Figure 6.2 A "chewy" matte like this is typically the result of clamping the foreground or background (or both) too far.

▶ **Protect edges at all costs.** This is the name of the game (and the focus of much of this chapter); the key to winning is to isolate and focus on the edges as much as possible to avoid crunchy, chewy mattes (**Figure 6.2**).

▶ **Keep adjustments as simple as possible, even starting over if necessary to simplify.** Artists spend hours on keys that could be done more effectively in minutes, simply by beginning in the right place. There are many complex and interdependent steps involved with creating a key; if you're hung up on one, it may be time to try a different approach.

▶ **Keep dancing: Check adjacent frames and zoom into detail.** When possible, start with the trickiest area of a difficult frame; look for motion blur, fine detail, excessive color spill, and so on, and keep looking around with a critical eye for what needs improvement.

▶ **Break it down.** This is the single most important concept that novices miss. Most mattes will benefit from separate garbage, core, and edge passes—a process detailed later in this chapter—and in many cases it helps to create a separate pass just for delicate edges: hair, a translucent costume, motion blur, and so on.

I encourage you to review this list again once you've explored the rest of the chapter.

Linear Keyers and Hi-Con Mattes

There are cases in which edge detail is less of a factor because the matte is used to adjust, not simply composite, an element. For example, you could hold out the highlight

---

CLOSE-UP

Linear Color Key vs. Roto Brush

In Chapter 7 we'll take a look at Roto Brush, which goes beyond what can be done with a simple linear key by combining many criteria (beyond luminance) for what makes up a selection. It is powerful enough that it may seem to supersede linear keying, but keep in mind that Roto Brush is always more expensive (in terms of processing power and setup). Sometimes a luminance key is all you need.

areas of an image for adjustment using a *high-contrast* (*hi-con*) matte. You might create this matte with a *linear keyer*.

Linear keyers are relatively simple and define a selection range based only on a single channel. This could be red, green, blue, or just overall luminance. They're useful in a wide variety of cases outside the scope of bluescreen and greenscreen shots, although similar principles apply with Keylight. (Keylight is covered later in this chapter.)

The most useful linear keyers, Extract and Linear Color Key, are unfortunately less intuitively named than the keyers to avoid at all costs—Luma Key and Color Key. The latter two are limited to a bitmap (black and white) selection; only by choking and blurring the result with Edge Thin and Edge Feather controls can you add threshold adjustment. It's a little unfortunate that Adobe hasn't let these ancient effects go into the bin marked "obsolete" since the other, less intuitively named effects supersede them (and yet those not in the know naturally reach for the ones with the obvious titles).

Extract and Linear Color Key

The Extract effect is useful for *luminance (luma) keying*, because it uses the black-and-white points of an image or any of its individual channels. Linear Color Key is a more appropriate tool for isolating a particular color (or color range).

Extract

If you're comfortable with the Levels effect, then Extract is no problem. It includes a histogram and sliders over a gradient. Try working with the chimp clip in this chapter's project folder. Before adjusting the effect, take a look at all three color channels (**Alt+1**, **2**, **3**/**Opt+1**, **2**, **3**). One of the three typically has the best initial contrast, while the default luminance channel is merely an average of the three and not as strong a choice. In this case, the blue channel has the most uniformly dark subject area, so in the Channel menu of Extract, choose that (**Figure 6.3**).

The Extract histogram gives you a strong clue as to the likely white or black thresholds on each channel. To set these, drag the upper right pair of square controls at the

Figure 6.3 Extract the luminance channel and you get all three channels blended together—but first examine those channels and it's easy to see that the foreground figure is most consistently dark in the blue channel. A gentle slope with Softness set to 75 (bottom) retains some of the softness and fine detail of the hair, and it certainly helps to comp over a light background.

All Channels Are Not Created Equal

If you set an RGB image as a luma matte, the red, green, and blue channels are averaged together to determine the luminance of the overall image. However, they are not weighted evenly, because that's not how the eye sees them. Details about how to work with this fact can be found in Chapter 12.

If you find yourself wanting to use a particular channel as a luma matte, use Effect > Channel > Shift Channels; set Take Alpha From as Full On and the other three channels to whichever channel—red, green, or blue—is most effective.

white end of the gradient, below the histogram. Watch the image itself as well as the histogram. Just as with Levels, you're bracketing the area where the foreground image data is held but stopping short of clipping—which in this case causes holes in the foreground.

The only way to decide how far to go is to add the target background. If you're removing a white set wall, the hope is that whatever is replacing it is also quite bright. If not, you may have to choke the edges more than is ideal to avoid white fringing. A bright sky behind this subject is much simpler than trying to make this matte work against black.

Once you've found the lowest white point setting that yields a nice edge (and if there are small holes in the foreground, don't worry too much about them yet), soften it by dragging the lower box in that pair of square controls to the right, raising White Softness. This adds threshold pixels to the matte naturally, by tapering between the fully opaque values at the white point and the transparent background.

If there are holes in the matte, duplicate the layer, and then in the duplicate, raise the White Point value so that the holes disappear. Now protect the edge by adding a Simple Choker effect on that duplicate layer and raising the Choke Matte value until you can toggle this layer on and off without seeing any effect on the edge. This is a core matte, and it will be essential with color keying ahead.

Linear Color Key

The Linear Color Key offers direct selection of a key color using an eyedropper tool. It's useful in cases where Keylight won't work, because the selected color is not one of the digital primaries (red, green, or blue) that Keylight relies on for its fundamental operations. You may never come up with a situation in which you need to key out a background made up of some secondary color, so this key can also be useful to select a certain range of color in an image for adjustment. The default 10% Matching Softness setting is arbitrary and defines a rather loose range. I often end up setting it closer to 1%.

Note that there are, in fact, three eyedropper tools in the Linear Color Key effect. The top one defines Key Color, and the other two add and subtract Matching Tolerance. I tend not to use these eyedroppers because they don't work in the Comp viewer; the main Key Color eyedropper and the Matching sliders work for me (**Figure 6.4**).

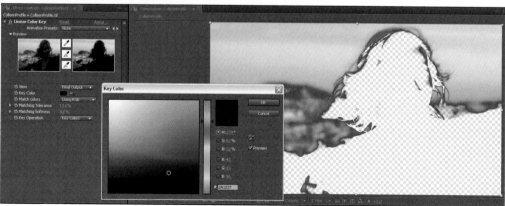

Figure 6.4 Suppose you want to make a change to the distant, out-of-focus area of this shot. By selecting a prominent object in the foreground, the sweater, and adjusting the selection (bottom), you can create a matte that separates the foreground and background. (Image courtesy of Eric Escobar.)

There's a hidden trick to getting better results with Linear Color Key. Because it is linear, it will pick up hues that seem unrelated. To reduce the effect of these, you can add a second instance of Linear Color Key. Under Key Operation, changing the default Key Colors setting to Keep Colors does nothing (if it's the first instance) except annul the effect. On the second instance, Keep Colors is unaffected by the first instance and can bring back hues that were already keyed. The one-two punch will often deliver the best result (**Figure 6.5**).

Figure 6.5 By using Linear Color Key set to Keep Colors again (left), I'm able to get rid of the extra selection areas in the background, apply the matte, and add a glow effect to just the background.

Color Keying: Greenscreen, Bluescreen, and (Very Rarely) Redscreen

And now, ladies and gentlemen, the main event. Past editions of this book have taken a high-level approach to explaining the art of keying along with specific advice about Keylight, the powerful keyer from the Foundry included with After Effects, but this time around, the two are combined in a practical example of a challenging key.

Keylight is useful in keying situations beyond studio-created bluescreen or greenscreen shots. For example, you

Figure 6.6 I was hoping to grab just the shadows on the floor with a Difference matte applied to the image on the left using the middle image as a Difference layer. Unfortunately, subtle stuff like that tends to be indistinguishable from noise, even with a clean, low-grain source.

can use Keylight for removal of a blue sky (**Figure 6.7**). You wouldn't use Keylight to pull a luminance key, however, or when you're simply trying to isolate a certain color range within the shot; it really is only effective at making one of the three primary colors transparent.

Keylight is most typically used on footage shot against a uniform, saturated, primary color background, where preservation of edge detail is of utmost importance.

To get started, make a new comp containing the blueScrn_mcu_HD clip. At first glance, this does not look like it will be a difficult shot to key: The background is a uniform, well-lit, and fully saturated blue, and the talent is well lit, with some nice warm edge lighting. The hair is edge lit in

Difference Mattes

The Difference matte is a little like Santa Claus. It would be nice to believe in it because it would give so much if it really existed, but it is mostly just a fantasy that a computer can compare two images, one with a foreground figure, one without, and extract that figure cleanly. It sounds like the kind of thing computers were made to do. But not only does this require a completely locked-off shot, but you'd also be shocked at how much one pixel of one frame that should be identical can vary due to compression grain and subtle variations of light. Low-lit areas, in particular, tend to gray out in a way that foils this technique, which works best with saturated, differentiated color. **Figure 6.6** amply demonstrates the problem and shows that Difference keying may be useful for the crudest type of isolation, but not much more.

Figure 6.7 Can a bright blue sky serve as an effective bluescreen? It's not ideal, but it can, indeed.

Figure 6.8 The plate is well shot and contains the kind of challenges that are fun to work with: nice hair details and beautiful motion blur.

a contrasting color from the left, containing wispy details to preserve, and the hands move quickly, creating motion blur (**Figure 6.8**).

Nowadays, it has become somewhat unusual to see bluescreen shots, which had their heyday in the pre-digital optical compositing era. Green is favored for digital shoots for several reasons, primarily that it is the dominant color in the visual spectrum and therefore most cameras are able to resolve it with far more image data than is found in the blue channel, which typically has less luminance and more noise.

Oddly enough, I've always preferred blue to green. For one thing, a nicely lit blue background is soothing to the eye, whereas digital green—the hue that is pure, luminant green, a specialty color not found at any ordinary paint store—is actually the most jarring color in the spectrum, one that has become a favorite of emergency services crews and warning signs around the world. The phenomenon known as "greenscreen psychosis," in which talented actors and directors struggle on a greenscreen set, has partly to do with it being such an empty environment, but I'm willing to bet it also has something to do with the vibe of that awful color.

The following steps apply to virtually any key, with specifics about this shot:

1. **Garbage matte** (mask) any areas of the background that can easily be masked out. "Easily" means you do not have an articulated matte (you don't have to animate

Figure 6.9 Even a quick-and-dirty garbage matte as simple as this isolates the action and eliminates the darker blue values in the corners.

individual mask points). As a rule of thumb, limit this to what you can accomplish in about 20 minutes or less (**Figure 6.9**).

This shot doesn't seem to need a garbage matte, but notice that the talent's action of raising her arms does not cover all areas of the frame, including at about 100 pixels from the left edge of the frame, 200 pixels from the right edge, and 100 pixels at the top. Notice also the slight vignette effect at the edges of the frame: move your cursor to the upper-right corner, for example, and take a look at the Info panel as you do so—you'll notice values are 10% to 15% lower in luminance than those along the edge of the talent.

If you didn't bother with a simple garbage matte in this case, you've already compromised the matte. The game is to key only the essential pixels, and those are the ones along the edge of the moving figure. Lazily keying the full frame compromises those edges by overweighting background pixels that don't matter, even on a shot as clean as this one. Draw a rectangular mask around the area containing the action as in Figure 6.9, and step through all frames of the clip to make sure no elbows are clipped out.

2. Use a side-by-side Composition and Layer view to create the **first pass** of the key with no extra adjustments.

This is a slightly new approach to this most essential step in Keylight—sampling the Screen Colour (that "u" gives away its British heritage). Before you even apply the effect, create a new workspace as follows: choose Minimal from View > Workspace (resetting it if necessary to get back to just a Timeline and a Composition viewer), and double-click the bluescreen clip in the timeline to open it in Layer view. Drag the Layer tab to one side of the panel or the other to create a new panel, so that you have two views of the clip side-by-side. Add an Effect Controls panel next to the timeline.

Go to a frame with some clear motion blur as well as hair detail in it, such as frame 5. Now try this. In Keylight, choose Status from the View menu. Both images will turn white, showing a solid alpha channel. In the Layer panel, uncheck Render to bring back the source image. Now click the Screen Colour eyedropper and, holding down the **Alt** (**Opt**) key, drag around the blue background in the Layer view and notice what happens in the other viewer.

Status view is an exaggerated view of the alpha channel matte. Opaque pixels are displayed as white, transparent pixels are black, and those containing any amount of transparency are gray (**Figure 6.10**). It's an easy way to see how well the background is keying (turning

> **TIP**
>
> The side-by-side layout is so useful, you should save it as a workspace named Keying or Matte.

Figure 6.10 You can't see it in a still figure, but by **Alt**-dragging (**Opt**-dragging) around the blue area of Layer view on the right, which is set to not render, a real-time update of Status view on the left allows you to discover the optimum background color.

black) on the first pass and whether any significant holes (in gray) appear in the foreground subject.

It's suddenly apparent that what looked like a straight-forward shot will be a challenging key. Although it is possible, with a little patience, to find a spot in the background that turns most of the background pixels black as in Figure 6.10, the dark areas of the shirt and the hair are nowhere near solid white. Still, having carefully chosen the best Screen Colour, you are free to move on and refine this matte.

3. Gently **refine the matte** and **preview** the result at full resolution, in full motion, against a contrasting color.

In previous editions of this book, I dutifully explained and made recommendations about the controls below Screen Colour: Screen Gain and Balance, Despill and Alpha Bias, and Screen Pre-blur. There's more information about these later in the chapter, but on the whole, my advice is, don't touch these. They all have one thing in common. They change the way the matte itself is calculated—and I have come to believe that manipulating them does more harm than good.

Skip down to Screen Matte and twirl down those controls. From here down, all of the Keylight controls are working with the matte after it has already been generated. In other words, adjusting these controls is no different than applying a separate effect after Keylight to refine its matte, and that's a good thing in this case.

Raise Clip Black by dragging to the right across the value to bring it upward. Stop when you see all of the gray pixels in the background turn black in Status view. (Even though you'll also see some of the gray pixels around the hair—the ones you want to keep gray—turn black as well. We'll deal with those next.) In my attempt, I ended up with a value of 26.0, and as a rule of thumb, anything above 20 is a bit high—another reason to take more care with this matte than just pulling the key in one pass.

Now lower Clip White by dragging to the left across that value to bring it downward. Here you may find that you have to go pretty far—like down into the 50s—in order to see all of the gray or green pixels in the torso become white. I ended up with a value of 57.0. You'll also see some green pixels remaining around the edges of the figure, particularly around the wisps of hair.

The green pixels in Status view are Keylight's signal that the color values of those pixels have changed in the keying process. Focus on the wisps of hair on the light side, and switch between Final Result and Intermediate Result in the View menu. The former suppresses that blue spill that you see in the latter to the natural hair color as part of the keying process.

Intermediate Result shows the source footage with the matte applied as an alpha channel but no alteration to the RGB pixels at all, while Final Result adds color suppression as a natural by-product of Keylight's method of removing the background color. Final Result seems to be the one you want, but there's an unfortunate side effect to watch out for: It can dramatically enhance graininess in the result. **Figure 6.11** shows a before and after in which the suppression process clearly pushes pixels to a much contrastier shade even though the source is well-lit footage from the RED camera. For this reason, don't let Keylight do your spill suppression for you.

Figure 6.11 Flashing the image with the exposure control at the lower right reveals a horrific amount of grain in Final Result view of this Keylight operation (left). Intermediate Result (right) omits any alteration to the source color, revealing that the original image, even flashed like this, is nicely shot, with smooth, tolerable grain.

Spill suppression will have to wait until after we're done with this key, and at this point, we're not even close. Getting that shirt to key has ruined the detail in the hair and the motion of the hands. Had the talent been wearing a different costume and not moved around as much, the steps taken to this point might have resulted in a completed key. But with anything more complicated—and most effects shots seem to be much more complicated—it's now necessary to break this operation into component parts (or be painted into a corner.) Neither holes in the matte nor crunchy edges on the hair is acceptable, and right now the two are fighting one another (**Figure 6.12**).

Figure 6.12 Closing all those little gaps in the foreground will mean destroying that hair detail if this matte is attempted in one pass.

4. This is the moment to **separate the plate for multiple passes**. In every case there are two basic ways to do this:

   ▶ Separate one part of the foreground from the rest with a mask or other selection. For example, in this case you could rotoscope a mask around the hair, and possibly another one around the moving hands.

   ▶ Create multiple passes of the same matte: one as a garbage matte (or gmatte), one as a core matte (or cmatte), and the final one featuring only the isolated edge.

In this case, we know that there are prominent holes in the foreground, so the latter approach—to create at least a core matte so that the interior areas are isolated from the all-important edge—is the way to go.

This method of breaking down the shot would work with any software keyer, but we're sticking with Keylight, as it is the most powerful keyer included with After Effects and this maximizes what it can do.

a. Duplicate the layer to be keyed.

At this point, our bluescreen shot has a garbage mask and an instance of Keylight applied to it. Leave these on the upper of the two layers, rename that layer "edge matte," and turn off its visibility—we'll deal with it later.

b. Rename the lower layer "cmatte" and refine the core matte (Figure 6.13).

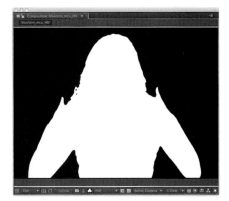

Figure 6.13 A heavily choked source matte, turning all areas of the alpha channel either white or black, makes a good core matte to sit behind the edge matte.

To begin, reset Clip Black by context-clicking on that property in the Effect controls and choosing Reset.

We're keeping our Screen Colour selection, but will now crush the matte. Switch back to Status view and lower Clip White until the torso and hair are completely filled in with white (around 66.0 may work). Now raise Clip Black all the way to one unit below the Clip White value (65.0 if the previous value was 66.0).

You now have the worst matte possible, with no edge subtlety whatsoever. What possible good is this?

Switch to Intermediate Result. Yep, horrible matte. Now close the Keylight controls and apply the Simple Choker effect. Toggle Alpha Channel view in the Composition viewer (**Alt+4/Opt+4**) and take a snapshot (**Shift+F5** or **F6**, **F7**, or **F8** all work).

Raise the Choke Matte value into the low double digits—say, around 15. The matte shrinks. Press F5 to toggle back and forth with the unchoked matte, and make sure that all of the choked matte's edges are several pixels inside that of the unchoked matte. This is important: There must be no edge pixels in the core matte that overlap with those of the edge matte.

This matte may behave better if it's softer—for now, you can take my word for that, since we're not yet putting it into use. As an extra precaution, apply Channel Blur and raise Alpha Blurriness to 15.0. This provides an extra threshold between the chunky core and the fine edge (**Figure 6.14**).

c. Kill the spill.

Leaving the View on Intermediate Result is great for avoiding side effects such as enhanced graininess, but the layer almost always then requires some sort of spill suppression. More often than not, you have to do this anyway.

There's a Spill Suppressor effect in After Effects; how great it would be if all you had to do was sample the color, change Color Accuracy from Faster to Better,

TIP

Switch a RAM preview to Alpha Channel view (**Alt+4/Opt+4**) and the cache is preserved; you can watch a real-time preview of the alpha channel without re-rendering the preview.

Figure 6.14 This isn't how the actual comp looks; it's showing the core matte as the white center with the plate translucently revealing that nicely isolated edge, where all efforts are to be focused.

leave Suppression at 100, and be done. But heck, you can crank Suppression up to 200 if you want (who knew?) and still see your talent looking green (or in this case, blue) around the gills (**Figure 6.15**).

You could also use the Edge Colour Correction in Keylight, but it has no effect other than in Final Result mode, and—gotcha—that's likely to mess with your footage too much, remember?

Spill suppression is a big enough deal that it merits its own section a little later in this chapter. The key (please excuse the pun) is not simply to suppress or desaturate it, but in fact to bring it back around to its natural hue. For that you need an effect a lot like Hue/Saturation and the skills to use it (coming up).

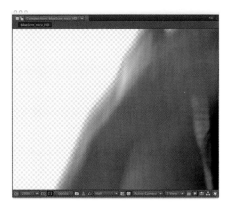

Figure 6.15 Blue matte line around the edges.

5. **Evaluate the shot in full motion.**

How are the details holding up? And how does the foreground look in the actual composite? It's easy to get so wrapped up in creating the perfect matte that you forget that some problems are harder to spot against some backgrounds. If she's headed for a bluish environment, why trouble yourself too much with spill suppression? Would more blending of the background into the foreground (see the "Edge Selection" section later in this chapter) or even light wrap help sell this composite (**Figure 6.16**)?

Figure 6.16 At this stage, prior to any color matching, the detail is well preserved but the matte lines along the torso and arms, in particular, remain.

Holdout Matte

A *holdout matte* isolates an area of an image for separate treatment. I recommend that you think of a color key as an isolated edge matte surrounded by two holdout mattes: one for the core, one for the background. Details on creating these can be found ahead in the "Fine-Tuning and Problem Solving" section.

The controls atop Keylight (from Screen Colour down to Screen Pre-blur) alter the actual generation of the matte. Everything from Screen Matte down adjusts the result of that first step.

6. Isolate and refine further.

Do you need to isolate the hair for its own keying pass? How about those motion-blurred hands? Are there holes in the matte, or problems with the core pass? Does the talent, heaven forbid, make direct contact with the background, for example lying down on the colored floor?

For these types of issues, create *holdout mattes*.

Keylight: The After Effects Keying Tool

The core of Keylight is *screen matte* generation, and as mentioned, the most essential step is choosing the exact color to key. From that, Keylight makes weighted comparisons between its saturation and hue and that of each pixel, as detailed in **Table 6.1**. From this, you see that the ideal background is distinct and saturated.

My current advice is to leave all other top controls in Keylight alone, but in case you're curious about them, the following provides a bit of extra information on how each works.

Screen Gain

The ideal Screen Gain setting is 100, no change from the default. This adjustment is compensation for a poorly lit matte or a foreground contaminated with background color. While raising it may make the matte channel look better, you are also likely to see increased color grain and loss of edge detail with values above the default. The alternative with fewer side effects is to raise Clip Black.

TABLE 6.1 How Keylight Makes Its Key Decisions

Compared to screen color, pixel is	Keylight will
of a different hue	consider it foreground, making it opaque
of a similar hue and more saturated	key it out completely, making it transparent
of a similar hue but less saturated	subtract a mathematically weighted amount of the screen color and make it semitransparent

Screen Gain boosts (or reduces) the saturation of each pixel before comparing it to the screen color. This effectively adds more desaturated background pixels into the keyed color range.

Screen Balance

Keylight relies on one of the three RGB color values being the dominant background color. It is even more effective when it knows whether one of the two remaining colors is more prevalent in the background—and when it knows which color. Screen Balance makes use of a dominant secondary background color.

The software automatically sets a balance of 95% with bluescreens (which typically contain a good deal of green) and leaves it at 50% for greenscreens (which tend to be more monochromatic). If you want to try adjusting it yourself, try alternate settings of either 5.0 or 95.0 to take it close to one or the other secondary color.

Figure 6.17 The Rosco colors: Ultimatte Blue, Ultimatte Green, and Ultimatte Super Blue. Blue is not pure blue but double the amount of green, which in turn is double the amount of red. Ultimatte Green is more pure, with only a quarter the amount of red and no blue whatsoever. Lighting can change their hue (as does converting them for print in this book).

Bias

The Bias settings color correct the image by scaling the primary color component up or down (enhancing or reducing its difference from the other two components). The Foundry recommends that, in most cases, you leave Alpha Bias at the default and that you click the Despill Bias eyedropper on a well-lit skin tone to be preserved; despill pivots around this value.

Bias has the unpleasant side effect of significantly increasing graininess. If this happens to your footage, try other despill methods discussed later in this chapter.

NOTES

A Rosco Ultimatte Blue screen contains quite a bit of green—much more than red, unless improperly lit. Ultimatte Green screens, meanwhile, are nearly pure green (**Figure 6.17**).

TIP

Hold down **Alt** (**Opt**) to center a zoom around your cursor.

Refinement

When you spot an area that looks like a candidate for refinement, save (to hold an undo point should you need to use File > Revert), zoom in, and create a region of interest around the area in question.

Now take a look at the tools provided by Keylight to address some common problems.

Clip White, Black, Rollback

The double-matte method (core and edge) eliminates a lot of the tug of war that otherwise exists between a solid foreground and subtle edges. Even with this advantage, both mattes may require adjustments to the Clip White or Clip Black controls.

Keep the largest possible difference (or *delta*, if you prefer) between these two settings, as this is where all of the gray, semitransparent alpha pixels live. The closer the two numbers get, the closer you are to a bitmap alpha channel, in which each pixel is pure black or white—a very bad thing indeed (**Figure 6.18**).

Figure 6.18 Here's how the hair looks without a separated edge matte. Not nice.

If you push too far, restore back toward the initial matte with Clip Rollback. Its value is the number of pixels from the edge that are rolled back relative to the original, unclipped screen matte. So if your edges were subtle but sizzling on the first pass, and removing noise from the matte hardened them, then this tool may restore subtlety.

Noise Suppression

For seriously sizzling mattes, Keylight includes a Screen Pre-blur option that I reserve for footage with a clearly evident noise problem, such as heavy compression. Blurring source footage before keying adds inaccuracy and is something of a desperation move. The footage itself does not appear blurred, but the matte does.

A better alternative for a fundamentally sound matte is Screen Softness, under the Screen Matte controls. This control blurs the screen matte itself, so it has a much better chance of retaining detail than a pre-blur approach. As

Figure 6.19 The source (top left) can be converted to YUV with Channel Combiner and the UV (chroma) or Y (luminance) blurred individually, then round-tripped back to RGB with Channel Combiner again. With heavy blur to the color data (top right) the image is still clear—albeit stylized—if the luminance is untouched, but blur the luminance and leave the color and the result is far less recognizable (lower left).

**Chroma Subsampling:
The 411 on 4:1:1, 4:2:2, and 4:2:0**

Video images are RGB on your computer, but video devices themselves use YCrCb, the digital equivalent of YUV. Y is the luminance or brightness signal (or "luma"). Cr and Cb are color-difference signals (roughly corresponding to red-cyan and blue-yellow)—you could call them chrominance or "chroma."

It turns out that the human eye is much more particular about gradations in luma than chroma, as is amply demonstrated in **Figure 6.19**.

The standard types of digital video compression take advantage of this fact. **Figure 6.20** shows the difference between straight RGB and 4:2:2 compression, which is common to popular formats including DVCPRO HD and DVCPRO50, ProRes 422, and cameras such as the Sony F900. The figure also shows 4:1:1, which is used by wisened, ancient DVCPRO and NTSC DV formats. Almost as bad for keying purposes is 4:2:0, used by the MPEG-2 (DVD), HDV, and PAL DV format as well as most variants of XDCAM and AVCHD (common to DLSR and related cameras).

As you might imagine, chromatic compression is far less than ideal for color keying, hence the work-arounds in this section.

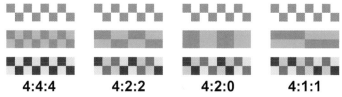

4:4:4   4:2:2   4:2:0   4:1:1

Figure 6.20 4:4:4 is just pixels, no chroma subsampling, where 4:2:2 and 4:1:1 group the nearest neighboring pixels, giving them identical luminance according to the patterns shown here.

shown in Chapter 3, edges in nature are slightly soft, and a modest amount of softness is appropriate even with a perfectly healthy matte.

The Despot cleanup tools are meant to fill matte holes, but at high levels they add blobbiness, so they are rarely useful. An alternative approach, particularly with DV formats (which, by the way, are guaranteed to add compression noise and are not recommended for bluescreen and greenscreen work), is to do as follows:

1. Convert the footage to YUV using Channel Combiner (the From menu). This will make the clip look very strange, because your monitor displays images as RGB. Do not be alarmed.

2. Apply Channel Blur to the green and blue channels only, at modest amounts. To gauge this, examine each channel as you work—press **Alt+2** (**Opt+2**) or **Alt+3** (**Opt+3**) while zoomed in on a noisy area. Make sure Repeat Edge Pixels is checked.

3. Round-trip back from YUV to RGB, using a second instance of Channel Combiner.

4. Apply Keylight.

Matte Choke

Besides mismatched lighting, fringing (excess edge opacity) and choking (lost edge detail) are the most common tells of a greenscreen comp. Screen Grow/Shrink deals with this issue directly. Don't be afraid to use it, gently (a setting of around 1.0, or one pixel, won't do your matte much harm, especially if combined with a bit of matte softness).

This is not the last resort for choking and spreading a matte; alternatives follow in "Fine-Tuning and Problem Solving."

Spill Suppression

Keylight suppresses color spill (foreground pixels contaminated by reflected color from the background) as part of the keying operation when displaying the final result. Thus spill-kill can be practically automatic if you pull a good initial key.

There are a surprising number of cases in which Keylight's spill suppression is not what you want, for the following reasons:

▶ Dramatic hue shifts occur to items whose colors are anywhere near green (for example, cyan) or opposite green (for example, magenta). It's challenging enough to keep green off of a green set, let alone its neighboring and opposite hues.

▶ These hue shifts can also add graininess, even to footage that was shot uncompressed and has little or no source grain.

Figure 6.21 Her face doesn't even look the same without the highlights reflected with the green. Even worse, at this magnification, it's easy to see that the amount of grain noise has increased significantly (right). It's a definite case for pulling the matte on one pass and applying spill suppression separately.

In **Figure 6.21**, notice how the whole shape of the woman's face seems to change due to the removal of highlights via spill suppression.

Should Keylight's spill suppression become unwieldy or otherwise useless for the preceding reasons, there is an easy out: Ordinarily, the View is set to Final Result, but set it to Intermediate Result for the matte applied to the alpha without any change to RGB. The CC Composite effect does the same thing, eliminating all RGB changes from preceding effects but keeping the alpha.

Keylight itself also includes spill suppression tools, under Edge Colour Correction, that influence only the edge pixels. Enable its check box and adjust the controls below, softening or growing the edge as needed to increase the area of influence. Sometimes adjusting the Luminance or Saturation of edges is a quick fix.

The next section, which goes beyond this tool, describes better ways to kill spill.

Fine-Tuning and Problem Solving

The key here is to break it down. The above steps apply to most ordinary keying situations, but extraordinary ones happen all the time. The trick is to find the areas that are closer to ordinary, deal with those, and isolate the extraordinary stuff separately. In this section we focus on how to break apart a key with various types of holdout mattes and keep procedural keys effective.

Although each shot is different, there are really only a few challenges that consistently come up with a color matte:

▶ Lighting: If the shot was not lit properly, everything that follows will be much more difficult.

▶ Image quality: Bluescreen and greenscreen keys put footage quality to the test, and the worst cameras are those that lose the most data right at the time of capture. MiniDV cameras used to be the main culprits, but nowadays it is sadly the mighty DSLR that is most often inappropriately used to shoot effects plates.

These two points are determined at the shoot itself; for more about that, see the next section, "Fix It On Set."

▶ Fine detail such as hair, motion, or lens blur.

▶ Costume contamination: shiny, reflective, or transparent subjects, or those simply containing colors close to that of the background, can present a fun keying challenge but can also turn out to be more of a nightmare (**Figure 6.22**).

▶ Set contact is always a huge challenge, whether simply a full-body shot including feet, or talent interacting with objects painted green, sitting on a green stool, or lying on the green floor.

Figures 6.22 Stylized view of a real comp in which it was necessary not only to key for core and edge but to do so in five individual areas of the frame, each masked out, keyed individually, and recombined in Alpha Add to avoid gaps in the overlapping identical mask edges. Layer label colors correspond to individual matte colors.

▶ Shadows are typically all or nothing—one either carefully lights to keep them or needs to be prepared to remove them, despite being by nature areas of low contrast and difficult to key.

These require separate holdout passes in order to be keyed, and the really stubborn situations may even require roto (Chapter 7).

Holdout Matte

Check out grnScrn_mcu_HD on the book's disc—this time it's the yellow stripes in the shirt that wreak havoc due to their similarity to green. There's no way to get a good key of the hair without pulling that key on a separate pass—so how exactly is that done?

Create a garbage matte—a mask—around all the hair edges only, carefully animating it so that they are fully isolated and nothing is missed. This layer then gets its own key using the same criteria and steps as you would use to derive the main matte. The Clip White and Black settings are much more mild than for the overall matte, allowing more detail.

That's clear enough—the place where artists sometimes get confused is then combining this with the main matte. Once this matte is complete, copy its mask and all keyframes and paste them on the main matte layers, but choose Subtract so that they hold out the inverse area. Now—and this is the step that's easily missed—switch the hair matte layer's blending mode to Alpha Add. This causes the mask and its inverse to blend together seamlessly without leaving a gap along the semitransparent edges (**Figure 6.23**).

Procedural Garbage Matte

Often the background is anything but uniform and the action is fast, so making a garbage matte to isolate the edge is quite a chore. In such cases, the same process that was used to create the core matte above can also be used to create a garbage matte, or gmatte, without drawing more than an elementary mask. In many cases Roto Brush will serve this purpose as well, but it too prefers uniform motion.

TIP

If a key requires several holdout mattes, this can become a bit heavy to manage. You do have the option to link Mask Shape properties with an expression (Chapter 10) so that if you change the mask animation in the holdout matte you don't have to remember to recopy the keyframes.

Figure 6.23 The mask is applied to the top layer to hold out the hair for a separate pass (top left), and the master layer has the same mask, inverted (or in Subtract mode). A telltale hairline appears where the two mattes overlap (top right) until the upper layer is set to Alpha Add mode (lower left).

NOTES

Refine Matte is a sophisticated bit of technology that can remove traces of the background from the edges of a matte, even if it's not a uniform color; what it's not so good at is the less-automated but more consistent usage being advocated here.

The clip from Figure 6.23 can be garbage matted procedurally in this manner. Just as with the cmatte, create a hard, chewy matte that pushes all of the background pixels to black and the foreground to white. Now spread that matte using one of the following methods.

Simple Choker allows you to spread the alpha channel using a negative number. You can push it hard and even use more than one instance if the 100-pixel limit gets in your way, as it can with garbage mattes.

Minimax is the choice if Simple Choker isn't effective enough. It provides a quick way to spread or choke pixel data, even without alpha channel information, and it has a powerful effect. It can also operate on individual channels of luminance.

Matte Choker sounds more pro than Simple Choker but it's really just unnecessarily complicated.

Now comes the part you won't like: Create three duplicates of the plate and label them, top to bottom as gmatte, edgematte, and cmatte, then precomp them. The reason for this is that the next step requires it.

Set the blending mode of that gmatte you just spread, the top layer, to Stencil Alpha. The layer disappears but its alpha channel cuts all the way through the comp—like a stencil! **Figure 6.24** shows why it's necessary to precomp; otherwise, the stencil operates on the background as well.

Figure 6.24 This is a great way to isolate an edge without hand-animating the garbage matte. The top layer is another crushed dirty matte that has been spread with Simple Choker with a value of –100.00. If it's not enough you can use two instances of Simple Choker or Minimax. Stencil Alpha blend mode then applies the result to the layers below.

Now, once you refine the core matte according to the Color Keying section above, the edge matte pass is truly as isolated as it can be, leading to a much more effective result or your money back. Actually, if you're not done at that point, it must mean you need holdout passes for specific areas of the frame. Keep breaking it down.

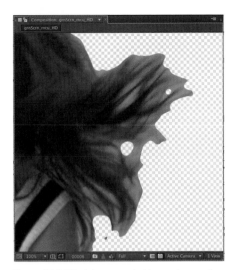

Figure 6.25 Mind the gaps; choking and spreading a matte, or using tools to do so automatically, such as the third-party Key Correct tools, is likely to close small gaps.

TIP

A useful third-party alternative to Minimax is Erodilation from ObviousFX (www.obviousfx.com). It can help do heavier choking (eroding) and hole filling (dilating), and its controls are simple and intuitive (choose Erode or Dilate from the Operation menu and the channel—typically Alpha).

Close Holes

Suppose you can't close a hole in the core matte using just Keylight. You can close them by choking then spreading the matte as follows:

1. Choke (garbage matte) or Spread (core matte) the holes until they disappear.

2. Spread or Choke (the reverse of whatever was the previous step) an equivalent or greater amount.

This will of course destroy any edge subtlety, which is why it only works well on a core or garbage matte. It will also cause small gaps near an outside edge to close (**Figure 6.25**), in which case you have to rotoscope. It can help to use the Roto Brush (Chapter 7) or track in a paint stroke (Chapter 8).

Edge Selection

Sometimes it's simpler to just select the edge and subtly blur the blend between foreground and background using that selection. **Figure 6.26** shows a comp in which it would be simpler to soften matte lines (rather than choke the matte) and add subtle light wrap.

Here's how it's done:

1. **Apply Shift Channels**. Set Take Alpha From to Full On and all three color channels to Alpha.

2. **Apply Find Edges** (often mistaken for a useless psychedelic effect because, as with Photoshop, it appears in the Stylize menu, and many goofy artists of the early 1990s thought it would be cool to apply it to an entire color image). Check the Invert box for an edge highlighted in white.

   Minimax can help choke or spread this edge matte since it's luminance data, not an alpha channel. The default setting under Operation in this effect is Maximum, which spreads the white edge pixels by the amount specified in the Radius setting. Minimum chokes the edge in the same manner. If the result appears a little crude, an additional Fast Blur will soften it (Figure 6.26).

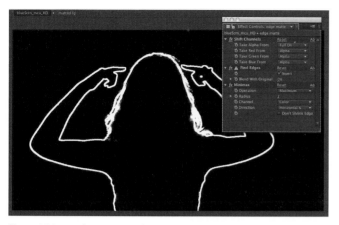

Figure 6.26 An edge matte can be used to blur background and foreground together, or to match the intensity and saturation to the background. The matte can itself be softened with a blur, Minimax, set to Maximum. Color can be used to grow the matte by increasing the Radius setting.

3. **Apply the result via a luma matte to an adjustment layer.**
   You should not need to precomp before doing so.

You can then use Fast Blur to soften the blend area between the foreground and background, which often works better than simply softening a chewy matte. A Levels adjustment will darken or brighten the composited edge to better blend it. Hue/Saturation can be used to desaturate the edge, similar to using a gray edge replacement color in Keylight.

Color Spill

I promised earlier to share an alternative to the tools that simply suppress color spill to gray, using the Hue/Saturation effect as follows.

1. Apply Effect > Color > Hue/Saturation.

2. Under Channel Control, choose the background primary (Greens or Blues).

3. This will sound odd, but raise the Saturation value for that channel to 100.0.

4. Adjust the Channel Range sliders until all spill is pushed to 100.0 saturation (**Figure 6.27**).

Figure 6.27 By maximizing saturation in the Greens, it's easier to adjust the range to encompass the green spill on the side of the shirt but leave out most of the yellow stripes.

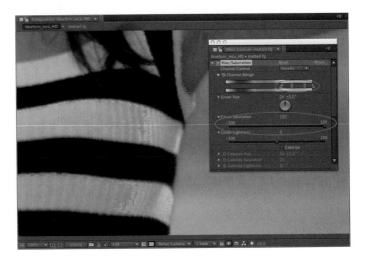

5. Now try some mixture of the following to eliminate spill:

   ▶ Lower the Saturation (still on the individual color channel) somewhere from −40.0 to −80.0.

   ▶ Shift the Hue between about 30 and 50 degrees in the warmer direction of skin tones. Positive values (clockwise) produce a bluescreen; negative values (counterclockwise) produce a greenscreen.

This combination of desaturation and hue shift with a carefully targeted range should do the trick once you get the hang of using the Channel Range, which is why it helps to crank Saturation at first. The inside rectangular sliders are the core range, and the outside triangular sliders determine the threshold area between the two sliders on each end. It's usually a good idea to give the selection range a good bit of thresholding (**Figure 6.28**).

There will be cases where it is impossible not to contaminate some part of the costume or set with spill suppression; for example, a cyan-colored shirt will change color when the actor is corrected for green. The above method is a better work-around than most of the automated tools (especially Keylight itself), but there are cases where you might have to add some loose roto to isolate the contaminated bits and adjust them separately.

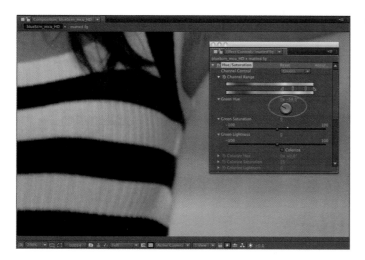

Figure 6.28 The actual adjustment brings Saturation back down to 0, and instead of suppressing that, shifts the green hues back toward their true, warmer hues.

Fix It on Set

Here are a few steps to take to ensure a good matte if you happen to be on set or, even better, involved in preproduction.

The Camera

Not all digital cameras are ideal for shooting a greenscreen or bluescreen, and with the advent of the DSLR, we have a prime example of a camera that can shoot a lovely looking image that does not hold up so well for effects work. Since the last version of this book, hundreds of thousands of DSLR cameras have entered the world, and they are capable of shooting high-definition video that can look incredibly cinematic and gorgeous, if well shot.

The reason DSLR footage looks so good has mostly to do with the optics. Pair this camera with a high-quality lens and the lens resolves an excellent image, which the sensor is able to capture at full HD—but not without throwing away every other line of data and trashing data that is essential to a clean edge. While a still photo from a DSLR such as the Canon 5D or 7D is a dream to key, the sensor is not capable of streaming video at 24 or more fps without drastically reducing the amount of data being produced before it ever leaves the sensor.

Someday, a camera like this will be available that won't simply melt down when shooting a lightly compressed HD clip. Meanwhile, there are other video cameras that produce much better effects footage if it's well lit and shot. RED and the new (as of this writing) Arri Alexa are two cameras that create effects plates you would use on a movie of any budget. You can rent these cameras inexpensively.

After Effects even has the means to work natively with RED .r3d files so you can key them in their full source color space at full 4K (or more) resolution. The previous version of After Effects could import an .r3d, but any attempt to key it natively would inevitably run into the memory limit that is no longer applicable in a 64-bit application. By keying an .r3d file natively at full resolution, you get the best possible matte even in the likely case that you will scale the plate down to a more reasonable HD size later on.

The bottom line about cameras is to choose the least compressed recording format possible and to work with someone (or be someone) who has created effects footage on that camera before and knows how to light for it.

On Set

If you have the opportunity to supervise on set, I highly recommend it. Be careful to bring a good bedside manner and refrain from disrupting the proceedings, develop the best possible relationship with the director of photography, and discreetly take as many reference images and clips with your DSLR as you can. It's pretty great to get out from behind the desk and have an adventure.

A hard *cyclorama*, or *cyc* (rhymes with "like") is far preferable to soft materials such as paper or cloth, especially if the floor is in shot. If you can't rent a stage that has one, the next best thing might be to invest in a roll of floor covering and paint it to get the smooth transition from floor to wall, as in **Figure 6.29** (assuming the floor is in shot).

Regarding the floor, don't let anyone walk across it in street shoes, which will quickly contaminate it with very visible dust. There are white shoe-cover booties often used specifically to avoid this, and you can also lay down big

---

NOTES

I hate to tell you this and make you the party-pooper, but as a post-production professional focused on visual effects, it's your job to educate the production team that DSLR is not as pristine as it's perceived to be. If there's any possibility of shooting with a less-compressed format, my advice is to push hard for that. Do it for the sake of the edges.

Figure 6.29 On a set with no hard cyclorama, you can create the effect of one—the curve where the wall meets the floor—using a soft bluescreen instead. It doesn't behave as well (note the hotspot on the curve), but it will certainly do in a pinch and is preferable to removing the seam caused by the corner between the wall and floor.

pieces of cardboard for the crew to use while setting up. Be insistent about this if you're planning to key shadows.

Lighting is, of course, best left to an experienced director of photography (DP) and gaffer (bonus points if they've shot effects before and understand the process even a little), and any kind of recommendations for a physical lighting setup are beyond the scope of this book. Because you'll spend more time examining this footage than anyone else, here are a few things to watch for on set:

▶ Light levels on the foreground and background must have matching intensity, within a stop or so of one another. A spot light meter tells you if they do.

▶ Diffuse lights are great for the background (often a set of large 1K, 2K, or 5K lights with a silk sock covering them, **Figure 6.30**), but fluorescent Kino Flo lights have become increasingly popular as they've become more flexible and powerful. With fluorescents, you may need more instruments to light the same space, but they consume relatively low power and generate very little heat.

▶ Maintain space, along with separate lighting setups, between the foreground and background. Ten feet as a minimum is a good rule of thumb.

▶ Avoid unintentional shadows, but by all means light for shadows if you can get them and the floor is clean.

Figure 6.30 The larger the set, the more diffuse white lights you'll see in the grid.

Note that this works only when the final shot also has a flat floor. Fill lights typically mess up floor shadows by creating extras.

▶ Where possible, avoid having talent sit, kneel, or lie down directly on the floor or any other keyable surface; not only does an astonishing wash of shadow and reflection result, but there is no realistic interaction with the surface, which is especially noticeable if they are to end up on carpet, grass, or the beach. If possible, use real sets and furniture in these cases.

▶ Here's a novel idea: Shoot exteriors outside where possible, forgoing the set and controlled lighting environment for chromatic tarps and the sun, which is a hard lighting source to fake.

▶ Record as close to uncompressed as possible. Even "prosumer" HD cameras such as the Sony EX-3 often have an HDMI port that outputs a live, uncompressed signal; pair this with a workstation or laptop containing a video capture card and high-speed storage, and you can get 4:2:2 or better practically for free.

▶ Shoot clean plate: a few frames of the set only, particularly on a locked-off shot and each time a new setup occurs.

In this day and age of quick camera to laptop transfer, it's great to have the means on the set to pull test comps;. These not only help ensure that the result will key properly, they also give the Director of Photography (DP) and talent a better idea of where they are, and where they can lead to more motivated light from the DP and more motivated action from the talent, who otherwise must work in a void.

More Alternatives for an Impossible Key

If you have tried keying a difficult shot and find yourself wishing for a better tool for the job, the first thing to do is make sure you've really read this chapter. The one-button or one-pass approach to keying very often needs to be broken down, and this can be done in two fundamental ways. I'm giving these bullet points, because they are significant and easily missed despite seeming simple.

▶ Divide the whole image into sections and work on each one individually as if it were its own whole image, so that you don't ruin the edges with lowest-common-denominator settings.

▶ Divide the edges of each keyed element into multiple passes: core and edge, or gmatte (garbage matte), cmatte (core matte), and edge.

Other tools allow other approaches. Flame, Autodesk's high-end compositing suite, is known for having a powerful keyer. A prime difference between its Master Keyer and related tools and Keylight is that instead of relying predominantly on slider controls, it works with direct selection and evaluates not only contrast between the three color channels but also things such as luminance. Primatte Keyer, from Red Giant Software, operates more like this.

You may have tried keying a color that falls between the three digital primaries (green, blue, or red) such as yellow or purple and found Keylight ineffective. The Keylight model is fundamentally based on weighing a single color channel (blue, in the case of a bluescreen) with the next-most-present (green, of which there is quite a bit in

NOTES

Shoot a lot of reference of the set, including anything and everything you can think of. If you plan to re-create the lighting, it's also a great idea to take HDR images using bracketed exposures—the same image shot at various f-stops. Photoshop includes the File > Automate > Merge to HDR function to combine these into a 32-bpc linear light image.

CLOSE-UP

The Right Color?

The digital age lets shooters play fast and loose with what they consider a keyable background. You will likely be asked (or attempt) to pull mattes from a blue sky, from a blue swimming pool (like I did for *Pirates of the Caribbean*), and from other monochrome backgrounds. However, you're probably asking for trouble if you paint your blue or green background with a can of paint from the hardware store; they're generally designed to be more neutral—grayer and less saturated. Rosco and Composite Components designs paints specifically for the purpose of color keying, and those are the ones to go with when painting a set.

How different must the background color be from the foreground? The answer is, not as much as you probably think. I have had little trouble keying a girl in a light blue dress or a soldier in a dress blue uniform. This is where it can be hugely helpful to have any type of capture device on set—even a point-and-shoot camera—to pull a test matte.

bluescreen blue) against the most absent (red). It simply isn't designed to isolate colors that fall between the color channels, nor to base the key as much or more on luminance (brightness) as chrominance (color intensity).

This is a case where Primatte Keyer is a fully legitimate Keylight alternative. Primatte can work with a whole range of colors, not just a single target. Imagine a cube whose axes are red, green, and blue, and imagine that your target background colors occupy a region within that cube. This region can be any color and any shape, and those specifics are determined by directly sampling color in the frame with eyedropper tools rather than refining settings with numerical sliders.

I like Primatte a lot for situations where, for example, a mistake was made and the talent or other foreground on a greenscreen stage contains some of the background color: for example, a costume is green, or the scene was underlit so there is not sufficient saturation. There are three main disadvantages to using it: It lacks numerical controls that can easily be shared and re-entered, it costs extra, and I have found that it takes a day or so to get into the groove of cranking keys with Primatte. Its initial learning curve is not insignificant, but help is available.

The next chapter offers hands-on advice for situations where procedural matte generation must be abandoned in favor of hand matte generation, also known as *rotoscoping*. There are also situations where rotoscope techniques, and in particular the Roto Brush tool, can be used to augment a difficult key.

7

Rotoscoping and Paint

It's a small world, but I wouldn't want to paint it.

—Steven Wright

Rotoscoping and Paint

Rotoscoping (or *roto*) is the process of adjusting a shot frame by frame. The selections might be made with the manual use of masks, introduced in Chapter 3. You may also clone and fill with frame-by-frame paint tools.

After Effects is not commonly known as the go-to rotoscoping tool, yet surprisingly there is no one preferred approach to roto, and many artists use it effectively for just that purpose. To its credit, the After Effects development team continues to improve the rotoscoping process with each new release, and in CS6 we have the long-awaited addition of variable mask feather, essentially an optional set of mask points just to vary edge softness. Combine paint and roto with tracking and keying, or let the software do so for you with Roto Brush, and you have in After Effects a powerful rotoscoping suite.

Here are some overall guidelines for roto and paint:

- The basic options are as follows, from most automated and least difficult to the higher-maintenance techniques:
    - Roto Brush
    - keying (color and contrast)
    - motion-tracked masks and paint
    - hand-animated masks (conventional roto)
    - paint via individual brushstrokes
- Paint is generally the last resort, although it can in certain cases be quite expeditious indeed.
- Keyframe deliberately: My own ideal is to create as few keyframes as possible. Other artists insist it is more efficient or effective simply to keyframe every frame. Either approach is valid for a given mask or section, and most artists use a bit of both.

- ▶ Review constantly, and maintain an approach that is as responsive as possible to support the roto process.

- ▶ Notice opportunities to switch and combine strategies, as alone none of them is exactly a silver bullet.

It can be satisfying to knock out a seamless animated matte, and once you have the tools under your fingertips, it can even be pleasant to kind of zen out and roto for a few hours, even as a full-time occupation.

Roto Brush for the Diligent (or Lazy)

Wouldn't it be awesome if your software could learn to roto so effectively that you never had to articulate a matte by hand again? Call a tool the Roto Brush and that's what everyone will think it does, when it is in fact more helpful as a useful component of the matting process. It reduces rather than omits the need to roto by hand. It may also lead you generally to create and use articulated selections more often for tasks where complete isolation isn't needed. Roto Brush doesn't magically erase the world's rotoscoping troubles, but it opens new possibilities for using selections that you might not otherwise consider.

To get a feel for how Roto Brush works, let's work with a clip that shows how to use it, and how you can go too far trying to make it perfect. Create a new composition containing the model_track.mov clip found in the folder for Chapter 7 on the book's disc, which is 1920 × 1080 24p 23.976 fps source from a Canon DSLR. Make sure that you're at full resolution (**Ctrl+J/Cmd+J**) and preview the clip.

Double-click to open the layer in the Layer viewer. Notice what challenges are involved in extracting the talent from the background: organic shapes, constantly changing angles, wispy hair and eyelashes, and clearly no chance at any kind of color or luminance key, given how muted the entire scene is. You can flip through the color channels (**Alt+1, 2, 3/Opt+1, 2, 3**) and confirm how little contrast there is in any of them.

To try Roto Brush to matte the talent, you can follow these steps:

1. Trim the clip so that it begins (**Alt+[**/**Opt+[**) at frame 92 (03:20) and ends (**Alt+]**/**Opt+]**) at frame 282 (11:18).

2. Go to a frame around the middle of the clip, such as frame 187.

3. Click the Roto Brush tool in the toolbar to make it active.

4. Scale the brush if necessary by **Ctrl**-dragging (**Cmd**-dragging) the brush in the Layer panel. Make it about the size of the ear (**Figure 7.1a**).

5. Roughly outline the interior of the talent's form, never touching its edges (**Figure 7.1b**). As soon as you release, the tool shows the *segmentation boundary* in pink, its first guess as to where the foreground boundaries may be.

6. Notice any areas missed—wisps of hair and an eye in **Figure 7.1c**. Gently fill these in, resizing the brush if necessary to paint only in the center of the missing area. If you paint into the background at all, it's best to undo and try again. Don't attempt to make this perfect; you're learning about the strengths and limitations of this tool.

7. Eliminate any other background included in the original boundary by **Alt**- or **Opt**-swiping those areas, again being careful not to cross the foreground edges.

   The result on this frame may look lumpy and bumpy, but it should at least be reasonably complete (**Figure 7.2**) within a pixel or two of the actual edge. Thoroughly defining the shape on this base frame gives you the best chance of holding the matte over time without an inordinate number of corrections.

8. Press the spacebar and watch as the matte updates on each frame.

   It's pretty cool how well the tool tracks the figure as the camera moves around her, but you may see areas of the

---

TIP

When swiping with Roto Brush, the idea is explicitly not to paint right along the outline, which is likely only to cause problems, but rather to suggest areas that help the tool guess what to include.

TIP

RAM preview shortcuts have been augmented for the purpose of working with Roto Brush spans. **Alt+0** (**Opt+0**) (on the numeric keypad) begins the preview a specific number of frames before the current one—the default 5-frame setting can be changed in Preferences > Previews.

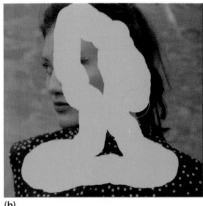

(b)

Figure 7.1 Size the Roto Brush by **Ctrl-** or **Cmd**-dragging **(a)**, then paint the form of the foreground inside its boundaries **(b)** to get an initial segmentation boundary, outlined in pink **(c)**.

left (camera right) side of her head emerge unselected after 8 to 10 frames or so.

9. As each detail emerges that isn't properly selected, return to the frame where the problem first occurs, closest to the original base frame, and fix it there.

   Roto Brush works outward, backward, and forward from the *base frame,* (that first frame you drew, marked in yellow), and refers inward toward that frame, hence you want to correct problems on the closest frame to the base frame.

10. Once you've worked your way forward to the end of the span (20 frames out), return to the base frame and work your way backward in the same fashion, adding (or subtracting) from the selection at the first sign of a problem.

    Don't sweat details like wisps or gaps in the hair; these are the Achilles heel of Roto Brush. Generally, you shouldn't need to make more than a dozen or so adjustments. Once you've completed the span, backward and forward, you have the option either to draw another one somewhere else in the timeline, or extend the one you have. The latter option should be sufficient in this case.

(c)

Figure 7.2 You can tell it's not perfect, but this is a good beginning with Roto Brush.

Figure 7.3 A stroke right inside the edge restores the hard contours of the shoulders (eliminating the white pattern of stars in the dress). Hair detail is a different story.

Figure 7.4 By this frame, the figure is so different from the source that it is probably time to limit the previous span and begin again with a new base frame.

SCRIPT

Purview is included in the Additional_Scripts_CS4-CS6 folder in the Scripts folder on the disc and via download from Adobe Exchange. It places the Alternate RAM Preview setting right in a UI panel so you can change the number of preceding frames previewed without digging into Preferences. You might create a workspace for Roto Brush with this panel open and the Layer panel prominent.

11. Drag each end of the span so that it matches the full selected length of the clip.

Complete the timeline and try not to fight too hard for details; there is a point of diminishing returns when it comes to specific details (**Figure 7.3**).

As you work, note that you do have a couple of other ways to view matte, using icons in the second row from the bottom of the Layer panel. Alpha Overlay (, **Alt+6/Opt+6**) fills the background with translucent red, for a rubylith-style holdout view. This view is not interactive, but it's easier to see than the pink outline (**Figure 7.4**). There's also the Alpha view (, **Alt+4/Opt+4**), and even an option to outline with a color other than pink.

Strengths and Limitations

Roto Brush is not a one-trick pony that simply replicates the matte you could derive yourself with contrast (like a luma or extract matte), color (like Linear Color Key or Keylight), or even automated tracking of pixels (Timewarp). It has surprising success in situations where other tools fail completely, but you need to stop short of trying to make it perfect on the first pass. It's clearly wise to stop when you find yourself repeating a correction on successive frames, since at that point you begin to lose the benefits of automation and start to feel like a slave to the grind (**Figure 7.5**).

You can't finalize a Roto Brush selection without enabling Refine Matte under the Roto Brush controls in the Effect Controls. The effect is set automatically as soon as you paint a stroke, but the refine setting is off because it takes longer to calculate and actually changes the segmentation boundary. As a general rule, work with it off; preview with it on (**Figure 7.6**).

The Propagation settings atop the Roto Brush effect controls are easily missed, but they change how the matte itself is calculated and so can be as important as getting the initial selection color correct in Keylight (Chapter 6). By default, Edge Detection is Balanced between using data from the previous and current frame. Favor Predicted

Figure 7.6 The unrefined matte can look pretty rough, but don't waste time fixing it with more brushstrokes. Instead, work on the Refine Matte settings for a much better result with the exact same outline.

Figure 7.5 It's impressive how well Roto Brush follows the fine contours of the figure, but not yet quite correct.

Edges (which uses data from the previous frame) can make a positive difference with an edge that is well defined and consistent. Favor Current Edges (which works only with the current frame) is designed for situations in which the edge is difficult to distinguish from the background.

The rest of the options are more like fix-it solutions. Smooth and Reduce Chatter settings reduce boiling edges. They're not magic, of course, so you will lose detail by raising those values, but with a foreground subject that has few pointy or skinny edge details, you can increase it without creating motion artifacts. If you're trying to remove the object from its background entirely, edge decontamination is remarkably powerful and adaptable, particularly when your background and foreground contain contrasting colors (not really the case here). Upon rendering, you can enable Higher Quality under Motion Blur if your subject has a good deal of motion, which this one does not. What this subject mostly has is a lot of detail (**Figure 7.7**).

TIP

The Use Alternate Color Estimation option can make a big difference in some cases as to how well Roto Brush holds an edge.

Figure 7.7 She's looking better with edge feather and decontamination, but the hair and eyelashes remain stubborn.

In case it's not obvious by this time, Roto Brush, while remarkable, is no substitute for greenscreen or even the types of articulated roto techniques to follow in this chapter. For cases where you truly need to fully extract a foreground figure from a background without the benefit of the types of mattes described in Chapter 6, you won't generally ever get as refined a result with Roto Brush as you will with actual hand rotoscoping.

In this case, however, the purpose of creating this matte was to hold out the talent from the background for a 3D track that is detailed in Chapter 8, and that goal is now achieved. If you needed a full extraction, you could consider using this result as a basis for refinement, or just start over with a hand-articulated matte (**Figure 7.8**).

Figure 7.8 With high detail, low contrast, or in this case, both, no single procedural solution matches hand-articulated roto. You can, however, combine the two to leverage what each gives you.

Articulated Mattes

An "articulated" matte has individual mask points, each adjusted one by one to detail a shape in motion. For selections that are only partially solved by Roto Brush, this is the professional solution. Articulated roto is a whole skill set of its own and a legitimate artistic profession within the context of large-scale projects such as feature films. Many feature film compositors have made their start as rotoscopers, and some choose to focus on roto as a professional specialty, whether as individuals or by forming a company or collective.

Keyframing began at Disney in the 1930s, where top animators would create the keyframes—the top of the heap, the moment of impact—and lower-level artists would add the in-between frames thereafter.

Ready, Set, Roto

Following are some broad guidelines for rotoscoping complex organic shapes.

▶ As with keying, approaching a complex shot in one pass will compromise your result. You can use multiple overlapping masks when dealing with a complex, moving shape of any kind (**Figure 7.9**).

Suppose, for example, you drew a single mask around a gator's head, similar to the one created with Roto

There's one major downside to masking on a layer with its visibility off: You cannot drag-select a set of points (although you can **Shift**-select each of them).

Figure 7.9 It is crazy to mask a complex articulate figure with a single mask shape; the sheer number of points will have you playing whack-a-mole. Separated segments let you focus on one area of high motion while leaving another area, which moves more steadily, more or less alone.

Brush on the woman in the previous set of steps. You're fine until the gator's mouth opens, but at that point it's typically more effective to work instead with at least two masks: one for the top and one for the bottom jaw.

It's not that you can't get everything with one mask, but the whole bottom jaw moves in one direction as a single basic piece, and the upper part of the head moves in the opposite direction. Here are some guidelines:

▶ Begin on a frame requiring the fewest possible points or one with fully revealed, extended detail, adding more points as needed as you go. Frame 77 is the frame with the most fully open mouth.

▶ As recommended previously, create a solid layer above the plate layer, turn off its visibility, and lock the plate.

▶ Now, with that layer selected, enable the Pen tool (shortcut **G**), click the first point, and begin outlining the top jaw, dragging out the Bezier handles as you place each point, if that's your preference. You may prefer to place points and adjust Beziers after you've completed the basic shape.

In this particular case, the outline is motion-blurred, which raises the question of where exactly the boundary should lie. The rigid rule used to be that you aim the mask outline right down the middle of the blur area, between the inner core and outer edge, to accommodate the rather rigid Mask Feather settings in After Effects. Variable mask feather offers more of a choice; nonetheless, here it's probably best to be consistent and center it.

▶ Block in the natural keyframe points first, those which contain a change of direction, speed, or the appearance or disappearance of a shape.

Here, you can place the first keyframe on the frame on which the mouth is open at its widest. **Alt+M** (**Opt+M**) sets a Mask Path keyframe at this point in time, so that any changes you make to the shape at any time are also recorded with a keyframe. The question is where to create the next keyframe.

Some rotoscopers prefer *straight-ahead* animation and create a shape keyframe on each frame, working in succession. I prefer to get as much as possible done with *in-between* animation, so I suggest that you go to the next extreme, or turning point, of motion.

▶ Animate the mouth in its closed position to either side of the open position, beginning at frame 73. Select a set of points and use the Transform Box to offset, scale, or rotate them together instead of moving them individually (**Figure 7.10**).

Most objects shift perspective more than they fundamentally change shape, and this method uses that fact to your advantage.

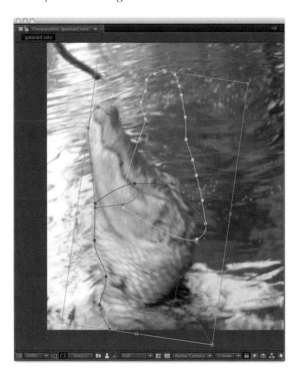

Figure 7.10 Gross mask transformations can be blocked in by selecting and double-clicking all, then repositioning, rotating, and scaling with the free-transform box, followed by finer adjustments to each mask.

▶ At frame 73, with nothing but the layer containing the masks selected, double-click anywhere on one of the masks and a transform box appears around all of the highlighted points. With any points selected, the box appears around those points only, which is also useful.

Basic Steps to Successful Keyframe Animation

▶ Use a mouse—a pen and tablet system makes exact placement of points difficult.

▶ Stick with the **G** key, plus the **Ctrl** (**Cmd**) and **Alt** (**Opt**) modifiers.

▶ Use the arrow keys and Zoom tool for fine point placement. The increments change according to the zoom level of the current view, down to the subpixel level when zoomed above 100%.

▶ You can lock unselected masks to prevent inadvertently selecting their points when working with the selected mask. Context-click to lock either the selected mask or all other masks. You can similarly hide locked masks.

▶ The Target menu in the Layer panel exists to allow you to select a mask and completely redraw (and replace) the shape at the current frame.

Figure 7.11 Overlapping Bezier handles result in kinks and loopholes (left); switching the mask to Rotobezier (right) eliminates the problem.

NOTES

Look carefully at any mask, and you'll notice one vertex is bigger than the rest. This is the first vertex point. To set it, context-click on a mask vertex and choose Mask and Shape Path > First Vertex (Chapter 3 has details).

In this case, freely position (dragging from the inside) and rotate (dragging outside) that transform box so that the end and basic contour of the snout line up.

This is a tough one! The alligator twists and turns quite a bit, so although the shape does follow the basic motion, it now looks as though it will require keyframes on each frame. In cases where it's closer, you may only need to add one in-between keyframe to get it right. Most creatures—human, mammalian, and beyond—move in continuous arcs, with hesitation at the beginning and often overshoot at the end. Other than when you're stuck with instances of sudden movements, in-betweening replicates these arcs.

Rotobeziers

Rotobezier shapes are designed to animate a mask over time; they're like Bezier shapes (discussed in Chapter 3) without the handles, which means less adjustment and less chance of pinching or loopholes when points get close together (**Figure 7.11**). Rotobeziers aren't universally beloved, partly because it's difficult to get them right in one pass; adjoining vertices change shape as you add points.

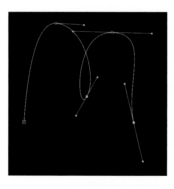 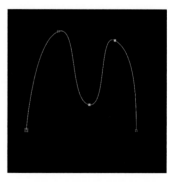

Activate the Pen tool (**G** key) and check the Rotobezier box in the Tools panel, then click the layer to start drawing points; beginning with the third point, the segments are, by default, curved at each vertex.

At any point as you draw the mask, or once you've completed and closed it by clicking on the first point, hold

Alt (Opt) to access the Convert Vertex tool . Drag it to the left over a mask point to increase tension and make the vertex a sharp corner, like collapsed Bezier handles. Drag in the opposite direction, and the curve rounds out. You can freely add ✦ points by clicking a vertex between points or subtract ✦– points as needed with the **Ctrl** (**Cmd**) modifier.

Rotobeziers exist for two main reasons. One is to speed mask animation by reducing adjustable points, and the other is to eliminate mask kinking. Other than that, rotobeziers are essentially what could be called "automatic" Beziers (**Figure 7.12**). The alternative is to draw enough Bezier points to keep the handles short, so you don't have to adjust them.

Refined Mattes: Feathered, Tracked

Beyond the basics already covered, there are several refinements to rotoscoping in After Effects.

▶ The long-awaited new Mask Feather Tool makes complex selections much more efficient.

▶ After Effects has no built-in method for applying a tracker directly to a mask, but there are now several ways to track a mask in addition to Roto Brush. See details below and more in Chapter 8, which deals specifically with tracking.

▶ Adding points to an animated mask has no adverse effect on adjacent mask keyframes. Delete a point, however, and it is removed from all keyframes, deforming them.

▶ There is no dedicated morphing tool in After Effects. The tools to do a morph do exist, though, along with several deformation tools that are described in a separate PDF for this chapter on the book's disc (07_AnimatingwithPuppet.pdf) and applied in Section III of the book.

▶ The automated Refine Matte tools within Roto Brush are available as a separate Refine Matte effect that can be used on any transparency selection, not just those created with Roto Brush.

Details follow.

TIP

You can freely toggle a shape from Bezier to Rotobezier mode and back, should you prefer to draw with one and animate with the other. Either by right-clicking or in the Layer menu, it's Mask and Shape Path > RotoBezier.

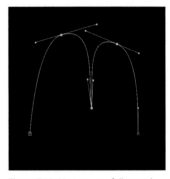

Figure 7.12 You can carefully avoid crossing handles with Beziers (left); convert this same shape to rotobeziers (right) and you lose any angles, direction, or length set with Bezier handles.

TIP

If the Selection tool (V) is active, **Ctrl+Alt** (**Cmd+Opt**) activates the Adjust Tension pointer.

Mask Feather and Motion Blur

An After Effects mask can be feathered (**F** key). This softening of the mask edge by the specified number of pixels occurs both inward and outward from the mask border in equal amounts, and it is applied equally all the way around the mask. An ordinary mask around a hard-edged object in a high-definition image generally requires 2 or 3 pixels of feathering to appear natural in full focus.

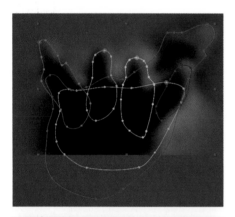

There are, of course, cases where it is preferable to, say, feather only outward from the edge, or to feather specific sections of a mask more heavily, and the Mask Feather tool introduced in After Effects CS6 allows you to do just that. What might have required combining, expanding, and contracting half a dozen masks as a work-around can now be done with a single mask and variable feather (**Figure 7.13**).

It's easy to try. The **G** keyboard shortcut has been redesigned in CS6 with only two modes, so with the Pen tool active, pressing **G** toggles to Mask Feather. Click anywhere on the mask and drag inward or outward; until you release, it can go either way; once. Once it's set, it remains an "innie" or an "outie" thereafter.

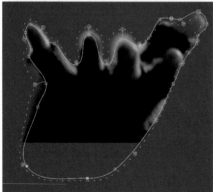

Figure 7.13 Check out how much more tight and efficient the single Mask Path property with variable feather is (top) than the alternative (bottom). Now imagine what a difference that makes when animating it.

Add a second feather point by clicking and dragging on the dotted mask feather boundary. As you drag inward or outward, you vary the feather. To get specific about the shape around a softer area of the boundary, add as many points as needed. These can correspond directly to mask points, but only if you draw each one out yourself.

It might seem at first like feather points should have a one-to-one relationship to mask vertices, and you can certainly set it up that way. In addition to allowing you to simply feather the entire mask inward or outward, you are reducing the number of points to track as you animate the mask. Sometimes it's enough just to soften the entire mask in a specific direction, as with a cast shadow.

Mask feather points do not keyframe quite like mask points. Instead of requiring that you carefully manage each Mask feather point from frame to frame, the mask feather points maintain tangency and distance from the edge. As you animate the mask shape, they more or less come along for the ride. You can adjust them over time, but otherwise the feather distance of a particular section of the mask is maintained.

The Mask properties all still work more or less as they always did: you can set a baseline feather amount and then expand it in certain areas, and then contract the entire matte with the Mask Expansion property.

The Feather, Expansion, and Opacity settings are still there and can be used in conjunction with the new feather tools, although it could get confusing to combine the two liberally. You can do crazy stuff like feather outward and then set a negative Mask Expansion value if you really feel like breaking this feature, but in most real-world situations, you're probably just occasionally adjusting overall variable feather (**F key**).

Animated masks in After Effects obey motion blur settings. Match the source's motion blur settings correctly (Chapter 2)), and you can match the blur of any object in motion by enabling motion blur on the layer containing the animated mask. Animate the mask with edges matching the center of the blurred edge, enable motion blur with the right settings, and it just works.

Track and Translate

You can track a mask in After Effects, and you can take an existing set of Mask Path keyframes and translate them to a new position, but neither is the straightforward process you might imagine. There's no way to apply the After Effects tracker directly to a mask shape, nor can you simply select a bunch of Mask Path keyframes and have them all translate according to how you move the one you're on (like you can with the layer itself).

You can track a mask using any of the following methods:

▶ Copy the mask keyframe data to a solid layer with the same size, aspect, and transform settings as the source, track or translate that layer, then apply it as a track matte.

TIP

A single mask feather point allows you to determine not only the amount but the basic feather direction, inward or outward. The Feather value in the timeline further adjusts the amount of softness (**Figure 7.14**).

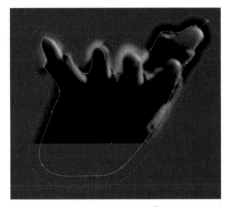

Figure 7.14 Set the entire matte to feather outward by a particular amount using an open Layer panel and a single mask feather point that is a specific distance from the outside or inside of the mask shape.

SCRIPT

TrackerViz by Charles Bordenave (http://aescripts.com/trackerviz/) originated as a tool to average motion data, so that several track attempts could be averaged together to make a single animation. Additional new features allow you to use mask shapes and tracker points interchangeably, or link a mask shape to the position of selected layers.

SCRIPT

KeyTweak by Mathias Möhl (http://aescripts.com/keytweak/) achieves the seemingly impossible: Edit a keyframed mask globally simply by pointing on one or two mask keyframes, and the rest are automagically changed accordingly. It works not just for Mask Shape keys but for any keyframed property. This means it can be used, for example, to correct a drifting track.

▶ If movement of a masked object emanates from camera motion and occurs in the entire scene, you can essentially stabilize the layer, animate the mask in place, and then reapply motion to both. See Chapter 8 for details.

▶ Use Roto Brush to track a matte selection, as described previously.

▶ Use mocha AE to track a shape and apply the tracked shape in After Effects via the mocha shape plug-in.

▶ Use mocha AE to track a shape and copy and paste it as mask data in After Effects. Yes, you understood correctly—you can do that.

Mask shapes can be linked together directly—instanced, really (aka "slaved")—with expressions. **Alt**-click (**Opt**-click) the Mask Path stopwatch, then use the pick whip to drag to the target Mask Path. Only a direct link is possible, no mathematical or logical operations, so all linked masks behave like instances of the first.

Paint and Cloning

NOTES

Check out the file on the disc, 07_AnimatingwithPuppet.pdf, for a bonus section on using the Puppet tool to deform footage.

Paint is generally a last resort when roto is impractical, for a simple reason: Use of this tool, particularly for animation, can be painstaking and more likely to show flaws than approaches involving masks. There are, of course, exceptions. You can track a clone brush more easily than a mask, and painting in the alpha channel can be a handy quick fix.

For effects work, then, paint controls in After Effects have at least a couple of predominant uses:

▶ Clean up an alpha channel mask by painting directly to it in black and white.

▶ Use Clone Stamp to overwrite an area of the frame with an alternate source.

Once you fully understand the strengths and limitations of paint, it's easier to decide when to use it.

Paint Fundamentals

Two panels, Paint and Brush Tips, are essential to the three brush-based tools in the Tools panel: , Clone Stamp , and Eraser . These can be revealed by choosing the Paint workspace.

The After Effects paint functionality is patterned after equivalent tools in Photoshop, but with a couple of fundamental differences. After Effects offers fewer customizable options for its brushes (you can't, for example, design your own brush tips). More significantly (and related), Photoshop's brushes are raster-based, while After Effects brushes are vector-based. Vector-based paint is more flexible, allowing you to change the character of the strokes—their size, feather, and so on—even after they're drawn.

Suppose that you have an alpha channel in need of a touch-up like the matte shown in **Figure 7.19.** This is a difficult key due to tracking markers and shadows. With the Brush tool active, go to the Paint panel and set Channels to Alpha (this panel remembers the last mode you used); the foreground and background color swatches in the panel become grayscale, and you can make them black and white by clicking the tiny black-over-white squares just below the swatches.

Figure 7.19 Touch up an alpha channel matte (for example, to remove a tracking marker): In the Paint panel, select Alpha in the Channels menu, then display the alpha channel (**Alt+4/Opt+4**).

To see what you are painting, switch the view to Alpha Channel (**Alt+4/Opt+4**); switch back to RGB to check the final result.

When using the paint tools keep in mind:

▶ Brush-based tools operate only in the Layer panel, not the Composition panel.

▶ Paint strokes include their own Mode setting (analogous to layer blending modes).

▶ With a tablet, you can use the Brush Dynamics settings at the bottom of the Brush Tips panel to set how the pressure, angle, and stylus wheel of your pen affect strokes.

▶ The Duration setting and the frame where you begin painting are crucial (details follow).

▶ Preset brushes and numerical settings for properties such as diameter and hardness (aka feather) live in the Brush Tips panel.

For a more effective workflow experience, try the following shortcuts with the Brush tool active in the Layer viewer.

▶ Hold **Ctrl (Cmd)** and drag to scale the brush.

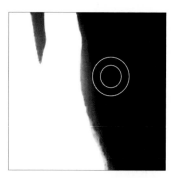

Figure 7.20 Modifier keys (**Ctrl/Cmd** to scale, **Alt/Opt** to feather, all with the mouse button held down) let you define a brush on the fly. The inner circle shows the solid core; the area between it and the outer circle is the threshold (for feathering).

There is a major gotcha with Constant (the default mode): Paint a stroke at any frame other than the first frame of the layer, and it does not appear until that frame during playback. It's apparently not a bug, but it is certainly an annoyance.

As in Photoshop, the **X** key swaps the foreground and background swatches with the Brush tool active.

▶ Add the **Shift** key to adjust in larger increments and **Alt (Opt)** for fine adjustments.

▶ With the mouse button held down, release **Ctrl** (**Cmd**) to scale hardness (an inner circle appears representing the inside of the threshold, **Figure 7.20**).

▶ **Alt**-click (**Opt**-click) to use the eyedropper (with brushes) or clone source (with the clone brush).

By default, the Duration setting in the Paint menu is set to Constant, which means that any paint stroke created on this frame continues to the end of the layer. For cleaning up stray holes on given frames of an alpha channel, this is probably not desirable because it's too easy to leave the stroke active too long. The Single Frame setting confines your stroke to just the current frame on which you're painting, and the Custom setting allows you to enter the number of frames that the stroke exists.

The other option, Write On, records your stroke in real time, re-creating the motion (including timing) when you replay the layer; this stylized option can be useful for such motion graphics tricks as handwritten script.

The Brush Tips panel menu includes various display options and customizable features: You can add, rename, or delete brushes. You can also name a brush by double-clicking it if it's really imperative to locate it later; searching in the Timeline search field will locate it for you. Brush names do not appear in the default thumbnail view except via tool tips when the cursor is placed above each brush.

For alpha channel cleanup, then, work in Single Frame mode (under Duration in the Paint panel), looking only at the alpha channel (**Alt+4/Opt+4**) and progressing frame by frame through the shot (**Pg Dn**).

After working for a little while, your Timeline panel may contain dozens of strokes, each with numerous properties of their own. New strokes are added to the top of the stack and are given numerically ordered names; it's often simplest to select them visually using the Selection tool (**V**) directly in a viewer panel.

Figure 7.21 Clone source overlay is checked (left) with Difference mode active, an "onion skin" that makes it possible to precisely line up two matching shots (middle and right images). Difference mode is on, causing all identical areas of the frame to turn black when the two layers are perfectly aligned.

Cloning Fundamentals

When moving footage is cloned, the result retains grain and other natural features that still images lack. Not only can you clone pixels from a different region of the same frame, you can clone from a different frame of a different clip at a different point in time (**Figure 7.21**), as follows:

▸ **Clone from the same frame:** This works just as in Photoshop. Choose a brush, **Alt**-click (**Opt**-click) on the area of the frame to sample, and begin painting. Remember that Duration is set to Constant by default, so any stroke created begins at the current frame and extends through the rest of the composition.

▸ **Clone from the same clip, at a different time:** Look at Clone Options for the offset value in frames. Note that there is also an option to set spatial offset. To clone from the exact same position at a different point in time, set the Offset to 0 on the X and Y and change the Source Time.

▸ **Clone from a separate clip:** The source from which you're cloning must be present in the current composition (although it need not be visible and can even be a guide layer). Simply open the layer to be used as source, and go to the current time where you want to begin; Source and Source Time Shift are listed in the Paint panel and can also be edited there.

▸ **Mix multiple clone sources without having to reselect each one:** There are five Preset icons in the Paint panel; these allow you to switch sources on the fly and then switch back to a previous source. Just click on a Preset icon before selecting your clone source and that source remains associated with that preset (including Aligned and Lock Source Time settings).

That all seems straightforward enough; there are just a few things to watch out for, as follows.

NOTES

The Aligned toggle in the Paint panel (on by default) preserves 1:1 pixel positions even though paint tools are vector-based. Nonaligned clone operations tend to appear blurry.

TIP

To clone from a single frame to multiple frames, toggle on Lock Source Time in the Paint panel.

Clone is different from many other tools in After Effects in that Source Time Shift uses frames, not seconds, to evaluate the temporal shift. Beware if you mix clips with different frame rates, although on the whole this is a beneficial feature.

Tricks and Gotchas

Suppose the clone source time is offset, or comes from a different layer, and the last frame of the layer has been reached—what happens? After Effects helpfully loops back to the first frame of the clip and keeps going. This is dangerous only if you're not aware of it.

Edit the source to take control of this process. Time remapping is one potential way to solve these problems; you can time stretch or loop a source clip.

You may need to scale the source to match the target. Although temporal edits, including time remapping, render before they are passed through, other types of edits—even simple translations or effects—do not. As always, the solution is to precompose; any scaling, rotation, motion tracking, or effects to be cloned belong in the subcomposition.

Finally, Paint is an effect. Apply your first stroke and you'll see an effect called Paint with a single check box, Paint on Transparent, which effectively solos the paint strokes. You can change the render order of paint strokes relative to other effects. For example, you can touch up a green-screen plate, apply a keyer, and then touch up the resulting alpha channel, all on one layer.

The View menu in the Layer panel (**Figure 7.22**) lists, in order, the paint and effects edits you've added to the layer. To see only the layer with no edits applied, toggle Render off. To see a particular stage of the edit—after the first paint strokes, say, but before the effects—select it in the View menu, effectively disabling the steps below it. These settings are for previewing only; they will not enable or disable the rendering of these items.

You can even motion-track a paint stroke. To do so requires the tracker, covered in the next chapter, and a basic expression to link them.

Figure 7.22 Isolate and solo paint strokes in the View menu of the Layer panel.

Wire Removal

Wire removal and rig removal are two common visual effects needs. Generally speaking, wire removal is cloning over a wire (typically used to suspend an actor or prop in midair). Rig removal, meanwhile, is typically just an animated garbage mask over any equipment that appeared in shot.

After Effects has nothing to compete with the state-of-the-art wire removal tool found in the Foundry's Furnace plug-ins (which, sadly, are available for just about every compositing package except After Effects).

The CC Simple Wire Removal tool is indeed simple: It replaces the vector between two points by either displacing pixels or using the same pixels from a neighboring frame. There are Slope and Mirror Blend controls, allowing you a little control over the threshold and cloning pattern, and you can apply a tracker to each point via expressions and the pick whip (described in Chapter 10).

The net effect may not be so different from drawing a two-point clone stroke (sample the background by **Alt-** or **Opt**-clicking, then click one end of the wire, and **Shift**-click the other end). That stroke could then be tracked via expressions.

Rig removal can very often be aided by tracking motion, because rigs themselves don't move—the camera does. The key is to make a shape that mattes out the rig, then apply that as a track matte to the foreground footage and track the whole matte.

Dust Bust

This is in many ways as nitty-gritty and low-level as rotoscoping gets, although the likelihood of small particles appearing on source footage has decreased with the advent of digital shooting and the decline of film. Most of these flaws can be corrected only via frame-by-frame cloning, sometimes known as *dust busting*. If you've carefully read this section, you already know what you need to know to do this work successfully, so get to it.

Photoshop Video

Photoshop offers an intriguing alternative to the After Effects vector paint tools, as you can use it with moving footage. The After Effects paint tools are heavily based on those brushes, but with one key difference: Photoshop strokes are bitmaps (actual pixels) and those from After Effects are vectors. This makes it possible to use custom brushes, as are common in Photoshop (and which are themselves bitmaps). You can't do as much with the stroke overall once you've painted it as you can in After Effects, but if you like working in Photoshop, it's certainly an option. However, irony of ironies, Photoshop's allegedly new and improved video isn't compatible with Adobe's video applications. Render these in a separate moving-image format (or, if as Photoshop files, a .psd sequence).

Dust busting can be done rapidly with a clone brush and the Single Frame Duration setting in the Paint panel.

Silhouette is available as both a standalone application and a shape import/export plug-in for After Effects. The software is designed to rotoscope and generate mattes using the newest research and techniques. If you're curious about it, there is a demo you can try on the disc.

Avoid Roto and Paint

You would think that, at the high end, there must be standard tools and all kinds of extra-sophisticated alternatives to roto, but that's not entirely true. There are full-time rotoscope artists who work predominantly in After Effects.

In many studios, roto is regarded as an entry-level job from which you move on as soon as you can demonstrate the necessary skills to advance to a different department (usually compositing). I also know some really smart people who have made roto a bread-and-butter focus (and inevitably they end up doing a bunch of compositing as well). It's a skill that is in constant demand, perhaps not as easily commodified and sent to the cheapest bidder as some might think. For a detail-oriented person who likes pure visual problem solving, it's a good gig.

Call it laziness, but I am somewhat known for how inventive I can be to avoid ending up in pure roto. What's the alternative? Focus on the best possible procedural approach—which can, truth be told, be just as much work—and incorporate motion tracking, the subject of the next chapter.

8

Effective Motion Tracking

I'm sick of following my dreams. I'm just going to ask them where they're going and hook up with them later.

—Mitch Hedberg

Effective Motion Tracking

Matchmoving is the art of seamlessly adding elements to a scene in motion. There is more to this art than simply sampling some motion of one layer and applying it to another, even though that's fundamentally how motion tracking works. The human eye is much more sensitive to subtleties of motion than of color or even edges, the main foci of Section II up to this point. Mismatch color and the shot looks bad, mess up edge composites and it looks fake, but mismatch motion and the audience will be screaming for a silver platter with your head upon it. The ability to sense anomalies in motion is key to our very survival as a species.

And now there's more to motion tracking in CS6, thanks to the addition of a couple of key tools, for which previous editions of this book offered highly manual (and "hackier") work-arounds. The 3D Camera Tracker brings fully automated 3D camera tracking directly into After Effects, no third-party plug-in or application required. The Warp Stabilizer effect also automatically analyzes the scene, but for the purpose of removing unwanted camera motion.

These new tools join the built-in point tracker and the bundled mocha AE from Imagineer Systems. The latter is a planar tracker, a fundamentally unique approach that solves the problem of corner pinning. In fact, corner pinning had been somewhere between difficult and impossible with the After Effects tracker, but it is now possible via the 3D Camera Tracker.

All of these trackers sample motion at a level of detail that would be very difficult to replicate by hand. Whether you rely on the automated tools or the ones that require you to begin with a selection, this chapter is a thorough look under the hood at what these various tools do and how to get the most out of them—including how to choose the right tool for the job, and how to solve common problems that cause tracks to go astray.

Track a Scene with the 3D Camera Tracker

Composited shots had been predominantly lock-offs, until procedural 3D tracking was first devised just prior to the dawn of the 21st century, initially as a custom tool for feature films (such as effects Oscar-winner *What Dreams May Come*) and then as high-priced specialty software (2d3's Boujou came along at around the same time OS X was born). Previous versions of After Effects forced a similar trade-off: either lock off the camera so that the compositing tool could easily handle it, or deal with all of the complexities of adding motion tracking.

Motion tracking is now built right into After Effects, making camera motion in the source plate less of a problem and more of an opportunity. You can place an object in a moving scene simply by giving it the appropriate 3D coordinates. Any shot in which the camera tracks (moves up, down, left, or right), dollies (moves backward and forward), or cranes (moves through space in all six directions) is a candidate for camera tracking. You can also use it on a nodal pan shot (typically camera rotation on a tripod), even though the lack of perspective robs the camera tracker of the data it needs to properly analyze the scene.

The After Effects 3D Camera Tracker has strengths and weaknesses, which are closely interrelated. It is easy to use and can often be a two-click solution, no further tweaks required. But this also makes it less full-featured when up against problems such as motion blur and other low detail, or elaborate camera choreography.

Track a Scene

The 3D Camera Tracker is designed to be simple to use. Select the source layer that contains the original camera motion and choose Track Camera from the Animation menu. The clip is analyzed automatically, and you can continue working while the track is completed in the background, or track a number of shots (or shot sections) simultaneously.

Once automatic analysis is complete, in the effect controls, you can simply click Create Camera and make immediate use of the resulting animated 3D camera. This camera contains Position, Orientation, and, if applicable, Zoom keyframes that match the motion, rotation, and Angle of View of the original shot. Thereafter, any 3D layer aligns with the motion of the scene without itself requiring any keyframes.

In order to position an object, you select a tracked point or set of 3D solved points and create text, a solid, a null object, or what is known as a shadow catcher aligned with the position, scale, and angle of those points. With the 3D Camera Tracker effect selected and Layer Controls visible in the Composition panel, by default you will see a number of colored targets populate the scene (**Figure 8.1**).

Figure 8.1 If you don't see markers populating the scene like this after a track, make sure the layer and effect are selected and View Options are all on (in the Composition panel menu).

In the default 3D Solved view, these track points are scaled to reflect their perceived relative distance from the camera, and similar-sized points are roughly coplanar to the camera. Move your cursor between any three of these points, and you can't miss a bright red target that reveals their orientation; you might also notice a subtler translucent white polygon connecting the three highlighted points (**Figure 8.2**).

You can specify your own set of points to position a static target by simply dragging a selection around those points, which highlights them in yellow (**Figure 8.3**). If the target's position isn't aligned at the proper angle, you can **Shift**-select and deselect points, looking for those that are slightly larger or smaller than the rest to eliminate

Figure 8.2 Move your cursor around the track points and you'll see where the tracker perceives points to be coplanar.

Figure 8.3 Select three or more points to align the object created with the plane formed by those points.

by clicking Delete. Once the angle is correct, you can drag the middle of the target—look for the icon with the four arrows to appear ⯭—and reposition it aligned to that plane.

Context-click on the target and you can create a camera and 3D layer (text, solid, null, or shadow catcher). After Effects ignores any camera you've already created and starts over to ensure that the object position is correct relative to the camera, allowing for edits and changes you might make to the track data.

Refine the Camera Track

Twirl down the Advanced section of the 3D Camera Tracker effect and you will find a few essential pieces of data. The first thing to look at, assuming the Method Used reads Typical, is the Average Error. This setting is common

Stuff That Helps Camera Tracker

▶ If you know the angle of view (typically saved with camera data), you can specify it to remove a variable.

▶ Delete points that slip in 3D view, or that are clearly on moving foreground objects in 2D view, then re-solve and create a new camera.

▶ Watch Average Error as you delete points; undo if it goes up.

▶ Give it shots with foreground and background detail. A couple of objects in the foreground can often be more useful than a dozen extra markers in the background.

▶ Be smooth! You can pull a jerky motion track, but there's nothing better than a clean camera move, and mixing Warp Stabilizer and camera tracker is officially a no-no (but unofficially will sometimes work fine).

3D Camera Tracker has no object tracking mode as such. If you want to track items to a moving object, you can choose to mask out the other nonmoving parts of the shot instead. Prepare for it to feel a bit kludgey, as any nulls derived from the trackers will be static with the motion translated to the camera.

to all 3D trackers; it measures the extent to which the tracker itself found inconsistencies that it cannot resolve. This number is directly related to tracks that slip. Ordinarily, with a value below 1.0 or even 1.5, you are unlikely to see much slippage that requires correction. Higher numbers can be the result of a moving object in the scene, or defocused or otherwise fuzzy areas of the frame.

If Auto Detect creates a Tripod Pan shot, you are working with a scene in which the camera rotated around a more or less static position. Even if the camera was handheld, if the shooter more or less stayed in place, it is the same to the tracker as if it were parked on sticks and panned. The problem for any 3D tracker is that a pan lacks parallax, making triangulation of depth impossible. A Mostly Flat Scene is a milder version of the same basic difficulty: a lack of any difference between foreground and background motion. These scenes may still give you results you can use, but the scene will lack 3D depth. If that's a problem, the only real solution is to shoot with X, Y, and/or Z motion of the camera.

But it is possible to improve on the Average Error number. If the track basically looks good and the scene has a lot of fine detail, you can check Detailed Analysis in the Advanced twirl-down and see if the number lowers. If so, and you've created a camera, replace it with a new one before moving on. However, be forewarned: Detailed Analysis is not a slam-dunk improvement, and it will reset any other refinements you have already made, such as deleted points.

In **Figure 8.4** the talent reminds me of an apiarist with a beard of giant colored bees. The points stick well, and the talent is relatively still. The Average Error is nonetheless 2.19, and the points along the back wall appear uneven, so the clear solution in this case is to knock out the moving foreground subject with a matte.

This is where the Roto Brush matte created in Chapter 7 comes into play. You can apply a matte to a foreground and invert it to force the 3D Camera Tracker to ignore that part of the frame. You just have to precomp (or render)

Figure 8.4 Unless the subject is as still as a statue, foreground movement decreases the accuracy of the camera. In this case, the foreground is so dominant that the tracker effectively object tracks the talent—which sometimes may even be what you want.

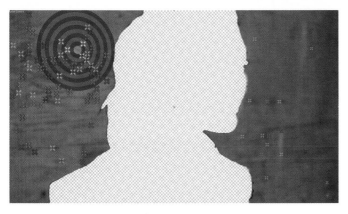

Figure 8.5 Apply and invert a foreground matte in a precomp and the transparent area of the frame is ignored by the tracker. In this case, the track is far more accurate and the points on the wall are coplanar.

the clip with the matte, because the tracker looks at the raw layer, ignoring effects and masks. You can get away with a pretty loose matte, and there is no need to add edge softness. Re-tracked with this matte, the error drops to 0.87, with most of the trackers now following the wall behind (**Figure 8.5**).

Unsolvable Shots

As you continue to work with the 3D Camera Tracker, you will find high error rates that can't be lowered with hold-out mattes and other adjustments. You may even see a red banner indicating that the tracker has failed for a given set of frames, or even the entire analysis (**Figure 8.6**).

Other than a foreground figure dominating the frame, the After Effects tracker really hates motion blur. If you have any control over how action footage is shot and you plan to track

(a)

(b)

Figure 8.6 Some shots **(a)** fail altogether, while others **(b)** only fail on certain frames. In either case, it can help to trim or split the shot—but if you split it, you have to create multiple cameras that will not line up automatically.

CLOSE-UP

Stuff 3D Camera Tracker Hates

▶ Lack of parallax (nodal pans, a dominant flat plane)

▶ Low-detail and, in particular, heavy motion blur

▶ Sudden, dramatic changes of POV

▶ Prominent figures (characters or objects) that dominate the foreground

it, you should raise the camera shutter speed, assuming that the resulting look of the footage is something you want or can live with. After Effects can also have trouble with scenes in which there is total discontinuity between the start and end frames, which is normal. In all of these cases, specialized third-party trackers such as Syntheyes and PF Track offer a much more sophisticated problem-solving toolset.

If one section of a shot seems to cause it to fail, shorter individual layers will often fix the problem—but it can be a pyrrhic victory. 3D Camera Tracker only aims to solve the entire trimmed shot, start to finish, which becomes an impossibility for it with a camera move that is particularly complex. All you can really do to control the delta between the first and last frame is reduce it. A long shot broken into trimmed sections will succeed. There's only one problem: The position and orientation of each camera is relative, and so an object that sits at the center of one camera's last frame will disappear in the following frame tracked by the next sequential camera.

Since, above all, the After Effects tracker was designed to be easy to use above all, convenience comes at the expense of solutions for every type of shot. Incorporating its track data is much simpler than with any third-party tool, an integration process that is outlined toward the end of this chapter. The tool will no doubt result in 3D-tracked composites becoming more ubiquitous, but if convenience and ease-of-use aren't the top priority, it may not disrupt production pipelines that rely on dedicated alternatives.

Warp Stabilizer: Smooth Move

Warp Stabilizer is a completely unique tool that requires no initial setup in order to stabilize or lock off a shot with camera motion. It is therefore easy to use and can remove all indications that stabilization was added. There are still uses for the older techniques from prior editions of this book, such as to manually stabilize and retrack a shot, principally because this new tool produces no usable data. The Warp Stabilizer methodology is akin to wholesale replacement of the original shot with a new improved version, and often that's more or less what you want.

What makes Warp Stabilizer completely unique from other tracking methods available in After Effects is that it analyzes patterns in the scene automatically. "Patterns" are not quite the same as objects analyzed by the 3D Camera Tracker, nor are they planes as in mocha AE they're more like a combination of the two.

Analyzing the progression of individual sets of pixels makes it possible to reduce camera shake while preserving a camera move, and even to fill in missing image data when foreground and background motion do not match. Like the 3D Camera Tracker, Warp Stabilizer anticipates and works with the phenomenon of parallax, and accounts for different rates of motion based on the varied distance of objects from the camera.

Point stabilization, by contrast, centers the entire scene around one point: a single, trackable feature in the scene of a given size. Sure, you can add a second tracking point, but it exists only to determine offsets in scale or rotation from the original point. This is clearly an effective way to lock down a single object—but with multiple planes of motion, this approach can lead the stabilization process to emphasize rather than diminish motion.

Figure 8.7 shows how parallax comes into play with shot tracking. The camera cranes up and forward, causing the foreground figure to move to the left while the lights in the background more or less maintain their position. With point tracking, you choose to stabilize one or the other, foreground or background—not both.

Figure 8.7 Notice how the background holds its place, while the foreground (right) dramatically changes its angle. Consider how you would solve this oppositional movement with normal tracking.

NOTES

A stabilized shot is not automatically preferable to a handheld one; it's a choice that can directly influence the story and emotion of a scene. A handheld shot typically conjures a firsthand witness whose view we might empathetically share. A smooth or locked-off shot, by contrast, often implies a more omniscient, anonymous perspective, allowing the emotion of the scene to take over.

If you were to stabilize either the foreground or background alone in a shot like this, making one more stabile would make the other less so, because the motion of the two is in opposition. Warp Stabilizer is designed to account for this.

Stabilize a Shot

There are a few different ways to access Warp Stabilizer. My method is to context-click the source layer in the timeline containing the excess camera motion and choose Stabilize Motion. This command is also available under the Animation menu, or you can apply the Warp Stabilizer effect.

As soon as Warp Stabilizer is applied, it automatically begins the two-stage stabilization process. A blue bar appears across the image to let you know the first step, analysis, is in progress (**Figure 8.8**). You can also monitor progress as a frame count or percentage completed in the Effect Controls panel. Once this first phase completes, the second (and typically much faster) step of stabilizing the shot occurs, accompanied by an orange bar across the image.

Stabilization is applied for the duration of the layer, within the bounds of the composition work area. If you have a long source clip, trim the clip layer itself, not the work area, to limit the area that is stabilized. With a long and cumbersome shot, you are free to let this process run in the background while you work in another area of After Effects, or stabilize more than one shot at once.

Figure 8.8 The blue banner informs you not only that stabilization is in progress but that it is a background process, leaving you free to work on a different layer or comp within After Effects.

Once the stabilization process is complete, the framing of the shot changes as it is scaled up to compensate for the changes in camera motion. An Auto-scale value (in parentheses) in the Effect Controls panel shows the exact amount of scaling to the shot. If you're at all uncertain about why this scaling occurs, change Framing to Stabilize Only and watch the boundaries of the original shot move around; without cropping and scaling the shot, these ragged edges would remain.

Warp Stabilizer creates no keyframes, even though it clearly affects the shot frame by frame. On the one hand, there are no keyframes to manage. On the other hand, if you find it useful to manage (or tweak or reuse) keyframe data, you're out of luck.

In a visual effects context, the lack of any means to reverse the process is a major limitation. If you need this, there is a manual means to lock a shot, match elements, and reintroduce motion, which will be discussed in "The Point Tracker: Still Useful" section.

If the initial result looks good to you, use the result just like a new source shot, with no render penalty for doing so; once the effect is applied, it does not need to reanalyze or restabilize.

Issues that you may wish to resolve after an initial stabilization include

▶ degree of scaling of the source shot

▶ amount of smoothness (inversely related to scaling)

▶ distortion, whether present in the source shot or added by the effect, including rolling shutter artifacts

Issues that Warp Stabilizer can't improve include

▶ motion blur: Yes or no? How much?

▶ irregular rolling shutter artifacts, including vertical pans and circular camera motion

You can avoid introducing these in the first place, if you are free to take the source shot with Warp Stabilizer in mind.

Overall, Warp Stabilizer can be a godsend, taking footage from unusable to final, although in many cases it changes the character of a shot. Handheld shots remind the viewer of the person behind the camera, but they also look amateurish, particularly from lightweight digital video cameras. Stabilized, the production value often increases dramatically.

Improve on Auto-Scale

Say a typical Auto-scale value of an initial result is 110%. There is no effective limit on the initial amount of scaling used to stabilize a shot, so initial values can be considerably higher on less-stable shots. Nevertheless, 110% is more scaling than would be applied in a professional visual effects situation; one expects noticeable softening and other quantization above 105%. Options to diminish up-scaling include

▶ reducing smoothness, since scaling occurs to add it

▶ cropping the image

▶ synthesizing new edges for the unscaled, cropped image

You can try each of these options, one by one, without losing the fundamental stabilization data.

Adjust Smoothness

Smoothness controls the amount of stabilization applied to the clip, and lowering it is one way to also lower the degree of scaling. By default, it is always set to 50%, which is a way of saying that the application begins with its best attempt at a compromise between desirable smoothness and presumably undesirable scaling. Adjusting the Smoothness control triggers a reappearance of the orange banner as the clip is stabilized using the same initial analysis—this is a redo of the second, quicker part of the two-step process.

Lower this control to a value of 0 and the result usually looks very similar to the original with some stabilization, as indicated by an Auto-scale value that remains above 100.

You'll rarely want that lowest Smoothness setting. Most HD footage is more noticeably degraded by excess motion than by a bit of extra scaling because we are so accustomed to seeing footage at various scales on a single monitor. Most viewers cannot tell the difference between 1280 × 720 footage and 1920 × 1080, but you can bet they'll all be distracted by a bouncy camera on what should be a smooth shot. It's preferable to find a sweet spot by adjusting Smoothness downward, rather than adjusting the Maximum Scale under Auto-scale directly, which leads to cropping. It's a little tedious to play hunt-and-guess with this control.

Under the Advanced controls is a property labeled Crop Less < – > Smooth More. This changes not only scale but position. Instead of restabilizing the clip like the Smoothness setting, this one simply adjusts the extent to which the image is recentered to require the least amount of scaling. The closer to 0% you set this, the more you're letting it move the image around to cover those gaps.

If low-frequency motion in the shot is okay with you, try lowering this value. The camera may appear to sway a bit more without reintroducing too much unwanted higher-frequency motion—the jiggle and jitter of the camera (which, after all, are more distracting). If scaling above a certain amount is unacceptable, you can crop it instead.

TIP

If you want a clip to be even smoother (and more scaled) than the default, you are free to raise its value beyond 100, all the way to 1000. This is often just short of locking off the shot, to be discussed later.

Crop

The effect of Smoothness on Auto-scale is indirect. If you have a scaling limit in mind—say, 105%—twirl down Auto-scale and enter it as a Maximum Scale value. This leads instantly to cropping—an even, black border around the edges of the image. Maximum Scale isn't the last resort, but it is the most straightforward solution if image fidelity is of utmost importance.

There is more than one method to crop the image. Just below Maximum Scale, you can use the Action-safe Margin control to determine a margin by percentage—say, 10%—for that black border. It's unusual to be able to say with confidence that your viewers will never see outside the action safe area, but if you have the advantage of working with that kind of padding around the edges of frame, heck, take it.

Want to kick it old-school and take over the decisions about how to deal with cropping and scaling yourself? Switch Framing to Stabilize Only, and the shot appears with its ragged edges showing at 100% scale, offering a pretty clear idea of where and how much the image is cropped. You can then keyframe the Additional Scale property under Auto-scale, or simply work with the layer Transform properties to scale and offset it until it's right.

Synthesize Edges

The Framing menu also includes an alternative so sophisticated it isn't enabled, which is to say that it would seem almost magical if, in fact, it worked more often. Synthesize Edges guarantees an Auto-scale setting of 100% without cropping the image—by actually filling in missing areas of the frame with its best guess of what belongs there.

Warp Stabilizer relies on tracked pixel data to work its magic, and it can guess what some of those pixels would do continuing at the same velocity, beyond the current image borders. So rather than try to fill in the blanks with data from the current frame, it analyzes adjacent frames and gathers missing images from them.

CLOSE-UP

Shooting for Stabilization

As you become more comfortable with how to shoot for stabilization, aim to shoot in formats that are of higher resolution than the target output, knowing that you'll crop the image later. Shoot in HD (1080p) if final output is 720p, remembering to frame the shot somewhat loosely.

When it works, you get a stable shot without any trade-off in resolution or framing. It's amazing to see that even objects that are moving diagonally in perspective are properly tracked into the shot. When it doesn't work, the bad guesses show up as crude, steppy pixels, gaps in the background, and ripples around the edges of objects near the border of the frame.

In the Advanced section of the effect, try extending the Synthesis Range, the number of frames (in seconds) the effect looks for matching footage, to average in. With irregular motion, this may help locate more missing pieces. Synthesis Edge Feather softens the blend of the effect and is only really useful with out-of-focus or otherwise obscured edges.

Overall, Synthesize Edges works best with a shot containing regular motion over a static background—even with the forward, curving motion of the example shot (**Figure 8.9**), but also an ordinary pan or dolly shot without a lot of extraneous movement at the edges of frame.

NOTES

One crucial step to get Synthesize Edges to work is to add handles to the shot. Because it relies on surrounding frames in both directions to guess what's next, the worst results are often at the start and end of the shot, simply because of a lack of data.

Figure 8.9 Particularly when a shot moves in a more or less uniform direction and there are handles—extra frames at the top and tail—Synthesize Edges can fill in missing background detail. This shot moves uniformly toward the upper left, leaving gaps in the upper-right and lower-left corners where there's no source from which to synthesize.

Lock the Shot

A second option atop the effect controls, under Result, locks the shot completely: No Motion. No means no in this case; the result is a shot with no camera motion whatsoever, with no option to reintroduce motion.

This really only works with a shot that was more or less meant to be locked off, and for whatever reason wasn't. Try to lock off a shot with significant motion, and the result is pretty strange—and not in a generally appealing way. If you need minimal camera motion of a gently unlocked camera, you're better off with the default Smooth Motion and a high Smoothness setting.

No Motion is awesome to keep in mind anytime you find yourself stuck without a tripod. In such a case, do your best to hold the shot steady against your body or a stationary object; try at least to minimize the amount of motion blur and perspective shift, and lock it off in post. The handheld_SFFD shot (available on the disc) was taken with a minimal amount of camera motion and requires only a modest amount of scaling. Stabilizing the background here is no big deal but there is a railing is in the immediate foreground (**Figure 8.10**).

Figure 8.10 The action of the scene is in the background, but stabilizing only at that depth would cause excess motion to the rail in the extreme foreground. Subspace Warp corrects for this by default.

Compare this with the Method: Perspective setting. Toggle between the first and last frames, or any two frames in which the source is significantly different, and you will clearly see the change in angle to that railing.

Now try locking off gator_lunch, which reveals the strengths and pitfalls of locking off a handheld shot. The result is amazing in the sense that very little in this scene is static, yet the lock-off does eliminate the camera motion. In this case, the railing at the left of frame, in particular, changes its angle more significantly than in the first one, so much so that correcting this perspective is just too much to ask. Here the best idea is probably to scale and offset the image so that the boat can be eliminated from the shot entirely. And when that's not an option?

When the Result Is Worse Than the Source

With a good source for stabilization, scaling is the only real issue. When stabilization goes really wrong, it leaves behind distracting motion artifacts, making the shot as a whole or areas of the frame appear as if projected onto jello. Here, it really helps to know your options.

Eliminate Warping

Take a look at the Method menu. Subspace Warp is the default. It's the only one on the list that actually rearranges the orientation of objects in the scene to compensate for parallax. It actually moves pixels around within the source frame. Bump this down to Perspective and—although the shot can be skewed to counter changes in camera angle along with position, rotation, and scale—the pixels themselves are not warped. Any "jello" you see with this setting is due to a combination of rolling shutter ripple and changes in the camera angle.

Only pixel warping can correct parallax. Try this: Hold your thumb up a few inches from your face and bob your head around. The relative motion of your thumb in your field of view is much higher than that of objects in the background, many feet away. An ordinary stabilization cannot compensate for this; you can stabilize the background and a lot of thumb motion remains, or you can stabilize the thumb and actually *add* to the relative motion of the background.

Subspace Warp is at the heart of what's truly new about Warp Stabilizer. The After Effects tracker has long allowed you to create a single-point (Position), two-point (Position, Scale, and Rotation), or four-point (Perspective) track. The names in parentheses are the Method settings that correspond to those types of tracks, and all of them are limited to stabilizing only around one plane of depth in the image, or averaging between planes. To do otherwise is effectively to reach around behind the foreground objects and fill in the blanks revealed by changing the orientation of the background.

Rolling Shutter Repair is new to CS6 and designed specifically to remove rolling shutter artifacts (**Figure 8.11**).

Figure 8.11 Rolling Shutter artifacts can be subtle and easily missed by the casual viewer—and can also be completely maddening to the postproduction professional. The edge of frame makes it easier to see where there is skewing in the source, which Rolling Shutter Repair automatically fixes.

Advanced Options

Your shot is stable but you see strange, distracting motion artifacts with Subspace Warp enabled; without it, some portion of the shot, probably the background, wobbles due to the lack of compensation for parallax. Feeling stuck? You still have the Advanced settings.

If the shot looks like jello, and was taken with a camera that uses a CMOS sensor with a rolling shutter, such as a DSLR, try Enhanced Reduction under Rolling Shutter Ripple. This lets Warp Stabilizer know that if something looks distorted, it should assume the possibility of rolling shutter and try to compensate for it.

Enable Detailed Analysis, which causes Warp Stabilizer to reanalyze the shot by breaking it down into finer features, typically meaning that it requires more track points (that you never see) and thus more time. This is the first thing to try when the results are unexpected and uneven, but just as with the Camera Tracker, there's no reason simply to assume it's better and should be used all the time. In some cases, it leads to more distortion in shot detail rather than less, and it can add significantly to processing time with, say, a fast-moving pan shot.

You Can't Fix These Problems

This section should, above all, teach you how to shoot when you anticipate the need to add stabilization in After Effects. The number one unfixable flaw in a stabilized shot is motion blur. If there was sufficient camera shake at the time the shot was taken to generate it, there is unfortunately no software publically available to remove it, from Adobe or anyone else—although some recent technology previews indicate you may well see it within your lifetime, even relatively soon.

Shoot for Stabilization

Finally, some guidelines for situations in which you find yourself shooting handheld and think you might later wish to stabilize or lock the shot.

To avoid unwanted motion blur, raise the shutter speed on the camera. Yes, young nerd, if you're shooting at 24 fps, a ⅟₄₈ second shutter is the cinematic look, but to avoid motion blur you need to at least double that shutter speed. To add motion blur based on pixel motion, check out the Timewarp effect information in Chapter 2 of this book, as well as a third-party plug-in designed expressly for this purpose: Reel Smart Motion Blur.

When shooting with a DSLR, RED, iPhone, or other CMOS sensor camera, try to avoid rapid vertical pans or circular camera motion. These cause irregular rolling shutter artifacts that are difficult to analyze and remove, even for the tools designed especially to deal with this problem. Rapid horizontal pans, or scenes containing rapid horizontal movement, are bad enough and should be kept slow when possible.

Overall, you're best off shooting handheld or with some other reasonable stabilization and doing your best to keep the shot steady. For example, with a traveling shot out the back of an open vehicle, you can avoid the high frequency jitter and motion blur of a hard mount by instead shooting handheld, or by cushioning the camera rig. Sure, there will be more dips and sways in the motion, but you'll have more control over the factors that can render the shot unsalvageable.

The great news is that you can get away with a lot of stuff with this toolset. My first personal success story was with a complicated dolly shot done crudely on a cherry picker. The operator bravely did his best, but the director wanted to retime the shot, which required that both the timing and the motion be smooth. By first retiming the shot using Timewarp so that the motion was continuous, then compressing those keyframes to compress time, and finally stabilizing the result, I was able to more or less steal back a shot that, on set, was more or less a failure.

Point Stabilization: Is There a Point?

Check out the clip in **Figure 8.12**, a handheld close-up with a foreground, a midground mostly in sharp focus, and a background. The source was taken handheld; it's not super wobbly, but it's not unreasonable to think you might want a locked-off version.

Figure 8.12 Stabilization with the point tracker allows you to specify that a specific plane of the image—in this case, the foreground—should be completely locked.

Warp Stabilizer averages together all of the planes of motion, but fails specifically to lock off the foreground, where the motion is most apparent to the viewer (since it is the focus of this shot). The result does not appear locked off. You can instead lock off this shot with a simple point track.

Huh? The problem for the effect is simple; it always attempts to lock off the entire shot, which means it averages foreground, midground, and background, and only one section—the midground—gets the No Motion treatment. Even Subspace Warp with all of its *Star Trek* technology can't resolve a shot like this.

The problem isn't with the stabilization per se, but rather with the fact that you have no means to aim it at a plane of depth. It is often the case that a shot will appear locked off when motion is removed from either the background or the foreground.

In this shot, it's the foreground that needs to be locked off, because if it wobbles around, the motion is so exaggerated and prominent you don't even notice that at some other depth, the shot is in fact locked off. While it's theoretically possible for Subspace Warp to resolve all planes of motion, this type of situation simply blows its mind.

Guess what? It's a good thing you can still stabilize a shot like this by hand, even though it's no longer obvious how to do it. Stay tuned and we'll look at exactly how in the next section.

The Point Tracker: Still Useful

After Effects still has a point tracker, which still has a couple of big advantages. One is that it lets you match the motion of a layer directly to features that you specify within the scene. And that, in turn, means that you can choose the basis for a track or stabilization rather than leave it to an automated tool, which can sometimes be necessary, as we'll see.

Tracking is a two-step process: The tracker analyzes the clip and stores its analysis as a set of layer properties that don't actually do anything. The properties are then applied to take effect. Both steps, setting the tracking target and applying the track, occur in the Tracker panel when matching or stabilizing motion in After Effects. There are also ways to work with raw unapplied tracking data, typically with the use of expressions.

Choose a Feature

Success with the After Effects tracker relies on your ability to choose a feature that will track effectively, as we saw earlier in Figure 8.15.

Ideally, the feature you plan to track

▶ is unique from its surroundings

▶ has high-contrast edges—typically a corner or point— entirely within the feature region

▶ is identifiable throughout the shot

▶ does not have to compete with similar distinct features within the search region at any point during the track

▶ is close to the area where the tracked object or objects will be added.

The manual lock-off comp is intended to be stabilized by hand because the automated Warp Stabilizer pass fails to lock off the foreground shown in Figure 8.15.

Context-click the plate layer, or under the Animation menu, choose Track Motion. This opens the Layer panel— where tracking is done in After Effects—and reveals the

Tracker panel with a default tracker. Double-check that you're on the first frame (for simplicity), then carefully drag the middle of the feature region (the smaller square, identified in **Figure 8.13**) so that the whole control moves as one, and place it over the target feature. It's very easy to grab the wrong thing, so pay close attention to the icon under your cursor before you drag.

Figure 8.13 Many interactive controls are clustered close together in the tracker. Identified here are: **A.** Search region; **B.** Feature region; **C.** Keyframe marker; **D.** Attach point; **E.** Move search region; **F.** Move both regions; **G.** Move entire track point; **H.** Move attach point; **I.** Move entire track point; **J.** Resize region. Zoom in to ensure you're clicking the right one.

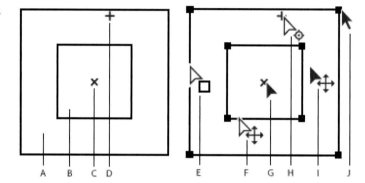

Click Stabilize Motion to switch from a motion track, used to match motion from a detail in the scene to a layer, to a point stabilization of the layer.

Click ▶ in the Tracker panel and watch as After Effects tracks the feature from frame to frame. The Track Point icon only moves in whole pixel increments, so don't assume you have a bad track if you see it jittering a bit. If you chose a well-defined feature with edges inside the feature region, you should quickly and automatically derive a successful track.

Now the only thing left to do is apply it. Click the Apply button in the Tracker panel, then click OK to the inevitable Motion Tracker Apply Options (to specify that this track does indeed apply to X and Y).

Back in the Composition viewer, compare the point stabilization with the result yielded by Warp Stabilizer; it's an improvement, in the sense that the foreground, which is more prominent, is more stable.

Before we move on, though, the main decisions when setting up a track regard the size and shape of the search and feature regions. Keep the following in mind:

▶ A large feature region averages pixel data, producing a smoother but possibly less accurate track (**Figure 8.14**).

▶ A small feature region may pick up noise and grain as much as trackable detail. This will lead to an accurate but (jittery and therefore unusable) track.

▶ The bigger the search region, the slower the track.

▶ The feature region doesn't have to contain the area of frame you want to match. One way to offset a track is to move the attach point—that little x at the center of the tracker. A better solution is to apply the track to a null (discussed later).

Tracked features can often be unreliable, changing perspective, lighting, or color throughout the course of the shot. The following sections solve the initial difficulty experienced in this first attempt, and explain what to do when you don't have a constant, trackable feature exactly where you want the target to go, as was the case here.

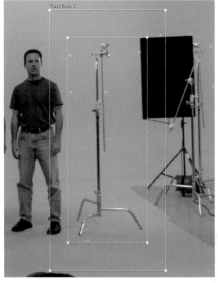

Figure 8.14 Thinking of tracking a large object? This may make the track smoother, because it averages more data, but less accurate (for the same reason).

Tweak the Tracker

There are five types of track listed under the Track Type menu in the Tracker panel. Before moving ahead one at a time, here is an overview of what each does. *Stabilize* and *Transform* tracks are created identically but applied uniquely. Edit Target shows the singular difference between them: Stabilize tracks are always applied to the *anchor point* of the tracked layer. Transform tracks are applied to the *position* of a layer other than the tracked layer (or the effect point control of any effect in any layer).

Using Stabilize, the animated anchor point (located at the center of the image by default) moves the layer in opposition to Position. Increasing the anchor point's X value (assuming Position remains the same, which it does when you adjust the Anchor Point value directly in the Timeline) moves the layer to the left, just as decreasing the Position value does.

TIP

Keep in mind that you can track in reverse, for situations where the feature being tracked is larger, more prominent, or more clearly visible at the end of a shot.

Corner Pin tracks are very different. In After Effects, these require three or four points to be tracked, and the data is applied to a Corner Pin plug-in to essentially distort the perspective of the target layer. Because these tracks are notoriously difficult and unreliable, the happy truth is that mocha AE, which also generates data that can be applied to a corner pin, has more or less superseded Corner Pin tracking.

A *Raw* track generates track data only, graying out the Edit Target button. It's simply a track that isn't applied directly as Transform keyframes. What good is unapplied track data? For one thing, it can be used to drive expressions or saved to be applied later. It's no different than simply never clicking Edit Target; the raw track data is stored within the source layer.

Position, Rotation, and Scale

You can't uncheck Position in the Tracker panel (thus avoiding the unsolvable riddle, What is a motion track without Position data?), but you can add Rotation and Scale. Enable either toggle, and a second track point is automatically added.

Additional tracking of rotation and scale data is straight-forward enough, with two track points instead of one. Typically, the two points should be roughly equidistant from the camera due to the phenomenon of parallax (**Figure 8.15**).

Solve Problems with Nulls

You may have tried simply moving a target layer after tracking data was applied to it. Because there is a keyframe on each tracked frame, moving the object at any point moves only that keyframe, causing a jump. You can instead select all Position keyframes by clicking that property in the Timeline panel, then moving them all (but it's easy to forget to do this, or for the keyframes to become deselected as you attempt it).

CLOSE-UP

Combine Tracking and Roto with Expressions and Scripts

Expressions and tracking data go together like Lennon and McCartney: harmoniously, not without friction, and to great effect. You don't even have to apply raw tracking data in order to put expressions to use; the expressions pick whip can be used to link any property containing X and Y position data directly to the X and Y of a motion track.

Chapter 10 contains specific tips to maximize the numerical data you get from the tracker for roto and paint.

Figure 8.15 A Scale or Rotation track will not succeed with two points that rest at completely different distances from the camera.

Apply track data to a null object layer and then parent to apply the motion. This gains you the following advantages:

▶ Freely reposition tracked layers. It doesn't matter whether the track attach point is in the right location; the null picks up the relative motion, and any layer parented to it can be repositioned or animated on its own (**Figure 8.16**).

▶ Once a track is set you can lock the tracked layer so that it's not inadvertently nudged out of position.

Figure 8.16 The null contains the applied motion data and is not touched. The foreground portal layer is parented and contains no keyframes, so you are free to move, scale, and rotate it without worrying about disrupting the track.

TIP

Stopping and restarting a track resets Feature Region at the frame where you restart. Use this to your advantage by restarting a track that slips at the last good frame; it often works.

▶ A Stabilization track can be used to peg multiple objects to a scene (see next section).

▶ One set of motion data can be parented to another to build tracks, parenting one to the next.

To fully solve 08_01_track_basic, take the following steps:

1. Create a null object (under the Layer menu).

2. Track Position and Scale using equidistant points on either tracking target (the c-stands that are there for this purpose).

3. Click Edit Target to make certain the null is selected, then apply the track to the null.

4. Parent the layer to the null (**Shift+F4** toggles the Parent column in the timeline); then select the null as the target from the foreground object being tracked.

Track a Tricky Feature

A shot with rotation or scale of more than a few degrees typically requires that you track a feature that does not look at all the same within the Feature Region box from the start to the end of the frame (**Figure 8.17**). For just such situations, Tracker > Options contains the Adapt Feature on Every Frame toggle.

By default, the tracker is set to adapt the track feature if the Confidence setting slips below 80%. Adapt Feature on Every Frame is like restarting the track on each and every frame, comparing each frame to the previous one instead of the one you originally chose. For ordinary tracks this adds an unwanted margin of error, but in a case where a feature is in constant flux anyway, this can help.

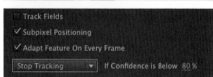

Figure 8.17 To the naked eye, the pattern being tracked in these two frames is nearly identical, but to a point tracker, which does not understand context, the two might seem almost unrelated due to changes in angle, blur, and scale. The solution with a point that changes due to rotation, scale, blur, or light changes may be to toggle Adapt Feature on Every Frame and have the tracker stop each time Confidence goes below the default threshold of 80%.

Confidence

At the bottom of Motion Tracker Options is a submenu of options related to After Effects' mysterious Confidence settings. Every tracked frame gets a Confidence setting, an evaluation of how accurate the track was at that frame. This may or may not be indicative of the actual accuracy, but my experience is that you're almost guaranteed to be fine with values above 90%, while real problems will cause this value to drop way, way down, to 30% or less (**Figure 8.18**).

Figure 8.18 The Confidence graph clearly indicates where this track has lost its target.

Depending on this setting, you can

▶ continue Tracking. Power ahead no matter what happens!

▶ stop Tracking. Reset the tracker manually right at the problem frame.

▶ extrapolate Motion. Allow After Effects to guess based on the motion of previously tracked frames, for cases where the tracked item disappears for a few frames.

▶ adapt Feature. Change the reference Feature Region to the previous frame if Confidence is low.

Whichever you choose, you also have the option to go back to the frame where a track went wrong, reset Feature Region by hand, and restart the track.

Motion Blur

Motion blur is also essential to matchmoving. A good track won't look right until its motion blur also matches that of the background plate. If you don't know the shutter speed with which a shot was taken, you can match it by eye, most often zooming in to an area of the frame where it is apparent in both the foreground and background. If you know, for example, that the shutter speed was one-half of the frame rate (the standard setting for a cinematic look), use a 180-degree shutter, and be sure to set the Shutter Phase to –0.5 of that number, or –90.

TIP

To reveal the current track in the Timeline with the Track Controls active, use the **SS** (Show Selected) shortcut.

SCRIPT

TrackerViz by Charles Bordenave (http://aescripts.com/trackerviz/) originated as a tool to average motion data, so that several track attempts could be averaged together to make a single animation. You can also use mask shapes and tracker points interchangeably, or to link a mask shape to the position of selected layers.

Figure 8.19 Motion tracking can't work without matching motion blur (right). This shot uses the standard film camera blur: a 180-degree shutter angle, with a phase of –90.

Subpixel Motion

The key feature of the After Effects tracker is *subpixel positioning*, on by default in Motion Tracker Options. You could never achieve this degree of accuracy manually; most supposedly "locked-off" scenes require stabilization despite the fact that the range of motion is less than a full pixel; your vision is actually far more acute than that.

As you watch a track in progress, the trackers move in whole pixel values, bouncing around crudely, unless you disable subpixel positioning. This does not reflect the final track, which is accurate to $^1/_{10000}$th of a pixel (four places below the decimal point).

Tracker2Mask by Mathias Möhl (http://aescripts.com/tracker2mask/) uses tracker data to track masks without the need for a one-to-one correspondence between the tracked points and the mask points. This script is a fantastic roto shortcut for cases where a rigid body in the scene is changing position or perspective.

Motion blur settings reside in Composition Settings (**Ctrl+K**/**Cmd+K**) > Advanced, and if you enable the Preview toggle at the lower left, you can see them update as you adjust them for eye matching. As described back in Chapter 2, adjust Shutter Angle and Shutter Phase until you see a good match, raising (or in the odd case, lowering) Samples per Frame and Adaptive Sample Limit to match (**Figure 8.19**).

If it's necessary to stabilize a scene that contains heavy motion blur, that's a bigger problem that needs to be avoided when shooting (even by boosting the shutter speed of the camera, where possible).

Mocha AE Planar Tracker: Also Still Quite Useful

Previous editions of this book heavily promoted mocha for After Effects, aka mocha AE, which in CS6 is now in its own version 3, and is more closely integrated with the After Effects UI—for better and worse. We have yet to see the version of mocha AE that is forgiving to beginners, but this version gamely tries to smooth the workflow.

Mocha is a *planar tracker*, which is truly and fundamentally different from a point tracker such as the one in After Effects. A planar tracker assumes that the area defined by the feature region is a plane in 3D space, and it looks for that plane not only to change its position, rotation, and scale, but also its orientation while remaining a consistent surface. The result is 2D data that can be used to emulate 3D, in particular Corner Pin and Shape tracks. A tracked plane can also be averaged to generate the same type of track data that the After Effects tracker creates.

Planar tracks are much more accurate than Point tracks, and the world is full of planes. Look around the environment where you are right now and you may notice them everywhere: walls, tabletops, the backs of chairs, the sides of hard-surface objects such as automobiles (**Figure 8.20**), even the trunk of a tree or the face of a hipster as she cycles past. If you were orbiting the earth reading this book from a space station, the surface of Earth, though curved, would track well as a unified plane, allowing you to map the outlines of nations on the natural topography.

Imagineer also offers mocha, a standalone version of the same software designed to integrate with other compositing and animation applications besides After Effects.

Figure 8.20 A plane does not have to be flat or rectilinear in order for mocha to track it; look around and you will see many coplanar objects.

The plainest use for mocha AE—pun very much intended—is Corner Pin tracking, or the replacement of a surface defined by a rectangle with another such surface. This type of track has long been the Achilles' heel of the After Effects tracker, and its use is now discouraged for this purpose, given the free availability of mocha AE. With the Camera Tracker, there is a contender for a more sophisticated screen-replacement option.

Mocha can, in fact, be used for just about any type of 2D tracking. The extra precision is often worth the extra steps of leaving the After Effects environment, if you can tolerate everything being nonstandard to Adobe—not just the UI and workflow but even the file handling and format support, not to mention the "simple" act of putting a mocha AE track to use in After Effects.

The footage and projects used for this mocha AE example can be found in the 08_mocha_corner_pin_basic folder on the book's disc.

The Basics

Mocha is an application unto itself, and this book is no substitute for the manual, which happily is an easy read despite being longer than this entire chapter (just choose Help > Offline Help in mocha). Seriously, it's not a bad read, and that's a good thing, because otherwise it would need a whole chapter here.

To try out the basic features:

1. Open the 08_mocha_basics project, and in it, the comp called Track in mocha AE.

2. Choose the source layer, 08_plt_cornerpin, and select Animation > Track in mocha AE.

3. Clear the dialog that appears in mocha AE by clicking OK. The frame range may seem odd, but the clip should match After Effects.

4. Use the right arrow key to go something like 18 frames into the shot in mocha AE. The exact amount doesn't matter, just enough to find a clean source frame. In this shot, the camera pans on and off the screen, so it will be necessary to begin a few frames in and track both forward and backward.

5. With the X-spline tool ▲X (or if you prefer, Bezier splines ▲B), click four corner points in succession just outside the monitor's boundaries (**Figure 8.21**), and then press **C** to close the shape.

    Note that the boundaries don't really matter here, but it is helpful if each point corresponds to some feature you can easily trace through the scene. This is the strange conundrum about mocha—it doesn't track points, but you can adjust the corner points to fix the planes. Capturing most of the foreground monitor, including its edges and even a bit of what's behind it, is fine.

6. Now track the shot, first forward ▶ to the end of the clip, then drag back to the beginning of the blue line of tracked frames and ◀ track backward to the opening of the shot.

Figure 8.21 Four corners are positioned outside the bounds of the item being tracked, without even taking the trouble to tighten the X-splines. The image on the monitor is washed-out enough that there's no need to hold out the source image (which would be done more carefully and is thoroughly explained in the mocha AE manual).

Note that, unlike the After Effects trackers, mocha AE has no trouble with motion blur, nor the moving content on the screen (because it's so faint in this case, the mocha AE manual has an example that requires a mask to hold out the screen). Perhaps most remarkably (compared with the After Effects point tracker, at least), it's no problem for the track area to exit frame.

7. Go back to the middle of the clip and enable the Surface button—the blue button atop the viewer. Drag the four blue corners so that the shape aligns with the edges of the screen. This is an important step.

8. Click the Adjust Track tab below the viewer, then scrub or play the clip to see how well the corners hold.

   Zoom Window's picture-in-picture views helpfully appear (**Figure 8.22**) with a given corner selected.

9. Use the Nudge controls under Adjust Track to gently push the corners back into place anywhere you see them slipping, or simply try the Auto button at the center of those controls. You may not have to do this at all, depending on your initial selection.

Figure 8.22 When it comes time to fine-tune the positions of the surface corners, mocha looks like a point tracker, but the crosshairs are only there to fine-tune the completed planar track.

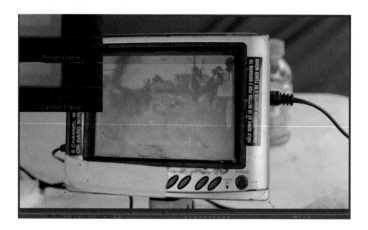

Mochalmport by Mathias Möhl (http://aescripts.com/mochaimport/) simplifies the process of applying mocha AE tracking data in After Effects. It also supports direct Corner Pin export from mocha AE.

Mocha is typically used for corner pinning, but you can instead choose to export After Effects Transform Data and use it like regular tracker data.

10. Once you are satisfied that the surface is locked in place, click Export Tracking Data from the lower right of the UI. From the dialog that appears, choose After Effects Corner Pin (which supports motion blur) and click Copy to Clipboard.

   If you instead choose to save a text file, you can then copy and paste its data from an ordinary text editor.

11. Back in After Effects, at the same starting frame, paste the keyframes to the target layer to be added (if you don't have one, create a new solid or placeholder layer).

12. Enable Motion Blur for both the layer and the Composition in the Timeline.

This track now has everything you need: an entry, exit, and motion blur, and the effect even matches the rolling shutter distortion caused by the Canon 7D CMOS sensor (which you can also remove beforehand with Rolling Shutter Repair). That change, and others that can be done prior to tracking in mocha AE, need to be pre-rendered.

The Nitty-Gritty

Although the method for moving a shot from After Effects into mocha AE seems simpler with the added menu command Animation > Track in mocha AE, you will find that any change you make to the shot—even trimming its in point, and of course adding any effect—requires pre-rendering. Mocha also doesn't support the full range of video and image formats that After Effects does.

In addition, tracking multiple shots simultaneously using the After Effects command opens multiple instances of mocha AE, and redoing a track pops up a dialog asking if you want to replace a project that you may not even be aware you created when you made the first attempt (it is saved by default and can be reopened).

It's also normal for a track to be slightly more complicated than this, usually due to motion or perspective shifts within the track area. This can be the result of foreground objects passing across the track region or the appearance of the region itself changing over time.

Figure 8.23 shows an otherwise straightforward track—a screen, like the last one—with the following challenges: flares and reflections play across the screen, the hands move back and forth across the unit, and the perspective of the screen changes dramatically. It's a 180-degree move on two axes using a technocrane that makes it too challenging a shot for the 3D Camera Tracker.

NOTES

The biggest competition to mocha AE is, in many cases, the 3D Camera Tracker, since it too allows you to do screen replacements and is automated and built right into After Effects.

Figure 8.23 The tracking markers on the screen are not necessary for mocha to track this handheld unit for screen replacement; it's the reflective screen itself, and the movement of the thumbs across it, that present mocha with a challenge.

There are two standard solutions to any track that slips:

▶ Sudden slippage is often the result of foreground motion (or light shifts) changing the appearance of the tracked area; the solution is to mask out the area containing the disturbance.

▶ Small, gradual slippage is often the result of shifts in perspective and can be keyframed.

Figure 8.24 Holdout masks are added to eliminate areas where the screen picks up reflections and the left thumb moves around. Notice that the tracking markers aren't even used; there is plenty of other detail for mocha to track without them.

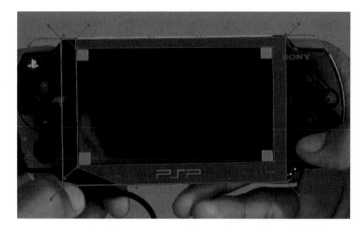

Shape Tracking

Mocha AE version 2 added shape tracking via the mocha Shape effect. There are a couple of features that are unique to it:

▶ Shapes tracked in mocha AE can be pasted into After Effects as mask shapes.

▶ Mocha shapes support adding feather to mask vectors (if applied with the mocha shape effect).

However, it has to be said that shape tracking is not the prime directive, if you will, of mocha AE; it can be challenging to set up the track (read the manual, as it involves linking shapes) and then to get the splines to conform to the actual contours of the item being tracked. Your mileage may vary.

The Red Giant Corner Pin effect included in the Warp collection (available on the book's disc both in the Effects Suite and Keying Suite installations found in the Red Giant Software folder) is designed specifically to be used with mocha AE .

Big shifts in the track region are caused by changes in the track area, so fix those first, adding an additional spline (or splines) containing the interruptive motion. The Add X-spline and Add Bezier Spline create a subtractive shape (or shapes) around the areas of the first region that contain any kind of motion. **Figure 8.24** shows that these can be oddly defined; they track right along with the main planar track.

Retracking with these additional holdout masks improves the track. All that is required to perfect this track is a single keyframe (at a point where the unit is tilted about 15 degrees toward camera), this time to the track mask itself, which creates a green keyframe along the main timeline. Mocha uses these keyframes as extra points of comparison, rather than simply averaging their positions.

In this example, it's also helpful to check Perspective under Motion in the Track tab; this allows the change in proportions from the tilting of the screen to be included in the Corner Pin export.

If you get into trouble, you'll want to know how to delete keys (under Keyframe Controls) or reference points (in the Adjust Track tab). You also need to know a few new keyboard shortcuts, such as **X** for the hand tool and arrow keys to navigate forward and backward one frame.

Camera Integration

After Effects can make use of 3D tracking data that comes from other applications as well. Many leading third-party motion tracking applications, including Pixel Farm's PF Track and SynthEyes, from Andersson Technologies, export 3D tracks specifically for After Effects. Imagineer's full version of mocha now includes a 3D camera tracker. And cameras from CINEMA 4D round-trip with the After Effects camera thanks to a set of add-ons from Maxon.

Generally, the 3D tracking workflow operates as follows:

1. Track the scene with a 3D tracking application. The generated 3D camera data and any associated nulls or center point can be exported as a Maya .ma file that After Effects can import directly.

2. Optionally, import the camera data into a 3D animation program and render 3D elements to be composited. Working with Maya or CINEMA 4D, you can also create a 3D animation and camera data from scratch, and export that.

3. Import the camera data into After Effects; you'll see a composition with an animated 3D camera and nulls (potentially dozens if they haven't been managed beforehand). A 2D background plate with the original camera motion can be freely matched with 3D layers.

Figure 8.25 shows a shot that also began with a 3D track in Boujou. The fires that you see in the after shot are actually dozens of individual 2D fire and smoke layers, staggered and angled in 3D space as the camera flies over to give the sense of perspective. More on this shot and how to set up a shot like this is found in Chapter 14.

3D Tracking Data

After Effects can import Maya scenes (.ma files) provided they are properly prepped and include only rendering cameras (with translation and lens data) and nulls. The camera data should be "baked," with a keyframe at every frame (search "baking Maya camera data" in the online help for specifics).

NOTES

After Effects can also extract camera data embedded in an RPF sequence (and typically generated in 3ds Max or Flame). Place the sequence containing the 3D camera data in a comp and choose Animation > Keyframe Assistant > RPF Camera Import.

Figure 8.25 Just because you're stuck with 2D layers in After Effects doesn't mean you can't stagger them all over 3D space to give the illusion of depth, as with this fly-by shot. Tracking nulls from Boujou helped get the relative scale of the scene; this was important, because the depth of the elements had to be to exact scale for the parallax illusion (right) to work. (Final fire image courtesy of ABC-TV.)

Because After Effects offers no proportional 3D grids in the viewers, nulls imported with a 3D scene are a huge help when scaling and positioning elements in 3D.

Besides Position and Rotation, Camera may also contain Zoom keyframes. Unless Sergio Leone has started making spaghetti westerns again, zoom shots are not the norm, and any zoom animation should be checked against a camera report (or any available anecdotal data) and eliminated if bogus (it indicates a push or even an unstable camera). Most 3D trackers allow you to specify that a shot was taken with a prime lens (no zoom).

Work with a Maya Scene

A .ma scene is imported just like a separate .aep project (make sure it is named with the .ma extension). You may see one or two compositions—two in the case of nonsquare pixels, including a nested square pixel version. The camera may be single-node, in which case the camera holds all of the animation data, or targeted, in which case the transformation data resides in a parent node to which the camera is attached.

The first challenge is that any null object with the word "null" in its name is also imported. Unedited, the scene may become massive and cumbersome. Any composition with 500 layers of any kind is slow and unwieldy, so eliminate all but the nulls that correspond to significant objects in the scene. If possible, do this in the tracking software or 3D program so you never have to see the excess in After Effects.

If too many nulls make their way into After Effects, once you've selected the dozen or so useful ones, context-click on them and choose Invert Selection to select the potentially hundreds of other unused nulls. Delete them, or if that makes you nervous, at least turn off their visibility and make them Shy layers.

The next challenge is that nulls often come in with tiny values (in the low single digits), which also means that they have 0, 0, 0 as a center point. This is standard in 3D but not in After Effects, which uses the coordinates at the center of the comp, such as 960, 540, 0.

Here's the honest truth: 0, 0, 0 is a much more sensible center point for anything 3D. If you think you can keep track of it and deal with the camera and other elements clustered around the upper-left corner in the orthographic views, it's more straightforward to handle a 3D scene with this center point and to reposition 2D layers to that point when they are converted to 3D.

This is also a way to tackle the problem of the tiny world of single-digit position values. Add a 3D null positioned at 0, 0, 0, then parent all layers of the imported Maya comp to it. Now raise the Scale values of the null. Once you have the scene at a healthier size, you can **Alt**-unparent (**Opt**-unparent) all of those layers, and the scaled values stick. This method will also invert a scene that comes in upside-down (as happens with After Effects, since its Y axis is centered in the upper-left corner and is thus itself upside-down).

Like the built-in 3D Camera Tracker, 3D matchmoving apps rely on the After Effects camera to recreate 3D data, and that feature and how it compares with the optics and behavior of a real-world camera is the subject of the next chapter.

9

The Camera and Optics

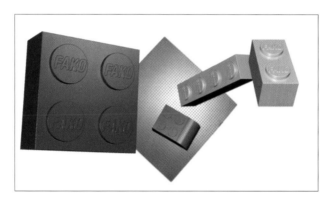

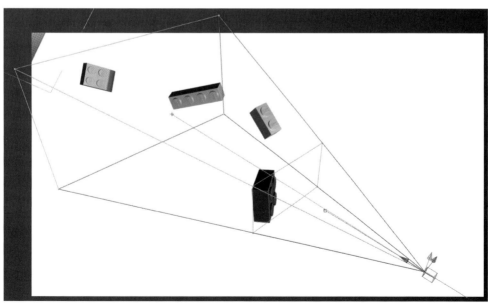

There is only you and your camera. The limitations in your photography are in yourself, for what we see is what we are.

—Ernst Haas

The Camera and Optics

When we say something in a movie looks realistic, we really mean it looks like it was a real scene photographed with a camera. The distinction is critical, because the photographed world looks different from the one your naked eye sees.

Cinematography is essential to compositing. Not only are you typically matching the look of a scene captured by a camera, but After Effects also lets you re-create and even change essential shooting decisions long after the crew has struck the set. A shot may be perfectly realistic on its own merits, but it doesn't belong in the story unless it works cinematically. Factors you can manipulate in After Effects include

- ▶ angle of view (or zoom)
- ▶ depth of field (or focal depth)
- ▶ the perceived shooting medium—poorly lit, grainy, handheld consumer video, or crisp cinematic widescreen—and what it reveals about the story and point of view
- ▶ parallax and perspective, including stereoscopic images
- ▶ camera motion (handheld, stabilized, locked) and what point of view it implies

The camera, after all, is part of the story.

Know Your Camera: Virtual and Real

The After Effects camera relates to an actual motion picture camera without being anything like one. There is a lens angle, but no lens, and the world that the camera sees is made up of an assortment of 2D and 3D objects.

See with the Camera

Toggle a layer to 3D and just like that, position, rotation, and scale have three axes instead of two—but 3D layers with no camera is like a race car with no manual clutch: You're fine on the straightaways, then at the first curve, boom, you hit the wall.

The Camera Settings dialog (**Figure 9.1**) includes a unique physical diagram to describe how settings in the 3D camera affect your scene.

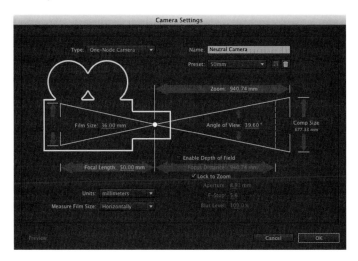

Figure 9.1 The Camera Settings dialog provides a visual method to elucidate the relationship between values. The 50 mm preset selected in the Preset menu is the neutral (default) setting; use it for neutral perspective.

Lens Settings

The true neutral default After Effects lens is the 50 mm preset in Camera Settings, although it is not labeled as such and After Effects defaults to any previous camera settings. This 50 mm setting (**Figure 9.2**) is neither wide (as with lower values, **Figure 9.3**) nor long (as with higher values, **Figure 9.4**), and in a scene that contains Z depth, it does not introduce a shift in perspective.

"50 mm" is literally meaningless, because virtual space doesn't contain millimeters any more than it contains kilograms, parsecs, or bunny rabbits. This is the median lens length of a 35 mm SLR camera, the standard professional still image camera.

Motion picture cameras are not so standardized. The equivalent lens on a 35 mm film camera shooting Academy

NOTES

The folder 09_3Dcamera_legos on the book's disc contains the cameras and 3D model used for the figures in this section.

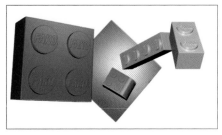

Figure 9.2 The default lens (50 mm setting). If settings are at the defaults, with Z Position value the exact inverse of the Zoom value, the resulting camera does not shift the comp's appearance.

Figure 9.3 An extreme wide field of view does not distort in the fish-eye manner of a short glass lens, but it does radically alter the perspective and proportions. If it looks wrong, this is probably because a computer has no "lens" and thus no curvature.

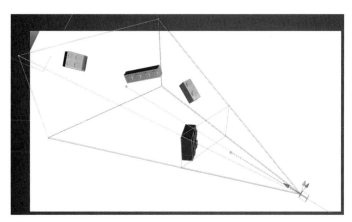

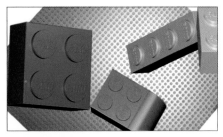

Figure 9.4 A narrow "telephoto" lens pushes the elements together and emphasizes dimensions.

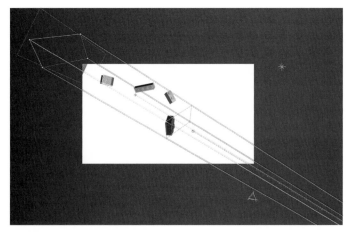

ratio itself has a 35 mm length. A miniDV camera, on the other hand, has a tiny neutral lens length of around 4 mm. The length corresponds directly to the size of the back-plate or video pickup, the area where the image is projected inside the camera.

Lens length, then, is a somewhat arbitrary and made-up value in the virtual world of After Effects. The corresponding setting that applies universally is Angle of View, which can be calculated whether images were shot in IMAX or HDV or created in a 3D animation package.

Real Camera Settings

To understand the relationship of the After Effects camera to that of a real-world camera, look again at the Camera Settings diagram introduced in Figure 9.1. Four numerical fields—Film Size, Focal Length, Zoom, and Angle of View—surround a common hypotenuse.

A prime (or fixed) lens has static values for all four. A zoom lens allows Zoom and Focal Length to be adjusted, changing Angle of View. Either lens will resolve a different image depending on the size of the sensor (or film back, or in this case the Film Size setting). These four settings, then, are interrelated and interdependent, as the diagram implies. Lengthen the lens by increasing Focal Length and the Angle of View decreases proportionally.

Angle of View is the radius, in degrees, from one edge of the view to the other. If you have calculated this number in order to match it, note that Camera Settings lets you specify a horizontal, vertical, or diagonal measurement in the Measure Film Size menu.

In After Effects, the Zoom value is the distance of the camera, in pixels, from the plane of focus. Create a camera and its default Z Position value is the inverse of the Zoom value, perfectly framing the contents of the comp at their default Z Position, 0.0. This makes for easy reference when measuring depth of field effects, and it lets you link camera position and zoom together via expressions (for depth of field and multiplane effects, to be discussed later).

A fifth numerical field in Camera Settings, Focus Distance, is enabled by checking Enable Depth of Field; it corresponds to a camera's aperture setting.

Emulate a Real Camera

Other considerations when matching a real-world camera include much of the material that follows in this chapter, such as

- ▶ **depth of field.** This is among the most filmic and evocative additions to a scene. Like any computer graphics program, After Effects naturally has limitless depth of field, so you have to re-create the shallow depth of real-world optics to bring a filmic look to a comp.

- ▶ **zoom or push.** A move in or out is used for dramatic effect, but a zoom and a push communicate very different things about point of view.

- ▶ **motion blur and shutter angle.** These are composition (not camera) settings; they were introduced in Chapter 2 and are further explored here.

- ▶ **lens angle.** The perspective and parallax of layers in 3D space change according to the angle of the lens used to view them.

- ▶ **lens distortion.** Real lenses introduce curvature to straight lines, which is most apparent with wide-angle or fish-eye lenses. An After Effects camera has no lens, hence no distortion, but distortion can be created or removed (see the section "Lens Distortion").

- ▶ **exposure.** Every viewer in After Effects includes an Exposure control ![icon]; this (along with the effect of the same name) is mathematically similar but different in practice from the aperture of a physical camera. Exposure and color range is detailed in Chapter 11.

- ▶ **bokeh, halation, flares.** All sorts of interesting phenomena are generated by light when it interacts with the lens itself. The appeal of this purely optical phenomenon in a shot is subjective, yet it can offer a unique and beautiful aesthetic and lend realism to a scene shot under conditions where we would expect to see it (whether we know it or not).

A *camera report* is a record of the settings used when the footage was taken, usually logged by the camera assistant (or equivalent).

Camera Lens Data

Maintaining an accurate camera report on a shoot (**Figure 9.5**) is the job of the second assistant camera operator (or 2nd AC). The report includes such vital information on a given scene and take as ASA and f-stop settings, as well as the lens used. Lens data is often vital to matching the scene with a virtual camera, although there are methods to derive it after the fact with reasonable accuracy. A great tip for a VFX supervisor is to take a shot of the camera itself on a given VFX shot so that there is visible reference of the lens and focal settings, in case they aren't recorded accurately.

The basic job of the visual effects supervisor is to record as much visual reference data as possible (typically using a DSLR camera) in addition to maintaining clear communications with the cinematographer, with whom the VFX supervisor is mutually dependent.

There are several other bits of data that can be of vital interest in postproduction, and these go beyond what is

Figure 9.5 An old-school film camera report and the contemporary version, EXIF data recorded on the Canon 7D and passed through to Lightroom. You don't necessarily get everything you need from ordinary metadata like this, but increasingly, devices are adding specialized VFX data such as the height of the camera and the distance to the subject.

recorded in an ordinary camera report. Focal distance (a measurement from camera to subject), camera height, any angle to the camera if it is not level, and any start and end data on zooms or focus pulls might be missing from the standard camera report. When supervising, be sure to ask that these be included, particularly if any 3D tracking will be necessary.

With accurate information on the type of camera and the focal length of a shot, you know enough to match the lens of that camera with an After Effects camera.

Figure 9.6 compares the sensor sizes of some popular moving image formats, and the book's disc includes a table with sensor sizes for a wide range of video and film cameras. If your particular brand and make of camera is on the list, and you know the focal length, use these to match the camera via Camera Settings (double-click the camera layer to reveal). The steps are as follows:

1. Set Measure Film Size to Horizontally. (Note that hFilmPlane in the expression stands for "Horizontal Film Plane.")

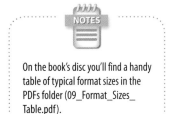

On the book's disc you'll find a handy table of typical format sizes in the PDFs folder (09_Format_Sizes_Table.pdf).

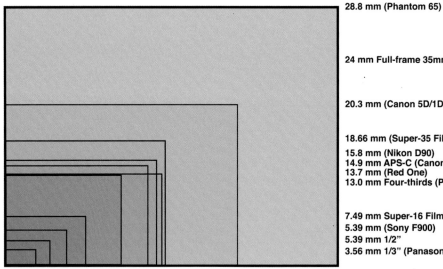

28.8 mm (Phantom 65)

24 mm Full-frame 35mm

20.3 mm (Canon 5D/1D X)

18.66 mm (Super-35 Film)
15.8 mm (Nikon D90)
14.9 mm APS-C (Canon 7D)
13.7 mm (Red One)
13.0 mm Four-thirds (Panasonic GH1)

7.49 mm Super-16 Film
5.39 mm (Sony F900)
5.39 mm 1/2"
3.56 mm 1/3" (Panasonic HVX-200)

Figure 9.6 Sensor size has a direct effect not only on angle of view at a given lens length, but on focal range and depth of field. Generally speaking, the larger the sensor, the shallower the raw depth of field.

2. Set Units to millimeters.

3. Enter the number from the Horizontal column of the chart that corresponds to the source film format.

4. Enter the desired Focal Length.

Once the Angle of View matches the footage, tracked objects maintain position in the scene as the shot progresses. It's vital to get this right when re-creating a camera move, especially if a particularly wide or long lens was used, or things simply may not line up correctly. It's even more important for camera projection (discussed later).

Lens Distortion

A virtual camera with a wide-angle view (like the one back in Figure 9.3) has a dramatically altered 3D perspective but no actual lens. A virtual camera is only capable of gathering an image linearly—in a straight line to each object.

A physical lens curves light in order to frame an image on the flat back plate of the camera. The more curved the lens, the wider the angle of view it is able to gather and bend so that it is perpendicular to the back of the camera. A fish-eye view requires a convex lens a short distance from the plate or sensor in order to gather the full range of view.

At the extremes, this causes easily visible lens distortion; items in the scene known to contain straight lines don't appear straight at all but bent in a curve (**Figure 9.7**). The barrel distortion of a fish-eye lens shot makes it appear as if the screen has been inflated like a balloon.

As you refine your eye, you may notice that many shots that aren't as extreme as a fish-eye perspective contain a degree of lens distortion. Or you might find that motion tracks match on one side of the frame but slip on the opposite side, proportions go out of whack, or things just don't quite line up as they should (**Figure 9.8**).

The Optics Compensation effect is designed to mimic lens distortion. Increasing Field of View makes the affected layer more fish-eyed in appearance; the solution in this case is to apply that effect to the red rectangle layer. You can even remove fish-eye distortion (aka barrel distortion)

NOTES

If lens data is missing for a given plate, it is possible to derive it if the vanishing point and a couple of basic assumptions about scale can be determined. Check the book's disc for a demonstration of how to do this courtesy of fxphd.com.

TIP

An alternative to the listed steps, for those who like using expressions, is to use the following expression on the camera's Zoom property:

```
FocalLength = 35 //
change to your value,
in mm
hFilmPlane = 24.892 //
change to film size,
in mm (horizontal);
multiply values in
inches by 25.4
this_comp.width*(Focal
Length/hFilmPlane)
```

NOTES

Check out 09_lens_distort_correction on the book's disc to try this for yourself.

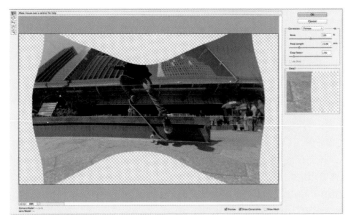

Figure 9.7 Compare this shot taken with a real wide-angle lens with the digital wide angle in Figure 9.3. The extreme curvature occurs because the lens has to be curved to gather the image; a computer has no lens or sensor and can gather the image linearly in any direction, so its distortion is linear. Photoshop CS6 can remove this curvature, but only one frame at a time.

Figure 9.8 The shot calls for the curb to be red, but a rectangular layer does not line up. Lens distortion is present in this shot.

by checking Reverse Lens Distortion and raising the Field of View (FOV) value, but the result is unnatural and the quantized pixels less aesthetically pleasing.

The setting is derived by eye, as follows:

Figure 9.9 The grid doesn't line up with the largely rectilinear background near the bottom and top of frame.

1. Having identified lens distortion (Figure 9.8), create a new solid layer called Grid. If you like, make it 10% to 20% larger than the source comp so that even when distorted, it reaches the edges of the frame.

2. Apply the Grid effect to the Grid layer. For a grid like the one in **Figure 9.9,** set Size From Width & Height and make the Width and Height settings equal, then give the grid the color of your choice.

3. Apply Optics Compensation and raise the FOV value until the grid lines up with the background. If necessary, rotate either the grid or the background image so that they are horizontally level with one another.

4. Note that the vertical lines don't match up, because the camera was tilted up when the shot was taken. Correct for this by making the Grid layer 3D and adjusting the X Orientation value (or X Rotation—these are interchangeable). **Figure 9.10** shows a matched grid.

5. Copy the Optics Compensation (and, if necessary, 3D rotation) settings to the foreground curb element and switch its blending mode to Color. It now conforms to the curb (**Figure 9.11**).

There's one unusual detail in this particular shot—study the distorted grid over the curb and notice that the curb curves away from it, as well as from the white lines out

Figure 9.10 Optics compensation is applied to the grid, which is also rotated in 3D to account for camera tilt (left). Even the shot from Figure 9.7 can be matched with the proper Optics Compensation setting (right).

Figure 9.11 The composited layer is distorted to match the curvature of the original background.

Camera Commands

A relatively recent addition in CS5.5, the Camera submenu (accessed either by context-clicking a camera layer or via the Layer menu) has some convenient, time-saving options.

Create Stereo 3D Rig, for stereo 3D creation, is discussed at length below. Create Orbit Null adds a null to which the camera is parented in place. Rotate this null and the camera pivots around it. Set Focus Distance to Layer with the camera and a selected layer automatically calculates the distance to that layer and can be keyframed. You can also link the two layers together with an expression using Link Focus Distance to Layer, which dynamically maintains focus over time. Link Focus to Point of Interest animates the point of interest to move from one area of the comp to another while maintaining focus around that point. Crank up the Aperture or Blur Level and you have pinpoint shallow focus for a dynamic scene.

TIP

If you are, in fact, creating a 3D logo in After Effects, one key new feature in CS6 is Layer > Create Shapes from Vector Layer, which allows you to start with an Illustrator or EPS file and end up with extruded 3D shapes that match it precisely.

in the street. The curb has a curve of its own in Z space, which we know for certain because we've corrected the lens distortion. You can freely edit the object for such details if necessary without compounding the problem by fighting lens distortion.

3D Layers Are Born

So you've heard that CS6 debuted fully three-dimensional layers in After Effects. It's exciting to know that within the fully three-dimensional world of an After Effects comp, the layers themselves are no longer completely flat; a text or shape can now be extruded. There is a cost in render time, but investing in a CUDA-enabled video card can cut down on that time by 10–20x or more.

A substantial number of After Effects artists have some access to other means (or a colleague) to create 3D objects using CINEMA 4D or Maya. Assuming that's the case, usage of ray-traced, extruded 3D objects in After Effects for visual effects composites may be limited; the most obvious thing you can do with extruded shapes is a flying logo.

Ray-Traced, Extruded 3D Fundamentals

The basic workflow to create a shape is simple once you know the rules. Make any layer 3D and a button appears at the upper right of the Composition panel, labeled Renderer. There are two modes in CS6: the familiar Classic 3D, and the new ray-traced 3D, which enables the extrusion features. Click the button and the Advanced tab of the Composition panel is opened for you to set the mode and adjust a few options associated with it (this is significant and will be explained later). The first time you select ray-traced 3D, you even get the rulebook (**Figure 9.12**).

Nothing changes until you extrude a text or shape layer, which is what the ray-traced 3D renderer allows you to do, revealing extra properties in these two types of layers. The additions include a whole new Geometry Options category. Raise Extrusion Depth and there you have it, an After Effects layer in full, glorious 3D.

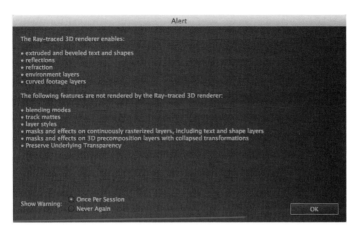

Figure 9.12 Why read this book when you can read this text-filled dialog with a concise list of the new renderer's capabilities and limitations? Is it because you never read the Read Me file either?

To paraphrase Henry Ford, you can have any mode you want as long as it's an extrusion. Forget about primitives such as sphere or cone; even the Legos depicted in this chapter are just a bunch of extruded layers grouped together in a subcomp and continuously rasterized (**Figure 9.13**).

There are also rudimentary options to improve upon the initial look of an extruded layer:

▶ **Bevels** that can make edges and corners appear more natural by reflecting light at an angle that you determine.

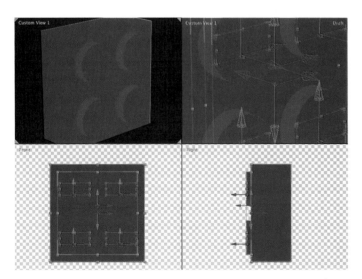

Figure 9.13 If you can build your model out of extrusions, you can build it in After Effects. Then leave it in its own subcomp with continuous rasterization enabled, so that the whole model can be manipulated as a single layer.

Figure 9.14 A good environment map does not have to look like an actual environment, but it should have the proper color and variation throughout, to avoid dead spots when reflected by a surface.

► **Lights** that create shading and, optionally, shadows.

► **Shadow Catcher** layers that are designed to add a shadow from a virtual object to a photographed surface. They are actually just solids with specific settings that cause only a shadow to be visible on them.

► An **Environment** layer that gives reflection layers something to reflect. You merely need to add it to a scene to do its work; although it should have the color and contrast range of the background, it is often best when somewhat abstract and full of detail (**Figure 9.14**).

► Additional **Material Options** that add Reflection, Refraction, and Transparency settings.

► Ray-traced 3D Renderer Options.

In a nutshell, you can create smooth metal, plastic, or glass surfaces. There are no presets for these, but Adobe does provide CS6MaterialProject.aep (on the disc and downloadable from Adobe Exchange), which has a dozen or so surface types. To use these, select one of the 3D objects, press **UU** to reveal all adjusted properties, highlight these by multiselecting them, copy, and paste to your own layer.

If you are among the few who carefully read that dialog in Figure 9.12, you know that a ray-traced comp has limitations beyond slower renders. The features you'll miss the most?

► **Blending modes**: the only way to apply one of these to an extruded 3D layer is to precomp it and *not* enable continuous rasterization, which is like pre-rendering it.

► **Effects, masks, or track mattes** cannot be applied directly to a ray-traced 3D layer either.

It's a trade-off, to say the least. And that's before we even talk about the speed.

Performance Anxiety

So you've set up your ray-traced scene to look just the way you want, and it's time to put things in motion. This is where, on even the most smokin' system, you rely on the Fast Previews options (). Everything in this menu becomes significant.

Five options are listed in order, and you can look at the list as slowest to fastest, or best to worst quality. The first two

TIP

One option to keep in your back pocket with ray-traced 3D is that it also lets you add curvature to any standard 3D footage layer or solid.

are way slower than the other three, because they fully ray-trace the scene. The difference between them is that Adaptive Resolution will render faster if resolution is set to half or lower, while Off (Final Quality) is always full resolution.

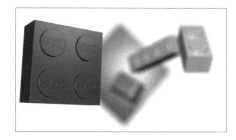

Before we talk about the other options, the bottom of the menu provides a separate control that has a huge influence on the speed and quality of a ray-traced scene. Choose Renderer Options from this menu, and check out the Ray-tracing Quality setting. This controls how many rays pass through a pixel. At the default of 3, there is graininess in the soft and shaded areas of the scene, and steppiness in the motion blur (**Figure 9.15**). This is too low a setting for a final render, but it will make the shaded scene much faster, so it's a decent working setting when you need to see reflections, translucency, and refraction look right.

Figure 9.15 Depth of field (shown here), motion blur, or just ordinary shading breaks up at a low Ray-tracing Quality of 3. Figure 9.3 is the same frame with a setting of 8.

You don't want to use these options while working unless you really care only about render quality; for animation they will bog you down. Wireframes shouldn't generally be necessary, but if you do use them, choose Fast Previews in Preferences and ensure that Show Internal Wireframes is checked. On the Fast Preview menu, that leaves the actual fast previews: Fast Draft, which lives up to its name but lacks even so much as specularity, and Draft, which looks a bit better but is really a bit neither/nor, if we're talking good and fast.

TIP

At render time, set Ray-tracing Quality to at least 8, and look for artifacts. In a scene with a lot of motion, detail, depth of field, and so on, you might need to go higher, to 11 or 12, for a clean result—and that will slow things down significantly. The anti-aliasing filter is at your discretion for edge appearance.

The big variable is inside your system. A CUDA-enabled NVIDIA graphics card is essential to gain maximum render performance at full quality. Ray-tracing calculates many times faster on these GPUs than on an unequipped system that must instead rely on the core processor alone. The visual result looks no different, but on a system without CUDA, like the MacBook Pro with an ATI card on which I type this text, you'll hear the fan get going immediately.

NOTES

Just as this book went to press, Element 3D was released by Video Copilot. Nominally a 3D particle system, this plug-in actually provides the means to import, animate, and texture 3D objects directly in After Effects. It offers no ray-tracing but will run with plain OpenGL, without the CUDA requirement.

Why is this the case? Betting on the GPU is choosing the favorite in the speed race; display processors have far exceeded Moore's Law for the past several years, and continue to do so, while CPUs have not. In a few years, the decision may look prescient, but for now, it leaves some otherwise speedy systems out in the cold.

Bear a CUDA

After Effects CS6 marks the sudden wake-up of GPU handling in the app, which in the past has tended to disappoint the owners of fancy dedicated graphics cards. Specific CUDA-certified cards, all of which currently are manufactured by NVIDIA, have gone from largely irrelevant to completely vital if you want anything like speedy render performance with even a modest ray-traced scene.

Wondering if you're invited to this party? Preferences > Previews has a GPU Information button that tells you the amount of memory and, more importantly, whether a CUDA GPU is available for rendering (**Figure 9.16**)

The list of certified cards includes a mixture of high-end (Quadro and Tesla) and low-end (GeForce) cards, mostly manufactured after 2010. There is a list of certified cards that Adobe has tested, and it does change and is even hackable. So if you like to run with the wolves, it is suggested you Google something like "After Effects CUDA hack"—you didn't think this book would advocate this kind of thing with a step-by-step, did you?

(a)

(b)

Figure 9.16 Got CUDA? This window tells you whether you do **(a)** or don't **(b)**, along with specifics about usable memory on the card.

Stereoscopic 3D Integration

Whether or not you still buy the hype on stereo 3D, you may need to deliver the 3D experience from After Effects. The application has been used to create stereographic 3D images since version 1.0 (ask Tim Sassoon), without much in the way of features to accommodate a dual-image pipeline. Do I sound like a crotchety grandpa complaining about you kids with your Ocula and your circular polarization?

I've worked on a few stereo 3D features using After Effects, from the trial-by-fire that was *Spy Kids 3D* to *Avatar*, which came with its own user guide. The pipeline we used for right and left channel on the former movie, which predates the current stereo craze kicked off by the latter, was one of our own devising. Since there was no built-in, automatic way to preview in stereo, we would just create the stereo preview with channel adjustments and blending modes. Where possible, we would use a pair of 3D cameras for the left and right images, and in other cases, we used expressions to tie together edits made to both channels.

Now After Effects does throw a bone or two in the direction of anyone looking for an easier time compositing for the output of left and right images. If you have no experience compositing in 3D, getting familiar with this process will also teach you a few things about how stereo compositing works.

Stereo Setup

To give it a whirl, begin with a 3D scene—it needs layers staggered in Z depth and preferable motion of the camera or elements. If you have a camera with animation, you can begin with that, provided it is set as a Two-Node Camera in Camera Settings. The example 3D.aep scene contains Z depth, visible with Custom View (**Figure 9.17**). Preview the scene without stereo to familiarize yourself with how it looks.

Select the camera layer, and choose Layer > Camera > Create Stereo 3D Rig. What just happened? Where there was one composition in the Timeline panel there are now four, and a preview of the 3D scene is displayed. This comp itself contains unfamiliar layers and controls.

NOTES

Too lazy to create a camera? Create Stereo 3D Rig makes you one with default settings, so nothing about the look of the scene itself changes.

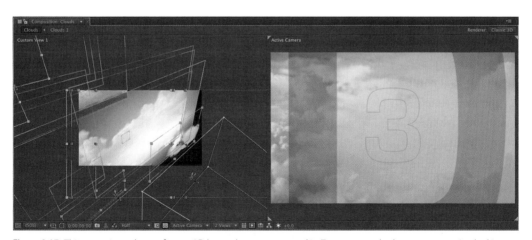

Figure 9.17 This scene is made up of many 3D layers that are staggered in Z space, not a bad way to create nice-looking billowy clouds even if you don't need to display them in stereo.

Click on the tab with the name of the original timeline and note that the source looks the same, but where there was one camera layer (or none) are now three. The two extra cameras are labeled Left Preview Cam and—wait for it—Right Preview Cam. Labels attached to these layers explain that the left and right views are "for preview and instructional purposes only."

Select the Left Preview Cam layer as an example and type **EE**—two **E**s in rapid succession—to reveal all of the expressions that link this camera to the other comps that were created when you initiated the rig. This is the basic way you now work in 3D in After Effects; it's automated so you don't have to make up those expressions and controllers yourself, and then organized into precomps for left and right view.

Use **Shift+ESC** to return to the Clouds Stereo 3D timeline, and select the Stereo 3D Controls. In the Effect Controls, Stereo 3D Controls affect the actual position and orientation of the cameras, while 3D Glasses influence how the shot is previewed in this comp only.

Any change to the Stereo 3D Controls effect links to the cameras in the subcomps via the expressions that you just glimpsed in the main comp. The Left Eye and Right Eye layers are turned off and locked, with their images used by the 3D Glasses effect to display the stereo preview. Put on your 3D glasses and take a look.

That leaves two other comps that were created for the Left Eye and Right Eye views. Each also contains a corresponding 3D camera with expressions. These two are the comps to render when everything is final, unless you are creating the single-frame stereo master, in which case you can use the 3D Glasses output. That's not how it's done professionally; left and right are generally rendered as regular 2D images in full color and combined separately.

Behold, Anaglyph

By default, the 3D Glasses effect displays *anaglyph* view, a slightly exotic sounding name that actually indicates you can view the scene with those paper red and blue glasses, the cheapest and most accessible way to view 3D on a 2D

Figure 9.18 In anaglyph view, it's clear that the clouds resolve fine, but the foreground letter D is too heavily separated due its position in the extreme foreground.

monitor (**Figure 9.18**). This view ruins color—pure red or blue are off-limits—but it will work with paper glasses on your regular display.

To make use of one of the other 3D View options provided in the 3D View menu, you need some special display equipment (**Figure 9.19**). The top set of options (above the first break in the list) contains views used by dedicated 3D display systems to view with passive polarized or active-scanning 3D glasses. Polarization reduces the brightness of the scene a full stop, but it doesn't otherwise corrupt the chromaticity of the image.

The rest of the 3D Glasses aren't often used: Scene Convergence is a temporary correction (the Convergence Options under Stereo 3D Controls move the cameras); Vertical

TIP

Balanced Red Blue LR effectively makes the scene monochromatic, but provides the maximum contrast on each color channel.

Figure 9.19 Some 3D hardware systems can take an interlaced stereo image created by the 3D Glasses effect such as this one, set in the 3D View menu, and make it viewable with polarized or active-scanning glasses.

Preview on a 3D Monitor

Although displaying 3D images on your computer hardware requires specialized hardware, 3D monitors intended for television display are able to pull in 3D via the HDMI cable for your viewing pleasure.

1. Connect the 3D TV to your computer using an HDMI cable (to DVI if your computer doesn't have HDMI).

2. Create a 3D composition in After Effects, make sure the composition size matches the current resolution of your output monitor, then Create Stereo 3D Rig.

3. Create a new comp viewer of your outputted Stereo 3D comp, lock it, and drag it onto your 3D monitor.

4. Make sure the viewer zoom value is set to 100%.

5. Click **Ctrl**+\ (**Opt**+\) (backslash in both) twice to full-screen the comp frame onto the 3D monitor. It should match the dimensions of the monitor exactly at this point.

6. Switch the 3D View in the 3D Glasses effect to Stereo Pair, Over Under, or Interlaced.

7. Turn On 3D mode for your 3D TV and match the format to what you set in 3D Glasses 3D View (Stereo Pair and Over Under are supported on most 3D TVs).

8. Put on your glasses and you should be able to edit your comp in true Stereo 3D.

Alignment is only necessary if the two cameras are somehow off axis; and of course Swap Left-Right is there just in case the scene is backward, which happens. The Balance control is useful with the Balanced 3D Views to deemphasize color and strengthen the 3D effect (or vice versa, of course).

Stereo 3D Convergence

The default orientation of the 3D cameras created by After Effects is parallel—both cameras point in the same direction. Generally speaking, you will want to go into Convergence Options and toggle Converge Cameras on in order to toe-in the camera angles, as your eyes do in the real world. The convergence point is the Z depth at which the views of the two cameras crosscross, as you can clearly see by selecting left and right in the source composition and switching to the Top view (**Figure 9.20**).

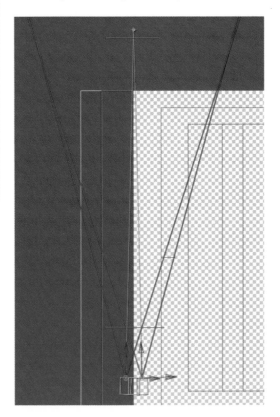

Figure 9.20 The cameras are converged on a single point, matching the way that human vision behaves when focused on a given distance.

Converging cameras a particular distance from the camera re-creates a phenomenon of binocular vision. When you focus on an object at a given distance, your eyes converge on it (so if you try and focus on the tip of your nose, you go cross-eyed). If the convergence point is far in the distance, it makes it difficult to resolve (see) objects in the near foreground, just as in a movie theater it's hard to see the screen when you're looking at someone seated in front of you. A close convergence point likewise makes it impossible to simultaneously view the infinite distance.

There are a couple of ways to adjust or even animate the convergence point. By default it converges to the Camera Point of Interest, but you can instead choose the Zoom Distance (which can be linked to the Point of Interest under Layer > Camera > Link Focus Distance to Point of Interest). You can also use the camera's position, after which you would presumably adjust the Convergence Z offset to specify a distance from the center of the camera; a 0.0 offset fails to resolve the scene.

The 3D movies I've worked on have chosen one or the other source camera as the "hero," the one used for 2D presentation. Robert Rodriguez uses the Left camera, James Cameron the Right. Michael Bay tends to use neither and to have his 3D created from scratch using clean plates from a single view. In After Effects, the two cameras are arrayed equidistant to either side of a single view.

Adjusting stereo scene depth actually repositions one or both stereo cameras, changing what is more commonly called the *interaxial distance* between the cameras. The default is chosen to more or less match the distance between human eyes, but there is some debate as to the perfect setting; it is, however, unlikely that you will adjust this other than in small fractions.

Copious Caveats

Even if all of your source elements are After Effects 3D layers, not all of them play along with this pipeline. In the example scene, camera depth of field and motion blur pass down properly through the pipeline, but lights and collapsed subcomps containing 3D layers do not. The

NOTES

The 6.5 cm distance between an average set of human eyes is too short for most bulky cameras, hence the use of a mirror to angle the second camera. Virtual elements created in Maya with this distance can use the expression value*(100.0 * 6.5 / thisComp.width) in the Stereo Scene Depth property in order to work in units that match, since Maya uses metric measurements.

only way to recover these is to cut them out of the source layer and drop them into the Left and Right Eye comps, where you then lose the benefit of controlling them from their original location—not to mention any other pipeline ordering that might have led you to create a subcomp in the first place. There are of course work-arounds involving the use of expressions.

And what about incorporating a 3D source from a 3D camera rig or 3D software rendering in stereo? You can simply drop the left and right eye views into the corresponding Left Eye and Right Eye comps, but they too won't respond to adjustments made with Stereo 3D Controls without a simple set of expressions.

With 3D footage placed into the left and right views, try the following:

1. Create a Slider Control by applying that effect on the Stereo 3D Controls layer.

2. Rename it Footage Offset.

3. Click the lock icon for the Effect Controls.

4. Open the Left Eye timeline.

5. Highlight the Position property for the footage layer and choose Animation > Separate Dimensions.

6. Set an expression for the resulting X Position Property by **Alt**-clicking (**Opt**-clicking) on its stopwatch icon.

7. Click at the end of the resulting expression to insert a cursor, and type a plus sign (+), then pick whip to the Footage Offset property displayed in the locked Effect Controls. Complete the expression by adding /100*width and clicking **Enter** (**Return**).

8. Go back to step 4 and do the same steps for the Right Eye timeline. In step 7, type a minus sign (–) after the default expression instead of a plus sign (+).

Now the Footage Offset expression can be used to adjust separation of the imported source layers independent of the rest of the comp.

The biggest challenge that is unmet by the current implementation of 3D in After Effects is any situation in which you need to alter convergence on imported footage. To do so is to mess with parallax and thus to reveal areas behind foreground objects that were previously concealed. Although Adobe has fantastic technology in Warp Stabilizer and Roto Brush, which could theoretically be used to create a tool like The Foundry's Ocula plug-in for Nuke, no such solution exists.

Stereo Render

To reemphasize a previous point, Stereo 3D comp is great for previewing and rendering a preview comp, but the two comps upstream from that one, marked Left Eye and Right Eye, are the ones you render for professional output. These comps reflect any adjustments made in the source comp, even after the Stereo Rig was created, as well as any adjustments to the Stereo 3D Controls.

You can double-check that everything looks okay by going to a hero frame, taking a snapshot from one of the views (**Shift**+**F5**), going to the same frame in the other eye, and toggling the view (**F5**). You'll notice the shift in perspective from left to right; if it's correct and convergence is on, it will typically look as though the whole scene is on a turntable, pivoting around the convergence point (counterclockwise from left to right).

The Camera Tells the Story

Locked-off shots are essential to signature shots by Welles, Hitchcock, Kubrick, and Lucas, among others, but these days they are the exception rather than the norm. Beginning in the 1970s, the neutral view of the static shot and the God-like perspective of the sweeping crane shot were no longer the only options, as the human documentary point of view of the handheld shot along with its smoother cousin, the steadicam, came to the fore.

In the bad old days of optical compositing, it was scarcely possible to composite anything but a static camera point of view. Nowadays, most directors aren't satisfied being limited to locked-off shots, yet the decision to move the camera might not happen on set, or it might have to be altered in postproduction.

Figure 9.21 Prominent though it may appear in this still image, the audience isn't focused on that San Francisco skyline outside the window. There's no multiplaning as the camera moves because the background skyline is a still image, but no one notices because viewer attention is on the foreground character. (Image courtesy of The Orphanage.)

TIP

Always keep in mind where the audience's attention is focused in order to best make use of the magician's technique—misdirection. If you're worried about a detail that is so obscure that the only way the audience would notice it is if they're bored with the story, your project has problems you'll never solve single-handedly!

It's helpful to create a rough assemble with camera animation as early in the process of creating your shot as possible, because it will tell you a lot about what you can get away with and what needs dedicated attention. The "Sky Replacement" section in Chapter 13 contains an example in which a flat card stands in for a fully dimensional skyline (**Figure 9.21**). The audience is focused on watching the lead character walk through the lobby, wondering what he has in his briefcase.

Camera Animation

The most common confusion about the After Effects camera stems from the fact that, by default, it includes a *point of interest*, a point in 3D space at which the camera always points, for auto-orientation. The point of interest is *fully optional*, and the toggle resides right in the Camera Settings.

A single-node camera is just like the ones we use in the real world, and thus is the one I find most useful and intuitive. For cases where you truly want the camera to orient around a point, the two-node camera's Point of Interest property can even be linked to that point with an expression (and the pick whip for a moving target).

The main problem with the two-node camera, besides that it has no direct equivalent in the physical world, is that it becomes cumbersome to animate a camera move that involves both the camera and its point of interest. To transform the camera and its point of interest together, don't attempt to match keyframes for the two properties—this is sheer madness! Parent the camera to a null and translate that instead. This can help with the other surprise about the auto-oriented two-node camera: that it always maintains an upright position. Cross over the X/Y plane above the center, and the camera flips unless you do so via a parented null (or just use a one-node camera).

The Y axis is upside-down in After Effects 3D, just as in 2D; an increased Y value moves a layer downward.

You can even orient the camera along its motion path, so that it maintains tangency (rotating in the direction it travels). For that, use the toggle in Layer > Transform > Auto Orient. You are still free to rotate a camera that is auto-oriented, but it usually gets a little hairy, since any change to a position keyframe changes the rotation, too.

The preceding points come into play only with more elaborate camera animations; more modest use of the 3D camera, such as a simple camera push, raises other more aesthetic questions.

TIP

The Unified Camera tool (**C**) lets you use a three-button mouse to orbit, track, and zoom the camera without having to cycle through the tools. The better your graphics card, the snappier this tool will be.

Push and Zoom

A camera *push* moves the camera closer to the subject; a *zoom* lengthens the lens, reframing the shot to be closer up while the camera remains stationary. **Figure 9.22** demonstrates the difference in perspective, which is just as noticeable with multiple 3D elements in After Effects as with objects in the real world. The zoom has a more extreme effect on the foreground/background composition of the shot and calls more attention to the camera itself. Zooming is most appropriate to reality or documentary shooting, as

Figure 9.22 Frame a similar shot with a long (left) and wide (right) lens and you see the difference between a zoom and a push. A zoomed image has a flattened perspective.

it makes the viewer aware of the camera operator reframing the shot. In a push, the point of view moves naturally through the space as a human (or other nonmechanical) view would.

Dramatic zooms for the most part had their heyday in 1960s-era Sergio Leone movies and have since declined dramatically in popularity, although they also re-create the live documentary feel of a camera operator reaching quickly for a shot. And that's really the point; because your eye does not zoom, this move calls attention to the camera apparatus itself, and to the camera operator. Its use is therefore limited.

The push, on the other hand, is a dramatic staple. The question when creating one in After Effects is whether it require a 3D camera when you can simply scale 2D layers?

Scaling a 2D layer (or several, parented to a null) works for a small move. However, to re-create progression through Z space, scaling is linear when it should be logarithmic—halve the distance from the camera to an object and it does not merely appear at twice its former size. A 3D camera move creates the proper scale difference naturally, making it simple to add eases, stops, and starts, a little bit of destabilization—whatever works, as if with an actual camera.

Natural camera motion contains keyframe eases (Chapter 2) for the human aspect. A little bit of irregularity lends the feeling of a camera operator's individual personality (**Figure 9.23**), or even dramatic interest (hesitation, caution, intrigue, a leap forward—the possibilities are many).

Lack of perspective can easily cause a move in or out of a completely 2D shot to look wrong. Likewise, all but the subtlest tracking and panning shots, crane-ups, and other more elaborate camera moves blow the 2.5D gag. Certain types of elements—soft, translucent organic shapes, such as clouds, fog, smoke, and the like—can be layered together and staggered in 3D space, fooling the eye into seeing 3D volume. Chapter 13 gives details.

NOTES

Animation > Keyframe Assistant > Exponential Scale is the old-school, pre-3D way to fake the illusion of a camera move on a 2D layer. There is no good reason to employ this feature when you can instead animate a 3D camera.

TIP

Do you have a bunch of coplanar layers you're making 3D just so you can push in on them? Precomp them together first to avoid little rounding errors that can easily occur where they overlap in 3D.

NOTES

For this example, check out 09_camera_projection_basic on the disc, or try 09_camera_projection_advanced for the more complicated setup from previous editions.

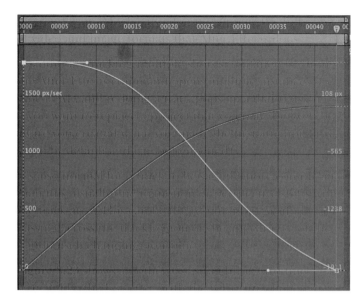

Figure 9.23 The Graph Editor shows where you've created organic motion in ease curves, although the smoothness of this camera push as it eases to a stop may itself lack that extra human imperfection, which would also show up in the curves.

Camera Projection

Camera projection (also sometimes called *camera mapping*, which is in fact a separate endeavor) begins with a still photo or locked-off (stabilized) moving image. Imagine this image to be a slide, projected onto three-dimensional blank surfaces that match the position of planes in the image. As you move around, the projection holds its place on the surfaces, providing the illusion of depth and perspective—right up until the illusion breaks by going too far and revealing missing or stretched textures.

Why do this? There are situations in which you simply can't crane or track the camera—for example, across the open water of McCovey Cove (**Figure 9.24**). As we have seen already in this chapter, a simple zoom (whether done

Figure 9.24 The difference between a simple reframe of the shot (left), which is a lot like a zoom (center), and a camera projection move, which is more like a dolly shot across the water (right), is not entirely subtle. The water surface appears soft in the projection because it is effectively scaled dramatically by the camera move.

with a camera or by scaling an image) merely reframes the image, completely ignoring the magic of parallax that indicates depth even without stereo.

A helicopter or possibly a very large crane can cross an open body of water, but expensively and not without disruption. For an infinitely lower price, you can plant the tripod you already own on the shore, take a locked-off plate like the one provided, and project the scene to animate it yourself (**Figure 9.25**).

Figure 9.25 It's easier to see what's really happening here in Perspective view: The water, the waterfront wall, and the stadium each have their own individual layer.

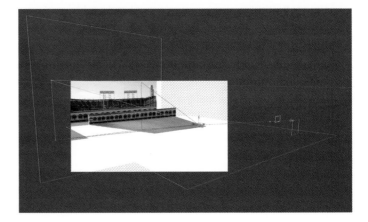

How is it that the one "texture" (the photo) sticks to the 3D objects? The steps to projecting any still image into 3D space are as follows:

1. Begin with an image that can be modeled as a series of planes. In this case, the water and stadium are at least two planes, but there is also the option of separating the front wall from the rest of the stadium, and even the sky and background skyscraper from that for a total of four or five planes. The more easily definable planes you can add, the more perspective you can derive.

2. Create a white solid for the first dimensional plane in the image, the background. Enable 3D, and under Material Options, change Accepts Lights to Off.

3. Add a camera named Projection Cam. If you know the Angle of View of your source image, add that value (but if you don't, it's not necessarily a big deal).

4. Add a Point light called Projector Light. Set its position to that of Projection Cam, then parent it to Projection Cam. Set Casts Shadows to On.

5. Duplicate the source image, naming this layer slide. Enable 3D, and in Material Options, change Casts Shadows to Only and Light Transmission to 100%.

6. Slide not located properly? Add a null object called Slide Repo; set its position to that of Projection Cam, and parent it to Projection Cam. Now parent your slide layer to it, and adjust its scale downward until the image is cast onto the white planes, as if projected.

   This much can be done for you by the CameraProjectionSetup script, other than specifying any unusual Angle of View (from step 3).

7. Now it's time to do a little—very little—3D modeling.

   The backing plane is already set, although it will be further edited, but the first layer to add is the ground plane. You can simply duplicate and rename the solid Plane, then enable multiple views to make it easy to rotate it 90 degrees, and move it down and outward until it lines up with the edge of the water against the dock.

   Having done that, I recommend at least one further breakdown. Duplicate the backing plane and name it wall. Create a masked shape around the low wall above the water on the backing plane. Move the other layer (in the original position with no masks) back in Z space, say 1000 pixels. Your setup should now begin to look something like that in Figure 9.19.

8. With a more complicated setup, if planes that you know to be at perpendicular 90-degree angles don't line up, adjust the Zoom value of the Projection Cam, scaling the model and slide as needed.

9. Once everything is lined up, duplicate and disable Projection Cam, and rename the duplicate Anim Cam. Freely move this camera around the scene.

A simple move forward across the water reveals a flaw: The top of the wall was doubled as the camera moved closer to

TIP

If a projected image looks softer than it should with the Classic 3D Renderer, go into the Advanced tab of Composition Settings, click Options, and change Shadow Map Resolution to at least double the frame size.

TIP

You can project an image onto an extruded shape if there is a box or column in your scene, using the same basic means. To do so requires use of the ray-traced 3D renderer, but the rest of the settings are the same.

Included on the disc in the Scripts folder is the rd_CameraProjectionSetup.jsx file, which is a script that Jeff Almasol and I designed to accomplish the basic camera projection setup automatically.

Projection (http://aescripts.com/projection/) is a script cleverly designed by Ben Rollason that does actual camera mapping, yielding a solid with a surface mapped to it that can be touched up and tracked into a scene.

it. A simple move downward, closer to the surface of the water, not only solves this problem, it also makes the effect of crossing the water more compelling.

There's no need to stop here. The bland, blue sky is just begging to be replaced, and that skyscraper to the right of frame could also use a plane of its own. Each of these presents a challenge: You need to mask or paint out the flag covering the building (I would just remove it) so it doesn't travel with the building. The sky can be keyed out, but you should do that in a precomp since you can't easily apply the matte to a projection.

You can freely add elements to the 3D environment of a camera-projected or camera-mapped scene. Here, a logo could hover over the water, or Godzilla could lumber along right field, properly positioned in XYZ space.

Focal Depth and *Bokeh* Blur

You may already be well aware that shallow depth of field is more than an occasionally an aesthetic trick in feature cinematography. Whole films are made up predominantly of shots that artfully focus your attention on the drama by keeping the camera's focal depth shallow, so that only objects within inches of the focal point of the scene are crisp and clear. The rest of the scene takes on abstract characteristics that can't be recreated simply by an ordinary blur. What is going on to create such a clear focal point for the drama?

With a real camera, particularly one with a large sensor such as a DSLR (or other APS-C or larger) format, you can both direct the viewer's attention and create a beautiful image with the use of shallow depth of field, whereby objects at a certain distance are in full focus, but those in the foreground and background appear soft and blurred.

The standard consumer video camera—a handicam, not a DSLR—has fairly limitless depth of field under normal shooting conditions, which can be seen as an advantage or a limitation. Shallow focal depth not only produces an image one would almost automatically call "cinematic," it tells the audience where to look, providing the director with a powerful storytelling tool.

Not everyone subscribes to this aesthetic, of course: Orson Welles and his cinematographer Gregg Toland invented their own camera to increase the focal depth of shots in *Citizen Kane* to the maximum possible amount. But even a casual look at cinema and dramatic television today reveals that they were going against the prevailing trend. You'll see a lot of beautiful shots with very shallow depth of field.

Limited focal range is a natural part of human vision. Camera lenses contribute their own unique blur characteristics that in the contemporary era are considered aesthetically pleasing the world over—particularly in Japan, where the term *boke* (literally meaning "fuzzy" and more commonly spelled *bokeh*) was coined to describe the quality of out-of-focus light as viewed through a lens.

A perfectly formed lens passes a defocused point of light to the back of the camera as a soft, spherical blur. A bright point remains bright but is enlarged and softened in the process (**Figure 9.26**).

A computer typically blurs an image by blending a pixel with neighboring pixels, but a defocused camera lens—or even your unfocused eye—creates blur artifacts that are the result of light passing through the lens, with more complicated associated physics.

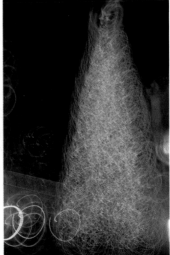

Figure 9.26 The strange yet entirely natural results of points of illumination shot out of focus with an open shutter are shown here. These images are all straight from the camera. Notice how different the result is from what you would get by blurring a sharp version of the same image.

Most camera lenses are not perfect, so instead of perfect blurred spheres, bokeh spheres may be brighter toward the edges than in the middle. An anamorphic lens will show squashed spheres, and as with lens flares, the shape of the aperture itself may be visible in the circles, making them hexagonal (or pentagonal, and so on, depending on the number of blades in the opening). Believe it or not, if you skip this level of detail, the result is far less likely to resonate even with the casual viewer. "I don't know bokeh, but I know what I like."

Specific depth-of-field effects such as these can be freely recreated in After Effects, using either the After Effects camera or the new Camera Lens Blur effect. Either of these handily outperforms the third-party options that used to be necessary, by making full use of the system's graphics processing unit.

A solid description of bokeh with links lives on the Web at http://en.wikipedia.org/wiki/Bokeh.

3D Compositing and Focal Depth

Suppose that you have a composition with 3D layers arrayed in Z space. Simply by enabling Depth of Field for the active 3D camera layer and dialing up the Aperture setting to taste, what is revealed is a focal blur that behaves much more like an actual defocused camera. Tune the lighting, iris shape, threshold, and saturation, and you can match some of the abstract characteristics of soft focus that are visible in Figure 9.26.

It wasn't always like this. Previous versions of the After Effects camera used an ordinary kernel blur. The softer the shot, the more things would generally become muddy and gray. But that's not really anything like the result with an actual camera, which boosts and blooms highlights.

The project 09_rack_focus.aep from this book's disc contains a simple foreground/background setup with a rack focus effect that was created with the CS4 version of the After Effects camera. Simply by opening this project, you begin with a better-looking image that can then be tuned.

Open the rackFocus no expressions composition and preview it. The camera settings here are near the defaults. Depth of Field is disabled by default, but here it has already been enabled, as can be seen by twirling down the rack cam layer settings. The Aperture setting of 200.0 is already plenty high enough to create soft focus, and everything else is still at the default. The two layers, foreground and background, are 700 pixels apart in Z space.

To create this rack focus effect from scratch:

1. In the composition called rackFocus no expressions, in 09_rack_focus.aep, either delete the existing rack cam layer or rename it rack cam old and choose Layer > New > Camera to create a camera from scratch.

2. Call this camera whatever you want—I chose "DOF cam" to make sure this isn't the same as the other one—and set it as a Two-Node Camera. Choose the 80 mm preset from the menu and, most importantly, make sure that Enable Depth of Field is checked (although you can always change this in the timeline).

3. The depth of field blur isn't too apparent yet; to see it clearly, twirl down the Camera Options under the layer you just created and raise the Aperture setting to something like 500.0. The background goes out of focus.

4. The rack focus shot should start focused on the background, so with the DOF cam layer selected, **Ctrl-click/Cmd-click** the cityBackground layer so both are selected, then choose Layer > Camera > Set Focus Distance to Layer (**Figure 9.27**).

5. Select just the DOF cam layer and press **UU** to reveal all properties that are not at the default. Click on the Focus Distance stopwatch that is revealed to set a keyframe at frame 0:00.

6. Use the **End** key to go to the final frame of the comp. This time, multiselect DOF cam and noSkateboards, the foreground image, and again choose Layer > Camera > Set Focus Distance to Layer. A keyframe is automatically set for Focus Distance.

7. Preview the rack focus animation. To see what's going on here, switch to the Top view with the same layers still selected and press the spacebar; you should see the plane of focus move from one layer to the other.

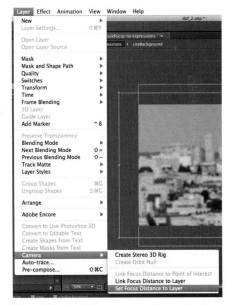

Figure 9.27 New Camera menu options include the ability to set focal distance to the distance between the camera and a selected layer. You can even choose Link Focus Distance to Layer if you have an animated target, and an expression will be set to update the setting dynamically.

8. Back in Active Camera view, you can improve on the look of the lens blur by twirling down all Camera Options and switching the Iris Shape to Octagon.

Fast Rectangle, the default Iris Shape, is meant for previewing purposes only. The difference made by switching to one of the polygon shapes is subtle here; a separate example will show this more clearly.

Narrow depth of field is created on a real camera by lowering the f-stop value, which lowers exposure as well. Not so with the After Effects 3D camera. Its Aperture and F-Stop settings (**Figure 9.28**) affect only focal depth, not exposure or motion blur, so raising aperture has no effect on the exposure of the scene, or any color data whatsoever.

Figure 9.28 Enable Depth of Field is checked in Camera Settings, activating Focus Distance (the distance in pixels of the focal point, which can be toggled to Lock to the Zoom). Raising Aperture lowers F-Stop, creating more blur without otherwise affecting the image; you can instead raise the Blur Level, even above 100%.

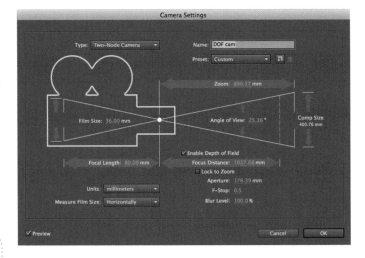

The two settings have an inverse relationship. F-stop is the term you might more likely hear as an industry standard, but it's Aperture that appears as a property in the Timeline panel. Raise Aperture and it's just like lowering the f-stop on a camera, widening the iris to create shallower depth of field.

Camera Lens Blur

You don't need to work in 3D in order to add soft focus effects; for compositing, a more likely need is to apply soft focus to a 2D footage layer or to an entire comp. The

NOTES

If you have a camera report that includes f-stop data, you can try starting with that value in Camera Settings (**Ctrl+Shift+Y/ Cmd+Shift+Y**, or double-click on the Camera in the Timeline panel) when matching existing footage. There are plenty of variables, such as pixel depth, that may necessitate changing this value, or you can rearrange objects in Z depth to look correct with that setting.

Camera Lens Blur effect can be applied directly to any layer (or adjustment layer) and contains the same controls that are found in the camera, plus the ability to create rack focus effects with the use of a 2D depth map.

On the disc and in this chapter's folder you'll find DOF_lensBlur_after.ae, which contains a comp with various focal settings that can be soloed and compared. Let's first try matching the Focus and Defocus layers.

1. Select the Focus layer and apply Camera Lens Blur. Because this is applied to the entire shot, be sure to check Repeat Edge Pixels.

2. Solo the Defocus layer and take a snapshot (**Shift**+F5, or use the Take Snapshot icon along the bottom of the comp viewer).

3. Unsolo Defocus so that Focus is displayed. With the Focus layer selected, apply the Camera Lens Blur effect.

4. Raise the Blur Radius to something like 12.0. You can check whether this is the proper amount of blur by toggling the snapshot (F5) and comparing the size of the *circles of confusion*—those big discs that bloom around the points of light.

5. Although it's not apparent here, when applying Camera Lens Blur to a full frame image, toggle Repeat Edge Pixels so that the blur goes all the way to the edges of the frame evenly.

6. The discs are clearly hexagonal shaped, but in the source they appear much more circular, so raise the Roundness value to 80% or higher.

7. Zoom in and compare the two images, and you may notice that the source circles are slightly narrower; to match these, you can lower Aspect Ratio to 0.9.

The main difference between the two images is all of the saturation in the highlights of the real focus; the circles appear amber and red, not white and pink. The Highlight controls affect how the highlights appear.

1. Boost Gain and Saturation to 100. It's Saturation we're after here, but this control is interdependent with Gain to have any effect.

   Even at this strongest setting, the saturation of the highlights is nothing like the real image.

2. Lower Threshold to have more highlights influenced by Gain and Saturation. Anything above this level of Threshold intensity is affected by the other two. Click and drag left on the value itself until you see a substantial change in the highlights.

   Clearly, the effect is not able to pull as much color out of the focused image as is present in the reference defocused image.

3. Apply a Vibrance effect and try raising both values to get more color into the highlights. Settings of 100.0 for Vibrance and 50.0 for Saturation makes the result more colorful, although the colors are completely different than the original (**Figure 9.29**).

Whatever you might think of this result, it's miles beyond what you might get with an ordinary kernel blur such as Gaussian Blur. On low-dynamic-range footage such as this,

(a)

(b)

Figure 9.29 Before bemoaning the fact that the colors don't match between the source image **(a)** and the one After Effects created with Camera Lens Blur **(b)**, notice how many things about the fabricated image do simulate the real-world optics. Compare this with a simple Gaussian Blur **(c)**.

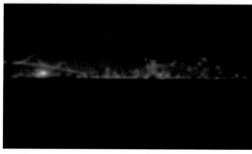

(c)

those types of blurs actually lower the intensity of the highlights when blurring them, making the result appear drab indeed.

Want to go even further? Try matching the Extreme source layer. This requires a blur radius more like 90.0, which, though slower than lower settings, is not the complete processor-killer that this effect has tended to be in third-party implementations.

Add a Blur Map

You aren't limited to blurring an entire layer, or slicing a comp into individual layers, in order to rack focus between them with a Camera Lens Blur animated on each. You can rack focus on a single 2D layer by adding a Blur Map layer.

A blur map generally has to be created specifically for a source layer. Depending on how complicated the scene is, it can require fairly intensive rotoscoping. When you rotoscope an image, you create an alpha channel that is white in the opaque areas and black where transparent. The gray levels create the subtle threshold between those extremes. A depth map is similar, but black and white signify the shallowest and deepest ends of the focal distance, and all of the gray levels are depth thresholds in between.

DOF_blurMap.aep contains a wide exterior source shot with a foreground, the rooftop, and a background. **Figure 9.31** shows a blur map that I created to match the depth of this image; it is made up of two layers, with a Ramp effect applied to each, and a mask applied to the foreground to match the rooftop area of the source shot.

Diffraction Fringe adds a bokeh characteristic you will sometimes see in source images, and one you might like to add to your own shots. It pushes intensity to the edges of the circles, creating rings around them. You can set it above 100.0 (**Figure 9.30**).

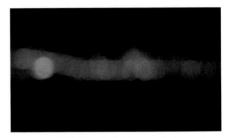

Figure 9.30 Bokeh is cranked to match the more heavily defocused lens. The rings around the edges of the circles are the result of a high Diffraction Fringe setting.

(a) (b) (c)

Figure 9.31 The depth map **(a)** signifies the distance of the 2D image with luminance values. White, in this case, corresponds to the areas of the rooftop closest to camera, and black to the infinite distance on the horizon. The break between them describes the difference between the edge of the rooftop and the buildings beyond. The result allows a rack focus from one **(b)** to the other **(c)**.

Figure 9.32 An image that is more or less made up of a flat plane stretching to the horizon allows you to use the simplest type of blur map.

The key with a depth map is to create a gradation between foreground and background: It's the gray areas that will provide a transition between extreme foreground and background, or the black and white areas of the depth map.

With an image that is essentially a flat plane, such as in **Figure 9.32**, you need only apply the default Ramp effect to a solid layer the size of the comp. Then precomp the layer with the effect applied, to instantly use the Blur Focal Distance setting to rack focus from foreground to background. You can even adjust the contrast of the map to help determine how abrupt the transition is from foreground to background.

It's even simple to roll your own postproduction tilt-shift lens effect using these same techniques. Real-world tilt-shift lenses (a prominent example of which was used for the boat race scene in *The Social Network*) are focused around one area of the frame, usually either the circular center or a single vertical or horizontal band of the frame.

1. Create a new composition containing the LV_timelapse.mov source shot. Timelapse shots of panoramic views such as this lend themselves particularly well to the Tilt Shift effect.

2. Create a solid layer called tilt/shift map.

3. Apply the Ramp effect.

4. Switch the Ramp Shape to a Radial Ramp.

5. Move the center of the Start Color (black) to the center of the Eiffel Tower in the image. If it helps, temporarily lower opacity so you can see both images.

6. Move the center of the End Color out to the left a bit to create a slightly more subtle gradation (**Figure 9.33**).

7. Precomp the map layer (making sure its opacity is back to 100%) with the Move All Attributes to the New Composition option checked.

8. Back in the main composition, turn off the tilt/shift map layers and apply Camera Lens Blur to the clip layer.

9. Choose the map layer under the Blur Map > Layer menu.

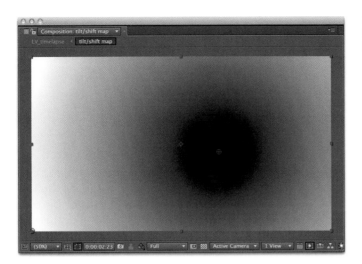

Figure 9.33 A Ramp effect set like this and precomped serves as the tilt/shift map.

10. Raise Blur Radius to 20.0.

11. Check Repeat Edge Pixels to get rid of the softness around the edges.

12. Apply the Levels Effect and raise Input Black and lower Input White to create heavy contrast and overexpose the image. Optionally, move Levels above Camera Lens Blur in the stack before the next step. Tilt Shift effects also seem to work best with high contrast and exposure.

13. Adjust Gain, Saturation, and Threshold to taste, along with any adjustments to the Iris settings.

Et voilà, the effect is complete—or as a friend remarked when I posted this image on Facebook, "it's a small world after all" (**Figure 9.34**).

Figure 9.34 Tilt Shift lens effects can be created with an actual lens designed to keep only a specific area of frame in focus; here the effect is re-created simply using built-in plug-ins included in After Effects.

Fix Blur Map Edges

Simple gradient-based blurs use types of maps that are easy to create. A more complex scene demands that each individual figure in Z space have its own proportional shade of gray. You don't want edge thresholds as you would with a good alpha channel, but rather sharp, pixel-accurate definitions around objects.

Even with crisp, precise roto in a blur map, any object that you isolate will display some edge artifacts with a blur applied using that map. The difficulty is that those edge pixels have to blur with a background that is actually behind the subject, and since we don't have those magic cameras that the Blade Runner predicted we'd be using by now, the foreground becomes contaminated with background colors that bleed in. For a scene with a high-contrast foreground and background, you will be compelled to create a clean plate of the background. This often can be done without too much trouble using Rotobrush, although the following technique also works with roto you create yourself.

Select a foreground item with Rotobrush if you're in a hurry, or with articulated roto as needed. If you have a good selection, check Refine Matte—or if working with your own roto instead of Rotobrush, apply the Refine Matte effect—and under Decontamination, use the Increase Decontamination Radius setting to bleed more of the background inside those foreground edges. For the background, invert foreground and background (there's a check box in the Rotobrush effect) and again increase the radius. The extra pixels created are more than good enough to use for blurring purposes, but the setup is now more complicated than a simple rack focus, because you have to apply it to both layers. You can use the pick whip to link Blur Focal Distance for both layers.

Bokeh and You

Study contemporary films that you like and you'll find all kinds of abstractions that appear in a live-action movie that incorporate shallow depth-of-field. Whether in a documentary or some visionary fantasy, otherwise ordinary backgrounds are completely transformed by soft focus. Not only can they look fantastic (depending on how fond you are of this look), but they also psychologically move the defocused area out of the viewer's conscious attention. A defocused background can be both lovelier and less distracting than one in sharp focus.

Note, finally, that although this type of blur has tended to extract a high price in render cycles, Camera Lens Blur is relatively tolerable even in high definition at high blur or aperture settings.

Don't Forget Grain

Once the image passes through the camera lens and is recorded, it takes on another characteristic of motion pictures: grain. Grain is essentially high-frequency noise readily apparent in each channel of most recorded footage, although progress in image-gathering technology has led to a gradual reduction of grain. Digitally produced animations such as Pixar movies have no native grain at all, save when the story calls for a deliberate re-creation of archival footage, as in the opening scenes of *The Incredibles*.

Grain can, however, be your friend, subtly adding life to a static background or camouflaging foreground edge detail. It is not simply switched on or off, but requires careful per-channel adjustment. There are two basic factors to consider:

▶ size of the grain, per channel

▶ amount of grain, or amount of contrast in the grain, per channel

The emphasis here is that these factors typically vary from channel to channel. Blue is almost universally the channel likeliest to have the most noise; happily, the human eye is less sensitive to blue than to red or green.

How much grain is enough? As with color in Chapter 5, the goal is typically to match what's already there. If your shot has a background plate with the proper amount of grain in it, match foreground elements to that. A computer-generated still or scene might have to be grain-matched to surrounding shots.

Excessive grain is often triggered by a low amount of scene light combined with a higher effective ASA, particularly with lower-quality image sensors.

Try grain matching for yourself with the material in the 09_grain_match folder.

Grain Management Strategies

After Effects includes a suite of three tools for automated grain sampling, grain reduction, and grain generation: Add Grain, Match Grain, and Remove Grain. Add Grain relies on your settings only, but Match Grain and Remove Grain can generate initial settings by sampling a source layer for grain patterns.

I don't always recommend the automated solution, but in this case, Match Grain usually comes up with a good first pass at settings; it can get you 70% to 80% there and is just as adjustable thereafter. To refine grain settings, follow these steps:

1. Look for a section of your source footage with a solid color area that stays in place for 10 to 20 frames. Most clips satisfy these criteria (and those that don't tend to allow less precision).

2. Zoom 200% to 400% on the solid color area, and create a Region of Interest around it. Set Work Area to the 10 or 20 frames with little or no motion.

3. Add a solid that's small enough to occupy part of the region of interest. Apply a Ramp effect to the solid, and use the eyedropper tools to select the darkest and lightest pixels in the solid color area of the clip. The lack of grain detail in the foreground gradient should be clearly apparent (**Figure 9.35**).

4. Apply the Match Grain effect to the foreground solid. Choose the source footage layer from the Noise Source Layer menu. As soon as the effect finishes rendering a sample frame, you have a basis from which to begin fine-tuning. You can RAM preview at this point to see how close a match you have. In most cases, you're not done yet.

5. Twirl down the Tweaking controls for Match Grain, and then twirl down Channel Intensities and Channel Size. You can save yourself a lot of time by doing most of your work here, channel by channel.

6. Activate the green channel only in the Composition panel (**Alt+1/Opt+1**) and adjust the Green Intensity

CLOSE-UP

Use Noise as Grain

Prior to the addition of Add Grain and Match Grain to After Effects version 6.5 Professional, the typical way to generate grain was to use the Noise effect. The main advantage of the Noise effect over Match Grain is that it renders about 20 times faster. However, After Effects doesn't make it easy for you to separate the effect channel by channel, and scaling requires a separate effect (or precomping).

You can use three solid layers, with three effects applied to each layer: Shift Channels, Noise, and Transform. Use Shift Channels to set each solid to red, green, or blue, respectively; set Blending Modes to Add; and set their Opacity very low (well below 10%, adjusting as needed). Next, set the amount of noise and scale it via the Transform effect.

If the grain is meant to affect a set of foreground layers only, hold them out from the background plate either via precomping or track mattes. If this sounds complicated, it is, which is why Match Grain is preferable unless the rendering time is really killer.

Figure 9.35 A gradient is placed right over the talent's head as a reference for grain matching the window above it. Even without slamming the image, it's clear that the added window looks too flat in this grainy scene, but slamming with the addition of a gradient gives you a clear target.

and Green Size values to match the foreground and background. Repeat this process for the green and blue channels (**Alt+2/Opt+2** and **Alt+3/Opt+3**). If you don't see much variation channel to channel, you can instead adjust overall Intensity and Size (**Figure 9.36**). RAM preview the result.

7. Adjust the Intensity, Size, or Softness controls under Tweaking according to what you see in the RAM preview. You may also find it necessary to reduce Saturation under Color, particularly if your source is film rather than video.

In most cases, these steps yield a workable result (**Figure 9.37**). The effect can then be copied and pasted to any foreground layers that need grain. If the foreground layer already contains noise or grain, you may need to adjust the Compensate for Existing Noise percentage for that layer.

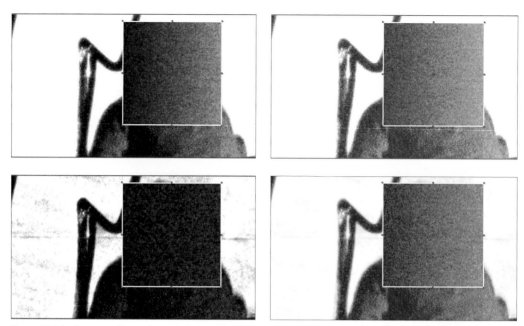

Figure 9.36 In this unusual case, there is little variation of grain channel to channel, and the automatic match is pretty good; a slight boost to the overall Intensity setting under the Tweaking controls does the trick.

Figure 9.37 Even in this printed figure, the matching grain is somewhat evident. Grain matching is often best reviewed in motion with a boosted exposure.

Obviously, whole categories of controls within Match Grain remain untouched with this approach. The Application category, for example, contains controls for how the grain is blended and how it affects shadows, midtones, and highlights individually. These are typically overkill, as are the Sampling and Animation controls, but how far you go in matching grain before your eye is satisfied is, of course, up to you.

Grain Removal

Removing grain, or sharpening an image in general, is an entirely different process from adding grain. On a well-shot production, you'll rarely have a reason to reach for the Remove Grain tool, but push hard on digital footage shot with a high ASA, and grain takes over.

Try the Remove Grain at the default settings and A/B the result with your source, looking for missing fine detail. If there is a problem, check into the Fine Tuning and Unsharp Mask settings to adjust the grain. Remove Grain is often best employed stealthily—not necessarily across the entire frame (**Figure 9.38**) or as part of a series of effects.

Figure 9.38 The left side of the frame is clearly less grainy than the right, as a result of applying Remove Grain and letting it automatically sample the footage.

There are newer and potentially better solutions for noise reduction in an image. Neat Video (www.neatvideo.com) is straightforward and effective.

When to Manage Grain

The most obvious candidates for grain addition are computer-generated or still image layers that lack the moving grain found in film or video footage. As soon as your shot has to match anything that came from a camera, and particularly in a large format such as HD or film, you must work with grain.

Blurred elements may also need grain addition, even if they originate as source footage. Blurry source shots contain as much grain as focused ones because the grain

TIP

If you're using Remove Grain to improve a bluescreen or greenscreen key, consider applying the result as an alpha track matte. This offers the best of both worlds: a clean matte channel and preservation of realistic grain on the source color layer.

Garbage In, Garbage Out

You don't need me to tell you how difficult it is to bring a poorly shot image back from the dead, but check *The DV Rebel's Guide* for a thorough rundown of factors that go into a well-shot image. If possible, go on set to help eliminate flaws that will be difficult to fix in post. Among the less-obvious points from the book:

▶ When shooting digitally, keep the contrast low and overall light levels well below maximum; you are shooting the negative, not the final.

▶ If using a small, light camera, mount it to something heavy to move it; that weight reads to the viewer as more expensive and more natural motion.

Stu has said that the update to *The DV Rebel's Guide* is his blog, www.prolost.com.

is an artifact of the medium recording the image, not the subject itself. Elements that have been scaled down in After Effects contain scaled-down grain, which may require restoration. Color keying can also suppress grain in the channel that has been keyed out.

Other compositing operations will instead enhance grain. Sharpening, unless performed via Remove Grain, can strongly emphasize grain contrast in an element—typically in a not-so-desirable manner. Sharpening also brings out any nasty compression artifacts that come with footage that uses JPEG-type compression, such as miniDV video.

Mismatched grain is one of the dead giveaways of a poorly composited shot. It is worth the effort to match the correct amount of grain in a shot even if the result isn't apparent as you preview it on your monitor.

Real Cameras Distort Reality

The real fun comes when you start to add your own recipe of looks to an image, whether to make it look as though it were shot on some different medium, or to make it look as cinematic as possible. In either case, you will find yourself effectively degrading your footage: adding effects related to lens limitations, cropping the image to be shorter (and thus appear wider), pushing the color into a much more limited, controlled range.

The question of how to create a cinematic image without a professional film crew (or budget) is greatly expanded upon in *The DV Rebel's Guide: An All-Digital Approach to Making Killer Action Movies on the Cheap* (Peachpit Press, 2006), by Stu Maschwitz. The first chapter lists the major factors that influence production value. Many of these, including image and sound quality, location, and lighting, cannot be "fixed in post," which must be why Stu's book includes a bunch of information on how to actually shoot.

Achieving a particular look is well within the realm of tricks you can pull off consistently in After Effects. You can take control of the following to develop a look and maximize production value:

▶ **Lens Artifacts.** We love defects! In addition to the afore-mentioned bokeh and other defocus imperfections, along with chromatic aberration, are such filmic visual staples as the vignette and the lens flare.

▶ **Frame Rate.** Change this to alter the very character of footage. For the most part, frame rate needs to be determined when shooting in order for things to go smoothly.

▶ **Aspect Ratio.** The format of the composition makes a huge perceptual difference as well. Wide connotes big-budget Hollywood epic and thus is not always appropriate.

▶ **Color Look.** Nothing affects the mood of a given shot like color and contrast. It's a complex subject revisited in Chapter 12.

Lens Artifacts and Other Happy "Accidents"

Reality as glimpsed by the camera includes *lens artifacts*—visual phenomena that occur only through a camera, not the lens of your eye—such as lens distortion and lens blur (or *bokeh*), but that's not all. Also on your palette are "flaws" that good cinematographers avoided right up until *Easy Rider* showed that a lens flare goes with a road movie the way mustard goes with a hot dog.

Vignettes, the darkening around the corners of the frame that results from a mismatch between a round lens and a rectangular frame (when the frame is too large for the image) are almost completely avoidable these days, yet they've never been more popular among designers and photo-graders.

Chromatic aberration is exactly the combination it sounds to be: an aberration (which sounds bad) of color (we all like that). It, too, is always the result of a mismatch between a lens and a camera and rarely shows up unless the shooter is doing something crazy or using a very cheap camera.

All of these effects provide texture, variety, and spontaneity to an image; in other words, they can bring a shot to life.

TIP

After Effects now includes Distort > Rolling Shutter Removal to remove this annoying effect; Chapter 8 has details.

The Lens Flare

When a bright light source such as the sun appears in shot it causes secondary reflections to bounce around among the lens elements. There's so much light, it reflects back on the surface of the many individual lenses that make up what we call a lens. Your eye can resolve an image using one very flexible lens, but camera lenses beyond the simplest Brownie (one lens) or pinhole (none) camera require a series of inflexible glass lens elements. A complex zoom lens might consist of 20 elements. Each is coated to prevent the reflections that create flares, but there's a limit.

Because they occur within the lens, lens flares appear superimposed over the image. If the light source is partially occluded by a foreground object or figure, the flare may diminish or disappear, but you'll never see a full-strength lens flare partially blocked by a foreground subject. Each flare appears as a complete disc, ring, star, or other shape.

Artists love lens flares and can develop the bad habit of playing a bit fast and loose with them. As with anything, the game is to keep it real first, and then bend the rules around to the look you want, if necessary. Fundamentally, only if the shot was clearly taken with a long lens do you have any business with the types of crazy multi-element flares you get by using the default setting of the paltry Lens Flare effect that ships with After Effects.

SCRIPT

Designing your own array of lens elements isn't out of the question. To array them in a classic multi-element zoom lens arrangement, you can use Trajectory (http://aescripts.com/trajectory/), a script from Michael Cardeiro, that aligns layers between two null objects.

In addition to the glass elements, aperture blades contribute to the appearance of flares. Their highly reflective corners result in streaks, their number corresponding to the number of blades. As with bokeh, the shape of the flares might correspond to the shape of the aperture (a pentagon for a five-sided aperture, a hexagon for six). Dust and scratches on the lens even reflect light.

The Lens Flare effect that ships with After Effects is limited to three inflexible 8-bits-per-channel presets and had become dated a decade ago. The Optical Flares plug-in from Video Copilot is a hot option these days, with Knoll Light Factory its well-respected elder.

Chapter 12 shows that flares can also be caused by bright specular pings and other reflected highlights in a scene, and that they offer a further opportunity to enhance the reality of a shot. These can be re-created with those same plug-in effects, or by creating your own and using a blending mode (typically Add) to apply it.

The Vignette

When the edges of the frame go dark, our attention becomes more focused on what's at the center. Lens manufacturers have gone to significant trouble to eliminate this effect during shooting, but pay attention to the corners of the images you see and you'll notice an awful lot of vignettes added in post these days.

Vignette controls are included with "film look" software such as Magic Bullet Looks, but this is also an easy effect to create:

1. Create a black solid the size of your frame as the top layer and name it vignette.

2. Double-click the Ellipse tool in the toolbar; an elliptical mask fills the frame.

3. Highlight the layer in the timeline and press **F** to reveal Mask Feather.

4. Increase the Mask Feather value a lot—somewhere in the low triple digits is probably about right.

5. Lower the Opacity value (**T**) until the effect looks right; you might prefer a light vignette (10% to 15%) or something heavier (40% to 50%).

A vignette would be elliptical or round, depending on whether it was shot with an anamorphic lens (**Figure 9.39**). There would be no reason for a lens vignette to be offset, but you're not confined to such realistic limitations if it suits your scene to offset and rotate a soft ellipse. Generally, vignettes look best just below the threshold where we would clearly notice that the corners and edges have gone a little dark.

Figure 9.39 A vignette is created with a feathered mask applied to a solid (top). If the image is reframed for display in another format, such as anamorphic, you may have to use that framing instead of the source (bottom).

SCRIPT

François Tarlier's ft-Cubic Lens Distortion (http://aescripts.com/ ft-cubic-lens-distortion/) is in fact, a pixel-bender plug-in. What it has in common with scripts is that it is donation-ware and freely available to try. It uses the Syntheyes cubic lens distortion algorithm and can not only add or remove lens distortion but also apply chromatic aberration to a shot.

Chromatic Aberration

Chromatic Aberration is an even rarer visual phenomenon. This fringing or smearing of light that occurs when a lens cannot focus various colors on the spectrum to a single point, because of the differing wavelengths, yields a rainbow of colors something like that of light passing through a prism. The effect is more pronounced closer to the edge of frame. It can occur during projection as well; alas, I have seen it in low-budget cinemas.

Like lens flares and bokeh, a little bit of aberration can bring a scene life and spontaneity. Some simple steps to re-create this effect at its most basic level:

1. Duplicate the layer twice and precompose all three.

2. Use the Shift Channels effect to leave only red, green, or blue on for each layer (so you end up with one of each).

3. Set the top two layers to Add mode.

4. Scale the green channel to roughly 101% and the blue channel to roughly 102%.

5. Add a small amount of Radial Blur (set to Zoom, not the default Spin).

A before-and-after comparison using this setup appears in **Figure 9.40**. Better yet, pick up Satya Meka's Separate RGB effect (http://aescripts.com/separate-rgb/), which lets you name your own price. This Pixel Bender plug-in lets you transform individual channels of color directly.

Figure 9.40 A simulation of chromatic aberration (right), the color ringing that is caused when different wavelengths of light have different focal lengths; most lenses correct for it with an added diffractive element (left).

Frame Rate and Realism

It's no accident that film images are still displayed at 24 frames per second nearly a century after this seeming limitation was imposed, and that even the newest electronic formats that can be optimized for 30 or 60 also tend to gain legitimacy when they add a 24p, or full frame 24 fps mode, but it makes no sense. Why not gather more data if you can?

The answer does not seem entirely logical. The truth seems to be that your eye has an effective "refresh rate" somewhere slightly upward of 60 times per second, and so the 60 interlaced fields of 29.97 American television feel a lot like direct reality. On the other hand, 24 fps is barely above the threshold where the eye loses persistence of vision, the phenomenon that allows it to see continuity from still images shown in series.

Cinema may have gone for 24 fps due to limitations of equipment and money. Fewer frames per second meant a sizable reduction in film stock costs. If so, with this compromise, they also accidentally got the more ephemeral and dreamlike quality that comes with it. As with shallow depth of field (discussed earlier in this chapter) and color reduction (ahead), less can be more. Once again, re-creating cinematic reality requires that you reduce data.

After Effects is quite forgiving about letting you change frame rates midstream compared with most video applications; details on how the conversion actually works appeared in Chapter 2. However, it is very difficult to convert 29.97 fps footage to 24 fps without introducing a lurching cadence to smooth motion, as every sixth frame is dropped. When working at 29.97 fps, it can still make sense to animate and render whole frames instead of interlacing to 60 fields per second, in order to give a little more of that cinematic quality to the result.

Format and Panoramas

As the world transitions from standard-definition to high-definition broadcast television, formats are undergoing the same transition that they made in film half a century ago. The nearly square 4:3 aspect as standard is being replaced

29.97 fps Is for Soap Operas and Reality Television

The debate about raising the frame rate above the 24 fps you see in the cinema has been raging since long before the digital era. The invention of videotape in the 1950s made it cheap and fast to record imagery more directly in the format of television.

One particular experiment from this era stands out. For six episodes, the producers of "The Twilight Zone" tried tape before they evidently realized it was ruining the show's mystique. Video's higher frame rate transformed this masterpiece of irony and suspense into something resembling a soap opera. Judge for yourself—check out any of Season 2's videotaped episodes: "Static," "Night of the Meek," "The Lateness of the Hour," "The Whole Truth," "Twenty-Two," or "Long Distance Call." The experiment was quickly ended, and in five total seasons the show never appeared on videotape again.

The numbers "1.85" and "2.35" or "2.4" give the width, relative to a height of 1, so it's like saying 1.85:1 or 2.39:1 (the actual widescreen ratio). The 16:9 format, which has become popular with digital video and HD, is equivalent to a 1.77:1 ratio, slightly narrower than Academy, but wide compared to the standard television format of 4:3 (1.33: 1), which is also that of old movies such as *Casablanca*.

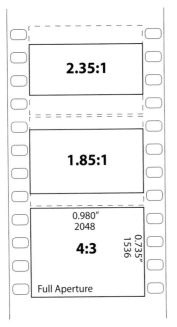

Figure 9.41 "Wide" film formats would more accurately be called "shorter," because they typically involve cropping the original 4:3 image.

by the wider 16:9 format, but 1.85 Academy aperture and 2.35 Cinemascope also appear as common "widescreen" formats.

In response to the growing popularity of television in the 1950s, Hollywood conjured up a number of different widescreen formats through experiments with anamorphic lenses and film stocks as wide as 70 mm. These systems—CinemaScope, VistaVision, Panavision, and so on—themselves faded away but not without changing the way films are displayed.

Standard 35 mm film has an aspect ratio of 4:3, which is not coincidentally the same as a television. Movies tend to be filmed in this format as if originally intended for the small screen. When shown in a theater using a widescreen aspect of 1.85:1 (also known as 16:9, the HDTV standard) or 2.39:1 (Cinemascope), the full 4:3 negative is cropped (**Figure 9.41**). The wider formats also tend to have been shot anamorphically, squeezing the wider image into the narrower frame.

Now 16:9 widescreen high-definition televisions and projectors have taken over, so clearly the wider aspect ratio won. Is 2.4:1 even better? This format seems to go best with sweeping vistas: the majestic desert of *Lawrence of Arabia* and the Millennium Falcon's jump to light speed. If you choose this format, you are saying to your audience that they should expect to see some pretty spectacular views, and if you don't deliver, the format choice may disappoint.

Ironically, when shown in HD, the widescreen image is the lowest resolution—only 800 pixels tall, making small detail less discernable, especially once compression has been applied.

Less Color Is More

This entire section has been about how corrupting, degrading, and reducing data in an image can bring it to cinematic life. Color grading can transform an ordinary image into one that resonates emotionally, and it does so, paradoxically, by reducing the accuracy and range of the hues in the source image.

In her book *If It's Purple, Someone's Gonna Die*, author Patti Bellantoni explores many scenes from cinema whose color palette is dominated by one color, and why this choice resonates with us, including analogues with other visual art forms such as paintings. It's surprisingly rare for a shot in a movie to be dominated by more than three shades, and there is no doubt that the dominant color influences the emotional impact of the scene.

Figures 9.42, **9.43**, and **9.44** offer a simple demonstration of how color choices can influence the look of a scene, along with showing the primary corrections that were made in Colorista to achieve them.

Figure 9.42 The source image does not by itself convey any particular emotion through its color palette, although the natural vignette-like effect caused by the backlight does focus one's attention. (Source clip courtesy of Eric Escobar.)

Figure 9.43 There is something miraculous in Grand Central Station.

Figure 9.44 It is a city of cold efficiency.

Primary color correction—creating the look in post—typically is done via a three-way color corrector, and Adobe SpeedGrade supplies that and much more. This process may reduce the range of hues in the shot, but emotionally, when done right, it will make the frame sing. However, this is merely one of many methods one could use to establish a look. For more ideas, watch others as they work in videos on color correction, which are freely available at Adobe TV.

Overall, if you're new to the idea of developing a color look for a film or sequence, look at references. Study other people's work for the effect of color on the mood and story in a shot, sequence, or entire film, and give yourself the exercise of re-creating it. Don't be hard on yourself—just notice what works and what's missing. Once you have that down, you're ready to create your own rules and even break those set by others.

Train Your Eye

And really, this chapter just scratched the surface of what's possible. The best way to expand upon these ideas is to close After Effects and pick up an actual camera; make sure it's one with a detachable lens that allows you full control of exposure, ASA, and focal depth. If you have a friend who is also willing to learn, you can make a daily practice of sharing a photo of something you noticed with the camera. This habit will not only make you a better shooter, it will give you lots of ideas you can use as a compositor and train your eye.

You can always look for new methods to replicate the way that the camera sees the world, going beyond realism to present what we really want to see—realism as it looks through the lens.

10

Expressions

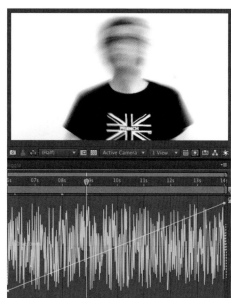

Music is math.

—Michael Sandison and Marcus Eoin
(Boards of Canada)

Expressions

Expressions are cool. You can use them to create amazing procedural effects that would otherwise be impossible (or at least impractical). You can also use them to create complex relationships between various parameters. Unfortunately, many After Effects users are afraid of expressions. Don't be.

The fact that you're reading this chapter indicates that you are at least curious about expressions. That's a good start. By the end of the chapter, you'll see how expressions can open new doors for you, and I hope you'll have the confidence to give them a try.

The best way to learn about expressions is to examine working examples to figure out what makes them tick. The examples in this chapter focus on how you can use expressions to create or control effects.

What Expressions Are

The After Effects expression language is a powerful set of tools with which you can control the behavior of a layer's properties. Expressions can range in complexity from ridiculously simple to mind-numbingly complicated. At the simple end of the spectrum, you can use expressions to link one property to another or to set a property to a static value. At the other extreme, you can create complex linkages, manipulate time, perform calculations in 3D space, set up tricky procedural animations, and more.

Sometimes you'll use expressions instead of keyframes (most properties that can be keyframed can be controlled by expressions). In other cases, you'll use expressions to augment the keyframed behavior. For example, you could use keyframes to move a layer along a specific path and then add an expression to add some randomness to the motion.

Creating Expressions

The easiest way to create an expression is to simply **Alt**-click (**Opt**-click) the stopwatch of the property where you want the expression to go. After Effects then creates a default expression, adds four new tool icons, changes the color of the property value to red (indicating that the value is determined by an expression), and leaves the expression text highlighted for editing (**Figure 10.1**).

At this point you have a number of options. You can simply start typing, and your text will replace the default expression. Note that while you're in edit mode, the **Enter** (**Return**) key moves you to a new line in the expression (this is how you can create multiline expressions) and leaves you in edit mode.

Another option while the text is highlighted is to paste in the text of an expression that you have copied from a text editor. This is the method I generally use if I'm working on a multiline expression. Instead of replacing all the default text by typing or pasting, you can click somewhere in the highlighted text to create an edit point for inserting additional text.

Alternatively, you can drag the expression's pick whip to another property or object (the target can even be in another composition), and After Effects will insert the appropriate text when you let go. Note that if an object or property can be referenced using the pick whip, a rounded rectangle appears around the name as you drag the pick whip over it. If this doesn't happen, you won't be able to pick whip it. Finally, you can also use the Expression Language menu to insert various language elements.

After creating your expression, exit edit mode by clicking somewhere else in the timeline or pressing **Enter** on the numeric keypad. If your expression text contains an error, After Effects displays an error message, disables the expression, and displays a little yellow warning icon (**Figure 10.2**). You can temporarily disable an expression by clicking on the enable/disable toggle.

CLOSE-UP

Expressions Have Limitations

Although the expression language presents you with an impressive arsenal of powerful tools, it's important to understand their limitations so you can avoid making assumptions that lead you astray.

▶ An expression may generally be applied only to a property that can be keyframed, and it can affect only the value of that property. This means there are no global variables. Also, although an expression has access to many composition and layer attributes (layer width and height, for example), as well as the values of other properties, it can only read not change them.

▶ Expressions can't create objects. For example, an expression cannot spawn a new layer, add an effect, create a paint stroke, change a blend mode, and so on.

▶ Expressions can't access information about individual mask vertices.

▶ Expressions can't access text layer formatting attributes, such as font face, font size, leading, or even the height and width of the text itself.

▶ Expressions can't access values they created on previous frames, which means expressions have no memory. If you've had a little Flash programming experience, you might expect to be able to increment a value at each frame. Nope. Even though you can access previous values of the property using valueAtTime(), what you get is the pre-expression value (the static value of the property plus the effect of any keyframes). It's as if the expression didn't exist. There is no way for an expression to communicate with itself from one frame to the next.

Note, however, just to make things more confusing, the postexpression value of a property *is* available to any other expression, just not the one applied to that property. In fact, the postexpression value is the *only* value available to expressions applied to other properties. To summarize: An expression has access only to the pre-expression value of the property to which it is applied, and it only has access to the postexpression values for other properties with expressions. It's confusing at first, but it sinks in eventually.

Figure 10.1 When you create an expression, After Effects creates a default expression with the text highlighted for editing, changes the color of the property value to red, and adds four new tool icons: an enable/disable toggle, a Graph Editor toggle, a pick whip, and an Expression Language menu.

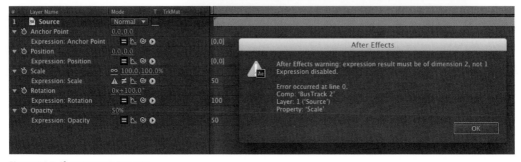

Figure 10.2 If your expression contains an error, After Effects disables the expression, changes the enable/disable toggle to the disabled state, returns the Property value to its normal color, displays an error icon, and displays an error message dialog box.

Working with existing expressions is as easy as creating them. Some common operations include

▶ **editing.** Click in the expression text area to select the entire expression; you now have the same options as when creating a new expression. If your expression consists of multiple lines, you may need to expand the expression editing area to be able to see all (or at least more) of it by positioning the cursor over the line below the expression text until you see a double-ended arrow and then clicking and dragging.

▶ **deleting.** Simply **Alt**-click (**Opt**-click) the property's stopwatch, or you can delete all the text for the expression and press **Enter** on the numeric keypad.

▶ **exposing.** Select a layer in the Timeline and press **EE** to expose any expressions applied to that layer.

▶ **copying.** In the Timeline panel, select a layer property containing an expression and choose Edit > Copy Expression Only to copy just the property's expression. You now can select as many other layers as you'd like and choose Edit > Paste to paste the expression into the appropriate property of the other layers.

The Language of Expressions

The After Effects expression language is based on a subset of JavaScript. JavaScript is a scripting language used largely for Web page design and includes many features specifically aimed at that task. The JavaScript implementation for expressions includes the core features only. That means there's a lot about JavaScript that you won't need to know, but it also means that any JavaScript reference you pick up (and you're going to need one if you really want to master expressions) is going to have a lot of content that will be of little or no use to you.

The rest of the expression language consists of extensions that Adobe has added specifically for After Effects. This means that in addition to a good JavaScript reference, you'll also be frequenting Help > Expression Reference, or www.adobe.com/support/aftereffects.

This chapter focuses on working examples rather than the details of JavaScript. The book's disc, however, contains an abbreviated JavaScript guide to glance through before you really dive into the sample expressions discussed here. Appropriate sections of that guide are referenced as Java-Script elements occur for the first time.

Linking an Effect Parameter to a Property

At the most basic level, expressions are used to link properties. Suppose you want to create a surreal scene in which instead of hearing music, the scene is dominated by a heartbeat, so much so that the scene pulses along with it.

Specifically, you want to link the Size parameter of the CC Lens effect to the amplitude of an audio layer. Expressions can't access audio levels directly, so first you have to use a keyframe assistant (Animation > Keyframe Assistant > Convert Audio to Keyframes) to create a null layer named Audio Amplitude with Slider Controls keyframed for the audio levels of the Left, Right, and Both channels (for a stereo source). Next, you just **Alt**-click (**Opt**-click) the stopwatch for the Size parameter of CC Lens and drag the pick whip to the Both Channels Slider property of the

Audio Amplitude layer (**Figure 10.3**). Doing so generates this expression:

```
thisComp.layer("Audio Amplitude").effect("Both
Channels")("Slider")
```

Take a closer look at its syntax: From JavaScript, the After Effects expression language inherits a left-to-right "dot" notation used to separate objects and attributes in a hierarchy. If your expression references a property in a different layer, you first have to identify the composition. You can use `thisComp` if the other layer happens to be in the same composition (as in this example). Otherwise, you would use `comp("other comp name")`, with the other composition name in quotes. Next you identify the layer using `layer("layer name")`, and finally, the property, such as `effect("effect name")("property name")` or possibly `transform.rotation`.

In addition to objects and properties, the dot notation hierarchy can include references to an object's attributes and methods. An attribute is just what you would guess: a property of an object, such as a layer's height or a composition's duration. In fact, in JavaScript documentation, attributes are actually referred to as properties, but in order to avoid confusion with the layer properties such as Position and Rotation (which existed long before expressions came along), in After Effects documentation (and here) they're referred to as attributes. For example, each layer has a height attribute that can be referenced this way:

```
comp("Comp 1").layer("Layer 1").height
```

Methods are a little harder to grasp. Just think of them as actions or functions associated with an object. You can tell the difference between attributes and methods by the parentheses that follow a method. The parentheses may enclose some comma-separated parameters.

It's important to note that you don't have to specify the full path in the dot notation hierarchy if you're referencing attributes or properties of the layer where the expression resides. If you leave out the comp and layer references, After Effects assumes you mean the layer with the expression. So, for example, if you specify only `width`, After Effects assumes you mean the width of the layer, not the width of the composition.

Back to the scene. You linked the amplitude of your audio layer to your effect parameter, but it's not really right until you increase the effect that the audio level has on the parameter. You can use a little JavaScript math to multiply the value by some amount, like this

```
thisComp.layer("Audio Amplitude").effect("Both
Channels")("Slider") * 2 + 100
```

Why is 100 added? This particular effect makes the layer disappear when size goes to zero. Adding 100 allows you to start at full size and increase from there. Toward the end of the chapter you'll see a much more complicated and powerful way of linking an effect to audio.

NOTES

If you're not familiar with arithmetic operators specific to JavaScript (such as the * for multiplication used in this example), you might want to take a look at the "Operators" section of the JavaScript guide on the book's disc.

Using a Layer's Index

A layer's `index` attribute can be used as a simple but powerful tool that allows you to create expressions that behave differently depending on where the layer is situated in the layer stack. The `index` attribute corresponds exactly to the number assigned to the layer in the Timeline panel. The `index` for the layer at the top of the stack is 1, and so on.

Time Delay Based on Layer Index

Suppose you want to re-create the time offset effect in **Figure 10.4**. The technique is simple: Create a bunch of identical layers, and temporally offset their animations by an amount that increases as you move down the layer stack. To do so, you first need to figure out what frame begins the sequence.

Time in expressions is measured in seconds, so it helps to switch the timeline to display time instead of frames. The jump begins at 12:00, a nice round number, so set Time Remapping (**Ctrl+T/Cmd+T**) and apply this expression to the top layer's Time Remap property:

```
delay = 12;
delay+(index-1)
```

Now, duplicate the layer a bunch of times. The animation of each layer will lag behind the layer above it by one-second intervals (**Figure 10.4**).

Figure 10.4 With the sky keyed out (see Chapter 6) the motorcycle jump displays at one-second intervals.

What's going on here? The first line defines a JavaScript variable named `delay` and sets its value to 12 seconds, the point where the jump begins. The second line represents the current layer time, in seconds.

Subtracting 1 from the layer's `index` gives the total delay (in seconds) for this layer. Subtracting 1 from `index` means that the delay will be 0 for the first layer. So, for Layer 1, the total delay is 0, for Layer 2 it is 1. However, if you prefer half-second intervals, you can make the value (index/2—0.5). The result of this is that Layer 1's animation still begins at 12:00; Layer 2's animation lags behind Layer 1 by 0.5 seconds; and so on.

Later in this chapter, you'll see how you can create a variable for any fixed value that you anticipate may change—the amount of time between frames, for example. You'll also learn how to assign a Slider Control so that instead of copying and pasting whole new copies of the expression, or re-creating the layer stack from scratch, you can simply try different settings with the slider, as if it were any other effect.

Looping Keyframes

The expression language provides two convenient ways to loop a sequence of keyframes: loopOut() and loopIn().

In a VFX context, the most often used of these is loopOut("continue"). This expression extrapolates the animation beyond the last keyframe, so the value of the property keeps moving at the same rate (and in the same direction, if you're animating a spatial property such as Position) as the last keyframe. Anytime you track an object that moves offscreen, or want to match the motion between any two given keyframes, this expression is your go-to (**Figure 10.5**).

TIP

To copy a change to one expression to an entire set, context-click on the property containing the expression and choose Copy Expression Only. Then select all of the effects containing the previous expression and paste—no need to select individual properties as a paste target.

Figure 10.5 An informal Twitter poll revealed that loopOut("continue"), which simply repeats the direction and velocity at the end of an animated sequence, may be the most-used expression in After Effects postproduction.

There are three other variations of loopOut():

▶ loopOut("cycle") Ever find yourself copying and pasting a set of keyframes to create a repeating loop? This expression eliminates the need for that.

▶ loopOut("pingpong") Runs your animation alternately forward, then backward.

▶ loopOut("offset") Works similar to "cycle" except that instead of returning to the value of the first keyframe, each loop of the animation is offset by an amount equal to the value at the end of the previous loop. This produces a cumulative or stair-step effect.

The loopIn() expression operates the same way as loopOut(), except that the looping occurs before the first keyframe instead of after the last keyframe. Both loopIn() and loopOut() will accept a second, optional parameter that specifies how many keyframes to loop. Actually, it's easier to think of it as how many keyframed segments to loop. For loopOut(), the segments are counted from the last keyframe toward the layer's In point. For loopIn(), the segments are counted from the first keyframe toward the layer's Out point. If you leave this parameter out (or specify it as 0), all keyframes are looped. For example, this variation loops the segment bounded by the last and next-to-last keyframes:

```
loopOut("cycle",1)
```

Two variations on the expressions—loopOutDuration() and loopInDuration()—enable you to specify the time (in seconds) as the second parameter instead of the number of keyframed segments to be looped. For loopOutDuration(), the time is measured from the last keyframe toward the layer's In point. For loopInDuration(), the time is measured from the first keyframe toward the layer's Out point. For example, this expression loops the two-second interval prior to the last keyframe:

```
loopOutDuration("cycle",2)
```

If you leave out the second parameter (or specify it as 0), the entire interval between the layer's In point and the last keyframe will be looped for loopOutDuration(). For loopInDuration(), the interval from the first keyframe to the Out point will be looped.

Conditional Events

Here are techniques that will further familiarize you with broader examples of time and index functions, including if/then statements and values that increment over time.

TIP

A small glitch in the cycle version of loopOut() drops the first keyframe from each of the loops. If you want the frame with the first keyframe to be included, add a duplicate of the first keyframe one frame beyond the last keyframe.

Using the attributes of layer (and composition) markers, you can establish or synchronize timing relationships between animated events.

The marker attributes that appear most frequently in expressions are time and index. As you might guess, the time attribute represents the time (in seconds) where the marker is located on the timeline. In this case, instead of the layer's number in the stack, the index attribute represents the marker's order on the timeline, where 1 represents the left-most marker.

You can retrieve the marker nearest to a time that you specify by using nearestKey(). For example, to access the layer marker nearest to the current comp time, use

```
marker.nearestKey(time)
```

This can be handy, but more often you'll want to know the most recent previous marker. The code necessary to retrieve it looks like this:

```
n = 0;
if (marker.numKeys > 0){
  n = marker.nearestKey(time).index;
  if (marker.key(n).time > time){
    n--;
  }
}
```

Note that this piece of code by itself is not very useful. When you do use it, you'll always combine it with additional code that makes it suitable for the particular property to which the expression will be applied. It's versatile and adaptable provided you know how it works.

The first line creates a variable, n, and sets its value to 0. If the value is still 0 when the routine finishes, it means that at the current time no marker was reached or that there are no markers on this layer.

The next line, a JavaScript if statement, checks if the layer has at least one marker. If there are no layer markers,

After Effects skips to the end of the routine with the variable n still set to 0. You need to make this test because the

TIP

You can set a marker to a layer or comp in real-time as you play back a RAM preview.

NOTES

For more explanation of if statements, check out the "Conditionals" and "Comparison Operators" sections of the JavaScript guide.

NOTES

If you're wondering about the JavaScript decrement operator (--), it's described in the "Operators" section of the JavaScript guide.

next line attempts to access the nearest marker with the statement

```
n = marker.nearestKey(time).index;
```

If After Effects attempted to execute this statement and there were no layer markers, it would generate an error and the expression would be disabled. It's good engineering practice to defend against these kinds of errors so that you can apply the expression first and add the markers later if you want to. Look at you, programmer!

If there is at least one layer marker, the third line of the expression sets n to the index of the nearest marker. Now all you have to do is determine if the nearest marker occurs before or after the current comp time with the statement

```
if (marker.key(n).time > time){
    n--;
}
```

This tells After Effects to decrement n by 1 if the nearest marker occurs later than the current time.

The result of all this is that the variable n contains the index of the most recent previous marker (or 0 if no marker has yet been reached).

So how can you use this little routine?

Trigger Animation at Markers

Suppose you're playing paparazzi and want a strobe to appear to go off at specific times. Here is a setup that allows you to preview the footage and press * on the numeric keypad wherever you want the flash to go off.

The Exposure effect can act like a flash. In this example, it's applied to the slow-motion footage that was used for the audio-driven animation above, so I'm going to stylize the flashes so that each one comes on at full strength and decays over a couple of frames (even though most photographers prefer strobe duration to be as brief as possible). My strobe animation is 5 frames long with 3 keyframes on the Exposure property: 0.0 on the first frame, 7.5 on frame 2, and 0.0 on frame 5, with an Easy Ease In on the final frame so the flash appears not to linger. Create your own, however you like it.

Then, apply this expression to the animated property:

```
n = 0;
if (marker.numKeys > 0){
  n = marker.nearestKey(time).index;
  if (marker.key(n).time > time){
    n--;
  }
}if (n == 0){
  valueAtTime(0);
}else{
  t = time - marker.key(n).time;
  valueAtTime(t)
}
```

As you can see, it's the previous marker routine with six new lines at the end. These lines tell After Effects to use the property's value from time 0 if there are no previous markers. Otherwise, variable t is defined to be the time since the most recent previous marker, and the value for that time is used.

The result is that the animation will run, beginning at frame 0, wherever there is a layer marker (**Figure 10.6**).

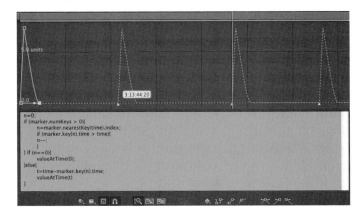

Figure 10.6 In the Graph Editor, the markers are admittedly teeny, but they were placed by simply playing through the clip. Using the displayed expression, each one triggers the appearance of a camera flash.

Play Only Frames with Markers

Suppose you have a long clip in which you want to condense specific frames so they play back together, without any gap between them.

First enable time remapping for the layer, then scrub through the Timeline and drop a layer marker at each frame that you want to include. Finally, apply this expression to the Time Remap property:

```
n = marker.numKeys;
if (n > 0){
  f = timeToFrames(time);
  idx = Math.min(f + 1, n);
  marker.key(idx).time
}else{
  value
}
```

In this expression, the variable n stores the total number of markers for the layer. The if statement next checks whether there is at least one marker. If not, the else clause executes, instructing After Effects to run the clip at normal speed. If there are markers, the expression first calculates the current frame using timeToFrames(), which converts whatever time you pass to it into the appropriate frame number. Here, it receives the current comp time and returns the current frame number, stored in variable f.

Next you need to convert the current frame number to a corresponding marker index for the frame you actually want to display. It turns out that all you need to do is add 1. That means when the current frame is 0, you actually want to show the frame that is at marker 1. When frame is 1, you want to show the frame at marker 2, and so on. The line

```
idx = Math.min(f + 1, n);
```

See "The Math Object" in the Java-Script guide for more information on Math.min().

calculates the marker index and stores it in the variable idx. Using Math.min() ensures the expression never tries to access more markers than there are (which would generate an error and disable the expression). Instead, playback freezes on the last frame that has a marker.

Finally, you use the idx variable to retrieve the time of the corresponding marker. This value becomes the result of the expression, which causes After Effects to display the frame corresponding to the marker.

Randomness

Another common usage for expressions in a VFX context is to generate random values. It turns out there are several flavors of randomness, and more often than not, the ones that are not completely random but rather tie adjacent values together organically (as with wiggle) or in a bell-curve distribution (Gaussian random) are more useful.

So, for example, you might apply a wiggle expression to camera position to make a smooth camera motion, or a camera with no motion at all, appear unlocked and hand-held. In such a case, a random expression would probably be way too jolting, but it would be useful to distribute a set of layers like particles; gaussRandom would do the same, but with Brownian motion.

Let's try applying randomness to footage to create unique specific results: turntable scratching with wiggle, and the violent, creepy head-shaking effect that was the signature of the classic movie *Jacob's Ladder*.

Wiggle Time

Wiggle is not a truly random number generator; similar to Perlin noise, it controls the amount of randomness to be more organic and interrelated. Each value relates to adjacent values, even at a more jittery higher frequency. For this reason, it is more useful than the random operators.

Chapter 8 introduced footage with a close-up of a record spinning on a turntable, and a couple of ways to stabilize it. This example uses After Effects to do some scratchin' on that record with a wiggle expression. The footage has no sound, so to get started, grab any .mp3 you find on your local system and precomp it with the source clip Turntable. mp4. Stabilize the turntable clip using one of the methods from that earlier section of the book; trust me, the result will be a lot more fun.

The footage is 60 fps and 1280i, but it moves around a lot, so place it in another comp at NTSC D1 Widescreen Square Pixel, 23.976 fps. The extra fps isn't wasted; in general, if you plan to slip the timing of a clip, it's preferable

Perlin noise works by defining an *n*-dimensional grid. Each grid coordinate stores a gradient of unit length in n dimensions. To sample, determine which grid cell you're in, and then compute the n-dimensional vectors from the sample location to each grid coordinate of the cell. This sets up a non-random relationship between the cells.

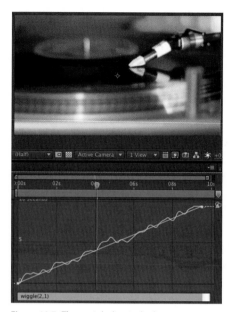

Figure 10.7 The straight line is the linear progression of time that setting Time Remap sets by default. The wiggly line is the result of the wiggle expression displayed below the graph. Where it dips below the straight line, the footage plays in reverse. Scratchin' 2, Electric Boogaloo!

to shoot it at a higher frame rate. In this case HD can be reduced and displayed smaller for stabilization.

The simple method is just to enable Time Remapping on the precomped layer in the master comp and apply a simple expression (**Figure 10.7**):

```
wiggle(2,1)
```

The `wiggle()` expression is an extremely useful tool that can introduce a smooth or fairly frenetic randomness into any animation, depending on your preference. Although `wiggle()` accepts five parameters, only `frequency` and `amplitude` are required. Check the After Effects documentation for an explanation of what the remaining three optional parameters do.

The first parameter, `frequency`, represents the frequency of the wiggle in seconds; for example, `wiggle(2,1)` varies the playback speed at the rate of twice per second. The second parameter is the amplitude of the wiggle, given in the units of the parameter to which `wiggle()` is applied, which in this case is also seconds. So, `wiggle(2,1)` lets the playback time deviate from the actual comp time by as much as one second in either direction.

Random Time

The movie *Jacob's Ladder* contained a unique effect that gave a clear indication that something surreal and creepy was going on in the world of the story: a body with a head that jerks around so violently it is just a blur (**Figure 10.8**). For this example, instead of having time move back and forth organically, the expression offsets each layer's playback time by a random amount. The expression you need for the Time Remap property is:

```
maxOffset = 8;
seedRandom(index,false)
random(maxOffset);
```

The first thing to notice about this expression is the use of `seedRandom()` and `random()` and the relationship between these functions. If you use `random()` by itself, you get a different random number at each frame, which is usually not what you want. The solution is seedRandom(), which takes two parameters. The first is the seed. It controls which random numbers get generated by random(). If you specify only this parameter, you will have different random numbers on each frame, but a sequence of numbers unique to this layer. It's the second parameter of seedRandom() that enables you to slow things down. Specifying this parameter as true tells After Effects to generate one random value on all frames. The default value is false, so if you don't specify this parameter at all, you get different numbers on each frame. So seedRandom() doesn't generate anything by itself. It just defines the subsequent behavior of random().

The first line creates the variable maxOffset and sets it to the maximum value, in seconds, that each layer's playback time can deviate from the actual comp time. The maximum for the example is 8 seconds.

The next line tells After Effects that you want the random number generator (random()) to generate the same random number on each frame.

The last line of the expression calculates the final Time Remap value, which is just the sum of the current comp time plus a random offset between 0 and 8 seconds.

Random Distribution

The seed random function allows you to distribute a bunch of layers around the frame randomly, and choose whether to have them hold their position. This position expression randomly moves a layer to a new location in the comp on each frame:

```
random([thisComp.width,thisComp.height])
```

This variation causes the layer to stay in one random location:

```
seedRandom(1,true);
random([thisComp.width,thisComp.height])
```

This version is the same as the previous one, except that it generates a single random location and the value of the seed is unique to the layer:

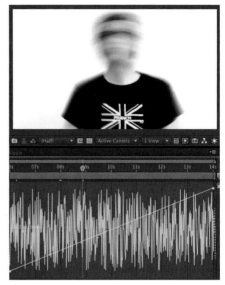

Figure 10.8 Need caption.

CLOSE-UP

More About random()

There are several ways to use *random()*. If you call it with no parameters, it will generate a random number between 0 and 1. If you provide a single parameter (as in the Random Time example), it will generate a random number between 0 and the value of the parameter. If you provide two parameters, separated by a comma, it will generate a random number between those two parameters. It's important to note that the parameters can be arrays instead of numbers. For example, this expression will give you a random 2D position somewhere within the comp

```
random ([thisComp.width,
thisComp.height])
```

In addition to *random()*, After Effects provides *gaussRandom()*, which operates in much the same way as *random()* except that the results have more of a Gaussian distribution to them. That is, more values are clustered toward the center of the range, with fewer at the extremities. Another difference is that with *gaussRandom()*, the values may actually be slightly outside the specified range, which never happens with *random()*.

```
seedRandom(index,true);
random([thisComp.width,thisComp.height])
```

Static random positions can be applied to any property that has a layer position in this manner.

Tracking Motion Between 2D and 3D

In the world of expressions, layer space transforms are indispensible, but they present some of the most difficult concepts to grasp. There are three coordinate systems in After Effects, and layer space transforms provide you with the tools you need to translate locations from one coordinate system to another.

One coordinate system represents a layer's own space. This is the coordinate system relative (usually) to the layer's upper-left corner. In this coordinate system, [0, 0] represents a layer's upper-left corner, [width, height] represents the lower-right corner, and [width, height]/2 represents the center of the layer. Note that unless you move a layer's anchor point, it too will usually represent the center of the layer in the layer's coordinate system.

The second coordinate system represents world space. World coordinates are relative to [0, 0, 0] the composition. This starts out at the upper-left corner of a newly created composition, but it can appear anywhere in frame if the comp has a camera and the camera has been moved, rotated, or zoomed.

The last coordinate system represents comp space. In this coordinate system, [0, 0] represents the upper-left corner of the camera view (or the default comp view if there is no camera), no matter where the camera is located or how it is oriented. In this coordinate system, the lower-right corner of the camera view is given by [thisComp.width, thisComp.height]. In comp space, the Z coordinate really doesn't have much meaning because you're only concerned with the flat representation of the camera view

So when would you use layer space transforms? One common use is to provide the world coordinates of a layer that is the child of another layer. When you make a layer the child of another layer, the child layer's Position value changes from the world space coordinate system to the layer space of the parent layer. In other words, the child layer's Position becomes the distance of its anchor point from the parent layer's upper-left corner. So a child layer's Position value is no longer a reliable indicator of where the layer is in world space.

For example, if you want another layer to track a layer that happens to be a child, you need to translate the child layer's position to world coordinates. Another common application of layer space transforms allows you to apply an effect to a 2D layer at a point that corresponds to where a 3D layer appears in the comp view.

Effect Tracks Parented Layer

To start, consider a relatively simple example: You have a layer named "star" that's the child of another layer, and you want to rotate the parent, causing the child to orbit the parent. You have applied CC Particle Systems II to a comp-sized layer, and you want the Producer Position of the particle system to track the comp position of the child layer. The expression you need to do all this is:

```
L = thisComp.layer("star");
L.toComp(L.transform.anchorPoint)
```

The first line is a little trick I like to use to make the following lines shorter and easier to manage. It creates a variable L and sets it equal to the layer whose position needs to be translated. It's important to note that you can use variables to represent more than just numbers. In this case, the variable is representing a layer object. So now, when you want to reference a property or attribute of the target layer, instead of having to prefix it with `thisComp.layer("star")`, you can just use L.

In the second line the `toComp()` layer space transform translates the target layer's anchor point from the layer's own space to comp space. The transform uses the anchor point because it represents the layer's position in its own layer space (**Figure 10.9**). Another way to think of this second line is "From the target layer's own layer space, convert the target layer's anchor point into comp space coordinates."

Figure 10.9 Only the null is keyframed, and the particles layer doesn't reference, but references the child layer to generate the sine wave that indicates animation of its position around the null.

This simple expression can be used in many ways. For example, if you want to simulate the look of 3D rays emanating from a 3D shape layer, you can create a 3D null and make it the child of the shape layer. You then position the null some distance behind the shape layer. Then apply the CC Light Burst 2.5 effect to a comp-sized 2D layer and apply this expression to the effect's Center parameter:

```
L = thisComp.layer("source point");
L.toComp(L.anchorPoint)
```

(Notice that this is the same expression as in the previous example, except for the name of the target layer: source point, in this case.) If you rotate the shape layer, or move a camera around, the rays seem to be coming from the position of the null.

Reduce Saturation Away from Camera

Let's change gears a little. You want to create an expression that reduces a layer's saturation as it moves away from the camera in a 3D scene to mimic the phenomenon of atmospheric haze. In addition, you want this expression to work even if the target layer and the camera happen to be children of other layers. You can accomplish this by applying the Color Balance (HLS) effect to the target layer and applying this expression to the Saturation parameter:

```
minDist = 900;
maxDist = 2000;
C = thisComp.activeCamera.toWorld([0,0,0]);
dist = length(toWorld(transform.anchorPoint), C);
ease(dist, minDist, maxDist, 0, -100)
```

The first two lines define variables that will be used to set the boundaries of this effect. If the target layer's distance from the camera is less than `minDist`, you'll leave the Saturation setting unchanged at 0. If the distance is greater than `maxDist`, you want to completely desaturate the layer with a setting of –100.

The third line of the expression creates variable C, which represents the position of the comp's currently active camera in world space. It's important to note that cameras and lights don't have anchor points, so you have to convert a specific location in the camera's layer space. It turns out that, in its own layer space, a camera's location is represented by the array [0,0,0] (that is, the X, Y, and Z coordinates are all 0).

The next line creates another variable, `dist`, which represents the distance between the camera and the anchor point of the target layer. You do this with the help of `length()`, which takes two parameters and calculates the distance between them. The first parameter is the world location of the target layer, and the second parameter is the world location of the camera, calculated previously.

All that's left to do is calculate the actual Saturation value based on the layer's current distance from the camera. You do this with the help of `ease()`, one of the expression language's amazingly useful interpolation methods. What this line basically says is "as the value of `dist` varies from `minDist` to `maxDist`, vary the output of `ease()` from 0 to –100."

Interpolation Methods

After Effects provides some very handy global interpolation methods for converting one set of values to another. Say you wanted an Opacity expression that would fade in over half a second, starting at the layer's In point, and you knew that In point might change. This expression would always trigger at that point, regardless. You could apply it to an unlimited set of layers so that they would all fade in gradually, and you are free to edit their In points without also having to edit their keyframes.

This is very easily accomplished using the `linear()` interpolation method:

```
linear(time, inPoint, inPoint + 0.5, 0, 100)
```

CLOSE-UP

Expression Controls

Expression controls are actually layer effects whose main purpose is to allow you to attach user interface controls to an expression. These controls come in six versions: Slider Control, Point Control, Checkbox Control, Color Control, and Layer Control.

All types of controls (except Layer Control) can be keyframed and can themselves accept expressions. The most common use, however, is to enable you to set or change a value used in an expression calculation without having to edit the code. For example, you might want to be able to easily adjust the `frequency` and `amplitude` parameters of a `wiggle()` expression. You could accomplish this by applying two slider controls to the layer with the expression (Effects > Expression Controls). It's usually a good idea to give your controls descriptive names; say you change the name of the first slider to frequency and the second one to amplitude (**Figure 10.10**). You would then set up your expression like this—and using the pick whip to create the references the sliders would be smart:

```
freq = effect("frequency")
("Slider");

amp = effect("amplitude")
("Slider");

wiggle(freq, amp)
```

Now, you can control the frequency and amplitude of the wiggle via the sliders. With each of the control types (again, with the exception of Layer Control) you can edit the numeric value directly, or you set the value using the control's gadget.

One unfortunate side note about expression controls is that because you can't apply effects to cameras or lights, neither can you apply expression controls to them.

Figure 10.10 Expression controllers let you tweak an expression as if it were a built-in effect, without editing the actual code.

As you can see, `linear()` accepts five parameters (there is also a seldom-used version that accepts only three parameters), which are, in order:

▶ input value that is driving the change

▶ minimum input value

▶ maximum input value

▶ output value corresponding to the minimum input value

▶ output value corresponding to the maximum input value

In the example, `time` is the input value (first parameter), and as it varies from the layer's In point (second parameter) to 0.5 seconds beyond the In point (third parameter), the output of `linear()` varies from 0 (fourth parameter) to 100 (fifth parameter). For values of the input parameter that are less than the minimum input value, the output of `linear()` will be clamped at the value of the fourth parameter. Similarly, if the value of the input parameter is greater than the maximum input value, the output of `linear()` will be clamped to the value of the fifth parameter. Back to the example: at times before the layer's In point, the Opacity value will be held at 0. From the layer's In point until 0.5 seconds beyond the In point, the Opacity value ramps smoothly from 0 to 100. For times beyond the In point + 0.5 seconds, the Opacity value will be held at 100. Sometimes it helps to read it from left to right like this: "As the value of time varies from the In point to 0.5 seconds past the In point, vary the output from 0 to 100."

The second parameter should always be less than the third parameter. Failure to set it up this way can result in some bizarre behavior.

Note that the output values need not be numbers. Arrays work as well. If you want to slowly move a layer from the composition's upper-left corner to the lower-right corner over the time between the layer's In point and Out point, you could set it up like this:

```
linear(time, inPoint, outPoint, [0,0], [thisComp.
width, thisComp.height])
```

There are other equally useful interpolation methods in addition to linear(), each taking exactly the same set of parameters. While easeIn() provides ease at the minimum value side of the interpolation, easeOut() provides it at the maximum value side, and ease() provides it at both. So if you wanted the previous example to ease in and out of the motion, you could do it like this:

```
ease(time, inPoint, outPoint, [0,0], [thisComp.width,
thisComp.height])
```

Fade While Moving Away from Camera

Just as you can reduce a layer's saturation as it moves away from the camera, you can reduce Opacity so the layer disappears in the distance. The expression is, in fact, quite similar:

```
minDist = 900;
maxDist = 2000;
C = thisComp.activeCamera.toWorld([0,0,0]);
dist = length(toWorld(transform.anchorPoint), C);
ease(dist, minDist, maxDist, 100, 0)
```

The only differences between this expression and the previous one are the fourth and fifth parameters of the ease() statement. In this case, as the distance increases from 900 to 2000, the opacity fades from 100% to 0%.

From Comp Space to Layer Surface

There's a somewhat obscure layer space transform that you haven't looked at yet, namely fromCompToSurface(). This translates a location from the current comp view to the location on a 3D layer's surface that lines up with that point (from the camera's perspective).

Imagine you have a 2D comp-sized layer named beam, to which you have applied the Beam Effect. You want a Lens Flare effect on a 3D layer to line up with the ending point of the Beam effect on the 2D layer. You can do it by

More About sampleImage()

You can sample the color and alpha data of a rectangular area of a layer using the layer method sampleImage(). You supply up to four parameters to sampleImage() and it returns color and alpha data as a four-element array (red, green, blue, alpha), where the values have been normalized so that they fall between 0.0 and 1.0. The four parameters are

▶ sample point

▶ sample radius

▶ post-effect flag

▶ sample time

The sample point is given in layer space coordinates, where [0, 0] represents the center of the layer's top left pixel. The sample radius is a two-element array (X radius, Y radius) that specifies the horizontal and vertical distance from the sample point to the edges of the rectangular area being sampled. To sample a single pixel, you would set this value to [0.5, 0.5], half a pixel in each direction from the center of the pixel at the sample point. The post-effect flag is optional (its default value is true if you omit the argument entirely) and specifies whether you want the sample to be taken after masks and effects are applied to the layer (true) or before (false). The sample time parameter specifies the time at which the sample is to be taken. This parameter is also optional (the default value is the current composition time), but if you include it, you must also include the post-effect flag parameter. As an example, here's how you could sample the red value of the pixel at a layer's center, after any effects and masks have been applied, at a time one second prior to the current composition time:

```
mySample = sampleImage([width/
height]/2, [0.5,0.5], true,
time - 1);
```

```
myRedSample = mySample[0];
```

applying this expression to the Flare Center parameter of the Lens Flare effect on the 3D layer:

```
beamPos = thisComp.layer("beam").effect("Beam")
("Ending Point");
fromCompToSurface(beamPos)
```

First, store the location of the ending point of the Beam effect into the variable `beamPos`. Now you can take a couple of shortcuts because of the way things are set up. First, the Ending Point parameter is already represented as a location in the beam layer's space. Second, because the beam layer is a comp-sized layer that hasn't been moved or scaled, its layer space will correspond exactly to the Camera view (which is the same as comp space). Therefore, you can assume that the ending point is already represented in comp space. If the Beam layer were a different size than the comp, located somewhere other than the comp's center, or scaled, you couldn't get away with this. You would have to convert the ending point from Beam's layer space to comp space.

Now all you have to do is translate the `beamPos` variable from comp space to the corresponding point of the surface of the layer with Lens Flare, which is accomplished easily with `fromCompToSurface()`.

You'll look at one more example of layer space transforms in the big finale—the "Extra Credit" section available on the book's disc in the PDFs folder.

Color Sampling and Conversion

Here's an example that demonstrates how you work with colors in an expression. The idea here is to vary the opacity of an animated small layer based on the lightness (or luminosity) of the pixels of a background layer that currently happens to be under the moving layer. The smaller layer will become more transparent as it passes over dark areas of the background and more opaque as it passes over lighter areas. Fortunately, the expression language supplies a couple of useful tools to help out.

Before examining the expression, we need to talk about the way color data is represented in expressions. An individual color channel (red, blue, green, hue, saturation, lightness, or alpha) is represented as a number between 0.0 (fully off) and 1.0 (fully on). A complete color space representation consists of an array of four such channels. Most of the time you'll be working in red, blue, green, and alpha (RGBA) color space, but you can convert to and from hue, saturation, lightness, and alpha (HSLA) color space. This example uses sampleImage() to extract RGBA data from a target layer called background. Then rgbToHsl() converts the RGBA data to HSLA color space so that you can extract the lightness channel, which will then be used to drive the Opacity parameter of the small animated layer. Here's the expression:

```
sampleSize = [width, height]/2;
target = thisComp.layer("background");
rgba = target.sampleImage(transform.position,
sampleSize, true, time);
hsla = rgbToHsl(rgba);
hsla[2]*100
```

First, you create the variable sampleSize and set its value as an array consisting of half the width and height of the layer whose opacity will be controlled with the expression. Essentially, this means that you'll be sampling all of the pixels of the background layer that are under smaller layers at any given time.

The second line just creates the variable target, which will be a shorthand way to refer to the background layer. Then sampleImage() retrieves the RGBA data for the area of the background under the smaller layer and stores the resulting array in the variable rgba. See the sidebar "More About sampleImage()" earlier in the chapter for details on all the parameters of sampleImage().

Next rgbToHsl() converts the RGBA data to HSLA color space and stores the result in variable hsla. Finally, because the lightness channel is the third value in the HSLA array, you use the array index of [2] to extract it (see the "Arrays" section of the JavaScript guide if this doesn't make sense to you). Because it will be a value between 0.0 and 1.0, you just need to multiply it by 100 to get it into a range suitable to control the Opacity parameter.

Become an Expressions Nerd

This chapter covered a lot of ground, but it only provided a hint of what's possible with expressions. Here are a few resources where you can find additional information:

▶ **www.aenhancers.com:** A forum-based site where you can get your questions answered and take a look at expressions contributed by others

▶ **http://forums.creativecow.net/forum/adobe_after_effects_expressions:** A forum dedicated to expressions

▶ **http://forums.adobe.com/community/aftereffects_general_discussion/aftereffects_expressions:** Adobe's own After Effects forum, which has a subforum on expressions

▶ **www.adobe.com/support/aftereffects:** The online version of After Effects Help

▶ **www.motionscript.com:** The site of the author of this chapter, which has a lot of examples and analysis

11

Advanced Color Options and HDR

Don't you wish there was a knob on the TV to turn up the intelligence? There's one marked "Brightness," but it doesn't work.

—Gallagher

Advanced Color Options and HDR

Perhaps you are somewhere near your computer monitor, and there is a window near that monitor. Perhaps there is daylight outside that window, and although like so many graphic artists you work with the shades closed, perhaps some of that light is entering the room. If you were to take a photo out that window from inside the room from where that monitor sits, and then display it on that monitor, would there be any difference between how the room appeared on screen and in reality?

No matter how good your camera or recording medium, and no matter how advanced the display, no way will that scene of daylight illuminating a room from the window look the same on a display and in actuality. But how exactly does the image fail to capture the full fidelity, range, and response of that scene, and what can you do about it? That is the subject of this chapter.

The point here is that you may be aware that the images you work with and the ways you work with them have limitations, but you may not be aware what those are or how to work with them. Specifically, digital images tend to fall short in the following ways:

▶ Color accuracy is not maintained, so hues and intensities slip and slide as an image makes its way through the pipeline.

▶ The dynamic range of the source image is limited, so that shadows and highlights lack the detail that exists in the real world.

▶ The very model used internally by your computer's graphics system is inaccurate in how it adjusts and blends colors, and highly limited in the colors that it can store or represent on the monitor.

To take an image all the way through the pipeline so that the screen matches the source is, of course, impossible. You create camera reality, not reality itself, and as soon as you capture an image, you create an optical point of view that doesn't otherwise exist.

But don't stop believing there's room for improvement; hold on to that feeling. As soon as you learn to work with light more like it actually exists in the world, you begin to realize the compromises and learn to work around the standard limitations of digital color. The computer's model of color is itself a limitation to overcome on the path from the rich outer world of visual data to the images in your final output.

This chapter looks at how higher bit depths, the built-in color management system of After Effects and 3D LUTs, and compositing in linear (1.0 gamma) color can enhance your work.

What Is High Dynamic Range, and Does Film Even Still Exist?

Let's suppose, as is certainly true, that the majority of After Effects artists work predominantly in 8 bits per channel, also known as *monitor color*. If you are among them, this section details the many ways in which you can do better. The simplest and least costly of these is to move from 8-bpc to 16-bpc mode.

16-Bit-Per-Channel Composites

After Effects 5.0 added support for 16-bpc color for one basic reason: to eliminate color quantization, most commonly seen as banding, where subtle gradients and other threshold regions appear in an image. The 16-bpc mode adds 128 extra gradations between each R, G, B, and A value of the familiar 8-bpc mode.

Those increments are typically too fine for your eye to distinguish (or your monitor to display), but the eye easily notices banding, and multiple adjustments to 8-bpc images will cause banding to appear in areas of subtle shading,

NOTES

All but the oldest and most outdated effects and plug-ins support 16-bpc color. To discern which ones do, with the project set to 16 bpc, choose Show 16 bpc-Capable Effects Only from the Effects & Presets panel menu. Effects that are only 8 bpc aren't off-limits, but it may be helpful to place them at the beginning (or end) of the image pipeline, where they are least likely to cause quantization by mixing with higher-bit-depth effects.

such as edge thresholds and shadows, making the image look bad. To raise project color depth, either **Alt**-click (**Opt**-click) the color depth setting at the bottom of the Project panel or use the Depth menu in File > Project Settings.

There are really only a couple of downsides to working in 16 bpc instead of 8. There is a performance hit from the increased memory and processing bandwidth, but on contemporary systems it is nowhere near as bad as it is made out to be.

The real resistance tends to come from the unfamiliarity of 16-bit color values, but switching to 16-bpc mode doesn't mean you're stuck with incomprehensible pixel values such as 32768, 0, 0 for pure red or 16384, 16384, 16384 for middle gray. The Info panel menu allows you to choose whichever numerical color representation works for you, including familiar 8-bpc values when working in 16 bpc (**Figure 11.1**). The following sections use the 8-bpc values of your monitor despite referring to 16-bpc projects.

The Info panel menu's color value settings determine color values everywhere in the application, including the Adobe Color Picker.

Figure 11.1 Love working in 16 bpc but hate analyzing 16-bit values that go up to 32768? Choose 8 bpc in the Info panel menu to display familiar 0 to 255 values. Or better yet, use Decimal values in all bit depths.

Even if your output is 8 bpc, the higher precision of 16 bpc will eliminate quantization and banding. However, there is more to color flexibility than toggling 16 bpc in order to avoid banding. You may even come to work with source images containing values beyond standard 8-bit color, and that's where the opportunities to shine literally begin.

Film and Cineon Files

Although film as a recording and display medium is on the wane, the standards and formats of film remain common in an entirely digital big screen pipeline. The 10-bit Cineon .dpx file remains a common format for storing feature film images. The process of working with film can teach us plenty about how to handle higher dynamic ranges in general, and even newer formats can output film-style .dpx sequences.

The world's most famous Cineon file remains Kodak's dearly departed original test image, affectionately referred to as Marcie (**Figure 11.2**) and available on the book's disc. To get a feel for working with film, drop the file called dlad_2048X1556.cin from the 11_output_simulation folder into After Effects, which imports Cineon files just fine.

The first thing you'll notice about Marcie is that she looks funny, and not just because that look on her face means that her favorite new Tears for Fears song just came on the radio. Cineon files are encoded using a logarithmic (log) tone response curve. To make Marcie look more natural, open the Interpret Footage dialog, select the Color Management tab, click Cineon Settings, and choose the Over Range preset (instead of the default Full Range). The log image is now converted to the monitor's color space.

It would seem natural to convert Cineon files to the monitor's color space, work normally, and then convert the end result back to log, but to do so would be to throw away valuable data. Try this: Apply the Cineon Converter effect and switch the Conversion Type from Linear to Log. This is a preview of how the file would be written on output back to a Cineon log file. Upon further examination of this conversion, you see a problem: In an 8-bpc (or even 16-bpc) project, the bright details in Marcie's hair don't survive the trip (**Figure 11.3**).

What's going on with this mystical Cineon file and its log color space that makes it so hard to deal with? And more importantly, why? To properly answer the question, it's necessary to discuss some basic principles of photography and light.

How Film Becomes Digital

After 35mm or 16mm film has been shot, the negative is developed, and shots destined for digital effects work are scanned frame by frame. During this *Telecine* process, some initial color decisions are made before the frames are output as a numbered sequence of *Cineon* files, named after Kodak's now-defunct film compositing system. Both Cineon files and the related format, DPX, store pixels uncompressed at 10 bits per channel. Scanners are usually capable of scanning 4K plates, and these have become more popular for visual effects usage, although many still elect to scan at half resolution, creating 2K frames around 2048 by 1536 pixels and weighing in at almost 13 MB.

Figure 11.2 This universal sample image has been converted from the film of a bygone era to the Cineon format found on the book's disc.

Also included on the book's disc is a Cineon sequence from the RED Camera (courtesy of fxphd.com), showing off that digital camera's dynamic range and overall image quality. This is one example of the Cineon format that is remaining viable with a digital source.

Figure 11.3 When you convert an image from log space (left) to linear (center) and then back to log (right), the brightest details are lost.

As becomes evident later in the chapter, the choice of the term "linear" as an alternative to "log" space for Cineon Converter is unfortunate, because "linear" specifically means neutral (1.0) gamma; what Cineon Converter calls "linear" is in fact gamma-encoded.

Dynamic Range

The pictures shown in **Figure 11.4** were taken in sequence from a roof on a winter morning. Anyone who has ever tried to photograph a sunrise or sunset with a digital camera should immediately recognize the problem at hand, even in an era in which a phone camera can allegedly deliver HDR images. With a standard exposure, the sky comes in beautifully, but foreground houses are nearly black. Using longer exposures, you can bring the houses up, but by the time they are looking good the sky is completely blown out.

The limiting factor here is the digital camera's small dynamic range, which is the difference between the brightest and darkest things that can be captured in the same image. An outdoor scene has a wide array of brightnesses, but the typical digital device can read only a slice of them. You can change exposure to capture different ranges, but the size of the slice is fixed.

Figure 11.4 Different exposures when recording the same scene clearly produce widely varying results.

Our eyes have a much larger dynamic range and our brains have a wide array of perceptual tricks, so in real life the houses and sky are both seen easily. But even eyes have limits, such as when you try to see someone behind a bright spotlight or use a laptop computer in the sun. The spotlight has not made the person behind any darker, but when eyes adjust to bright lights (as they must to avoid injury), dark things fall out of range and simply appear black.

White on a monitor just isn't very bright, which is one reason professionals work in dim rooms with the blinds pulled down. When you try to represent the bright sky on a dim monitor, everything else in the image has to scale down in proportion. Even when a digital camera can capture extra dynamic range, your monitor must compress it in order to display it.

A standard 8-bpc computer image uses values 0 to 255 to represent RGB values. If you record a value above 255—say 285 or 310—that represents a pixel beyond the monitor's dynamic range, brighter than white, aka overbright. Because 8-bpc pixels can't actually go above 255, overbright information is stored as floating-point decimals where 0.0 is black and 1.0 is white. Floating-point numbers, on the other hand, are virtually unbounded, 0.75, 7.5, or 750.0 are all acceptable values, even though everything above 1.0 will clip to white on the monitor (**Figure 11.5**).

Digital cameras have improved, and the best among them have 13–14 stops or more of latitude, enough to provide effective over range handling. It has also become simpler to create still HDR images from a series of exposures—files that contain all the light information from a scene (**Figure 11.6**). There is even a Photoshop operation (File > Automate > Merge to HDR Pro) to automate the process. In successive exposures, values that remain within range can be compared to describe how the camera is responding to different levels of light. That information allows a computer to connect bright areas in the scene to the darker ones and calculate accurate HDR pixel values that combine detail from each exposure.

But with all the excitement surrounding HDR imaging and improvements in the dynamic range of video cameras,

NOTES

Floating point decimal numbers (which are effective for storing a wide range of precise values efficiently) and high dynamic range numbers (which extend beyond monitor range) have tended to be lumped together, but each is a separate, unique concept. If your 8-bit color range is limited to 0 to 255, then as soon as you have a value of 256, or −1, you are in high dynamic range territory. Floating-point values are merely a method used to store those out-of-range values without hitting an absolute low or high cutoff.

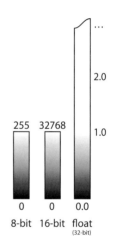

Figure 11.5 Monitor white represents the upper limit for 8-bpc and 16-bpc pixels, while 32-bpc values can go arbitrarily higher (depending on format) or lower; the range also extends below absolute black, 0.0—values that are theoretical and not part of the world you see (unless you're in outer space, staring into a black hole).

Darker Sky: 1.9

Bright Sky: 7.5

Dark Tree: 0.03

Houses: 0.8

Figure 11.6 Consider the floating-point pixel values for this HDR image; they relate to one another proportionally, and continue to do so whether the image is brightened or darkened, because the values do not need to clip at 1.0.

Even the modern DSLR camera lacks the dynamic range to capture an outdoor scene with heavy contrast such as Figure 11.13 on a single pass, so most of them include an option to shoot a series of stills with bracketed exposures above and below the target. The stills can be combined into a single high dynamic range image using Photoshop's Merge to HDR Pro feature.

many forget that for decades there has been another medium available for capturing dynamic range far beyond what a computer monitor can display or a digital camera can capture.

That medium is film, and although an increasing number of professionals consider it a dead medium, the film model remains a basis for how experienced pros store and discuss state-of-the-art captured digital images.

Cineon Log Space

Cineon Log in the DPX format remains the lingua franca of cinematic images. The Cineon format was cleverly developed (pun intended) by Kodak in 1993 for its innovative Cineon compositing system, which had to work with film images using a processor far less powerful than today's iPhone. The standards and language used to talk about this format come from film and how it works, and because that is also related to natural light and physics, those standards largely remain. A film negative gets its name because areas exposed to light ultimately become dark and opaque, and areas unexposed are made transparent during developing. Light makes dark. Hence, *negative*.

Dark is a relative term here. A white piece of paper makes a nice dark splotch on the negative, but a lightbulb darkens the film even more, and a photograph of the sun causes the negative to turn out darker still. By not completely exposing to even bright lights, the negative is able to capture the differences between bright highlights and really bright highlights. Film, the original image capture medium, has always been high dynamic range.

If you were to graph the increase in film "density" as increasing amounts of light expose it, you'd get something like **Figure 11.7**. In math, this is referred to as a *logarithmic curve*. I'll get back to this in a moment.

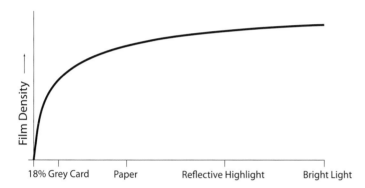

Figure 11.7 Graph the darkening (density) of film as increasing amounts of light expose it and you get a logarithmic curve.

Digital Film

If a monitor's maximum brightness was considered to be 1.0, the brightest value film can represent is officially considered by Kodak to be 13.53 (although using the more efficient ICC color conversion, outlined later in the chapter, reveals brightness values above 70). Note that this only applies to a film negative that is exposed by light in the world as opposed to a film positive, which is limited by the brightness of a projector bulb, and is therefore not really considered high dynamic range. A Telecine captures the entire range of each frame and stores the frames as a sequence of 10-bit Cineon files. Those extra two bits mean that Cineon pixel values can range from 0 to 1023 instead of the 0 to 255 in 8-bit files.

Having four times as many values to work with in a Cineon file helps, but considering there is 13.53 times the range to

All About Log

You may have first heard of logarithmic curves in high school physics class, if you ever learned about the decay of radioactive isotopes.

If a radioactive material has a half-life of one year, half of it will have decayed after that time. The next year, half of what remains will decay, leaving a quarter, and so on. To calculate how much time has elapsed based on how much material remains, a logarithmic function is used.

Light, another type of radiation, has a similar effect on film. At the molecular level, light causes silver halide crystals to react. If film exposed for some short period of time causes half the crystals to react, repeating the exposure will cause half of the remaining to react, and so on. This is how film gets its response curve and the ability to capture even very bright light sources. No amount of exposure can be expected to affect every single crystal.

record, care must be taken in encoding those values. The most obvious way to store all that light would simply be to evenly squeeze 0.0 to 13.53 into the 0 to 1023 range. The problem with this solution is that it would only leave 75 code values for the all-important 0.0 to 1.0 range, the same as allocated to the range 10.0 to 11.0, which you are far less interested in representing with much accuracy. Your eye can barely tell the difference between two highlights that bright—it certainly doesn't need 75 brightness variations between them.

A proper way to encode light on film would quickly fill up the usable values with the most important 0.0 to 1.0 light and then leave space for the rest of the negative's range. Fortunately, the film negative itself with its logarithmic response behaves just this way.

Cineon files are often said to be stored in a log color space. Actually, it is the negative that uses a log response curve, and the file is simply storing the negative's density at each pixel. In any case, the graph in **Figure 11.8** describes how light exposes a negative and is encoded into Cineon color values.

One strange feature in this graph is that black is mapped to code value 95 instead of 0. Not only does the Cineon file store whiter-than-white (overbright) values, it also has some blacker-than-black information. This is mirrored in the film lab when a negative is printed brighter than usual

Figure 11.8 Log encoding is so-called because its color values are expressed as a logarithmic curve, with labels for the visible black and white points that correspond to 0 and 255 in normal 8-bit pixel values.

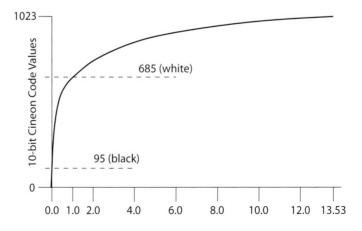

and the blacker-than-black information can reveal itself. Likewise, negatives can be printed darker and take advantage of overbright detail. The standard value mapped to monitor white is 685, and higher values are overbright.

Although the Kodak formulas are commonly used to transform log images for compositing, other methods have emerged. The idea of having light values below 0.0 is dubious at best, and many take issue with the idea that a single curve can describe all film stocks, cameras, and shooting environments. As a different approach, some visual effects facilities take care to photograph well-defined photographic charts and use the resultant film to build custom curves that differ subtly from the Kodak standard.

As much as Cineon log is a great way to encode light captured by film, it should not be used for compositing or other image transformations. This point is so important that it just has to be emphasized again:

Encoding color spaces are not compositing color spaces.

To illustrate this point, imagine you had a black pixel with Cineon value 95 next to an extremely bright pixel with Cineon's highest code value, 1023. If these two pixels were blended together (say, if the image was being blurred), the result would be 559, which is somewhere around middle gray (0.37 to be precise). But when you consider that the extremely bright pixel has a relative brightness of 13.5, that black pixel should only have been able to bring it down to 6.75, which is still overbright white! Log space's extra emphasis on darker values causes standard image processing operations to give those values extra weight, leading to an overall unpleasant and inaccurate darkening of the image. So, final warning: If you're working with a log source, don't do image processing in log space!

Video Gamma Space

Because log spaces certainly don't look natural, it probably comes as no surprise that they are bad color spaces to work in. But there is another encoding color space with which you definitely have a working familiarity, and which is also

The 3D color LUT is commonly designed to be applied directly to a standard Cineon log file to mimic the color response of a given stock or chemical process.

CLOSE-UP

Cineon Settings: Over Range or Full Range?

Tucked away in the Color Management tab of the Interpret Footage dialog with a .dpx or .cin file is a special Cineon Settings button that opens a settings dialog that is perplexing to just about everyone who encounters it for the first time. In After Effects, it is unique to Cineon, yet it is not standard in Nuke or other applications that handle Cineon.

There are four presets, one of which is not like the others. Which one will I choose? Standard sounds boring, Video sounds wrong, and Over Range looks virtually identical to Standard in the numerical settings, so why not the more attractive sounding Full Range?

Turns out there are basically two types of Cineon spaces: log and… non-log. This chapter amply demonstrates why it's not accurate to call the non-log color "linear." Yet, without log encoding, Cineon is merely a slightly more color-accurate, low dynamic range format. Nonetheless, the format is often used that way in the post-film era.

Bottom line: If the file has log encoding, don't use Full Range unless you plan to use some other means such as the Cineon Converter or Apply Color LUT effect to handle the image (which can be appropriate; see the section on LUTs later in the chapter).

The description of gamma in video is oversimplified here somewhat because the subject is complex enough for a book of its own. An excellent one is Charles Poynton's *Digital Video and HDTV Algorithms and Interfaces* (Morgan Kaufmann).

not naturally suitable for compositing: the video space of your monitor.

You may have always assumed that the 8-bit monitor code value 128, halfway between black and white, makes a gray that is half as bright as white. If so, you may be shocked to hear that this is not the case. In fact, 128 is much darker— not even a quarter of white's brightness on most monitors.

A system where half the input gives you half the output is described as *linear*, but monitors (like many things in the real world) are nonlinear. When a system is nonlinear, you can sometimes describe its behavior using the gamma function, shown in **Figure 11.9** and in the equation

```
Output = inputgamma 0 <= input <= 1
```

In this function, the darkest and brightest values (0.0 and 1.0) are always fixed, and the gamma value determines how the transition between them behaves. Successive applications of gamma can be concatenated by multiplying them together. Applying gamma and then 1/gamma has the net result of doing nothing. A curve with a gamma of 1.0 is linear.

In versions of Mac OS X prior to 10.6, the default system gamma value was 1.8., while Windows has long used the gamma value of 2.2, which is now also the Mac OS standard. Because the electronics in your screen are slow to react to lower levels of input voltage, a 1.0 gamma is simply too dark in either case; boosting this value compensates correctly.

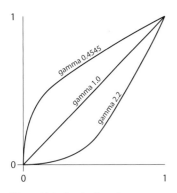

Figure 11.9 Graph of monitor gamma (2.2) with file gamma (0.4545) and linear (1.0). These are the color curves in question, with 0.4545 and 2.2 each acting as the direct inverse of the other.

The reason standard 8-bit digital images do not appear dark, however, is that they have all been created with the inverse gamma function baked in to prebrighten pixels before they are displayed (**Figure 11.10**). Yes, all of them.

Because encoding spaces are not compositing spaces, working directly with images that appear on your monitor can pose problems. Similar to log encoding, video gamma encoding allocates more values to dark pixels, so they weigh more than they should. Video color space is not much more valid than Cineon color space for re-creating the way light behaves in the world at large.

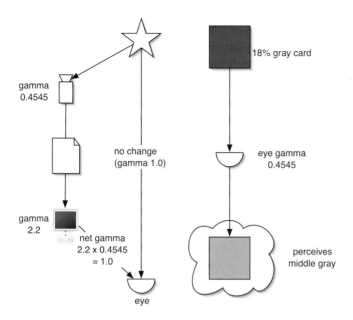

Figure 11.10 The gamma settings in the file and monitor complement one another to result in faithful image reproduction.

CLOSE-UP

Gamma-rama

In case all this gamma talk hasn't already blown your mind, marvel at how monitor gamma and human vision work together. The question often comes up—why is middle gray 18% and not 50%? And why does 50% gray look like middle gray on my monitor, but not on a linear color chart?

It turns out that your eyes also have a nonlinear response to color—your vision brightens low light, which helps you to see where it's dim, a survival advantage. The human eye is very sensitive to small amounts of light, and it gets less sensitive as brightness increases. Your eye effectively brightens the levels, and objects in the world are in fact darker than they appear—or, they become darker when we represent their true linear nature. The subjective observation that 18% gray, give or take a percentage point, appears to be the midpoint between black and white indicates that your eye (or more accurately, the human vision system) applies a gamma correction of 2.5, which can be calculated as follows: $0.5 = 0.18^{(1/2.5)}$.

Linearized Working Space

In the real world, light intensity is linear. Double the wattage and illumination perceptually doubles. Unless you work linear, with these *scene-referred* values, this is not how color intensity behaves on your computer's *monitor-referred* values, which also clip at an intensity well below the whitest white your eye can see. If only your computer had the same color and light model as the real world, you could use light values the same way they are used in nature.

Let's take a trip now to a magical land where computer and real-world light values are one; our destination lays no further than the Project Settings dialog.

Open Project Settings in any project and take a look at Color Settings. By default the dialog might look like the one in **Figure 11.11** (left). There are a couple of menus, a few check boxes (one or two of which might be grayed out), and some complicated looking fine print below.

If there's one thing I know about visual artists, it's that we're generally impatient with fine print and are enamored of visual examples, so try the following:

NOTES

To follow this discussion, choose Decimal from the Info panel menu (this is the default for 32 bpc): 0.0 to 1.0 values are those falling in low dynamic range, or LDR—those values typically described in 8 bit as 0 to 255. Any values outside this range are HDR, 32 bpc only.

NOTES

What's up with the name? sRGB's cumbersome full name tells us that it comes from the IEC, a standards management board founded a century ago by Lord Kelvin in the famously neutral country of Switzerland. Like so many engineering specs, its numerical name connects it to a version number of a long and detailed document—51 pages long, in this case, or roughly 10% longer than this chapter.

1. Set a working space to enable color management. It doesn't really matter for this exercise which you choose—more on the specific choice later—but if you want the most common and flexible one, choose sRGB (or use its more complete and impossible-to-remember name, sRGB IEC61966-2.1), which is designed to correspond to your monitor itself.

2. Note that the check boxes are now all live (none are grayed out), including Linearize Working Space. Enable that one, and leave Compensate for Scene-referred Profiles enabled, then click OK (**Figure 11.11**, right).

3. For simplicity's sake, make sure in Preferences > General that Use System Color Picker is disabled so that you're working with the Adobe Color Picker.

4. Create a new solid layer. Click on the color swatch to open the Adobe Color Picker. Notice that it looks different—strange and unfamiliar, even (**Figure 11.12**). Set Brightness to 50% and notice a tone much brighter than what would be considered middle gray.

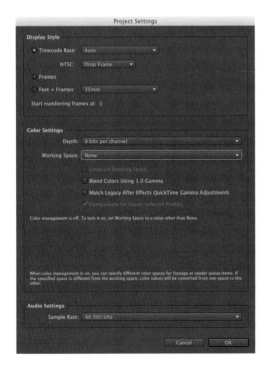

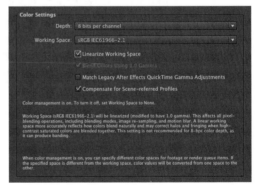

Figure 11.11 This is how default Color Settings might look in the Project Settings dialog.

Figure 11.12 When you set the working space to be linearized, the Adobe color picker responds in kind by presenting linear color values. Notice how far below center middle gray appears to be.

5. Now try switching that Brightness value to 18%.

Aha. In a linearized working space, After Effects accommodates the 18% middle gray of real-world color.

Now the question becomes, how does that help? This type of change should generally not be introduced to a project already in progress, since all of the solids and other color selections will shift and need to be reset, and any blends will also be linear, so even composites without color selections will shift. Plus, it's confusing not to have middle gray at 50%, isn't it?

What's the point?

Linear HDR Compositing: Lifelike

The examples in **Table 11.1** show the difference between making adjustments to digital camera photos in their native video space and performing those same operations in linear space. In all cases, an unaltered photograph featuring the equivalent in-camera effect is shown for comparison.

The table's first column contains the images brightened by one stop, an increment on a camera's aperture, which controls how much light is allowed through the lens. Widening the aperture by one stop allows twice as much light to enter. An increase of three stops brightens the image by a factor of eight ($2 \times 2 \times 2$, or 23).

To double pixel values in video space is to quickly blow out bright areas in the image. Video pixels are already encoded with extra brightness and can't take much more.

TABLE 11.1 Comparison of Adjustments in Native Video Space and in Linear Space

	BRIGHTEN ONE STOP	LENS DEFOCUS	MOTION BLUR
Original Image			
Filtered in Video Space			
Filtered in Linear Space			
Real-World Photo			

The curtain and computer screen lose detail in video space that is retained in linear space. The linear image is nearly indistinguishable from the actual photo for which camera exposure time was doubled (another practical way to brighten by one stop).

The second column simulates an out-of-focus scene using Fast Blur. You may be surprised to see an overall darkening with bright highlights fading into the background—at least in video space. In linear, the highlights pop much better. See how the little man in the Walk sign stays bright in linear, but it almost fades away in video because of the extra emphasis given to dark pixels in video space. Squint your eyes and you notice that only the video image darkens overall. Because a defocused lens doesn't cause any less light to enter it, regular 8-bpc blur does not behave like a true defocus.

The table's third column uses After Effects' built-in motion blur to simulate the streaking caused by quick panning as the photo was taken. Pay particular attention to the highlight on the lamp; notice how it leaves a long, bright streak in the linear and in-camera examples. Artificial dulling of highlights is the most obvious giveaway of nonlinear image processing.

Artists have dealt with the problems of working directly in video space for years without even knowing we're compensating all the time. A perfect example is the Screen transfer mode; while it's additive in nature, its calculations are clearly convoluted when compared with the pure Add transfer mode. Screen uses a multiply-toward-white function, which has the advantage of avoiding the clipping associated with Add. But Add's reputation comes from its application in bright video-space images. Screen was invented only to help people be productive when working in video space, without overbrights; Screen darkens overbrights (**Figure 11.13**). Real light doesn't screen, it adds. Add replaces Screen, Multiply supersedes Hard Light, and many other blending modes fall away entirely in linear floating point, where they are revealed for what they are: kludgey compensations for the limitations of 8 bit.

NOTES

According to Wikipedia, the "Kluge paper feeder" was an automatic paper feeder for printing presses, which was first manufactured by Brandtjen and Kluge in 1919. It supposedly had a Rube Goldberg machine reputation, and was "temperamental, subject to frequent breakdowns, and devilishly difficult to repair—but oh, so clever!"

Figure 11.13 Watch those highlights. Double up the explosion (top left) in video space while Add blows out (top right), but Screen in video looks better if washed out (bottom left). Adding in linear is best (bottom right).

NOTES

Examples on the disc with an over-range source can be found in 11_experiments_hdr_source and 11_hdr_overrange_RED_source; 11_hdr_from_ldr_afternoon and 11_hdr_from_ldr_sunrise are examples from previous editions making use of 32-bpc compositing of low dynamic-range source.

TIP

Linear blending is available without 32-bpc HDR; in Project Settings, choose Blend Colors using 1.0 Gamma. This feature is described in detail near the end of the chapter.

CLOSE-UP

Terminology

Linear floating-point HDR compositing uses *radiometrically linear*, or *scene-referred*, color data. For this discussion, this is perhaps best called "linear light compositing" or "linear." The alternative mode to which you are accustomed is "gamma-encoded," "monitor color space," or simply "video."

HDR Source and Linearized Working Space

Should you be fortunate enough to have high-bit-depth source images with over-range values, or even if you have reason to push images into HDR by adding overexposure, glows, and so on, working in 32-bpc linear has indisputable benefits—even if your final output uses a plain old video format that cannot accommodate these values.

In **Figure 11.14**, the lights are severely clipped by video space, which is not a problem so long as the image is only displayed; all of the images look fine printed on this page or displayed on your monitor. Add motion blur, however, and you see the problem at its most exaggerated; the points of light should not lose their intensity simply by being put into motion.

The benefits of floating point aren't restricted to blurs, however; those just happen to emphasize the difference. Every operation in a compositing pipeline gains extra realism from the presence of floating-point pixels and linear blending.

Figure 11.15 features an HDR image on which a simple composite is performed, once in video space and once using linear floating point. In the HDR version, the dark translucent layer behaves like sunglass lenses on the bright window, revealing extra detail exactly as a filter on

Figure 11.14 An HDR image (left) is blurred without floating point (center) and with floating point (right).

Figure 11.15 A source image with over-range values in the highlights (left) is composited in LDR (middle) and HDR (right).

a camera lens would. The soft edges of a motion-blurred object also behave realistically as bright highlights push through. Without over-range values, there is no extra information to reveal, so the exterior disappears and foreground objects don't.

32 Bits per Channel

You don't need an HDR source to take advantage of an HDR pipeline, but it does offer a clear glimpse of this brave new world. Open 11_treeHDR_lin.aep; it contains a comp made up of a single image in 32-bpc EXR format. With the Info panel clearly visible, move your cursor around the frame.

As your cursor crosses highlights—the lights on the tree, specular highlights on the wall and chair, and especially in the window—the values are seen to be well above 1.0, the maximum value you will ever see doing the same in 8-bpc or 16-bpc mode. Remember that you can quickly toggle between color depths by **Alt**-clicking (**Opt**-clicking)

NOTES

Included on the disc are two similar images, sanityCheck.exr and sanityCheck.tif. The 32-bpc EXR file is linearized, but the 8-bpc TIFF file is not. Two corresponding projects are also included, one using no color profile, the other employing a linear profile. These should help illustrate the different appearances of a linear and a gamma-encoded image.

Figure 11.16 Exposure is an HDR preview control that appears in the Composition panel in 32-bpc mode.

NOTES

Keep in mind that for each 1.0 adjustment upward or downward of Exposure, you double (or halve) the light levels in the scene. Echoing the earlier discussion, a +3.0 Exposure setting sets the light levels 8x (or 2³) brighter.

the project color depth identifier at the bottom of the Project panel.

You might assume that there is no detail in that window—it appears blown out to solid white forevermore in LDR. However, you may have noticed an extra icon and accompanying numerical value that appears at the bottom of the Composition panel in a 32-bpc project (**Figure 11.16**). This is the Exposure control; its icon looks like a camera aperture and it performs an analogous function—controlling the exposure (total amount of light) of a scene the way you would stop a lens up or down, adjusting its aperture.

Drag to the left on the numerical text and something amazing happens. Not only does the lighting in the scene decrease naturally, as if the light itself were being brought down, but at somewhere around –10.0, a gentle blue gradient appears in the window (**Figure 11.17a**).

Drag the other direction, into positive Exposure range, and the scene begins to look like an overexposed photo; the light proportions remain and the highlights bloom outward (**Figure 11.17b**).

The Exposure control in the Composition panel is a preview-only control (there is an effect by the same name that renders); scan with your cursor, and Info panel values do not vary according to its setting. This control offers a quick way to check what is happening in the out-of-range areas of a composition. With a linear light image,

(a)

(b)

Figure 11.17 At –10 Exposure **(a)**, the room is dark other than the tree lights and detail becomes visible out the window. At +3 **(b)**, the effect is exactly that of a camera that was open three stops brighter than the unadjusted image.

each integer increment represents the equivalent of one photographic stop, or a doubling (or halving) of linear light value.

Mixed Bit Depths and Compander

Many effects don't, alas, support 32 bpc, although there are dozens that do. Apply a 16-bpc or (shudder) 8-bpc effect, however, and the overbrights in your 32-bpc project disappear—all clipped to 1.0. Any effect will reduce the image being piped through it to its own color space limitations. A small warning sign appears next to the effect to remind you that it does not support the current bit depth. You may even see a warning explaining the dangers of applying this effect.

Of course, this doesn't mean you need to avoid these effects to work in 32 bpc. It may mean you have to cheat, and After Effects includes a preset allowing you to do just that: Compress-Expand Dynamic Range (contained in Effects & Presets > Animation Presets > Image – Utilities; make certain Show Animation Presets is checked in the panel menu).

This preset actually consists of two instances of the HDR Compander effect, which was specifically designed to bring HDR back into LDR range. The first instance is automatically renamed Compress, and the second Expand, which is how the corresponding modes are set. You set the Gain of Compress to whatever is the brightest overbright value you wish to preserve, up to 100. The values are then compressed into LDR range, allowing you to apply your LDR effect. Gain (as well as Gamma) of Expand is linked via an expression to Compress so that the values round-trip back to HDR (**Figure 11.18**).

This prevents clipping of over-range values. If banding appears as a result of Compress-Expand, Gamma can be adjusted to weight the compressed image more toward the region of the image (probably the shadows) where the banding occurs. Image fidelity is thus sacrificed in order to preserve a compressed version of the HDR pipeline.

You can set up a project to ensure that Compressor/Expander, known as Compander, play the most minimal role possible.

RED HDRx

Since the last edition of this book was published, RED has devised a method to conjoin two adjacent exposures in a single image and provide exposure latitude to rival film on their EPIC and SCARLET cameras, improving upon the 13 stops of latitude that RED already claims for its regular shooting format, with up to 18 stops of total latitude. Recollect from the film discussion earlier that Kodak conservatively set film latitude at just under 14 stops (may shooters claim higher numbers).

It's not a given that, simply because this option is available, productions universally take advantage of it, for a couple of reasons. One is that the associated data footprint is substantially larger, such that it limits all areas of the production process. Maximum frame rate, minimum REDCODE ratio, and maximum record time on media are all cut in half. Because of how the format works, it is also more breakable with fast motion of bright objects in a dark environment; these may not resolve without distortion.

Still… 18 stops lets you pull off some shots like you may have never seen before, moving freely from a dark interior to a bright exterior, or even shooting both at once.

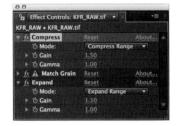

Figure 11.18 Effects & Presets > Animation Presets > Presets > Image – Utilities includes the Compress-Expand Dynamic Range preset, also known as the Compander (Compressor/Expander). Two instances of the HDR Compander effect are linked together with expressions to work in opposition, and the idea is to sandwich them around an 8- or 16-bpc effect (such as Match Grain).

Floating-Point Files

As you've already seen, there is one class of files that does not need to be converted to linear space: floating-point files. These files are already storing scene-referred values, complete with overbright information. Common formats supported by After Effects are Radiance (.hdr) and floating-point .tif, not to mention .psd, but the most universal and versatile is Industrial Light + Magic's OpenEXR format. OpenEXR uses efficient 16-bpc floating-point pixels, can store any number of image channels, supports lossless compression, and is already supported by most 3D programs thanks to being an open source format.

After Effects offers expanded support of the OpenEXR format by bundling plug-ins from fnord software, which provide access to multiple layers and channels within these files. EXtractoR can open any floating-point image channel in an EXR file, and Identifier can open the other, non-image channels such as Object and Material ID.

TIP

Any 8- and 16-bpc effects clip only the image that they process. Apply one to a layer, and you clip that layer only. Apply one to an adjustment layer, and you clip everything below. Add an LDR comp or layer to an otherwise HDR comp in a 32-bpc project, and it remains otherwise HDR.

As much as possible, group all of your LDR effects together, and keep them away from the layers that use blending modes where HDR values are most essential. For example, apply an LDR effect via a separate adjustment layer instead of directly on a layer with a blending mode. Also, if possible, apply the LDR effects first, then boost the result into HDR range to apply any additional 32-bpc effects and blending modes.

Blend Colors Using 1.0 Gamma

After Effects includes a fantastic option to linearize image data only when performing blending operations: the Blend Colors Using 1.0 Gamma toggle in Project Settings (**Figure 11.19**). This allows you to take advantage of linear blending, which makes Add and Multiply blending modes actually work properly, even in 8-bpc or 16-bpc modes.

Figure 11.19 This check box is all you need to get the benefits of linear light compositing without the extra overhead of 32-bpc floating-point color.

The difference is quite simple. A linearized working space—of which The Foundry's Nuke is a prime example, since unlike After Effects it only operates in linear—performs all image processing in gamma 1.0. In Nuke and in a linear After Effects project, footage is converted to a linear project space on import, and converted back to monitor color only for the purpose of, you guessed it, displaying the image on the monitor (while the data itself remains linearized).

Linearized blending, which is somewhat unique to After Effects, actually converts a layer to linear color during the blending stage, right after any masks, effects, or transforms have been applied. None of those benefits from the increased range and accuracy of linear color, but the blending modes do behave just as they do in a linearized working space. Add and Multiply look good when used this way. Try it, you'll like it.

Because effects aren't added in linear color, blurs using the blending-only model fail to interact correctly with overbrights (although they do composite more nicely), and you don't get the subtle benefits to Transform operations that seem to solve what are seen as basic limitations of After Effects. In a fully linearized working space, 3D lights behave more like actual lights.

After Effects is sometimes bashed for poor scaling quality when compared with Nuke, which has a number of available scaling operations; a scaled image behaves much better in a linearized working space. I love the linear blending option when working with entirely LDR footage, with no need to manage over-range values. It gives me the huge benefit of more elegant composites and blending modes without forcing me to think about managing effects in linear color, or confusing some other artist by handing them a project that only looks good at 32-bpc linear (although inevitably, some do). Certain key effects, in particular Exposure, helpfully operate in linear, 1.0 gamma mode even in a default 8-bpc project.

À la Carte

So to review, there are three fundamental ways to move beyond standard monitor color in After Effects. Simply by enabling 32-bpc color, you get out-of-range handling, without enabling linear blending. Or, you can enable linear blending and use it in all three color modes, not just 32 bpc. Finally, by setting a project working space, you can linearize the color of the entire project, as shown at the end of the previous section.

One thing you cannot do is enable 32 bpc just for one comp—it's the whole project or nothing. But you can work in 16 bpc and enable 32 bpc only when it's time to render, if the performance at the higher bit depth is too great. Not only do per-frame render times lengthen in 32 bpc, but RAM previews also become shorter as each frame is required to hold exponentially more data. Remember, 32 bits is not double 16; it doubles each pixel value eight times.

Output

What good is it working in linear 32-bpc color if the output bears no resemblance to what you see in the Composition viewer? Just because you work in 32-bpc color does not mean you have to render your images that way.

Keeping in mind that any given working space can be linear or not, if you work in a linearized color space and then render to a format that is typically gamma encoded (as most are), the gamma-encoded version of the working space will also be used. After Effects spells this out for you explicitly in the Description section of the Color Management tab (**Figure 11.20**).

Figure 11.20 Suppose you work in a color-managed 32-bpc linear project but want to dump out a simple reference QuickTime without thinking about it. After Effects does the right thing and even spells out in the fine print what it's doing: leaving the output gamma (because the format doesn't support 32 bpc) and baking in the profile (because the format can't embed it) so as best to preserve the appearance of the comp.

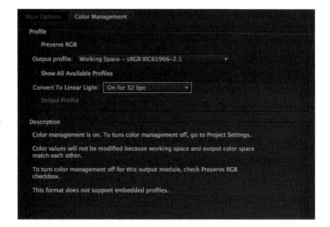

To this day, the standard method to pass around footage with over-range values, particularly if it is being sent for film-out, is to use 10-bit log-encoded Cineon/DPX. This is also converted for you from 32-bpc linear, but be sure to choose Working Space as the output profile, and in Cineon Settings use the Standard preset.

The great thing about Cineon/DPX with a standard 10-bit profile is that it is a universal standard. Facilities around the world know what to do with it even if they've never encountered a file with an embedded color profile. As detailed earlier in the chapter, it is capable of taking full advantage of the dynamic range of film, which is still the standard to which digital formats aspire in this particular regard.

Linear LDR Compositing, Color Management, and LUTs

Color only seems arbitrary because it is a phenomenon of human vision and seems to be perceived differently by each individual human. The light values that make up that color, however, are precisely measurable and replicable in absolute terms. You might not have so narrow a goal as to make output "exactly" match source, but taking control of the color pipeline necessitates that you eliminate variables.

While color is a phenomenon of vision and does not apparently exist in the absence of an eye to see it and a mind to process it, color also corresponds to measurable wavelengths and intensities that can be regulated and profiled. Your computer and its monitor, however, do not natively do this on your behalf.

We're all familiar with the concept of a digital image as three color channels, each containing an 8-bit luminance value. Web designers may convert this value into more concise hex color values (white is FFFFFF, black 000000, pure blue 0000FF, and so on), but they're merely the same 8-bit combinations described in a different language.

The fantasy is that these 8-bit RGB values are reliable, since they seem precise. The reality is they are tied directly to a highly imprecise and arbitrary device, your monitor, no two of which are completely identical in how they appear right out of the box. Those R, G, and B values are only monitoring how much current—electrical power—is given to each channel.

Color Management in After Effects

You may have noticed that you can't choose the Linearize Working Space option in Project Settings without choosing a Working Space. Which of the many should you choose, and why? It's a topic that seems to have caused at least as many questions as it has addressed since being added to After Effects along with 32 bit-per-channel HDR.

The short answer is that sRGB (aka sRGB IEC61966-2.1—say it five times fast) is most often the color space you want for feature projection and digital displays. HDTV

(Rec. 709) is similar in terms of response but limited to the broadcast TV gamut, which is actually helpful if you're working on a broadcast project. Although these color spaces are sometimes associated with a specific bit depth, you can you use any of them at any of the three color depths, including 32 bits per channel, in After Effects.

The bigger picture is that Adobe nobly took the lead on standardizing the color pipeline for video the way that Photoshop and Illustrator did for print beginning over a decade before. The model of embedding a color profile with an image file works well with still images for which color precision is essential (corporate logos come to mind), and theoretically can work just as well with moving images.

The difficulty for After Effects color management, however, is threefold. First of all, many people fail to understand or remember that it is for previewing only, unless you input and output images that support color profiles, and those color profiles are maintained in their final display format. That simply never happens, despite how cool it might be if it did.

Second, most moving image formats, devices, and applications don't support color profiles, so even if you want to put them to use, you're limited to image sequence formats such as TIFF and PSD that support them.

The full Color Management section that was included as part of this chapter in the previous edition has been moved to a PDF on the book's disc. This includes the entire pipeline, from Monitor Calibration to color-managed output.

The expectation that the choice of Working Space will affect the look of the final image is false; it only affects your perception of the look as you work in After Effects, and thus how you adjust it. This allows for the super-cool display simulation capabilities in After Effects, and those do work; you can adjust an image in the application and see right in the Composition viewer how it will look when printed to a particular film stock.

And that leads to the third and final difficulty with color management: It competes with another system that, while less flexible, has been around much longer, the color LUT. That After Effects has adopted and expanded LUT support—it is now the main form of integration between the application and SpeedGrade, Adobe's first dedicated color correction suite—is a tacit admission that the color management system, while cool, is not currently a contender to provide the whole answer.

Even worse, the real world also includes QuickTime, which can, on its own, further change or render nonstandard the appearance of a file, almost guaranteeing that the output won't match your composition without special handling.

QuickTime

QuickTime is a format on which a huge majority of post-production professionals rely. The QuickTime format is a moving target for color, because it has its own internal and seemingly ad-hoc color management system (whose spec Apple does not even reveal, which sometimes changes from one version of QuickTime to the next, and which also can change depending on which system or software is displaying it). Even Apple's own software applications have not proven reliably consistent about how they display QuickTime color, and if that's not a danger signal, what is?

The gamma of QuickTime files is interpreted uniquely by each codec, so files with Photo-JPEG compression can, for example, have a different gamma than files with H.264 compression. Even files with the default Animation setting, which are effectively uncompressed and assumedly neutral, have been known to display an altered (inconsistent) gamma.

The Match Legacy After Effects QuickTime Gamma Adjustments toggle in Project Settings is not only the longest-titled check box in the entire application, it is an option you should not need, in theory at least, unless you've opened up an old 7.0 (or earlier) project, or you need a composition to match what you see in QuickTime Player.

If in doubt, at least compare QuickTime output by eye to what you see in your After Effects comp, particularly if using a format notorious for gamma shifts, such as the otherwise useful H.264. If you see such shifts occur—and they will generally be obvious—either adjust gamma on output to compensate (squirrely but reliable), or set up a test using an image such as the included SanityCheck to try to track down where the shift can be eliminated. The author wishes to apologize for the lack of a universal quick-fix for QuickTime anomalies, and wishes in turn to acknowledge this as one more reason why professional visual effects facilities should render image sequences and use QuickTime as a review not delivery format.

Bypass Color Management?

Headaches like these make many artists long for simpler days. If you prefer to avoid color management altogether, even on files that contain color profiles, or to use it only selectively, you can disable the feature and return to After Effects 7.0 behavior (other than in 32-bit linear, which requires it):

1. In Project Settings, set Working Space to None (as it is by default, **Figure 11.21**).

Figure 11.21 The Working Space setting (along with the fine print) indicates that color management is disabled.

2. Enable Match Legacy After Effects QuickTime Gamma Adjustments.

   Being more selective about how color management is applied—to take advantage of some features while leaving others disabled for clarity—is tricky and tends to stump some pretty smart users. Here are a couple of final tips that may help:

   ▶ To disable a profile for incoming footage, check Preserve RGB in Interpret Footage (Color Management tab). No attempt will be made to preserve the appearance of that clip.

▶ To change the behavior causing untagged footage to be tagged with an sRGB profile, in interpretation rules.txt find this line

```
# soft rule: tag all untagged footage with an
sRGB profile
*, *, *, *, * ~ *, *, *, *, "sRGB", *
```

and add a # at the beginning of the second line to assign no profile, or change "sRGB" to a different format (options are listed in the comments at the top of the file).

▶ To prevent your display profile from being factored in, disable View > Use Display Color Management and the pixels are sent straight to the display.

▶ To prevent any file from being color managed, check Preserve RGB in Output Module Settings (Color Management tab).

Note that any of the preceding tips may lead to unintended consequences, and the hope is that such nerdery is never actually required.

LUT: Color Look-Up Table

LUTs are a worldwide standard for compositing, editing, and color software the world over. After Effects, which didn't even support them until CS5, now relies on them to bring you looks from SpeedGrade (not to mention LogC footage from the Arri Alexa).

What is a LUT? A color look-up table essentially takes one set of color values and translates them to another set of values; it is an array of values that can be saved and reapplied and shared on any system that supports a LUT. The classic usage of a LUT is to preview a 10-bpc log file on a monitor as if it were a film print using a particular film stock. In other words, it overlaps heavily with After Effects' own Color Management, as well as effects such as Cineon Converter. In fact, a LUT-based workflow generally replaces both of those.

There's a bit more to a LUT than there is to an effect preset. A one-dimensional LUT is a lot like levels—taking a single value and changing it to a different value—but

Figure 11.22 SpeedGrade includes a bunch of .look LUTs that work very well without adjustment if applied to flat footage (aka well-shot footage).

ARRI LogC

The .cube format is also used by ARRI and their online LUT generator, which allows you to set specific parameters in a Web interface with a series of preset categories, and download a set of LUT files that are designed to work with your source and destination formats of choice (**Figure 11.23**). There are a couple of reasons to use these; one is that After Effects doesn't have native handling of LogC, which isn't the same profile as Cineon Log. Also, there are a number of particulars for which the LUT generator will develop a specific LUT that allows you never to think about that part of the process again.

It's essential to know how your footage was shot and what type of image pipeline you're planning to use (video or linear) and in what color space (such as Rec.709). These variables make it impossible to recommend specific settings in a book for generalized usage rather than to steer you toward a 3D LUT that looks "good"—which is to say flat, and not overly dark or flashed—when you bring it in and apply the LUT. In a linear 32-bit workflow, you may also need to add the Linear Profile Converter effect with the Input Profile set to Linearize Input Profile and the appropriate Input Profile chosen.

the new Apply Color LUT plug-in supports a couple of the common 3D LUT formats. A 3D LUT adjusts all three color channels interdependently and nonlinearly, so that saturation and brightness can be adjusted independent of one another. This allows color adjustments to mimic different gamuts, such as the wider gamut of film. It's a much more sophisticated color model than could be recreated with 1D effects such as Levels and Curves.

You can create your own 3D LUT as a SpeedGrade .look file (**Figure 11.22**), or use one of the dozens provided with the application. You can also make adjustments to one of the provided looks and save that. After Effects can even work with a LUT in one of the Autodesk formats to create a .3DL file, or the Truelight .cube format, which is the one ARRI supplies for use with LogC footage from its Alexa camera.

What's the point? For one, the color adjustment is ubiquitous and can be interchanged with many other types of

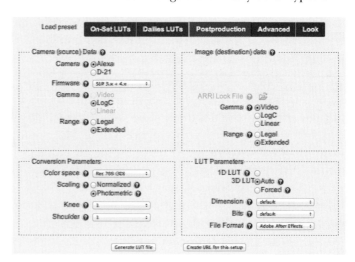

Figure 11.23 ARRI offers just enough options to hang yourself if you don't know what you're doing—but nowhere near as many as RED. This interface is used to create a LUT that you can use directly in After Effects in lieu of color management.

computer graphics systems. More importantly, if someone working in Lustre, Smoke, Flame, or Scratch wants to send you a LUT, he can do so without apologies, provided he chooses one of the compatible formats.

There are three basic usages of a LUT. A *Calibration LUT* is like color management and can in turn be used in a couple different ways—it can be meant only to preview how an image might look in a different setting, on a particular film stock, or with a particular process. To use a LUT this way in After Effects requires that you apply it to an Adjustment layer and set that layer as a Guide layer so that it doesn't render. You do this with the anticipation that later in the process you will actually be applying and viewing the footage in that setting (that is, printing to that particular stock).

A *Viewing LUT* is used to apply a color correction look to footage. This one is intended to alter and render the pixel values, not merely preview them. This can be established at the end of the pipeline in an application such as Speed-Grade and then applied for rendering out of After Effects (in this case, as a .look file exported from SpeedGrade).

An interesting contemporary usage of calibration in an all-digital pipeline that never ends up in a photochemical process, is to establish the entire look of a project with a LUT in preproduction, preview with it on set, then pre-apply it to all incoming footage and match to that footage as if it were already baked in, like starting with a film stock. Treating the flexible digital medium like a rigid film format such as this can actually free a production to shoot with a flat response—excellent practice with a digital camera—and feel confident how the final will look while on set.

Beyond Theory into Practice

This chapter concludes Section II, which has focused on the most fundamental techniques of effects compositing. In the next and final section, you'll apply those techniques. You'll also learn about the importance of observation, as well as some specialized tips and tricks for specific effects compositing situations that re-create particular environments, settings, conditions, and natural phenomena.

12

Color and Light

Light seeking light doth light of light beguile.

— William Shakespeare

Color and Light

There's more to light than physics and optics, although those are certainly essential components. The work of a compositor is akin to that of a painter or cinematographer, in that a combination of technical knowledge, interpretation, and even intuition all contribute to getting a scene "right."

Other areas of digital production rely on elaborate models to simulate the way light works in the physical world. Like a painter, the compositor observes the play of light in the three-dimensional world in order to re-create it in two-dimensions. Like a cinematographer, you succeed with a feeling for how lighting and color decisions affect the beauty and drama of a scene and how the camera gathers them.

Several chapters in this book have already touched upon principles of the behavior of light. Chapter 5 is about the bread and butter work of the compositor—matching the brightness and color of a foreground and background. Chapter 9 is all about how the world looks through a lens. Chapter 11 explores more advanced technical ways in which After Effects can re-create the way color and light values behave.

This chapter is dedicated to practical situations involving light that you as a compositor must re-create. It's important to distinguish lighting conditions you can easily emulate and those that are essentially out of bounds—although, for a compositor with a good eye and patience, the seemingly "impossible" becomes a welcome challenge and the source of a favorite war story.

A Light Source Has Quality and Direction

In many scenes, there is clearly more involved with light than matching brightness and contrast channel by channel. Light direction is fundamental, especially where the quality of the light might be *hard* (direct) rather than *soft* (diffuse).

Light is obviously complicated. It required no less than Max Planck and Albert Einstein to address a debate that had raged since the 17th century as to whether light was even made up of particles or waves. Even an ordinary scene lit by a single source—the sun—is filled with a number of characteristics that are rather painstaking to re-create from scratch on a computer. Nonetheless, there are some general guidelines and workflows for manipulating the light situation of a 2D scene, and for incorporating 3D lighting and objects.

Location and Quality of Light

In an ideal world, once you get to the After Effects stage you will have specific information about the lighting conditions that existed when source footage was shot. This could be a plan view of the placement and type of each light; on-set photos or notes from a director of photography, DIT (digital imaging tech), camera assistant, or on-set supervisor, if any of those were present; and on a low-budget production, all of those might be you. Otherwise, and with or without all of that data, you need to look for clues about the lighting from within the scene itself. How hard and dark are the shadows? Where are there reflections? How does the ambient light change from frame to frame?

Hard light aimed directly at a subject from the same direction as the camera actually flattens out detail, effectively decreasing contrast. And artificial lighting is usually from multiple sources in a single scene, which work against one another to diffuse hard shadows (**Figure 12.1**).

Alter Light Direction and Hotspots Like a Matte Painter

Mismatched direction or diffusion of light on a foreground element is clearly a fundamental problem for the compositor. This can only be the result of poor planning or limited resources, unless the composite has turned into something more like a digital matte painting, which might be made up of dozens of individual loosely matched sources. The solution is generally to neutralize the mismatch by isolating and minimizing it. Relighting the element in 2D generally

TIP

One of your primary responsibilities as an on-set visual effects supervisor is to record references and diagrams of light conditions on set, to elucidate what shows up in the image.

Figure 12.1 Interior sets, like interior environments, are typically lit by more than one source, creating multiple soft highlights and shadows.

offers a result that might technically be called "cheesy" if you leave your fingerprints all over it.

Every shot in the world has unique light characteristics, but a couple of overall strategies apply. Once you've exhausted simple solutions such as flopping the shot (if the lighting is simply backward), you can

▶ isolate and remove directional clues around the element, such as cast shadows (typically by matting or rotoscoping them out)

▶ isolate and reduce the contrast of highlights and shadows in the element itself, typically with a Levels or Curves adjustment (potentially aided by a luma matte, described later in this chapter)

▶ invert the highlights and shadows with a counter-gradient

The simple way to undo evidence of too strong a keylight in a scene is to create a counter-gradient as a track matte for an adjustment layer; a Levels or Curves effect on this layer affects the image proportionally to this gradient.

This is one area where the addition of falloff lighting to After Effects comes into play.

Light Falloff

TIP

Just as this book went to press, the Pixel Cloud plug-in was debuted by Blurrypixel. It allows you to relight a 3D generated image using a Position Pass and Normal Pass; these supply the data about the original rendered surface needed to relight it, a capability that had previously been considered off limits outside of Nuke. It works with renders from CINEMA 4D, Maya, and 3ds Max. Find out more at http://blurrypixel.com.

Suppose you need to add or match natural light falloff. Versions of After Effects previous to CS5.5 have more or less forced you to fake it, using tricks like multiplying together a couple of linear gradients to get anything like realism. With 3D lighting, you were out of luck if you wanted falloff, and that is the big change this time around. If your scene contains 3D layers that are meant to be lit realistically, or even just to contain some falloff that you control, After Effects lights now include a couple of options that will make—well, not a night and day difference, but certainly an afternoon and evening difference.

Enabling the new options is as simple as going into the Light layer controls, either when you create the light or by twirling down the layer thereafter, and choosing a Falloff option (**Figure 12.2**). None is After Effects lighting as you've known it since version 5.0—not CS5, but 5, when 3D layers were first added. Open a project from a prior version of After Effects and this will be the default.

Smooth Falloff allows control of the Radius, which you can think of as the size of the light, and Falloff Distance, beyond which no light is cast. The levels diminish in direct proportion to the difference between these two distances; halfway between one and the other, light intensity is 50% of its level within the radius.

So where are the vectors showing these two crucial radii around the Light icon in the comp viewer? Sadly, those must wait for a future version of the application. As useful as it would be simply to see how far a Radius of x pixels and a Falloff Distance of y would be, you instead must either calculate it using either Position data or expressions, or use visual evidence. Set a target as in **Figure 12.3** and it's a pretty close equivalent, not that you want to add a big ol' shape layer every time you create a light.

Smooth Falloff offers complete control, but as stated elsewhere in the book, it's not realistic. To re-create the behavior of an actual light in the natural world, twirl down Light Options and change Falloff to Inverse Square Clamped, a long-winded title that could be shortened to "Realistic." The "inverse square" portion of the name refers to the way light decays as discovered by none other than that kooky Cantabrigian Sir Isaac Newton.

In principle, the inverse-square law is straightforward. For each doubling of the distance, the intensity of light is one-quarter the source. At four times a given distance, or double-double, intensity is one-sixteenth, and Falloff Distance is grayed out to reflect that this rule is in play. The "clamped" portion of the name indicates that the values start calculating at the edge of the Radius; they are clamped to that number as the equivalent of zero, or the starting point.

In practice, Inverse Square Clamped lights can be mixed and matched at higher and lower intensities just as you might use light fixtures together on a set. It might take a number of lights to re-create the effect of a scene with

Figure 12.2 The Falloff menu and related Radius and Falloff Distance controls (here grayed out for inverse-square clamped) are new additions to the Light Settings dialog; these settings are also accessible from the Timeline.

Figure 12.3 This point light is simply positioned above the 3D target graphic with the Inverse Square Clamped falloff setting, resulting in this natural look.

multiple light sources, or a single light with an Intensity setting above 100%. When mixing multiple lights and pushing values above 100%, it is a good idea to consider 32-bpc mode to make their behavior and those of the layers they affect most natural.

Color Looks in After Effects and SpeedGrade

It's funny to me now that in earlier editions of this book I felt the need to convince readers of the importance of color correction. "Correction" probably isn't as good a term for what I'm talking about as "looks" or "conforms," which mean slightly different things. The point remains that I can no longer name a professional feature film or broadcast project these days that goes out without a grade, with the exception of news programs, sports, and reality TV, and even those are starting to see grades and color looks.

In the Foreword to this book, Stu Maschwitz asks the question, "who brings the sex" to a project ? The answer is clear. In his account, this person is the one who makes the shot look final by daring to make the color and contrast cinematic, so the shot evokes emotion.

So don't take my word for it; look at any production in a movie theater or on your television and compare it to what you were looking at just a decade ago, and see if you don't agree that the entertainment world seems to be deep in the throes of a love affair with color.

And at just this moment, along comes the first Adobe software dedicated specifically to color grading, SpeedGrade. Compared to what we've had from Adobe in the past, it's as if the company said, "Here, we bought you a Ferrari; take it for a spin and see what she can do."

Getting into SpeedGrade

Chapter 5 had the best information I know how to offer on using the three most popular color correction tools in After Effects—Levels, Curves, and Hue/Saturation—to match any two layers. Grading is a whole different deal,

TIP

Evoking emotion is sexy to a storyteller, even (especially?) if that emotion is hilarity, incredulity, or stark terror.

and the Ferrari metaphor is apt here: It seems way trickier at first, and feels unfamiliar and even dangerous, and then once you've gotten over that, it's the speed and thrills that you can't experience in an ordinary ride.

SpeedGrade deserves its own book, and is getting at least one, but I can hardly extol its virtues and then send you away to some other book to try out software that's probably sitting right there on your system, now can I? For a brief taste, here's the quickest advice I can offer in print to get you up and running.

The SpeedGrade UI

The first step with SpeedGrade is to get over the fact that its user interface is nothing like any other Adobe software (nor is it a copy of any other grading application). That's in many ways a good thing. For one thing, notice that the space the application takes on your drive is a small fraction of the other Adobe apps, and next note that the application launches in the blink of an eye.

Once it's open, everything is unfamiliar. It may not be instantly apparent that there are three basic sections: top, middle, and bottom. The middle is the timeline, the bottom contains the controls, and the top toggles between the Desktop, where you select clips to grade, and the Monitor, where you actually look at the image (**Figure 12.4**).

When you open the app, the Desktop is forward (and the Desktop tab highlighted) at the top of the screen, ready for you to choose a clip or project file. There are a bunch of options for how the file system is displayed, but the essential place to go is at the left, where you use a very un-Adobe user interface to navigate to the source material (it's just like Nuke's, allowing you to see all of the underlying hierarchy on your system).

To get started, navigate to the 2shot_intext_track.mov clip from Chapter 8 and double click on it to load it into the timeline. Click on the Monitor tab at the top and there it is, but the first thing you're wondering is, "how do I see it?" Find the Zoom to Fit icon in the tray below the image to see the full frame (**Figure 12.5**).

TIP

Overview videos that Patrick Palmer, Product Manager of SpeedGrade, can be found on Adobe TV.

NOTES

SpeedGrade has higher requirements than After Effects for monitor size and GPU. Minimum display size 1680 x 1050, and a supported GPU; www.adobe.com/go/speedgrade_ systemreqs has the latest list of supported cards.

TIP

You can also use the Toggle Grading Panel icon [icon] to hide the entire lower section of the UI, giving more space for the image itself.

TIP

You can open an edited sequence created with Adobe Premiere Pro in SpeedGrade.

Figure 12.4 The three areas of the SpeedGrade UI as it looks when you first launch the app are highlighted.

Figure 12.5 Once you select a file and are ready to grade, it appears in the timeline; switch to the Monitor tab at the top and the Look tab below, revealing the color wheels (also called "color pots") below. The Waveform and Histogram are also opened and flank the image.

Grade the Shot

Let's start with a little instant gratification to get you hooked. To go to another part of the shot, you can drag the rather unique time indicator with the frame number displayed right in it (**Figure 12.6**), or you can use the **L** key to play forward.

Figure 12.6 The unusual playhead shows the current time. It is numbered because you can have more than one, to show multiple frames side by side (drag that icon on the right, holding option **Alt+Ctrl/Opt+Ctrl**). Just like Adobe Premiere Pro, SpeedGrade has **JKL** playback: **J** and **L** play backward and forward, and clicking each more than once speeds playback in each direction, and **K** stops playback.

Stop on any frame you like, and click on the Look tab atop the bottom of the UI's three sections (third tab from the left). Along the bottom you should see some tabs with preset looks (the preview image is the woman in profile that appears on the cover of SpeedGrade's box). Click each image once to apply that look to the footage; for example, in the Cinematic category, try one of the looks labeled Cinematic. Oooh, that's nice.

In After Effects terms, this is not applying a color effect but just selecting a preset from a list. As you click each look, you do not add a new look on top of the previous one, but instead replace it altogether. Look at the Layers panel in the lower-left corner: Depending on the preset, you may see multiple layers appear with various names. There are three types of layers at play in these presets: Primary (which contain only color adjustments), LUT, and Custom Look presets. Some of the Style presets have scads of layers stacked together.

But we're getting ahead of ourselves. Every look has something going for it, partly because they're nicely designed, but also because this footage was properly shot (flat and low contrast) for these presets to look magical in one pass (hat tip to Vincent LaForet).

That's too easy. Suppose a shot (or some portion of it) should simply be warmer or cooler. With only a camera and some film, you might accomplish this transformation by adding a lens filter of a solid color (blue for cooler, amber to warm things up). The Look Examples/Temperature tab has presets named warm and cold—apply the Cold Mix preset and the scene goes cold indeed.

Figure 12.7 On a small monitor, you may have to drag out a section of the UI to see it properly.

If you can't see the color pots (**Figure 12.7**), drag upward on the boundary between the Look panel and the timeline (look for the double-headed arrow before doing so). This dramatic effect is entirely comprised of only two subtle color adjustments.

How do I know that? With the Overall tab selected above the color pots, the Gamma pot (in the center) is high-lighted and has a little corner marker at its lower right. The Midtones tab has an almost identical adjustment: in both, the crosshairs are just ever so slightly shifted toward blue. That's the whole look.

Now customize it. It's okay, you can touch as well as look. If you want to start fresh, click the amber Reset on the right of the Layer labeled Primary, or you can just play. Try the following:

▶ Drag your cursor around in a color pot. For example, drag the Gamma pot under Midtones toward green and Enter the Matrix.

▶ **Shift**-drag the cursor around the pot: the adjustment is much more dramatic. Ooh la la!

▶ Drag the teeny pointer atop the color pot counterclock-wise; not only does the corresponding range of the shot go darker, but a second corner triangle appears, this time to the lower left.

▶ Click on the triangle. It turns out that these are reset buttons for individual controls.

▶ Toggle on the Waveform ▐▐ and Histogram ▐▐, noting the little triangular pointer next to the title of the panel that flips it to the other side of the Monitor.

▶ Under the Overall tab (where adjustments are easy to see, both in the image and in the Waveform and Histogram), try adjusting the horizontal sliders along the top. These are labeled Contrast, Temperature, and Final Saturation—mostly familiar controls that turn out to do more or less what you would expect, yet it's all somehow more lucid and much harder to make the image look terrible. Again, holding the **Shift** key emphasizes the drag (if you do want to make it look terrible), and this time it's a lower-right rectangle that resets.

Okay, we're getting somewhere! Never mind for now fine distinctions such as the difference between Input Saturation and Final Saturation, or where to use Pivot. You have your hands on the fundamental controls to grade a shot in SpeedGrade, and it feels pretty good, doesn't it?

Add Presets

You could work in SpeedGrade with just the Primary controls, but you've already had a glimpse that there are other tools at your disposal. Let's take a quick look.

Along the bottom of the Layers panel are a series of icons (**Figure 12.8**). These are all unfamiliar, but there is nothing to be afraid of: You have an undo command, remember, and each has a tool tip if you hold your cursor over it.

Figure 12.8 Don't be scared by unfamiliar icons. A strange icon is just a friendly icon you haven't met. The ones highlighted in red create a new Primary, Secondary, or Look layer; those in amber manage layers; and the blue one saves your adjustments as a .look file for use in After Effects.

▶ Click the + icon and a list is revealed of the many custom look presets available in SpeedGrade. These are shortcuts to what can be a much stronger or more specific effect than a Primary grade. Each one you select creates a new layer, with the familiar eyeball 👁 on the left to toggle visibility and the all-important trash can 🗑 at the bottom right of the panel. Controls for each replace the color pots to the right.

▶ In that custom look menu, choose LUT. Here is access to a set of .cube and .ilut presets.

▶ Create your own LUT for use in After Effects. First, click the Save Look icon 📥 added to whatever page (tray) is forward among the presets. Move your cursor over the added look, and an E and an X icon appear: the X deletes, but the E allows you to export a LUT.

Of all of the LUTS on that list, the IRIDAS .cube LUT is your bridge back to After Effects. Whatever you've come up with in terms of a look can be applied in your After Effects comp with the file you save from this dialog. Whatever is checked is saved into a zipped folder with one of each item you choose, potentially including an example image.

Add Masks and Secondaries

This is an After Effects book, so you have a firm grasp of how to composite a color look you create with SpeedGrade into a comp. However, grading an individual shot is an interactive process, and there are selection tools right in SpeedGrade to help you apply unique color adjustments to specific areas of frame: to color correct or bring out just skin tones or a face, for example.

The secondary look layer is easy to use and completely unique compared to the hi-con matte selection in After Effects. Let's work with handheld_pinkDress.mov, which has a nice prominent color to select, a pink dress. You again choose it under the Desktop tab, and if you double-click, it's added to the timeline after the previous clip.

Figure 12.9 To work with secondaries, it helps to see the full controls, including the eyedroppers that make quick work of selecting the color or contrast range.

▸ Apply a Secondary layer with the +S icon in the Layers tray. Nothing changes other than the tools to the right of Layers.

▸ Make sure you can see all the tools; below the sliders are eyedroppers (**Figure 12.9**).

▸ Go to a frame where you can clearly see the pink dress, and use the eyedropper to select it: Click the + eyedropper and then the dress in the monitor.

▸ Nothing happens until you either adjust or preview the layer. Go crazy with the color pots to the right of the eyedroppers and sliders.

▸ The whole dress doesn't come along for the ride until you select the missing bits, again with the + eyedropper. To see what's happening, try the options in the Grayout menu (**Figure 12.10**).

Figure 12.10 Secondaries in SpeedGrade can helpfully be displayed in isolation, a feature that would be great to have in After Effects.

Here's where I'm obligated to say, you've only scratched the surface with SpeedGrade, but in fact, you're already pretty deep in at this point, particularly since you also know how to combine the application with After Effects. The two applications are a powerful one-two punch that neither can offer on its own.

Work with Popular Grades

All of the presets you found in SpeedGrade are available in After Effects, along with the ones you now know how to create yourself. But as your humble After Effects book author, my job is to make sure you know how to do things from the ground upward in that application, rather than having to rely on some preset. Here are specific situations you can solve with a preset grade from the SpeedGrade collection, or you can implement directly in After Effects.

Black and White

Counterintuitively, Hue/Saturation is not effective to create a black-and-white image because it maintains luminance proportions, and as mentioned in the "All Channels are Not Created Equal" sidebar back in Chapter 6, that's not how the eye sees color. **Figure 12.11** illustrates the difference.

If it's truly a black-and-white version of the color source that is required, several options will work better than lowering Saturation to 0.0:

- ▶ A tint effect at the default settings weights the color channels, as does a fully desaturated solid (black, white, or gray, it doesn't matter) with a Color blending mode.

- ▶ For more control of color weighting, you can make use of the Black & White effect. Because this effect originated in Photoshop, it doesn't support 32 bits per channel, but if you're applying it directly to 8- or 16-bit source, even in a 32-bpc project, that limitation won't cost the image any accuracy.

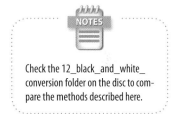

NOTES

Check the 12_black_and_white_ conversion folder on the disc to compare the methods described here.

Figures 12.11 This is the flag of Mars (left): it shows three fields of pure red, green, and blue. Tint (center) compensates for the perceptual differences in human color vision when desaturating, but Hue/Saturation (right) does not.

Figure 12.12 A real color-to-grayscale conversion may involve carefully rebalancing color, contrast, or saturation. Here, the face and lamp are important and get individual adjustments in color prior to conversion. (Images courtesy of 4charros.)

Taking care with the conversion from color to black-and-white and in particular the weighting of the color channels can heavily influence the look of the shot (**Figure 12.12**).

Day for Night

TIP

Many images benefit from a subtle reduction in overall Saturation using the Hue/Saturation tool. This moves red, green, and blue closer together and can reduce the "juicy" quality that makes bright-colored images hard to look at.

Stronger optical effects are often possible, such as making a daytime scene appear as if it were shot on a moonlit night. Known in French as *la nuit américaine* (and immortalized in Francois Truffaut's ode to filmmaking of the same name), this involves a simple trick. Shoot an exterior scene under ordinary daylight with a dark blue lens filter to compensate for the difficulty of successful low-light night shoots. If there is direct sunlight, it's meant to read as moonlight.

Lighting techniques and film itself have improved since this was a common convention of films, particularly Westerns, but digital cameras tend to produce noisy and muddy footage under low light.

Figure 12.13 shows the difference between a source image that is blue and desaturated and an actual night look. If

Figure 12.13 An ordinary twilight shot of a house at dusk (left) becomes a spooky Halloween mansion. Converting day for night avoids the problems associated with low-light shooting. (Images courtesy of Mars Productions.)

instead you're starting with a daylight image, look at the images on the book's disc, which take the image more in that direction. Overall, remember that the eye cannot see color without light, so only areas that are perceived to be well illuminated should have a hue outside the range between deep blue and black.

Source, Reflection, and Shadow in Compositions

Sometimes you work with source footage that contains strong lighting and thus offers a clear target. Other times, it's up to you to add a strong look. Either way, reference is your friend. You will be surprised how much bolder and more fascinating nature's choices are than your own.

Unexpected surprises that simply "work" can be the kiss of love for a scene—that something extra that nobody requested but everyone who is paying attention appreciates. Details of light and shadow are one area where this extra effort can really pay off.

Big, bold, daring choices about light don't call attention to themselves if appropriate to a scene, adding to the dramatic quality of the shot instead of merely showing off what you as an artist can do.

Backlighting and Light Wrap

The conditions of a backlit scene are a classic example of when a comped shot falls short of what actually happens in the real world.

SCRIPT

The light wrap formula outlined below has been converted to a script created by Jeff Almasol. You can find it on the book's disc as rd_ Lightwrap. Select the matted source layer and let this script do the work.

Figure 12.14 The silhouetted figure is color corrected to match but lacks any of the light wrap clearly visible around the figures seated on the beach.

This technique is designed for scenes that contain backlighting conditions and a foreground that, although it may be lit to match those conditions, lacks light wrapping around the edges (**Figure 12.14**).

A lot of people wish for an After Effects light wrap plug-in. Simply creating light around the edges of a figure just doesn't look right. The light needs to be motivated by what is behind the subject, and that presents a difficult procedural problem for a plug-in. The following method has you create your own color reference for light wrapping and use that.

Set up a light wrap effect as follows:

1. Create a new composition that contains the background and foreground layers, exactly as they are positioned and animated in the master composition. You can do this simply by duplicating the master comp and renaming it something intuitive, such as light wrap. If the foreground or background consists of several layers, it will probably be simpler to precompose them into two layers, one each for the foreground and background.

2. Set Silhouette Alpha blending mode for the foreground layer, punching a hole in the background.

3. Add an adjustment layer at the top, and apply Fast Blur.

4. In Fast Blur, toggle the Repeat Edge Pixels on and crank up the blurriness.

NOTES

Check out the 12_lightwrap folder on the disc to see this example in action.

5. Duplicate the foreground layer, move the copy to the top, and set its blending mode to Stencil Alpha, leaving a halo of background color that matches the shape of the foreground (**Figure 12.15,** top). If the light source is not directly behind the subject, you can offset this layer to match, producing more light on the matching side.

6. Place the resulting comp in the master comp and adjust opacity (and optionally switch the blending mode to Add, Screen, or Lighten) until you have what you're after. You may need to go back to your light wrap comp to further adjust the blur (**Figure 12.15,** bottom).

When there is no fill light, the foreground subject might appear completely silhouetted. Because the foreground subjects are often the stars of the scene, you might have to compensate, allowing enough light and detail in the foreground so that the viewer can see facial expressions and other important dramatic detail.

In other words, this might be a case where your reference conflicts with what is needed for the story. Try to strike a balance, but remember, when the story loses, nobody wins.

Flares

For our purposes a "flare" is any direct light source that appears in shot, not just a cheesy 17-element lens flare whenever the sun pokes around the moon in some science-fiction television show from the early 1990s (or even a few shots from *Hancock*). These don't come with After Effects; 3D lights don't even create a visible source if placed in shot until you add the Trapcode Lux effect (available on the disc in the Trapcode Suite installation in the Red Giant Software folder).

Real lens flares aren't cheesy but natural, even beautiful, artifacts the eye accepts without necessarily understanding anything about what actually causes them (**Figure 12.16**). ILM in particular seems to excel at great-looking light optics (but cannot be held responsible for the over-the-top look on the bridge of *Star Trek*).

Therefore, to get lens flares or even simple glints right, good reference is often key. Only a tiny percentage of your

Figure 12.15 The background is blurred into the matte area (top) in a precomp and added back into the scene to better integrate the silhouette (bottom).

NOTES

Prior to the 1970s-era of *Easy Rider* and moon shots, flares were regarded as errors on the part of the cinematographer, and shots containing them were carefully noted on the camera report and retaken.

What Causes a Lens Flare?

Unlike your eye, which has only one very flexible lens, camera lenses are typically made up of a series of inflexible lens elements. These elements are coated to prevent light from reflecting off of them under normal circumstances. Extreme amounts of light, however, are reflected by each element.

Zoom lenses contain many focusing elements and generate a complex-looking flare with lots of individual reflections. Prime lenses generate fewer.

Many factors besides the lens elements contribute to the look of a flare. Aperture blades within the lens cause reflective corners that often result in streaks; the number of streaks corresponds to the number of blades. The shape of the flares sometimes corresponds to the shape of the aperture (a pentagon for a five-sided aperture, a hexagon for six). Dust and scratches on the lens also reflect light. And few light elements look as badass as the anamorphic lens flare you might get shooting into a light source for 2.39:1 widescreen scope display.

Lens flares also appear very different depending on whether they were shot on film or video; excess light bleeds out in different directions and patterns.

Figure 12.16 You might think of a lens flare as one of those element rings caused by a zoom lens pointing at the sun, but flares occur anytime a bright light source appears in or near frame. Here, the green traffic light causes a large flare without even appearing in frame, and numerous other lights bloom and flare. (Image from *Quality of Life*, courtesy of Benjamin Morgan.)

viewers may know the difference between lens flares from a 50 mm prime and a 120 mm zoom lens, yet somehow, if you get it wrong, it reads as phony. Odd.

Here are some things you should know about lens flares:

▶ They are consistent for a given lens. Their angles vary according to the position of the light, but not the shape or arrangement of the component flares.

▶ The big complex flares with lots of components are created by long zoom lenses with many internal lens elements. Wider prime lenses create simpler flares.

▶ Because they are caused within the lens, flares beyond the source appear superimposed over the image, even over objects in the foreground that partially block the source flare.

Moreover, not every bright light source that appears in frame will trigger a lens flare—not even the sun.

The Lens Flare effect included with After Effects is useless, as it contains only three basic presets. The bright light of third-party effects, which seems to be no mere flash in the pan (okay, I'll stop) is Optical Flares from Video Copilot. That one has no demo, but the also excellent traditional champion Knoll Lens Flare does, and you can find it on the book's disc in the Effects Suite installation in the Red Giant Software folder. Either of these will improve dramatically upon what you can achieve with the built-in effect, so investing in one or the other is recommended for this purpose (assuming you're not the type of nerd to create your own lens flares as a 3D precomp, which would be much more time-consuming).

Reflected Light

Reflected light is another "kiss of love" opportunity for a scene. You might not notice that it's missing, but a glimmer, glint, or full reflection can add not only realism but pizzazz to a shot.

Glints are specular flares that occur when light is reflected toward the camera from shiny parts of an element in scene, such as the chrome of the taxi in **Figure 12.17**, taken from the Chapter 5 color matching example.

The same plug-ins used for flares (Optical Flare, Trapcode Lux, Knoll Light Factory, Tinderbox) can be used to create glints, with more modest settings that don't create all the lens reflections. **Figure 12.18** shows that there's not necessarily a whole lot to a single glint. An Add mode makes these work even in 32-bpc HDR (in which case they create over-range values, just as they would on film).

Figure 12.17 This sequence shows the glint that plays off the chrome areas of the taxi as it passes a spot in the frame where the sun is reflected directly into the camera lens.

Figure 12.18 There's not a whole lot to a glint when you look at it closely, but it helps sell the plane.

Light Scattering and Volume

Light scatters as it encounters particles in the air, most dramatically causing the phenomena of volumetric light or "God rays." Our atmosphere does not permit light to travel directly to the camera, uninterrupted, as it does in outer space. Instead, the light ricochets off tiny particles in the air, revealing its path.

The effect can be subtle. Lights that appear in the scene, casting their beams at the camera, tend to have a glowing halo around them. If the light traveled directly to the camera, the outline of the source light would be clear. Instead, light rays hit particles on their way to the camera and head off in slightly new directions, causing a halo (**Figure 12.19**).

Figure 12.19 You're so used to light halation (left) that it looks wrong to lower the exposure so that it disappears.

NOTES

To see the setup used to create volumetric light with built-in After Effects tools, check out 12_godrays_built_in_effects on the disc.

Add more particles in the air (in the form of smoke, fog, or mist), and a halo may appear, along with the conditions under which volumetric light occurs. God rays are the result of the fact that light from an omnidirectional source, such as the sun, travels outward in a continuous arc (**Figure 12.20**).

The CC Light Rays effect is probably most helpful among those included with After Effects to re-create volumetric light effects and even God rays. The honest truth is that Trapcode Shine outperforms it, but where possible, this book provides methods that don't involve buying a plug-in.

Light Rays not only boosts and causes halation around the source light, but it also adds rays coming straight at camera. These rays can be made more prominent by boosting radius and intensity, but in order to create a God rays

Figure 12.20 God rays, with which nature evokes the vast and eternal from an ordinary sunset.

effect and not overwhelm an entire image with rays, it's usually best to make a target source and apply the effect to that. Here are some examples:

1. Add a solid of your preferred color.

2. Apply Fractal Noise (default settings are acceptable to begin).

3. Mask the solid around the target God rays source area. Feather it heavily.

4. Apply CC Light Rays. Place Center at the God rays target. Boost Intensity and Radius settings until the rays are prominent.

5. For rays only (no fractal noise) set Transfer Mode to None.

6. Set a Subtract mask or Alpha Inverted track matte to create occluded areas for the rays to wrap around, as in **Figure 12.21**.

You can further hold out and mask out the rays as needed, even precomping and moving the source outside of frame if necessary. To make the rays animate, keyframe the Evolution property in Fractal Noise or add an expression such as `time*60` to make them undulate over time. Different Fractal Type and Noise Type settings will also yield unique rays.

NOTES

A more straightforward plug-in for volumetric light is Trapcode Lux, which can derive volume and a flare from any After Effects 3D light simply by applying it to an adjustment layer.

Figure 12.21 The included CC Light Rays effect is essential to creating your own volumetric light effects in After Effects. Masks or mattes can be used to occlude rays.

Three Ways to Blur

After Effects offers quite a few blur effects, but three are most common for general usage: Gaussian Blur, Fast Blur (which at best quality is no different), and Box Blur, which can match the other two but offers more flexibility.

At the default Iterations setting of 1, a Box Blur can seem crude and, well, boxy, but it can approximate the look of a defocused lens without all the more complex polygons of Lens Blur. You can also hold it out to the horizontal or vertical axis to create a nice motion blur approximation (where Directional Blur is actually too smooth and Gaussian).

Raising the Box Blur Iterations setting above 3 not only amplifies the blur but refines the blur kernel beyond anything the other two effects are capable of producing. What actually occurs is that the blur goes from a square appearance (suiting the name box blur) to a softer, rounder look. You're more likely to notice the difference working with over-range bright values in 32-bit HDR.

Fast Blur and Box Blur also each include a Repeat Edge Pixels check box; enable this to avoid dark borders when blurring a full-frame image. The same setting with these two effects will not, alas, produce the same amount of blur even if Box Blur is set to 3 iterations (to match Fast Blur).

NOTES

Some simple shadow-casting setups can be found in the 12_shadow_casting_basic folder on the disc.

Shadows

As there is light, so must there be shadows. Unfortunately, they can be difficult to re-create in 2D because they interact with 3D space and volume, none of which 2D layers have. The behavior of shadows can be unpredictable, but luckily, your audience typically doesn't know how they should look in your scene either (until there is some reference right there in the shot).

You can certainly cast a shadow from a matted layer onto a plane by positioning each of them in 3D space and properly positioning a light. Be sure that you first change Casts Shadows for the matted layer from its default Off setting to On or Only (the latter option makes it possible to create a precomp containing only the shadow).

You can instead corner pin the matte to the angle at which the shadow should fall and avoid the 3D setup altogether. In either case, the problem is that the illusion breaks if the light source is more than 10 degrees off-axis from the camera. The more you light a 2D element from the side, the more it just breaks (**Figure 12.22**).

There's also the possibility of cheating: If it's easy to add ground surface that would obscure a shadow (for example, grass instead of dirt), do so, and no one will even expect to see a shadow because it no longer belongs there.

Contact Shadows and Indirect Light

For the most part, successful shading in a 2D scene relies on achieving what you can practically, and getting creative when practical shadows aren't present. There are plenty of cases where a full cast shadow would be correct and no shadow at all would clearly look wrong, but a simple contact shadow can at least remove glaring contrast so that no one really notices.

A *contact shadow* is a lot like a drop shadow—basically just an offset, soft, dark copy directly behind the foreground. A *drop shadow*, however, is good only for casting a shadow onto an imaginary wall behind a floating logo, whereas a contact shadow is held out to only the areas of the foreground that have contact with the ground plane.

Figure 12.22 Compare the fake 3D shadow (left) with the real thing and you instantly grasp the problem with this approach. You can cast a good shadow head-on, but not at this steep an angle.

Figure 12.23 shows the foreground layer duplicated and placed behind the source. A mask is drawn around the base, and it is then offset downward. A blur is applied to soften the transparency channel. That gives you the matte. Red Giant Warp includes a Shadow effect that not only facilitates the process of creating this type of shadow, but adds the ability to project across a floor and a back wall, with an angle and position that are determined parametrically.

The Shadow Catcher

Among the additions that come along with ray-traced 3D in CS6 is the mystical shadow catcher. This may sound like a cross between the Loch Ness Monster crossed with Holden Caulfield, but it is merely a solid layer with some settings that allow it to do one thing and one thing only: cast a shadow created by a 3D object from a layer that is otherwise translucent.

There's no Layer > New > Shadow Catcher command; the Create Shadow Catcher, Camera, and Light option is among the types of layers you can create with the 3D Camera Tracker when you select multiple points. These points should be planar to the surface whereupon the shadow is to be cast. Yes, we Yanks sure are good with the king's English.

Thing is, there's only one ingredient in the Shadow Catcher secret sauce that makes it what it is: Accept Shadows is set to Only, guaranteeing that the layer, in fact, does nothing but accept a shadow. It's as simple as that.

If you're brave, you can try creating an extruded shape that stands in for an object in a scene that is to cast a shadow: the Casts Shadows property also has an Only setting.

Figure 12.23 A simple contact shadow (middle) can make the difference between an object that appears to sit on a surface and an object that appears to float in space.

Figure 12.24 By applying the shadow layer as a track matte to an adjustment layer, you can treat it as a color correction and match the color and contrast of the scene's existing shadows (left). Add a color correction pass and a day-lit American street takes on a more exotic vibe (right).

A real shadow is often not just black; it's an area of reduced light and therefore color. Instead of darkening down the matte itself to create the shadow, create an adjustment layer just below the contact shadow layer and set an alpha track matte. Add a Levels (or if you prefer, Curves) effect and adjust brightness and gamma downward to create your shadow. Treat it like a color correction, working on separate channels if necessary; the result is more interesting and accurate than a pool of blackness (**Figure 12.24**).

Reflected light is another type of contact lighting that plays a role in how things look in the real world, and thus can play a role in your composited scenes. Most objects in the world have diffuse surfaces that reflect light. When the object is prominent or colorful enough, your eye simply expects it to affect other more neutral neighboring surfaces, whether or not your brain is aware of the phenomenon (**Figure 12.25**).

In a dedicated 3D animation application, this situation is re-created via global illumination, which includes light and surface interactions in a render. If you're working with a

Figure 12.25 The color influence of indirect light is not always as evident as with a bright saturated object, but it is always in play in a natural setting.

computer-generated scene, aim for a pass that includes these types of light interactions. If you have to create the effect from scratch, the method is similar to that of shadows or color matching: Create a selection of the area reflecting light, including any needed falloff (that may be the hard part), and use color correction tools to color match the adjacent object reflecting color.

Multipass 3D Compositing

Lighting in computer-generated scenes has advanced to an astonishing extent, with stunning scenes from *Avatar* or *Toy Story 3* displaying all of the loveliness of natural light with no compositing needed. Nonetheless, when attempting to match a computer-generated element to a live-action backplate, it's more effective to divide the render of a single element into multiple passes.

This is different from simply rendering in layers, which though also useful for compositing is really only about separating foreground elements from the background.

Multipass rendering is the technique of isolating individual surface qualities and creating a separate render for each. "Surface qualities" are things such as specularity, shadows, and wear and tear (or grunge). In his excellent book *Digital Lighting & Rendering, Second Edition* (Peachpit Press, 2006), Jeremy Birn calls out multiple benefits yielded by rendering a model on multiple passes:

▶ **Changes** can be made with little or no re-rendering. If a shadow is too dark or a glow is the wrong color, the adjustment can be made right in After Effects.

▶ **Integration** often requires multiple passes where the model interacts with the scene, casting a shadow on the ground or being reflected in water. If the cast shadow is simply part of a single render, you lose all control over its appearance and cannot apply it as recommended in the previous section.

▶ **Reflections**, which often consume massive amounts of time to process, can be rendered at lower quality and blurred in After Effects.

RPF and EXR

RPF files are an Autodesk update to RLA. After Effects offers limited native support for these files (via the effects in the 3D Channel menu), but more robust support for some of the finer features of RPF such as Normal maps is available via third-party plug-ins. Commercially available plug-ins that can translate normal maps for use in After Effects include ZBornToy (which also does amazing things with depth maps) from Frischluft and WalkerFX Channel Lighting, part of the Walker Effects collection. There is a free option for Windows called Normality (www.minning.de/software/normality).

As mentioned in Chapter 8, After Effects can also extract camera data from RPF files (typically generated in 3DS Max or Flame); place the sequence containing the 3D camera data in a comp and choose Animation > Keyframe Assistant > RPF Camera Import.

The most popular way to get a multipass render into After Effects these days is via the EXR format, which can store all of the various passes and related data in a single file. EXR is now supported directly in After Effects via EXtractoR and IDentifier, two plug-ins from fnordware.

- **Bump Maps** can be applied more selectively (held out by another pass such as a highlight or reflection pass).

- **Glows** can be created easily in 2D by simply blurring and boosting the exposure of a specular pass.

- **Depth of Field** can be controlled entirely in 2D by using a Z pass as a matte for a blur adjustment layer.

- **Less render power and time** is required to render any one pass than the entire shaded model, so a lower-powered computer can do more, and redoing any one element takes far less time than redoing the entire finished model.

Putting multiple passes to use is also surprisingly simple; the artistry is in all of the minute decisions about which combination of adjustments will bring the element to life. **Table 12.1** (on the next page) describes some common render passes and how they are typically used.

Other passes for specific objects might include a Fresnel (or Incidence) pass showing the sheen of indirect light and applied to an adjustment layer with a luma matte (raise Output Black in Levels to re-create sheen); a Grunge or Dirt map, applied as a luma inverted matte, allowing you to dial in areas of wear and tear with Levels on an adjustment layer; a Light pass for any self-illuminated details; and a Normal pass showing the direction of surface normals for relighting purposes. Many, many more are possible—really anything that you can isolate in a 3D animation program. **Figure 12.26** shows a model set up for multipass rendering and a few of its component render layers.

None of these passes necessarily requires a transparency (alpha) channel, and in old-school effects it is customary not to render them, since multiple passes of edge transparency can lead to image multiplication headaches.

The general rules for multipass compositing are simple:

- Use the Diffuse layer as the base.

- Apply color layers meant to illuminate the base layer, such as specular and reflection, via Add or Screen blending modes.

- Apply color layers meant to darken the base layer, if any, via Multiply or Darken blending modes.

NOTES

Got UV Maps? After Effects has the means to use them with the RE:Map plug-in from RE:Vision Effects. This allows you to map a texture to an object, using the UV map for coordinates, without returning to the 3D app that generated it or waiting for Live Photoshop 3D to support mapping in After Effects.

NOTES

Check out the 12_multipass folder on the disc for a couple of setups, and try your own versions!

TABLE 12.1 Ten Typical Multipass Render Layer Types

TYPE	COLOR/ GRAYSCALE	TYPICAL BLENDING MODE	DESCRIPTION	USE
Diffuse	Color	Normal	Full color render; includes diffuse illumination, color correction, and texture; excludes reflections, highlights, and shadows	Color basis for the element; main target for primary color
Specular	Color	Add or Screen	Isolated specular highlights	Control how highlights are rendered; can be reused to create a glow pass by simply blurring and raising exposure
Reflection	Color	Add or Screen	Self-reflections, other objects, environment	Control the prominence and color of reflections
Shadow	Grayscale	Luma Inverted Matte	Isolated translucent shadows in scene	Control appearance, color, and softness of shadows; applied as a track matte to an adjustment layer with a Levels or Curves effect
Ambient	Color	Color	Color and texture maps without diffuse shading, specular highlights, shadows, or reflections	Color reference, can be used to make the color/texture of an object more pure and visible
Occlusion	Grayscale	Luma Inverted Matte	Shadows that result from soft illumination, simulating light from an overcast sky or well-lit room	Adds natural soft shadows to an object; these can be tinted to reflect the color of reflected light
Beauty	Color	Normal	A render of all passes	Reference: this is how the object or scene would appear if rendered in a single pass
Global Illumination	Color	Add or Screen	Indirect light added to the scene by global illumination, potentially including ray-traced reflections and refractions	Control intensity of indirect lighting in scene
Matte/ Mask/ Alpha	Grayscale	Luma Matte	Can be used to contain multiple transparency masks for portions of the object or scene, one each on the red, green, blue, and alpha channels	Straight alpha for any channel
Depth/Z-depth/ Depth Map	Grayscale or non-image floating point	Luma Matte	Describes the distance of surface areas from the camera	Can be used to control depth effects such as fog and lens blur, as well as light falloff

Figure 12.26 A basic multipass setup (**a**) with the beauty pass (**b**) as reference, made up of the following color passes: diffuse (**c**), specular (**d**), and reflection (**e**) as well as grayscale passes applied as luma mattes to adjustment layers. Each pass also contains a Levels effect: grunge (**f**), incidence (**g**), and occlusion (**h**). A depth matte (**i**) can be applied in various ways; here it is used as reference for a lens blur on an adjustment layer (to give the appearance of shallow depth of field).

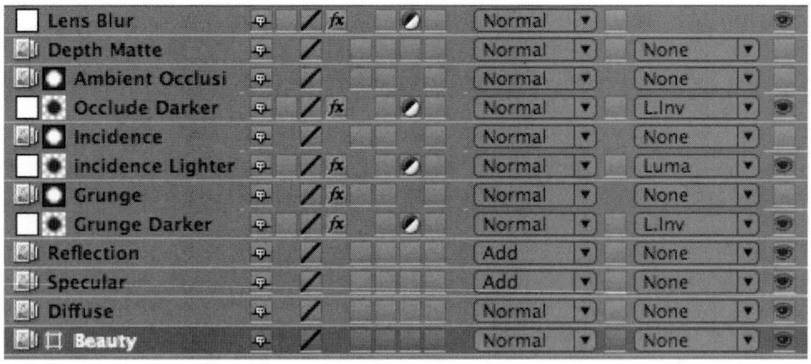

(a)

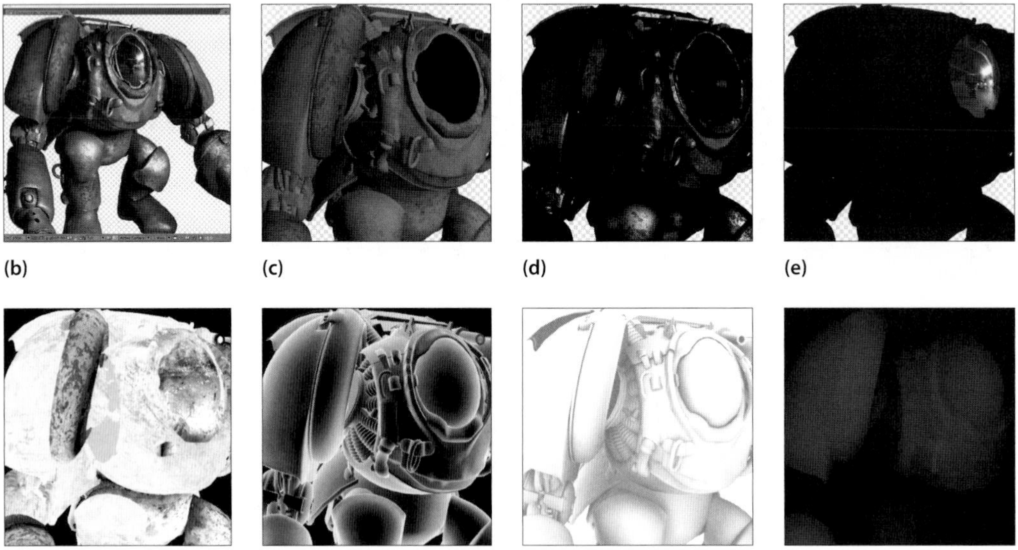

(b)

(c)

(d)

(e)

(f)

(g)

(h)

(i)

▶ Apply grayscale maps as luma mattes for adjustment layers. Apply Levels, Curves, and Hue/Saturation to allow these mattes to influence the shading of the object or scene.

▶ Control the strength of any layer using Opacity.

Multipass renders provide an excellent opportunity to enable Blend Colors Using 1.0 Gamma in Project Settings, whether or not you assign a working space (and whether or not that working space is linearized). With this setting enabled, specular and reflection passes naturally light the model via Add mode, and shadow, grunge, or ambient occlusion passes naturally darken it via Multiply.

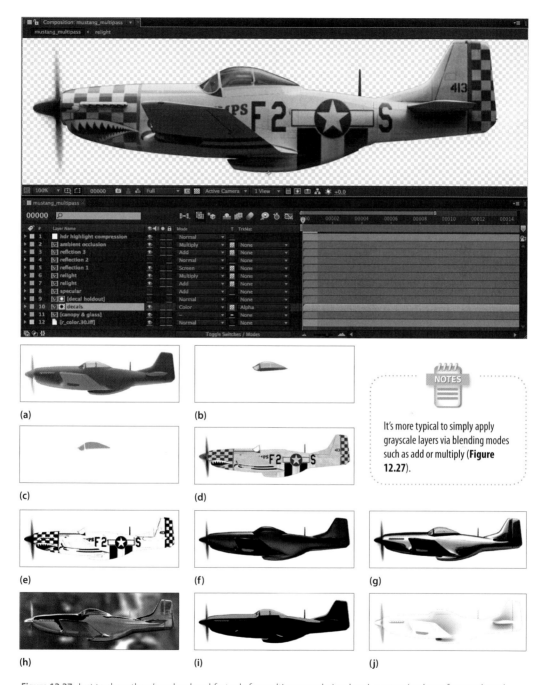

(a)

(b)

(c)

(d)

NOTES

It's more typical to simply apply grayscale layers via blending modes such as add or multiply (**Figure 12.27**).

(e)

(f)

(g)

(h)

(i)

(j)

Figure 12.27 Just to show there's no hard-and-fast rule for multipass rendering, here's a setup (and set of source layers) completely unique from the previous example. The color pass **(a)** is minimal. Precomping the canopy **(b)** and glass **(c)** separately with Collapse Transformations on gives individual control of that translucent element. The decals **(d)** are held out by a hi-con pass **(e)** to give the color pass most of its surface attributes. A specular **(f)** and three individual reflection passes **(g-i)** give full control over the plane's salient shininess. The ambient occlusion pass **(j)** is multiplied in to give weight to the shadows, and an adjustment layer applies HDR Highlight Compression to this 32-bpc assembly so that it can be rendered and used as an 8- or 16-bit element if necessary.

Multipass rendering is only partially scientific and accurate; successful use of multiple passes is a highly individualized and creative sport. I personally like to cheat heavily instead of going by the book as long as I'm happy with the result. With the correct basic lighting setup, you can use multipass renders to place a given 3D element in a variety of environments without the need for a complete re-render.

Varied environments are themselves the subject of the following chapter.

13

Climate and the Environment

Rainy days and Mondays always get me down.
— Roger Nichols and Paul Williams

Climate and the Environment

Even if you're not called upon to re-create extreme climate conditions, a casual glance out the window demonstrates that meteorological phenomena are part of any exterior scene: A breeze is blowing in the trees, or water and particulates in the air change the appearance of buildings and the landscape as it extends to the horizon.

It can be a fun and fascinating challenge to create natural elements such as particulates and wind effects, as well as to replace a sky, or add mist, fog, smoke, or other forms of precipitation in After Effects. Sometimes the required conditions simply don't materialize on the day of a shoot, and in other cases, you might need to create Roland Emmerich–level weather events. Mother Nature is, after all, notoriously fickle, and shooting just to get a particular environment can be extraordinarily expensive and random.

If the story needs are specific, it's rare indeed that a shoot can wait for perfect weather at a particular time of day, in a particular location. Transforming the appearance of a scene using natural elements is among the more satisfying things you can do as a compositor or matte painter.

Particulate Matter

Particulate matter in the air influences how objects appear at different depths. What is this matter? Fundamentally, it is made up of water as well as other gas, dust, or visible particulates usually known as pollution. In an ideal, pristine, pollution-free environment there is moisture in the air— even in the driest desert, where there also might be heavier forms of particulates like dust and sand. The amount of haze in the air offers clues as to

NOTES

Atmospheric haze occurs only in the presence of an atmosphere. Examine photos of the moon landscape, and you'll see that the blacks in the distance look just as dark as those in the foreground.

Figure 13.1 Same location, different conditions. Watch for subtleties: Backlighting emphasizes even low levels of haze and reduces overall saturation (left); more diffuse conditions desaturate and obscure the horizon while emphasizing foreground color (right).

- ▶ the distance to the horizon and of objects in relation to it
- ▶ the basic type of climate; the aridness or heaviness of the weather
- ▶ the time of year and the day's conditions
- ▶ the air's stagnancy (think *Blade Runner*)
- ▶ the sun's location (when it's not visible in shot)

The color of the particulate matter offers clues to how much pollution is present, what it is, and even how it feels: dust, smog, dark smoke from a fire, and so on (**Figure 13.1**).

Particulate matter in the air lowers the apparent contrast of visible objects; objects also take on the color of the atmosphere around them, generically becoming slightly bluer and also slightly diffuse. This is a subtle yet omnipresent depth cue: With any particulate matter in the air, objects lose contrast further from the camera; the apparent color can change quite a bit, and detail is softened.

Depth Cues

Figure 13.2 shows how the same object at the same size indicates its depth by its color. The background has great foreground and background reference for black and white levels; although the rear plane looks icy blue against gray, it matches the look of otherwise gray objects in the distance of the image.

Figure 13.2 One plane (circled in white) is composited as if it is a toy model in the foreground, the other (circled in black) as if it is crossing the sky further in the distance (far right). A look at just the planes (near right) shows them to be identical but for their color. The difference between a toy model airplane flying close, a real airplane flying nearby, and the same plane in the distant sky is conveyed with the use of Scale, but just as importantly, with Levels that show the influence of atmospheric haze.

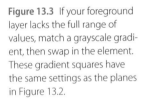

Figure 13.3 If your foreground layer lacks the full range of values, match a grayscale gradient, then swap in the element. These gradient squares have the same settings as the planes in Figure 13.2.

In this case, the foreground element seems to make life easier by containing monochrome colors, but here the color matching techniques from Chapter 5 come into play. Whether matching a more colorful or monochrome element, you can create a small solid and add the default Ramp effect using its predominant dark and light color values. With such a reference element, it is simple to add the proper depth cueing with Levels and then apply the setting to the final element (**Figure 13.3**).

Depth Maps

To re-create depth cues requires that the shot be separated into planes of distance. If the source imagery is computer-generated, the 3D program that created it can also generate a depth map for you to use. If not, you can slice the image into planes of distance, or you can make your own depth map to adjust the distance of the objects in frame (**Figure 13.4**).

A depth map can be applied to an adjustment layer as a luma (or luma inverted) matte. The adjustment layer contains a Levels or another color correction adjustment to create the color shifts associated with atmospheric depth by raising Output Black. With a day-lit exterior, you can also raise Blue Output Black and lower Blue Input White. Depth cueing applies to the most distant elements, so setting a luma inverted matte and then *flashing* the blacks

NOTES

The expression from Chapter 10 that assigns values according to the distance of an object from camera can be adapted to apply a depth-cueing effect.

Figure 13.4 This grayscale depth map is made up of individual roto shapes, each shaded for relative distance.

(raising the Output Black level in Levels) adds the effect of atmosphere on the scene.

Depth data may also be rendered and stored in an RPF file, as in **Figure 13.5**. RPF files lack thresholding in the edges, and for that reason have been superseded in many high-end visual effects pipelines with deep image compositing. *Deep images* contain multiple samples at varying depths of a given pixel position. Support for this type of image data is one area where After Effects lacks features available in Nuke, where handling of multiple channels is part and parcel of the application's very core.

TIP

Roto Brush is a perfect tool for quickly creating a decent depth map in 20% or less of the time it would take to do the roto by hand.

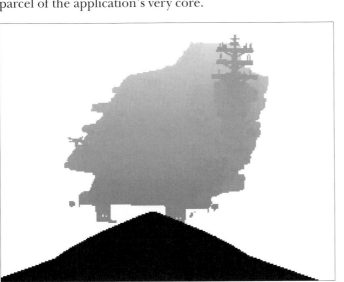

Figure 13.5 Note the jaggies in an RPF image. A depth map does not have to be perfectly pristine. (Created by Fred Lewis; used with permission from Inhance Digital, Boeing, and the Navy UCAV program.)

NOTES

One good reason to use a basic 3D render of a scene as the basis for a matte painting is that the perspective and lens angle can be used not only for reference but also to generate a depth map.

Examples of keying and replacing a sky are found in the 13_sky_replacement folder on the disc.

Sky Replacement

Sky replacement is an inexpensive and fundamental enhancement to a shot. Not only can a bland sky be improved to be prettier, you can also change the very location of the shot by changing its sky backdrop. This saves you from relying on the perfect conditions materializing at the perfect location, which is virtually guaranteed to be costlier and less efficient.

Skies are always part of the story—sometimes only subliminally, but often as a starring element. (*Independence Day* and *Vanilla Sky* are two movies that instantly come to mind as the character of the sky is essential to the story; you can no doubt think of many other examples.) An interior with a window could be anywhere, but show a recognizable skyline outside the window and locals will automatically gauge the exact neighborhood and city block of that location, along with the time of day, time of year, weather, outside temperature, and so on, possibly without ever really paying conscious attention to it.

The guerrilla method to add a view of Central Park at sunset in a picture window is to use a friend's apartment, shoot all day, and add the sunset view in post. In many cases, the real story is elsewhere, and the sky is a subliminal (even if beautiful) backdrop that must serve that story (**Figure 13.6**).

The Sky Is Not (Quite) a Blue Screen

Study the actual sky (perhaps there's one nearby) as well as reference images, and you may notice that the blue color desaturates near the horizon, cloudless skies are rare unless you live in the high desert, and even clear blue skies are not as saturated as they might sometimes seem. All of these factors compromise color keying a sky, but your major advantage is that your intention is to replace it with another sky. Even if the replacement isn't the same hue and brightness (going from mid-day to dramatic orange) the foreground can be adjusted to match it, since they interact so directly with one another (**Figure 13.7**).

Some combination of a color keyer, such as Keylight, and a hi-con luminance matte pass or a garbage matte, as

Figure 13.6 For an independent film with no budget set in San Francisco, the director had the clever idea of shooting it in a building lobby across the bay in lower-rent Oakland (top left), pulling a matte from the blue sky (top center), and match moving a still shot of the San Francisco skyline (from street level, top right) for a result that anyone familiar with that infamous pyramid-shaped building would assume was taken in downtown San Francisco (bottom). (Images courtesy of the Orphanage.)

Figure 13.7 The matte doesn't have to be perfect if the intensity of the replacement sky matches that of the original, and the hue of the foreground is corrected to match.

needed, can remove the existing sky in your shot, leaving nice edges around the foreground. Chapter 6 focuses on strategies that put these to use, and Chapter 7 describes supporting approaches when keys and garbage mattes fail.

The first step in sky replacement is to remove the existing sky (which may include garbage matting items such as buildings and clouds) by developing a matte for it. As you do this, place the replacement sky in the background. If you're replacing one blue sky with another, there's no need to create a matte that looks perfect against a contrasting color.

Infinite Depth

The next step to match in the replacement sky is to match the motion, and the Camera Tracker makes this a much more straightforward process than in the past. Here are a few things to keep in mind:

▶ *Parallax* occurs between the foreground scenery and the background sky, which is at infinite depth. Once a scene is 3D tracked, you can have some parallax for free by simply moving your background sky away from the camera on the Z axis (to a distance of, say, 4000 pixels with the typical scene), scaling the element to compensate for the distance (no problem scaling up in 3D, just remember that the definition of the source image has to be sufficient to support it), and keeping the foreground at its default 0.0 Z position. All of the parallax that was in the original foreground plate remains, and the background naturally contains the reduced motion of a distant element.

▶ A *nodal pan* contains no parallax, so an offset will make no difference with such a track.

▶ If the sky is much more proximal—the camera is flying through the clouds—a flat image of a sky won't do unless it is completely cloudless. The clouds and mist are foreground and mid-ground elements to be added in that case.

Fog, Smoke, and Mist

NOTES

Want smoke? A few modest examples are in the 13_smoke folder on the disc.

An animated layer of thin, translucent clouds or fog is easy to re-create in After Effects. The basic element can be fabricated by applying the Turbulent Noise effect to a solid. An Add or Screen blending mode gives the reflective light quality, and a separate Multiply pass can be used to add weight and thickness.

Turbulent Noise at its default settings already looks smoky; switching the Noise Type setting from the default, Soft Linear, to Spline improves it. The main extra ingredient is motion, which requires only a simple expression applied to the Evolution property: time*60 (I find 60 an appropriate rate in many situations; follow your own taste). The Transform properties within Fractal Noise can be animated, causing the overall layer to move as if being blown by wind.

Brightness, Contrast, and Scale settings influence the apparent scale and density of the noise layer. Complexity and Sub settings also affect apparent scale and density, but with all kinds of undesirable side effects that make the smoke look artificial. The look is greatly improved by layering at least two separate passes via a blending mode (**Figure 13.8**).

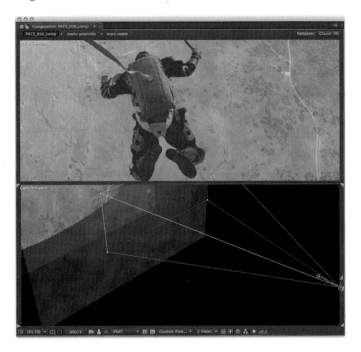

Figure 13.8 This bluescreen shot of a skydiver is made more convincing by layers of atmospheric haze that are staggered to provide depth as the camera follows him rapidly downward.

Masking and Adjusting

When covering the entire foreground evenly with smoke or mist, a more realistic look is achieved using two or three separate overlapping layers with offset positions (**Figure 13.9**). The unexpected byproduct of layering 2D particle layers in this manner is that they take on the illusion of depth and volume.

The eye perceives changes in parallax between the foreground and background and automatically assumes these

CLOSE-UP

Add vs. Multiply: Light and Occlusion

Multiply mode works well for elements such as smoke, mist, and fog—these are dark and occlude what is behind them—and Multiply enhances dark tones and omits light ones. Add mode is best for light elements (especially those shot against dark backgrounds such as pyrotechnics); it has the characteristic of brightening what is behind it. For an element with light and dark tones such as a thick plume of smoke, you may want to use a combination of both, at varying levels of opacity.

Figure 13.9 Overlay layers of fabricated smoke to add dimensionality and depth.

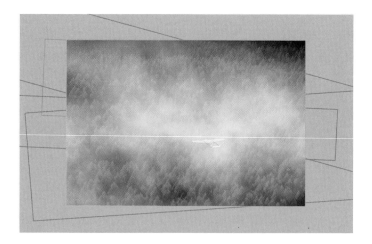

NOTES

Textures created with Fractal Noise maintain an advantage over those from Turbulent Noise in that they can loop seamlessly (allowing reuse on shots of varying length). In Evolution Options, enable Cycle Evolution, and animate Evolution in whole revolutions (say, from 0° 2 × 0.0°). Set the Cycle (in Revolutions) parameter to the number of total revolutions (2). The first and last keyframes now match, and a `loopOut("cycle")` expression continues this loop infinitely.

to be a by-product of full three-dimensionality, yet you save the time and trouble of a 3D volumetric particle render. Of course, you're limited to instances in which particles don't interact substantially with movement from objects in the scene, although that's not off-limits for one who is patient; techniques to shape the motion of liquid elements follow later in this chapter.

Particle layers can be combined with the background via blending modes, or they can be applied as a luma matte to a colored solid. As always, choose whichever gives the most control via the fewest steps.

To add smoke to a broad area of the frame, a big elliptical mask with a high feather setting (in the triple digits even for video resolution) does the trick; if the borders of the smoke area are apparent, increase the mask feather even further (**Figure 13.10**).

Figure 13.10 This mask of a single smoke element from the shot in Figure 13.8 has a feather value in the hundreds. The softness of the mask helps to sell the element as smoke and works well overlaid with other, similarly feathered masked elements.

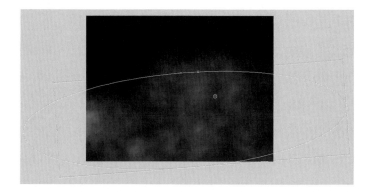

Moving Through the Mist

The same effect you get when you layer several instances of Turbulent or Fractal Noise can aid the illusion of moving forward through a misty cloud. That's done simply enough (for an example of flying through a synthetic cloud, see the Smoky Layers project, 13_smoke.aep, on the disc), but how often does your shot consist of just moving through a misty cloud? Most of the time, clouds of smoke or mist are combined with an existing shot.

The secret is that these organic "liquid" 2D layers take on the illusion of volume as they are overlaid and arrayed in 3D. By "liquid" we mean any element with flowing organic motion and no hard-surface shape, so even gases and fire are included. To make this work, keep a few points in mind:

▶ Each instance of Fractal Noise uses a soft elliptical mask.

▶ The mask should be large enough to overlap with another masked instance but small enough to hold its position as the angle of the camera changes.

▶ A small amount of Evolution animation goes a long way, and too much will blow the gag. Let the movement of the camera create the interest of motion.

▶ Depending on the length and distance covered in the shot, be willing to create at least a half-dozen individual masked layers of Fractal Noise.

The Smoky Flyover features just such an effect of moving forward through clouds. It combines the tracking of each shot carefully into place with the phenomenon of parallax, whereby overlapping layers swirl across one another in a believable manner. Mist and smoke seem to be a volume, but they actually behave more like overlapping, translucent planes—individual clouds of mist and smoke.

Billowing Smoke

Fractal Noise works fine to create and animate thin wispy smoke and mist, but it is of little help to fabricate thick, billowing plumes or clouds. Instead of a plug-in effect, all that's required is a good still cloud element, which you

CLOSE-UP

Selling the Effect with Diffraction

There is more to adding a cloud to a realistic shot than a simple A over B comp; liquid particles in the air, whether in spray, mist, or clouds, not only occlude light but diffract it. This diffraction effect can be simulated by applying Compound Blur to an adjustment layer between the fog and the background and using a precomposed (or pre-rendered) version of the fog element as its Blur layer.

This usage of Compound Blur is detailed further in Chapter 14, where it is used to enhance the effect of smoky haze.

can animate in After Effects. And all you need to create the element is a high-resolution reference photo—or even a bag of cotton puffs, as was used to create the images in **Figure 13.11**.

 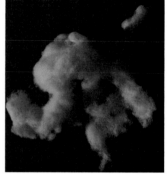

Figure 13.11 A good static image, even cotton puffs arranged on black posterboard, photographed in daylight, can be used as the foundation of billowing smoke.

To give clouds shape and contour, open the image in Photoshop, and use the Clone Stamp tool to create a cloud with the shape you want. You can do it directly in After Effects, but this is the kind of job for which Photoshop was designed. Clone in contour layers of highlights (using Linear Dodge, Screen, or Lighten blending modes) and shadows (with Blending set to Multiply or Darken) until the cloud has the look you're after (**Figure 13.12**).

So now you have a good-looking cloud, but it's a still. How do you put it in motion? This is where After Effects' excellent distortion tools come into play, in particular Mesh

Figure 13.12 The elements from Figure 13.11 are incorporated into this matte painting, and the final shot contains a mixture of real and composited smoke.

Warp and Liquify. The project containing just such a cloud animation is found on the disc, 13_smoke.aep.

Mesh Warp

Mesh Warp displays a grid of Bezier handles over the frame. To animate distortion, set a keyframe for the Distortion Mesh property at frame 0, then move the points of the grid and realign the Bezier handles associated with each point to bend to the vertices between points. The image to which this effect is applied follows the shape of the grid.

By default, Mesh Warp begins with a 7×7 grid. Before you do anything else, make sure that the size of the grid makes sense for your image; you might want to increase its size for a high-resolution project, and reduce the number of rows to fit the aspect ratio of your shot, for a grid of squares (**Figure 13.13**).

You can't typically get away with dragging a point more than about halfway toward any other point; watch carefully for artifacts of stretching and tearing as you work, and preview often. If you see stretching, realign adjacent points and handles to compensate. There is no better way to learn about this than to experiment.

I have found that the best results with Mesh Warp use minimal animation of the mesh, animating instead the element that moves it. This works well with any organic, flowing liquid or gas shape.

Liquify

Mesh Warp is appropriate for gross distortions of an entire frame. The Liquify effect is a brush-based system for fine distortions. The Smoke Cloud project includes a composition that employs Liquify to swirl a cloud. The following is a brief orientation to this toolset, but as with most brush-based painterly tools, there is no substitute for hands-on experience.

The principle behind Liquify is actually similar to that of Mesh Warp. Enable View Mesh under View Options and you'll see that you're still just manipulating a grid, albeit a finer one that would be cumbersome to adjust point by point—hence the brush interface.

NOTES

Mesh Warp, like many distortion tools, renders rather slowly. As you rough in the motion, feel free to work at quarter resolution. When you've finalized your animation, you can save a lot of time by pre-rendering it (see Chapter 4).

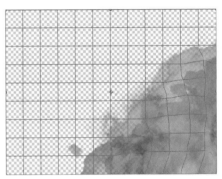

Figure 13.13 The Mesh Warp controls are simple, just a grid of points and vectors. You can preset the number and quality; more is not necessarily better. Points can be multiselected and dragged, and each point contains Bezier handles for warping the adjacent vectors.

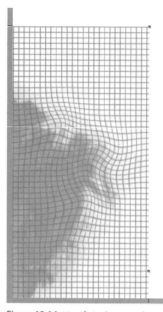

Figure 13.14 Liquify is also a mesh distortion tool, only the mesh is much finer than Mesh Warp's and it is controlled via brushes, allowing more specific distortions.

Puppet

The Puppet tool allows you to be extremely specific about what areas of a layer deform, which do not, and the timing of the deformation. It's called *Puppet* because it was designed to allow you to define "pins" at the joints of an articulated figure; see the 07_AnimatingwithPuppet.pdf file in the PDFs folder on the book's disc for information on how to do that.

Puppet is the right tool when you need specific areas of a layer to remain anchored while others deform, perhaps to bend it into a specific shape; this could also be a solid object such as a lamppost or tree that wobbles slightly in the wind.

Of the brushes included with Liquify, the first two along the top row, Warp and Turbulence, are most often used (**Figure 13.14**). Warp has a similar effect to moving a point in Mesh Warp; it simply pushes pixels in the direction you drag the brush. Turbulence scrambles pixels in the path of the brush.

The Reconstruction brush (rightmost on the bottom row) is like a selective undo, reversing distortions at the default setting; other options for this brush are contained in the Reconstruction Mode menu (which appears only when the brush is selected).

Liquify has the advantage of allowing holdout areas. Draw a mask around the area you want to leave untouched, but set the Mask mode to None, disabling it. Under Warp Tool Options, select the mask name in the Freeze Area Masked menu.

Liquify was a key addition to the "super cell" element (that huge swirling mass of weather) for the freezing of New York City sequence in *The Day After Tomorrow*. Artists at The Orphanage were able to animate matte paintings of the cloud bank, broken down into more than a dozen component parts to give the effect the appropriate organic complexity and dimension.

Wind and Ambience

What is wind doing in this chapter? Although wind is not itself visible, its effects are omnipresent in most any exterior shot. Therefore, suggesting the influence of wind can help bring a matte painting or other static background to life.

Most still scenes in the real world contain ambient motion of some kind. Objects directly in the scene as well as reflected light and shadow might be changing all the time in a scene we perceive to be motionless. The next time you are at a good outdoor vantage point, notice what subtle motion you see in the environment and think about what you could easily re-create.

As a compositor, you often look for opportunities to contribute to the realism of a scene without stealing focus. Obviously, the kinds of dynamics involved with making the leaves and branches of a tree sway are mostly beyond the realm of 2D compositing, but there are often other elements that are easily articulated and animated ever so slightly. Successful examples of ambient animation should not be noticeable, and they often will not have been explicitly requested, so this can be an exercise in subtlety.

Adding Elements and Animation

You also have the option of acquiring and adding elements that indicate or add to the effect of wind motion. **Figure 13.15** is an element of blowing autumn leaves shot against a black background for easy removal and matting. Granted, you could add an element this turbulent only to a scene that either already had signs of gusts in it or that contained only elements that would show no secondary motion from wind whatsoever.

Remember, too, that you can grab an effects element if a bright blue sky is your background (although you can never count on having one on the shooting day, of course). **Figure 13.16** shows the matte used to create the timelapse effect seen earlier in the book.

Primary and Secondary

Primary animation is the gross movement of the object, its movement as a whole. *Secondary animation* is the movement of individual parts of the object as a result of inertia. So, for example, a helicopter crashes to the ground: That's the primary animation. Its rotors and tail bend and shudder at impact: That's the secondary animation.

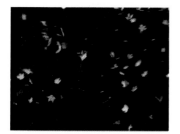
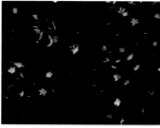

Figure 13.15 Sometimes you can find elements that will enliven your scene when comped in, such as this clip of blowing leaves shot over black. (Footage courtesy of Artbeats.)

Figure 13.16 If you dare to depend on a sky as your bluescreen, you will have to contend with the areas where its color is reflected into your foreground, and where it is less than perfectly monochrome. On the other hand, there's no reason the resulting sky wouldn't also yield those same characteristics.

Smoke Trails, Plumes, and More

Many effects, including contrails, don't necessarily require particle generation in order to be re-created faithfully. This example shows how, with a little creativity, you can combine techniques in After Effects to create effects that you might think require extra tools.

Initial setup of such an effect is simply a matter of starting with a clean plate, painting the smoke trails in a separate still layer, and revealing them over time (in this case, presumably behind the aircraft that is creating them). The quickest and easiest way to reveal such an element over time is often by animating a mask, as in **Figure 13.17**. Or, you could use techniques described in Chapter 8 to apply a motion tracker to a brush.

Figure 13.17 No procedural effect is needed; animating out masks is quick, simple, and gives full control over the result.

The second stage of this effect is dissipation of the trail; depending on how much wind is present, the trail might drift, spread, and thin out over time. That might mean that in a wide shot, the back of the trail would be more dissipated than the front, or it might mean the whole smoke trail was blown around.

One method is to displace with a black-to-white gradient (created with Ramp) and Compound Blur. The gradient is white at the dissipated end of the trail and black at the source (**Figure 13.18**); each point can be animated or tracked in. Compound Blur uses this gradient as its Blur Layer, creating more blur as the ramp becomes more

Figures 13.18 To dissipate a contrail the way the wind would, you can use a gradient and Compound Blur, so that the smoke dissipates more over time, or use the Turbulent Displace effect (right) that, like Turbulent Noise, adds fractal noise to displace the straight trails from Figure 13.17.

white. Another method, also shown in Figure 13.18, uses a different displacement effect, Turbulent displace, to create the same type of organic noise as in the preceding cloud layers.

Precipitation

You might want to create a "dry for wet" effect, taking footage that was shot under clear, dry conditions and adding the effects of inclement weather. Not only is it impractical to time a shoot so that you're filming in a storm (in most parts of the world, anyway), but wet, stormy conditions limit shooting possibilities and cut down on available light. Re-creating a storm by having actual water fall in a scene is expensive, complicated, and not necessarily convincing.

I like Trapcode Particular (available in the Trapcode Suite installation in the Red Giant Software folder on the book's disc) for particles of accumulating rain or snow. This effect outdoes After Effects' own Particle Playground for features, flexibility, and fast renders. As the following example shows, Particular is good for more than just falling particles as well.

The Wet Look

Study reference photographs of stormy conditions and you'll notice some things that they all have in common, as well as others that depend on variables. Here are the steps taken to make a sunny day gloomy (**Figure 13.19**):

NOTES

Want to see this project already set up? Look at 13_dry_for_wet on the book's disc.

Figure 13.19 An ordinary exterior where it "never rains" (left) becomes a deluge.

1. Replace the sky—placid becomes stormy (**Figure 13.20a**).

2. Adjust Hue/Saturation—LA becomes Dublin—to bring out the green mossiness of those dry hills. I've knocked out the blues and pulled the reds down and around toward green (**Figure 13.20b**).

3. Exchange Tint—balmy becomes frigid—to create the bluish cast that's common to rainy scenes (**Figure 13.20c**).

4. Fine-tune Curves—daylight becomes low light—aggressively dropping the gamma while holding the highlights makes things even moodier (**Figure 13.20d**).

That's dark, but it looks as dry as a lunar surface. How do you make the background look soaked? It seems like an impossible problem, until you study reference. Then it becomes apparent that all of that moisture in the air causes distant highlights to bloom. This is a win-win adjustment (did I really just type that?) because it also makes the scene lovelier to behold.

You can simply add a Glow effect, but it doesn't offer as much control as the approach I recommend.

Follow these steps:

1. Bring in the background layer again (you can duplicate it and delete the applied effects—**Ctrl+Shift+E/ Cmd+Shift+E**).

2. Add an Adjustment Layer below it and set the dupli-cated background as Luma Matte.

3. Use Levels to make the matte layer a hi-con matte that isolates the highlights to be bloomed.

4. Fast Blur the result to soften the bloom area.

5. On the Adjustment Layer, add Exposure and Fast Blur to bloom the background within the matte selection.

(a)

(b)

Create Precipitation

Trapcode Particular contains all the controls needed to generate custom precipitation (it contains a lot of controls, period). A primer is helpful, to get past the default anima-tion of little white squares emanating out in all directions (click under Preview in Effect Controls to see it). To get started making rain, create a comp-sized 2D solid layer and apply Particular. Next:

(c)

1. Twirl down Emitter and set an Emitter Type. For rain, I like Box so that I can easily set its width and depth, but anything besides the default Point and Grid will work.

2. Set Emitter Size to at least the comp width in X to fill the frame.

3. Set Direction to Directional.

4. Set X Rotation to –90 so that the particles fall downward.

5. Boost velocity to go from gently falling snow speed to pelting rain.

(d)

You might think it more correct to boost gravity than veloc-ity, but gravity increases velocity over time (as Galileo dis-covered) and rain begins falling thousands of feet above. Don't think too hard, in any case; what you're after here is realistic-looking weather, not a physics prize.

You do, however, need to do the following:

1. Move the Emitter Y Position to 0 or less so that it sits above frame.

2. Increase the Emitter Size Y to get more depth among those falling particles.

(e)

Figure 13.20 The progression to a heavy, wet day (top to bottom). Image E shows the result—it now looks like a wet, cold day, but where's the rain?

3. Crank up the Particles/Sec and Physics Time (under Physics) to get enough particles, full blast from the first frame.

4. If the particles are coming up short at the bottom of frame, increase the Life setting under Particle.

5. Enable Motion Blur for the layer and comp to get some nice streaky rain (**Figure 13.21**).

From here, you can add Wind and Air Resistance under Physics. If you're creating snow instead of rain, you might want to customize Particle Type, even referring to your own Custom layer if necessary for snowflakes.

Composite Precipitation

What is the color of falling rain? The correct answer to this Zen Koan–like question is that raindrops and snowflakes are translucent. Their appearance is heavily influenced by the background environment, because they behave like tiny falling lenses. They diffract light, defocusing and lowering the contrast of whatever is behind them, but they themselves also pick up the ambient light.

Figure 13.21 In the "good enough" category, two passes of rain, one very near, one far, act together to create a watery deluge. Particular could generate this level of depth with a single field, and the mid-ground rain is missing, but planes are much faster to set up for a fast-moving shot like this. The rain falls mainly on two planes.

Therefore, on *The Day After Tomorrow* our crew found success with using the rain or snow element as a track matte for an adjustment layer containing a Fast Blur and a Levels (or Exposure) effect, like a reflective, defocused lens. This type of precipitation changes brightness according to its backlighting, as it should. You may see fit to hold out specific areas and brighten them more, if you spot an area where a volumetric light effect might occur.

The final result in Figure 13.19 benefits from a couple of extra touches. The rain is divided into multiple layers, near and far, and motion-tracked to match the motion of the car from which we're watching this scene. Particular has the ability to generate parallax without using multiple layers, but I sometimes find this approach gives me more control over the perspective. Although you rarely want one without the other, it's one more example of choosing artistry over scientific accuracy.

Because we're looking out a car window, if we want to call attention to the point of view—because the next shot reverses to an actor looking out this window—it's only appropriate that the rain bead up. This is also done with Particular, with Velocity turned off and Custom particles for the droplets.

And because your audience can always tell when you have the details wrong, even if they don't know exactly what's wrong, check out **Figure 13.22** for how the droplet is designed.

Once again, it is attention to detail and creative license that allow you to simulate the complexities of nature. It can be fun and satisfying to transform a scene using the techniques from this chapter, and it can be even more fun and satisfying to design your own based on the same principles. Study how it really works, and notice details others would miss. Your audience will appreciate the difference every time.

The next chapter heats things up with fire, explosions, and other combustibles.

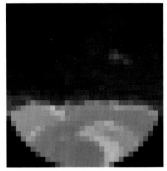

Figure 13.22 It looks jaggy because you don't want particles to be any higher resolution than they need to be, or they take up massive amounts of render time. There are two keys to creating this particle: It uses the adjusted background, inverted, with the CC Lens effect to create the look. Take a look at raindrops on a window sometime and notice that, as little lenses, they invert their fish-eye view of the scene behind them.

14

Pyrotechnics:
Heat, Fire, Explosions

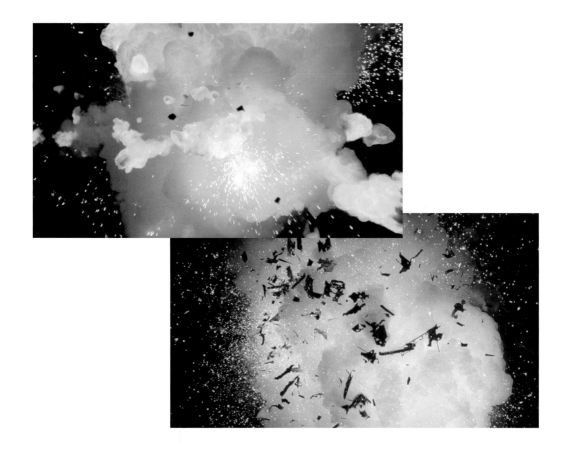

My nature is to be on set, blowing things up.
> —Ken Ralston, winner of five
> Academy Awards for visual effects

Pyrotechnics:
Heat, Fire, Explosions

It may not be the true majority, but plenty of people—guys mostly—first become interested in a visual effects career as borderline pyromaniacs or even gun nuts. You have to follow your passion in life, I suppose. Creating a conflagration on the computer isn't quite as much fun as simply blowing shit up, but maybe it keeps these people off our streets.

The truth is that many types of explosions are still best done through a combination of practical and virtual simulations. There are, however, many cases in which compositing can save a lot of time, expense, and hazard. Blowing up models and props is fun, but it involves extensive setup and a not insubstantial amount of danger to the cast and crew. Second chances don't come cheap.

On the other hand, there's often no substitute for the physics of live-action mayhem. I hope it doesn't come as a disappointment to learn that not everything pyrotechnical can or should be accomplished start to finish in After Effects. Some effects require actual footage of physical or fabricated elements being shot at or blown up, and good reference of such events is immensely beneficial. Practical elements might rely on After Effects to work, but pyrotechnical shots are equally reliant, if not more so, on practical elements.

Firearms

Blanks are dangerous, and real guns are deadly. To safely create a shot with realistic gunfire requires

- ▶ a realistic-looking gun prop in the scene
- ▶ some method to mime or generate firing action on set

▶ the addition of a muzzle flash, smoke, cartridge, or shell discharge (where appropriate)

▶ the matching shot showing the result of gunfire: debris, bullet hits, even blood

After Effects can help with all of these to some extent, and handles some of them completely, relieving you of the need for more expensive or dangerous alternatives.

The Shoot

For the purposes of this discussion, let's assume that you begin with a plate shot of an actor re-creating the action of firing a gun, and that the gun that was used on set produces nothing: no muzzle flash, no smoke, no shell. All that's required is some miming by the actor of the recoil, or kick, which is relatively minor with small handguns but a challenge with a shotgun or fully automatic weapon.

Happily, there's no shortage of reference, as nowhere outside of the NRA is the Second Amendment more cherished than in Hollywood movies and television. Granted, most such scenes are themselves staged or manipulated, not documentary realism. But remember, we're going for cinematic reality here, so if it looks good to you (and the director), by all means use it as reference.

Figure 14.1 shows something like the minimal composite to create a realistic shot of a gun being fired (albeit artfully executed in this case). Depending on the gun, smoke or a spent cartridge might also discharge. As important as the look of the frame is the timing; check your favorite reference carefully and you'll find that not much, and certainly not the flash, lingers longer than a single frame.

NOTES

Stu Maschwitz's book, *The DV Rebel's Guide* (Peachpit Press), is definitive on the subject of creating an action movie, perhaps on a low budget, with the help of After Effects. Included with the cover price, you get a couple of nifty After Effects tools for muzzle flashes and spent shells, and some serious expertise on the subject of making explosive action exciting and real.

Figure 14.1 Much of the good reference for movie gunfire is other movies; you typically want the most dramatic and cinematic look, which is a single frame of muzzle flash and contact lighting on surrounding elements (right).

The actual travel of the bullet out of the barrel is not generally anything to worry about; at roughly one kilometer per second, it moves too fast to be seen amid all the other effects, particularly the blinding muzzle flash.

Muzzle Flash and Smoke

The clearest indication that a gun has gone off is the flash of light around the muzzle, at the end of the barrel. This small, bright explosion of gunpowder actually lasts about $\frac{1}{50}$ second, short enough that when shot live it can fall between frames of film (in which case you might need to restore it in order for the action of the scene to be clear). Real guns don't discharge a muzzle flash nearly as often movie guns do.

A flash can be painted by hand, cloned in from a practical image, or composited from stock reference. The means you use to generate it is not too significant, although muzzle flashes have in common with lens flares that they are specific to the device that created them. Someone in your audience is bound to know something about your gun, so get reference: Certain guns emit a characteristic shape such as a teardrop, cross, or star (**Figure 14.2**).

Figure 14.2 The angle of the shot and the type of gun affect the muzzle flash effect. The image at left is from an M16 rifle; the one on the right is from a handgun. (Images courtesy of Artbeats.)

Any such explosion travels in two directions from the end of the barrel: arrayed outward from the firing point and in a straight line out from the barrel. If you don't have a source that makes this shape at the correct angle, it's probably simplest to paint it.

The key is to make it look right on one frame; this is a rare case where that's virtually all the audience should see, and where that one frame can be almost completely different from those surrounding it. If it looks blah or only part of the way there, it's too well matched to the surrounding frames. Focus on the one frame until you believe its explosiveness and dramatic flourish.

Technically speaking, some guns—rifles, for example—may cause quite a bit of smoke, but most emit little or none at all. If you do make a smoke puff with Turbulent Noise held out by a soft mask, which you certainly could, my advice is to make it evaporate relatively quickly so you don't blow the gag.

Shells and Interactive Light

If the gun in your scene calls for it, that extra little bit of realism can be added with a secondary animation of a shell popping off the top of a semiautomatic. **Figure 14.3** shows how such an element looks being emitted from a real gun and shot with a high-speed shutter.

It's definitely cool to have a detailed-looking shell pop off of the gun. However, the truth is that with a lower camera shutter speed, the element will become an unrecognizable two-frame blur anyway, in which case all you may need is a four-point mask of a white (or brass-colored) solid.

The bright flash of the muzzle may also cause a brief reflected flash on objects near the gun as well as the subject firing it. Chapter 12 offers the basic methodology: Softly mask a highlight area, or matte the element with its own highlights, then flash it using an adjustment layer containing a Levels effect or a colored solid with a suitable blending mode.

As a general rule, the lower the ambient light and the larger the weapon, the greater the likelihood of interactive lighting, whereby light (and shadows) contact surrounding surfaces with the flash of gunfire. A literal "shot in the dark" would fully illuminate the face of whomever (or whatever) fired it, just for a single frame. It's a great dramatic effect, but one that is very difficult to re-create in post. Firing blanks on set or any other means of getting contact lighting of a flash on set would be invaluable here.

By contrast, or rather by reduced contrast, a day-lit scene will heavily dampen the level of interactivity of the light.

Figure 14.3 A shell pops off the fired gun, but it could just as well be a shape layer with motion blur (or check *The DV Rebel's Guide* for a Particle Playground–based setup to create it automatically). (Images courtesy of Artbeats.)

Figure 14.4 This sequence of frames shows a second bullet hitting the cab of the truck, using two elements: the painted bullet hit (top) and the spark element, whose source was shot on black and added via Screen mode.

Instead of a white hot flash, you might more accurately have saturation of orange and yellow in the full muzzle flash element, and the interactive lighting might be minimal. This is where understanding your camera and recording medium can help you gauge the effect of a small aperture hit by a lot of light.

Hits and Squibs

Bullets that ricochet on set are known as squib hits because they typically are created with *squibs,* small explosives with the approximate power of a firecracker that go off during the take. Squibs can even be actual firecrackers. It is possible to add bullet hits without using explosives on set, but frenetic gunplay will typically demand a mixture of on-set action and postproduction enhancement.

Figure 14.4 shows a before-and-after addition of a bullet hit purely in After Effects. Here the bullet does not ricochet but is embedded directly into the solid metal of the truck. In such a case, all you need to do is add the results of the damage on a separate layer at the frame where the bullet hits; you can paint this (it's a few sparks). The element can then be motion-tracked to marry it solidly to the background.

At the frame of impact, and for a frame or two thereafter, a shooting spark and possibly a bit of smoke (if the target is combustible—but not in the case of a steel vehicle) will convey the full violence of the bullets. As with the muzzle flash, this can vary from a single frame to a more fireworks-like shower of sparks tracked in over a few frames (**Figure 14.5**).

A bullet-hit explosion can be created via a little miniature effects shoot, using a fire-retardant black background (a flat, black card might do it) and some firecrackers (assuming you can get them). The resulting flash, sparks, and smoke stand out against the black, allowing the element to be composited via a blending mode (such as Add or Screen) or a hi-con matte (Chapter 6). Better yet, try a pixel bender effect designed for the purpose of both keying out and unmultiplying the black areas of the image. If dangerous explosives aren't your thing, even in a

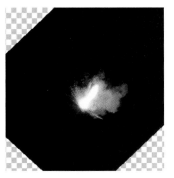
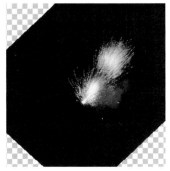

Figure 14.5 A source spark element shot against black can be composited using Add or Screen blending mode—no matte needed. (Images courtesy of markandmatty.com.)

controlled situation, stock footage is available. If debris is also part of the shot, however, the more that can practically be done on set, the better (**Figure 14.6**).

So to recap, a good bullet hit should include

▶ smoke or sparks at the frame of impact, typically lasting between one and five frames

▶ the physical result of the bullet damage (if any) painted and tracked into the scene

▶ debris in cases where the target is shatterable or scatterable

Later in this chapter, you'll see how larger explosions have much in common with bullet hits, which are essentially just miniature explosions. In both cases, a bit of practical debris can be crucial to sell the shot.

Energy Effects

There is a whole realm of pyrotechnical effects that are made up of pure energy. At one end of the (very bright) spectrum is lightning, which occurs in the atmosphere of our own planet daily; on the other end are science fiction weapons that exist only in the mind (not that the U.S. military under Ronald Reagan didn't try to make them a reality).

Figure 14.6 Animating debris is tedious and unrewarding when compared with shooting a BB gun at breakaway objects and hurling debris at the talent.

A lightning simulation and a light saber composite have quite a bit in common, in that they rely on fooling the

Figure 14.7 Spectacular dueling action from *Ryan vs. Dorkman*. (Sequence courtesy of Michael Scott.)

NOTES

The 14_lightsaber_ryan_vs_dorkman folder on the disc contains this effect as well as the sequence containing these clips.

eye into seeing an element that appears white hot. The funny thing about human vision is that it actually looks for the decay—the not-quite-white hot areas around the hot core—for indications that an element is brighter than white and hotter than hot.

The Hot Look: Core and Decay

The recipe for creating a filmic light saber blur used to be considered top secret by the people who worked on them, as closely guarded as the recipe for Coca-Cola. But the proper approach has long since been popularized by superstars of the low-budget light saber Ryan and Dorkman, who have provided an entire light saber battle on the disc (**Figure 14.7**).

You may find the light saber to be somewhat played out after three decades, but the techniques you need to make a good light saber battle apply to any other energy-driven effect. There is also still plenty of interest these days in a funny *Star Wars* parody or takeoff such as *Ryan vs. Dorkman*, from which the example used in this section is taken (**Figure 14.7**).

The Beam effect (Effect > Generate > Beam) automatically gives you the bare minimum, a core and surrounding glow. It is 32 bpc and can be built up, but like so many automated solutions, it's a compromise. The real thing is created by hand, and it's not all that much more trouble considering how much better the result can be. Greater control over the motion and threshold areas equals a much better look.

Figure 14.8 shows the basics for a single light saber effect:

1. In the first comp, make the background plate (**Figure 14.8a**) a guide layer, because this is not the final comp, and create a masked white solid. In this case, the position and arcs of the light sabers are all rotoscoped by hand (**Figure 14.8b**), as detailed in Chapter 7.

2. Drop (or precomp) this comp into a new comp, apply Fast Blur to the resulting layer (turn on Repeat Edge Pixels), and set the blending mode to Add (or Screen).

(a)

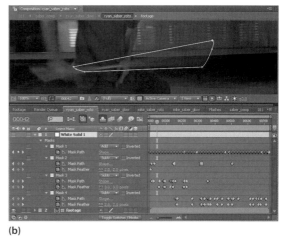

(b)

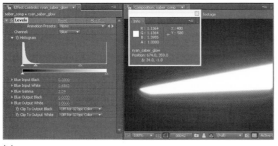

(c)

(d)

(e)

Figure 14.8 The initial roto comp is set up with generous padding **(a)** so that masks can move out of frame without being cut off. The roto itself is shaped to frame the full area of motion blur, where applicable, from the source **(b)**. The glow effect **(c)** comes from layering together several copies of the roto, each with different amounts of Feather on the mask. This is then tinted as a single element **(d)** and tweaked in Levels **(e)** for the proper glow intensity.

3. Duplicate this layer several times, and adjust Fast Blur so that each layer has approximately double the blur of the one above it. With six or seven layers, you might have a Blur Radius ranging from 5 on the top level (the core) down to 400 or so.

   To automate setup, you could even apply this expression text to the duplicate layer's Blurriness setting:

   ```
   thisComp.layer(index-1).effect("Fast Blur")
   ("Blurriness")*2
   ```

   This takes the Blurriness value from the layer above and doubles it so that as you duplicate the layer, each one below the top is twice as soft (**Figure 14.8c**).

4. Drop this comp into your main composition to combine it with footage and give it color (**Figure 14.8d**). The *Ryan vs. Dorkman* approach uses Color Balance and is composited in 16 bpc; one 32-bpc alternative (because Color Balance doesn't work in HDR) is simply to use Levels, adjusting Input White and Gamma on individual red, green, and blue channels. You could also apply Tint and Map White To values brighter than white (**Figure 14.8e**).

That's the fundamental setup; here are some other ways to really sell a scene like this. You can use

▶ motion blur; notice how by rotoscoping the arc of movement and adding the edge threshold you get this for free in the preceding figures

▶ contact/interactive lighting/glow (**Figure 14.9**)

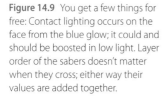

Figure 14.9 You get a few things for free: Contact lighting occurs on the face from the blue glow; it could and should be boosted in low light. Layer order of the sabers doesn't matter when they cross; either way their values are added together.

Figure 14.10 Flashes occur dozens of times throughout the battle; each one appears to have a unique shape, but they all use the same four-frame flare, and its unique shape comes from being composited with the rest of the scene.

▶ physical damage/interaction with the environment; the same types of interactions described for bullet hits apply, so add sparks, flares, and other damage to the surrounding environment

▶ flashes/over-range values (**Figure 14.10**)

I don't even need to tell you that these techniques are good for more than light sabers; suppose you intend to generate a more natural effect such as lightning. Reference shows this to possess similar qualities (**Figure 14.11**), and the same techniques will sell the effect.

Figure 14.11 Actual reference images contain energy effects with realistic thresholding and interaction with the surrounding environment. (Image courtesy of Kevin Miller via Creative Commons license.)

There are a couple of built-in effects that will create lightning in After Effects. With either Lightning or Advanced Lightning, you're not stuck with the rather mediocre default look of the effect itself; you can adapt the light saber methodology here and elsewhere. Turn off the glow and use the effect to generate a hard white core, and follow the same steps as just described. It's worth the trouble to get beyond the canned look, and it opens all of the possibilities shown here and more.

In some cases, you might go beyond these examples and create an element that throws off so much heat and energy that it distorts the environment around it.

Heat Distortion

Heat distortion, that strange rippling in the air that occurs when hot air meets cooler air, is another one of those effects compositors love. Like a lens flare, it's a highly

Figures 14.12 Heat haze by itself can look a little odd (top) but adds significantly to the realism of a scene containing a prominent heat source (bottom).

Check out 14_heat_displacement on the disc for this setup.

visible effect that, if properly adjusted, adds instant realism even if your viewers don't know that hot gas bends light.

Figures 14.12 shows the fabricated results of heat distortion in a close-up of a scene that will also incorporate fire. When your eye sees heat distortion, it understands that something intense is happening, just like with the decay/threshold of bright lights, as described earlier.

What Is Actually Happening

Stare into a swimming pool, and you can see displacement caused by the bending of light as it travels through the water. Rippled waves in the water cause rippled bending of light. There are cases in which our atmosphere behaves like this as well, with ripples caused by the collision of warmer and cooler air, a medium that is not quite as transparent as it seems.

As you might know from basic physics, hot air rises and hot particles move faster than cool ones. Air is not a perfectly clear medium but a translucent gas that can act as a lens, bending light. This "lens" is typically static and appears flat, but the application of heat causes an abrupt mixture of fast-moving hot air particles rising into cooler ambient air. This creates ripples that have the effect of displacing and distorting what is behind the moving air, just like ripples in the pool or ripples in the double-hung windows of a 100-year-old house.

Because this behavior resembles a lens effect, and because the role of air isn't typically taken into account in a 3D render, it can be adequately modeled as a distortion overlaid on whatever sits behind the area of hot air.

How to Re-create It

The basic steps for re-creating heat distortion from an invisible source in After Effects are as follows:

1. Create a basic particle animation that simulates the movement and dissipation of hot air particles in the scene.

2. Make two similar but unique passes of this particle animation—one to displace the background vertically, the other horizontally—and precomp them.

3. Add an adjustment layer containing the Displacement Map effect, which should be set to use the particle animation comp to create the distortion effect. Apply it to the background.

   Particle Playground is ideal for this purpose because its default settings come close to generating exactly what you need, with the following minor adjustments:

   a. Under Cannon, move Position to the source in the frame where the heat haze originates (in this case, the bottom center, as the entire layer will be repositioned and reused).

   b. Increase Barrel Radius from the default of 0.0 to the width, in pixels, of the source. Higher numbers lead to slower renders.

   c. Boost Particles Per Second to something like 200. The larger the Barrel Radius, the more particles are needed.

   d. Under Gravity, set Force to 0.0 to prevent the default fountain effect.

   The default color and scale of the particles is fine for this video resolution example, but you might have to adjust them as well according to your shot. A larger format (in pixels) or a bigger heat source might require bigger, softer particles.

4. Now duplicate the particles layer and set the color of the duplicated layer to pure green. As you'll see below, by default, the Displacement Map effect uses the red and green channels for horizontal and vertical displacement. The idea is to vary it so that the particles don't overlap by changing Direction Random Spread and Velocity Random Spread from their defaults.

It can be useful to generate the particles for the displacement map itself in 3D animation software, when the distortion needs to be attached to a 3D animated object, such as a jet engine or rocket exhaust. The distortion is still best created in After Effects using that map.

The 14_fire folder on the disc contains the still comps used for these figures, as well as a moving image shot that can be used to create your own dynamic shot with the same fire elements.

Figure 14.13 This displacement layer, matted against gray merely for clarity, was created with the included steps and used with the Displacement Map effect to produce the effect shown in Figure 14.12.

5. The heat animation is almost complete; it only needs some softening. Add a moderate Fast Blur setting (**Figure 14.13**).

Now put the animation to use: Drag it into the main comp, and turn off its visibility. The actual Displacement Map effect is applied either directly to the background plate or preferably to an adjustment layer sitting above all the layers that should be affected by the heat haze. Displacement Map is set by default to use the red channel for horizontal displacement and the green channel for vertical displacement; all you need to do is select the layer containing the red and green particles under the Displacement Map Layer menu.

Heat displacement often dissipates before it reaches the top of the frame. Making particles behave so that their life span ends before they reach the top of the frame is accurate, but painstaking. A simpler solution is to add a solid with a black-to-white gradient (created with the Ramp effect) as a luma matte to hold out the adjustment layer containing the displacement effect. You can also use a big, soft mask.

Fire

Within After Effects, fire synthesis (from scratch) is way too hot to handle; there's no tool, built-in or plug-in, to make convincing-looking flames. If fire is at all prominent in a shot, it will require elements that come from somewhere else—most likely shot with a camera, although 3D animators have become increasingly talented at fabricating alternatives here and there.

Creating and Using Fire Elements

Figure 14.14 shows effects plates of fire elements. The big challenge when compositing fire is that it doesn't scale very realistically—a fireplace fire will look like it belongs in the hearth, no matter how you may attempt to scale or retime it.

Fire elements are ideally shot in negative space—against a black background, or at least, at night—so that they can be

  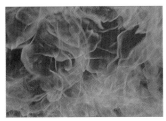

Figure 14.14 Fire elements are typically shot in negative (black) space or occasionally in a natural setting requiring more careful matting. By adjusting Input Black in Levels, you can control the amount of glow coming off the fire as it is blended via Add mode, lending the scene interactive lighting for free. (Images courtesy of Artbeats.)

composited with blending modes and a minimum of roto-scoping. Fire illuminates its surroundings—just something to keep in mind when shooting.

This, then, is a case where it can be worth investing in proper elements shot by trained pyrotechnicians (unless that sounds like no fun—although there's more involved with a good fire shoot than a camera rental and a blow-torch). In many cases, stock footage companies, such as Artbeats (examples on the book's disc), anticipate your needs. The scale and intensity may be more correct than what you can easily shoot on your own. Like anything, pyro is a skill whose masters have devoted much trial and error to its practice.

All Fired Up

Blending modes and linear blending, not mattes, are the key to good-looking fire composites. Given a fire element shot against black (as in the Artbeats_RF001H_fireExcerpt.mov included on the disc and used for the depicted example), the common newbie mistake is to try to key out the black with an Extract effect, which will lead to a fight between black edges and thin fire.

The first step is to simply lay the fire layer over the background and apply Add mode. To firm up a fire, flare, or other bright element you can

▶ ascertain that Blend Colors Using 1.0 Gamma is enabled in Project Settings

> Compound Blur simply varies the amount of blur according to the brightness of a given pixel in the Blur layer, up to a given maximum. It's the right thing to use not only for fire and smoke but for fog and mist; heavy particulates in the air act like little tiny defocused lenses, causing this effect in nature.

- ▶ fine-tune the result with a Levels effect, pushing in on Input White and Black (and color match as with any foreground element)
- ▶ add an Exposure effect (with a boosted Exposure setting) to create a raging inferno
- ▶ add interactive lighting for low-lit scenes (next section)
- ▶ create displacement above the open flames (as detailed in the previous section)
- ▶ add an adjustment layer over the background with a Compound Blur effect, using the transparency of the fire and smoke as a blur layer (**Figure 14.15**).

Where there's fire there is, of course, smoke. At a modest level, smoke can be created with a Fractal Noise effect as described in the previous chapter, bringing this shot home (**Figure 14.16**).

Figure 14.16 All of the techniques described here build to a result that gives the furniture motivation to jump out the windows.

Figure 14.15 The effect of steam or fog can be re-created with a subtle Compound Blur effect.

Light Interacts

Provided that your camera does not rotate too much, a 2D fire layer, or a set of them, offset in 3D space, can read as sufficiently three-dimensional. The key to making it interact dimensionally with a scene, particularly a relatively dark one, is often interactive light. As stated earlier, fire tends to illuminate everything around it with a warm, flickering glow.

Figure 14.17 Input White and Black on the RGB and red channels of the Levels effect offer control of the natural glow around the element. The better the dynamic range of the source image, the harder you can push this—another case for a higher-bit-depth source.

As shown in **Figure 14.17**, a fire element may include a certain amount of usable glow. Input White and Input Black in Levels control the extent to which glow is enhanced or suppressed (right), respectively.

Note, however, that this glow isn't anything unique or special; you can re-create it by using a heavily blurred duplicate of the source fire or a masked and heavily feathered orange solid, with perhaps a slight wiggle added to the glow layer's opacity to flicker the intensity.

Dimensionality

You can pull off the illusion of fully three-dimensional fire, especially if the camera is moving around in 3D space, directly in After Effects. I was frankly surprised at how well this worked when I created the shot featured in **Figure 14.18,** back in the early days of After Effects 3D.

As shown, the background plate is an aerial flyover of a forest. Because of the change in altitude and perspective, this shot clearly required 3D tracking (touched upon at the end of Chapter 8). The keys to making this shot look fully dimensional were to break up the source fire elements into discrete chunks and to stagger those in 3D space, so that as the plane rose above them, their relationship and parallax changed (**Figure 14.19**).

TIP

For a shot featuring a character or object that reflects firelight, there's no need to go crazy projecting fire onto the subject. In many cases, it is enough to create some flickering in the character's own luminance values, for example, by wiggling the Input White value at a low frequency in Levels (Individual Controls).

Figure 14.18 Before-and-after sequential stills of a flyover shot. Because of the angle of the aerial camera, the shot required 3D motion tracking, in this case done with 2d3's Boujou. (Images courtesy of ABC-TV.)

Figure 14.19 A top view of the 3D motion-tracked camera from Figure 14.18 panning past one set of fires (of which the final composition had half a dozen). The pink layers contain fire elements, the gray layers smoke.

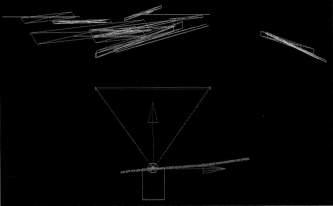

It is easy to get away with any individual fire element being 2D in this case. Because fire changes its shape constantly, there is nothing to give away its two-dimensionality. Borders of individual fire elements can freely overlap without being distracting, so it doesn't look cut out. The eye sees evidence of parallax between a couple dozen fire elements and does not think to question that any individual one of them looks too flat. The smoke elements were handled in a similar way, organized along overlapping planes. As mentioned in the previous chapter, smoke's translucency aids the illusion that overlapping smoke layers have dimensional depth.

Explosions

The example forest fire shot also contains a large explosion in a clearing. There is not a huge fundamental difference between the methods for compositing an explosion and mere fire, except that a convincing explosion might be built up out of more individual elements. It is largely a question of what is exploding.

All explosions are caused by rapidly expanding combustible gases; implosions are caused by rapid contraction. Just by looking at an explosion, viewers can gauge its size and get an idea of what blew up, so you need to design the right explosion for your situation or your result will be too cheesy even for 1980s television sci-fi. How do you do it?

Light and Chunky

Each explosion you will see is unique, but to narrow the discussion, I'll organize all explosions into two basic categories. The easier one to deal with is the gaseous explosion—one made up only of gas and heat. These explosions behave just like fire. In fact, in the shot shown on the left in **Figure 14.20** the explosion is fire, a huge ball of it, where something very combustible evidently went up very quickly.

Some shots end up looking fake because they use a gaseous explosion when some chunks of debris are needed. This is a prime reason that exploding miniatures are still in use, shot at high speed (or even, when possible, full-scale explosions, which can be shot at standard speed). The slower-moving and bigger the amount of debris, the bigger the apparent explosion.

If your shot calls for a chunky explosion, full of physical debris, and the source lacks them, you need an alternate source. Many 3D programs these days include effective dynamics simulations; if you go that route, be sure to generate a depth map as well because each chunk will be

Figure 14.20 Pyrotechnics footage is just the thing when you need a big explosion filled with debris. The explosion on the left is gaseous and firey, while the one on the right contains much more actual debris, as when a solid object is blown up. (Images courtesy of Artbeats.)

revealed only as it emerges from the fireball. Many other concerns associated with this are beyond the scope of this discussion because they must be solved in other software.

One effect that seems to come close in After Effects is Shatter, but it's hard to recommend this unless you're simulating a pane of glass or some other pane breaking. Shatter isn't bad for a decade-old dynamics simulator, but its primary limitation is a huge one: It can employ only extruded flat polygons to model the chunks. A pane of glass is one of the few physical objects that would shatter into irregular but flat polygons, and Shatter contains built-in controls for specifying the size of the shards in the point of impact. Shatter was also developed prior to the introduction of 3D in After Effects; you can place your imaginary window in perspective space, but not with the help of a camera or 3D controls.

A wide selection of pyrotechnic explosions is available as stock footage from companies such as Artbeats. In many cases, there is no substitute for footage of a real, physical object being blown to bits (**Figure 14.20, right**).

In a Blaze of Glory

With good reference and a willingness to take the extra step to marry your shot and effect, you can create believable footage that would require danger or destruction if taken with a camera. Even when your project has the budget to actually re-create some of the mayhem described in this chapter, you can almost always use After Effects to enhance and build upon what the camera captures. Boom. Sometimes you do get to go out with a bang.

Index

What's on the DVD?

Although this book is designed not to rely on tutorials, many of the techniques described in the text can be further explored via the dozens of projects and accompanying footage and stills included on the disc. These range from simple demonstrations of single concepts to completed shots, and make use of live action effects footage custom shot for the book or borrowed from a professional shoot. Wherever possible, HD (1920 × 1080) clips are incorporated; other examples use NTSC footage or stills if that is all that's required to get the point across.

Additionally, the DVD includes demos of more than a dozen plug-ins and applications. These demos are similar to the real software for everything but output, allowing you to experiment with your own footage. In the Scripts folder on the disc, you'll also find a PDF with a list of scripts mentioned in the book and links to download them from aescripts.com, a donation-ware site.

▶ **Custom scripts from redefinery**. A number of custom scripts created by Jeff Almasol are included with this edition in the Scripts folder on the disc, including Lightwrap and CameraProjectionSetup, which duplicate the exact steps described to set those up (Chapters 12 and 9, respectively); three scripts described in the appendix on the accompanying disc; and two scripts included with previous editions: Duplink, which creates "instance" objects, and Merge Projects, which integrates the structure of an imported project into the master project. More information on these is included as comments in the scripts themselves (which can be opened with any text editor).

▶ **Kronos** (*The Foundry*) is an alternative to After Effects' built-in Timewarp effect for optical-flow-based retiming of footage. Learn more at http://www.thefoundry. co.uk/products/kronos/.

- **Effects Suite** (*Red Giant Software*) includes Knoll Light Factory Pro and is used to generate lens flares, glints, and glows, and to create custom effects using individual lens components. Also included are Warp, for easier handling of corner pins and shadows, and Composite Wizard.

- **Magic Bullet Suite** (*Red Giant Software*) offers you color tools and includes Colorista II, Looks, and Mojo, as well as Denoiser and Instant HD.

- **Keying Suite** (*Red Giant Software*) features Primatte, the primary alternative to Keylight, which uses an entirely unique model for color differentiation that is particularly useful with uneven, poorly lit, or nonstandard backgrounds.

- **Trapcode Suite** (*Red Giant Software*) includes Particular, which is so useful as to practically be an application all of its own; the related Form; Lux for visible volumetric lights; and Horizon for creating skies and multicolor gradients. Shine is a great option for "god rays," and effects such as 3D Stroke and Sound Keys are useful for motion graphics.

- **Silhouette v4** (*SilhouetteFX*) is available as both a stand-alone application and a shape import/export plug-in for After Effects. It's designed to rotoscope and generate mattes.

- **ReelSmart Motion Blur** (*RE: Vision Effects*) allows you to procedurally generate motion blur for moving elements in a shot that lacks it (or lacks enough of it). After Effects' built-in motion blur is available only on animated elements.

- **Twixtor** (*RE: Vision Effects*) is an alternative to After Effects' built-in Timewarp effect for optical-flow-based retiming of footage.